An Introduction

An Introduction to MicroStation 95

A. Yarwood

LONGMAN

Addison Wesley Longman Limited
Edinburgh Gate, Harlow
Essex CM20 2JE, England
and Associated Companies throughout the world

First published 1996

British Library Cataloguing in Publication Data
A catalogue entry for this title is available from the British Library

ISBN 0-582-29979-9

Set by 24 in 10/13pt Melior
Produced by Longman Singapore Publishers (Pte) Ltd
Printed in Singapore

Contents

List of plates

Colour plates are between pages 114 and 115.

Preface

MicroStation 95 is a first class CAD (Computer Aided Design) software package in worldwide use. It is particularly strong in the architectural industries. The software package was published in 1996 as an update to MicroStation Version 5.

This book is intended to describe to students in education and beginners in industry how to use the software for the construction of 2D (two-dimensional) technical drawings, mainly based in mechanical engineering practice. Its contents form a course of work suitable for students required to learn CAD when undertaking vocational courses, in City and Guilds and mechanical engineering first-year courses in universities. Students and their teachers in Sixth Forms of secondary schools who are taking CAD as part of technology courses may also find the book to be of value. The book should also be suitable for those new to and wishing to learn CAD methods involving MicroStation 95 in industry.

Except for the final four chapters, the book's contents are based on 2D constructions. The software contains excellent 3D (three-dimensional) facilities for the construction and rendering of 3D models and an introduction to 3D modelling is given in the final four chapters of the book. These four chapters include numerous renderings. The author hopes to prepare a book on the construction and rendering of 3D models with the aid of the software as a follow up to this book.

An eight-page full colour section containing 16 colour plates is included to show the use of colour when constructing drawings with the aid of MicroStation 95. The colour section includes several renderings of 3D models.

The book's contents are based on the use of the software as loaded on a PC (Personal Computer) working under Windows 95. Its contents are also suitable for those working with the DOS version of the software. Its contents are however applicable to MicroStation 95 operating on other platforms.

A. Yarwood
Salisbury 1996

Acknowledgements

Trademarks

MicroStation® is a registered trademark, and AccuDraw™ and SmartLine™ are trademarks, of Bentley Systems, Incorporated.

IBM® is a registered trademark of International Business Machines Corporation.

MS-DOS® and Windows® are registered trademarks of Microsoft Corporation.

CHAPTER 1

Introduction

What is this book about?

This book has been written as an introduction to pupils in schools, students in colleges and other beginners who wish to learn how to construct technical drawings with the aid of the Computer Aided Design (CAD) software package **MicroStation 95**. To fully describe how to work with a complex CAD system such as MicroStation 95 would require a book considerably larger than this one. It is hoped however that readers of this book will be encouraged to use MicroStation and once introduced to constructing drawings with its aid, become sufficiently interested to go on to learn more about how to use the software to construct complex drawings.

When the software is first installed, it can be loaded into a computer either as an MS-DOS or as a Windows 95 application. Here we are only concerned with the Windows 95 version. Despite this, the DOS version is sufficiently similar to enable the operator to work from the descriptions contained in this book. Also, although the contents of the book are suitable for use with the software working in other platforms, we are only concerned here with working with a fully compatible PC (Personal Computer).

Hardware requirements

Operating chip: This should be at least an Intel (or similar) 80836 chip or better. If an 80836 or an 80846SX, then a math co-processor chip must also be fitted. If an 80846DX, then the math co-processor chip is integral to the operating chip. If a Pentium (or similar) operating chip is fitted, faster working will be possible.

Hard disk size: There should be at least 30 Mbytes free space, preferably more. MicroStation files require a minimum of 14 Mbytes, with a maximum of 70 Mbytes – depending upon the type of installation required. At least a further 15 Mbytes of disk space is required when running the software.

Random Access Memory (RAM): At least 8 Mbytes of RAM are required, but 16 Mbytes will allow for larger drawing files and faster operation. The amount of RAM required basically depends upon the size of the drawing. As far as the drawings described in this book are concerned, 8 Mbytes RAM will be sufficient.

Digitiser: This book deals only with a Microsoft compatible mouse with two buttons – a *left* button and a *right* button. MicroStation can be worked with the aid of a three-button mouse or a digitising tablet and puck, but their use is not described here.

Visual Display Unit: All work described here will be based upon the use of a single VDU (monitor or screen), although two VDUs can be fitted – one for graphics, the other for alphanumeric (text and figures) information. It is advisable for the VDU to be at least SVGA (Super Video Graphics Array) standard, working to at least 800 by 600 pixels. In all graphics work such as CAD, the bigger the VDU screen the better. Although one can work with a 14 inch screen, a 17 inch, 20 inch or larger screen is advisable. The problem is however cost. Screens larger than 14 inch are considerably more expensive.

Why use CAD anyway?

1. A CAD software package such as MicroStation can be used to construct any technical drawing which could be produced 'by hand' methods.

2. Drawings are constructed much more quickly than when working 'by hand'. A speed of 10 times (or more) faster is possible when worked by a skilled CAD operator.

3. Drawing with CAD is far less tedious than when working 'by hand'. Two examples may suffice – entering text into a drawing by hand is extremely tedious. Text goes in when working in CAD as fast as one can type. One of the most tedious jobs is hatching areas 'by hand'. With CAD hatching is almost instantaneous. Other examples could be quoted.

4. Drawings or their parts can be copied, scaled, rotated, mirrored, moved with ease. Drawings or parts of drawings can be inserted in other drawings almost instantaneously.

5. When working in CAD, get into the habit of never drawing the same thing twice. It can always be drawn, then copied, mirrored, inserted, etc. This is one of the major reasons why working in CAD is so fast.

6. Erasure of unnecessary parts or errors or even the whole of a drawing can be performed speedily without the need to mechanically erase.

7. Dimensioning of drawings is fast and accurate.
8. Considerable storage space is saved by not having to store drawings on paper or as tracings. They can instead be stored on disks.
9. Any drawing on disk can be plotted or printed to any scale required, without the drawing having to be redrawn to the required scale.
10. When using a system such as MicroStation, 3D models can be constructed to give realistic three-dimensional views of a model which has been drawn. Such 3D models can also be *rendered* to give photo-like realistic 'pictures' of the model in three dimensions.

In fact, if there is a drawback to using CAD for producing technical drawings, it can be said that the initial setting up costs are high compared to the setting up costs involved in drawing 'by hand'. However the drawing output per operator is considerably increased, resulting in greater productivity as well as increasing the accuracy of the resulting drawings.

Terms used throughout this book

As stated earlier, a two button mouse is used for all operations described in this book. The mouse may also be used at times in conjunction with the computer keyboard. The following terms are used to describe frequently performed operations when working in MicroStation:

Cursor: A variety of cursors of different shapes are employed in working both Windows 95 and MicroStation 95. Some of these are shown in Fig. 1.1.

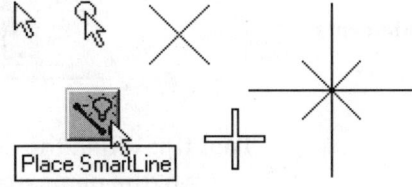

Fig. 1.1 Some of the cursor types used in MicroStation 95

Window cursors: Another group of cursors which may be used are those concerned with the sizing of windows. These cursors are shown in Fig. 1.2.

Enter: Type the letters, figures or word(s) that follow at the keyboard.

Key-in: *enter* names or abbreviations in the **Key-in** window.

Left-click: Press the left-hand button of the mouse.

Right-click: Press the right-hand button of the mouse.

Fig. 1.2 Cursors for *dragging* windows to new sizes

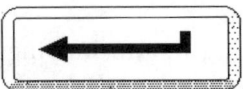

Fig. 1.3 The **Return** key on some keyboards

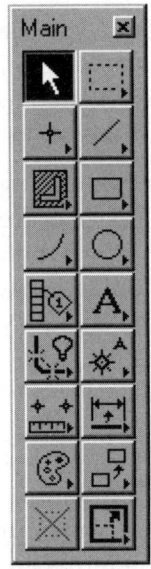

Fig. 1.4 The **Main** tool palette containing the tool icons for the tools in most frequent use

Fig. 1.5 The **Linear Elements** flyout

Drag: Position the cursor under mouse control over the feature to be *dragged*. Press and hold down the mouse button. Move the mouse and the feature will move in response.

Double-click: Press a mouse button twice in quick succession.

Both-click: Press both buttons of the mouse at the same time. (A MicroStation **tentative point**.)

Return: Press the **Return** key of the keyboard. This key is often marked with **Enter** instead of **Return**, or may have an arrow as shown in Fig. 1.3.

Palette: A set of tool icons within a box. Figure 1.4 shows the **Main** tool palette. Also referred to as a **tool box**.

Flyout: When an outward pointing arrow is seen in the right-hand bottom corner of a tool icon in a palette, holding down a *left-click* on the icon a *flyout* showing a sub-palette in line with the icon appears. Figure 1.5 shows the **Linear Elements** flyout.

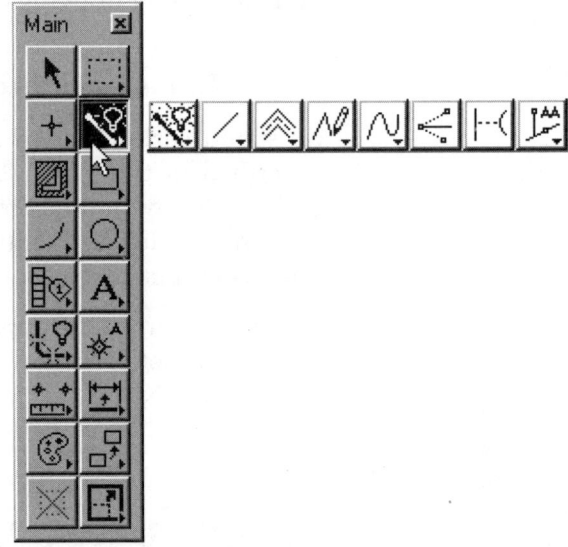

Tool tip: When the cursor, under mouse control, is placed over a tool icon, the name of the tool represented by the icon appears as a tool tip. Figure 1.6 shows the tool tip for the **Place Circle by Center** tool icon.

Element: This is a feature drawn in MicroStation with the aid of a tool. Figure 1.7 shows some typical elements. Note, however, that some elements may consist of several, when in a block or a group.

Highlight: A feature changes its colours and background. Examples are shown in Figs 1.4 and 1.5 in which tool icons have been selected by a *left-click* on the icons. The icon colour reverses from black to white and the background reverses from grey to black.

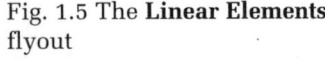

Fig. 1.6 The tool tip for the **Place Circle by Center** tool icon

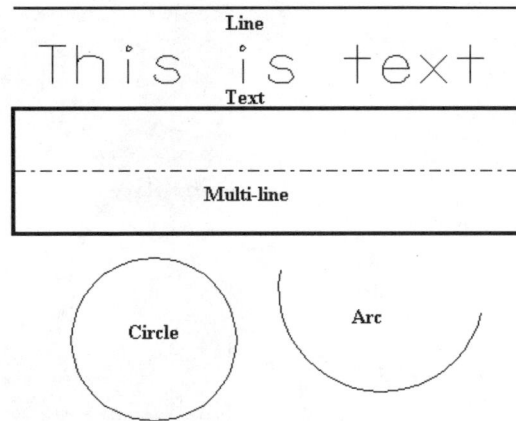

Fig. 1.7 Some typical
MicroStation elements

Opening MicroStation 95

1. *Left-click* on **MicroStation 95** in the **Windows 95** start-up window
   (Fig. 1.8). The **MicroStation 95** logo appears (Fig. 1.9). The logo
   stays on screen for about 30 seconds. The logo then disappears to
   be replaced by the **MicroStation Manager** dialogue box (Fig. 1.10).
2. *Left-click* on **File** in the menu bar of the dialogue box (Fig. 1.11). In
   the **File** dialogue box which appears, *left-click* on **New** (Fig. 1.12).
   The **Create Drawing File** dialogue box appears. In this dialogue
   box, *left-click* on **Select...** in the **Seed File** box (Fig. 1.13).

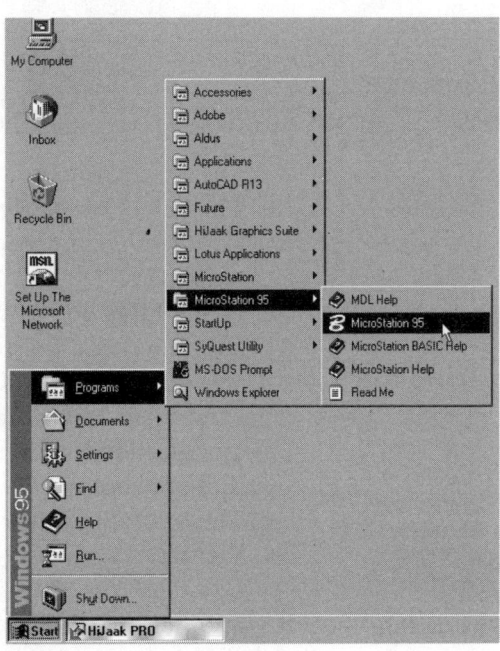

Fig. 1.8 *Left-click* on
MicroStation 95 in the
Windows 95 startup screen

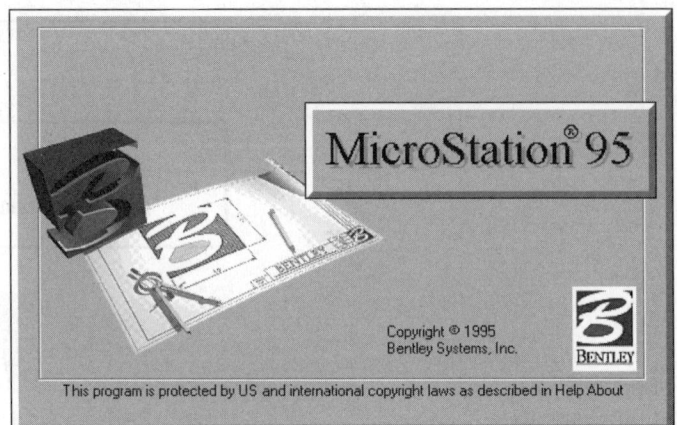

Fig. 1.9 The **MicroStation 95** logo appears on screen

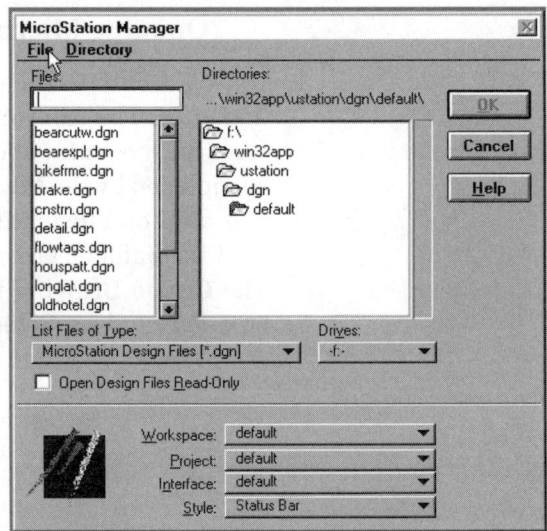

Fig. 1.10 The **MicroStation Manager** dialogue box

3. The **Select Seed File** dialogue box then appears. In the **File** list box, *double-click* on **seed2d.dgn**. The **Create Design File** dialogue box reappears.

4. In the **Files** box of the **Create Drawing File** dialogue box, *enter* a suitable name for your design file. I am using my initials (ay) as shown in Fig. 1.14. *Left-click* on the **OK** button of the dialogue box. When the **MicroStation Manager** dialogue box reappears with ay.dgn showing in the **Files:** box, *left-click* on the **OK** button of the dialogue box.

5. The MicroStation window appears carrying the design file ay.dgn. Figure 1.15 shows the screen at this stage.

6. *Left-click* on **Main** in the **Tools** pull-down menu, followed by another on **Main** in the sub-menu as shown in Fig. 1.16.

Fig. 1.11 *Left-click* on **File**

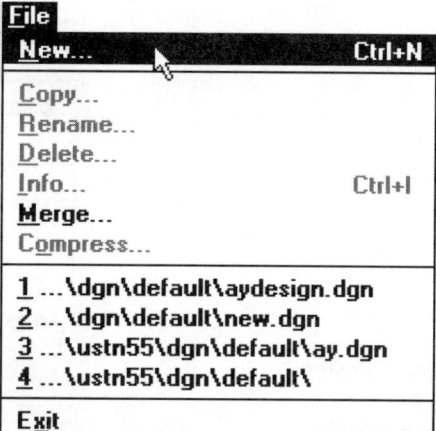

Fig. 1.12 *Left-click* on **New...** in the **File** pull-down menu

7. The **Main** tool palette appears (Fig. 1.17). Your screen will probably be black. For the purposes of clearly illustrating screens in this book they are all shown white.
8. *Left-click* on the **X** in the top right-hand corner of **Window 2** to remove that window from the screen. We only require **Window 1** for our purposes.

A note about seed files

Seed files are templates forming the basis for the settings when creating design files in which one can construct drawings. As can be seen in the **Select Seed File** dialogue box, shown in Fig. 1.13, MicroStation 95 contains a number of these files. More about seed files later (page 15)

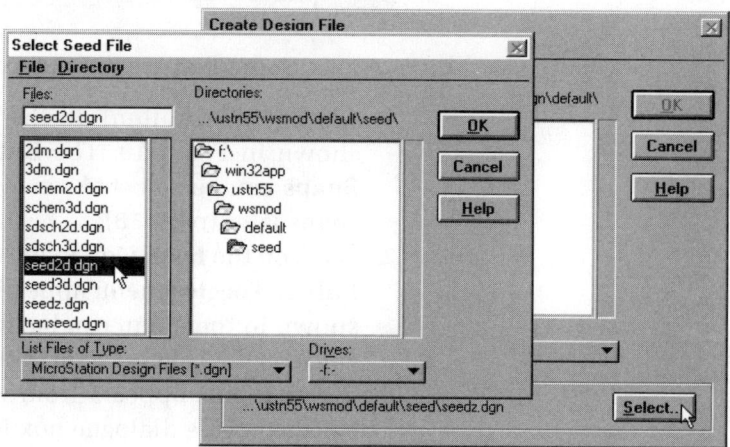

Fig. 1.13 *Left-click* on **Select** and in the **Select Seed File** dialogue box, *double-click* on **seed2d.dgn**

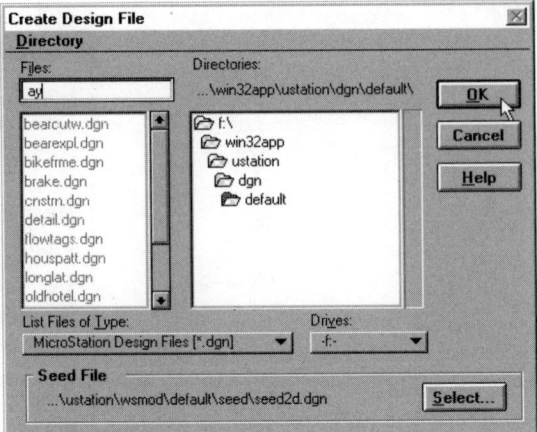

Fig. 1.14 In the **Create Design File** dialogue box, *enter* a suitable name in the **Files** box

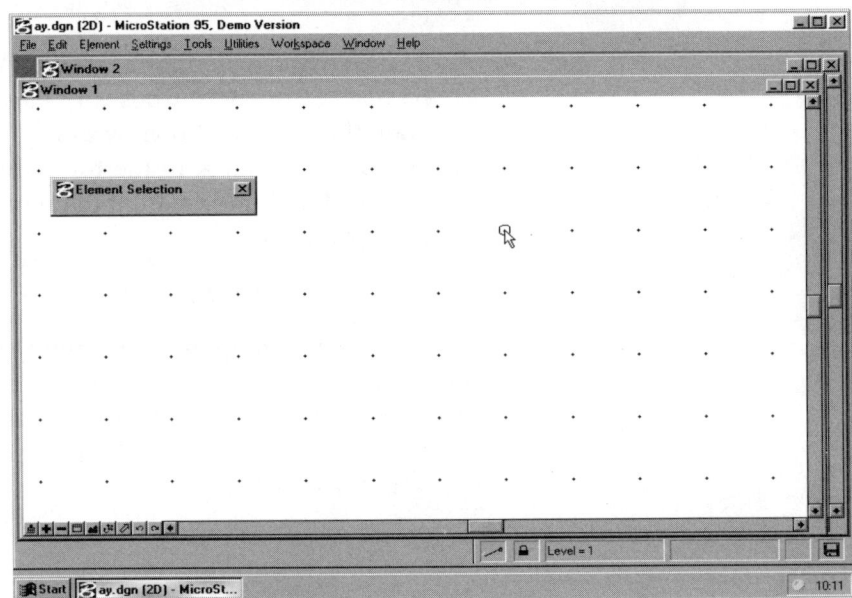

Fig, 1.15 The ay.dgn file as it appears in the MicroStation window

Some features of the ay.dgn screen

1. *Click* (either button) on the **Keypoint** icon in the Status Bar as shown in Fig. 1.18. The **Button Bar** menu appears from which **Snaps** can be selected when constructing drawings. More about snaps later (page 58).

2. *Click* on the **Lock** icon in the Status Bar as shown in Fig. 1.19. The **Full** or **Toggles** menu appears from which settings of the features shown in the menu can be made.

3. *Click* on the **Level=1** icon in the Status Bar and the **Set Active Level** dialogue box appears from which the level (layer) to be used is selected. This dialogue box is shown in Fig. 1.20.

Fig. 1.16 *Left-click* on **Main** in the **Tools** pull-down menu, followed by another on **Main** in the sub-menu

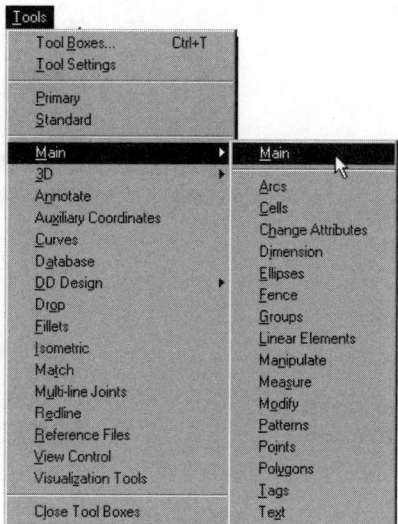

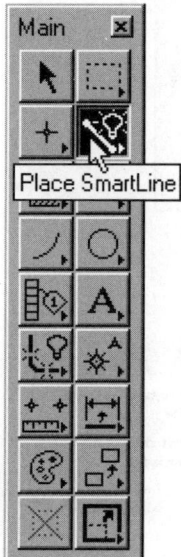

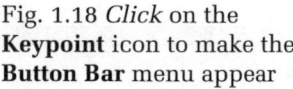

Fig. 1.17 The **Main** tool palette

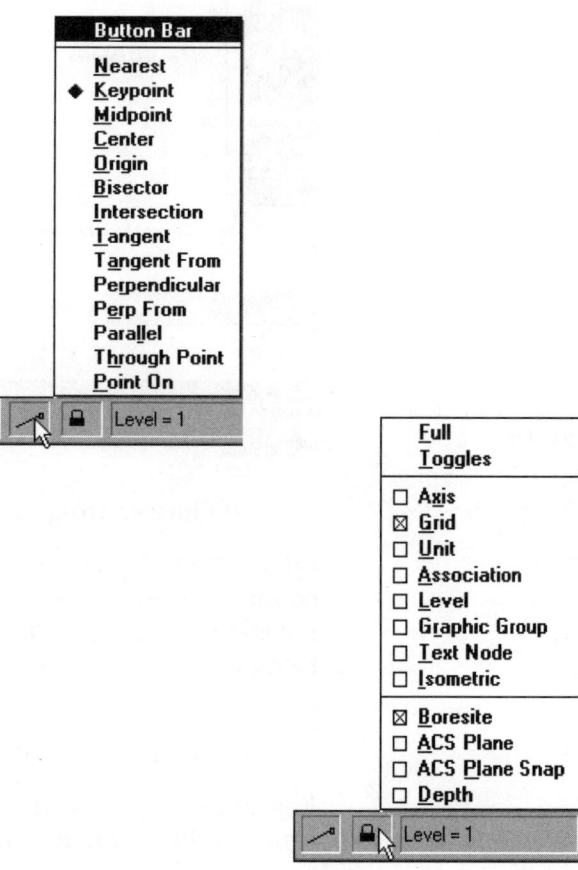

Fig. 1.18 *Click* on the **Keypoint** icon to make the **Button Bar** menu appear

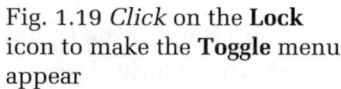

Fig. 1.19 *Click* on the **Lock** icon to make the **Toggle** menu appear

Fig. 1.20 *Click* on the **Level=1** icon and the **Set Active Level** dialogue box opens

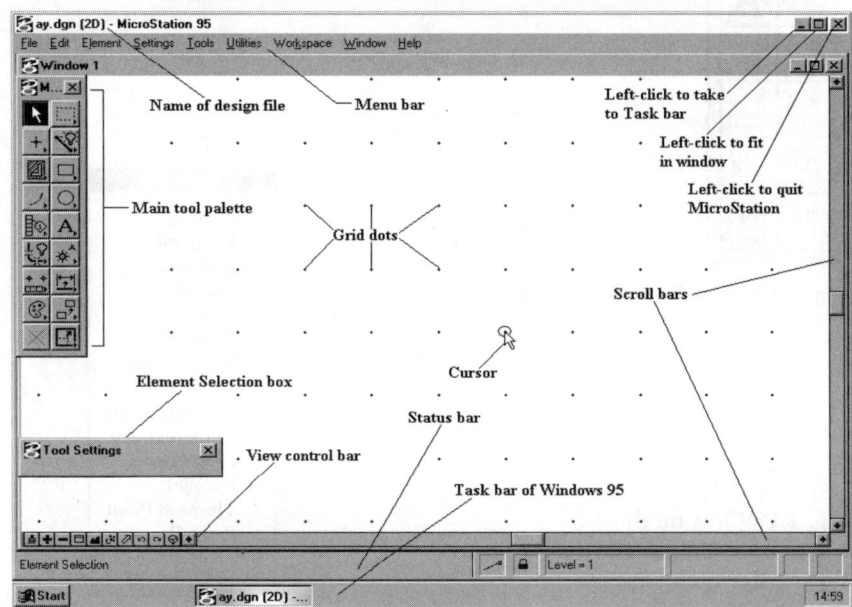

Fig. 1.21 Details of the final design file **ay.dgn**

The resulting ay.dgn screen

Figure 1.21 shows the resulting screen in which one could now commence constructing drawings. If the **Elements Selection** box is not showing, from the **Tools** pull-down menu select **Tool Settings** to bring it on screen, as shown in Fig. 1.21.

Calling or selecting tools

Figure 1.4 on page 4 showed the **Main** palette and Fig. 1.5 the flyout from the **Place Smart Line** tool icon in the **Main** palette. Fig. 1.6

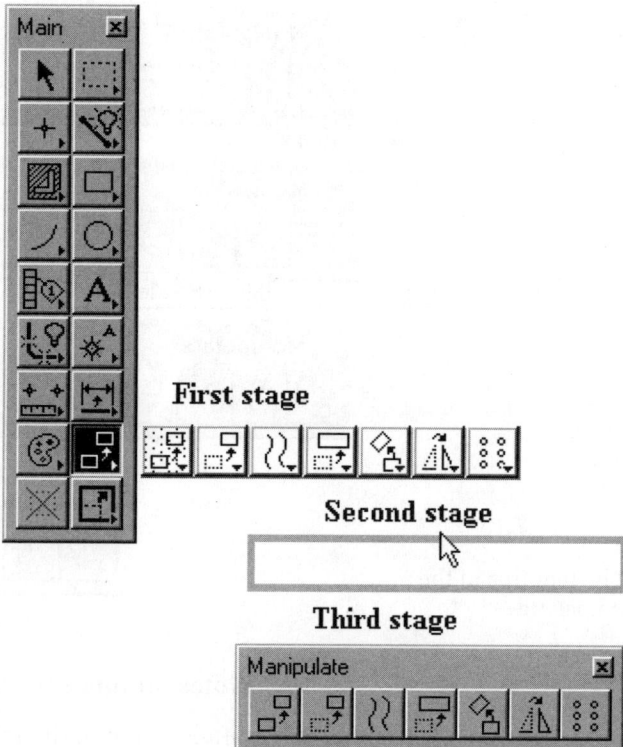

First stage

Second stage

Third stage

Fig. 1.22 Moving the
Manipulate palette

showed a tool tip associated with the **Place Circle by Center** tool
icon. The tools shown in these three illustrations are probably those
most commonly used when constructing drawings in any CAD
system.

Another set of important tools in frequent use are those contained
in the **Manipulate** palette. To select (call) a tool for use from this
palette, the following procedure can be adopted, as shown in Fig.
1.22:

> **First stage**. In the **Main** palette, hold a *left-click* over the **Copy**
> tool icon. The icon highlights and the **Manipulate** flyout
> appears.
> **Second stage**. Move the cursor under mouse control over the
> palette and *drag* the palette to a new position.
> **Third stage**. Release the mouse button and the palette appears in
> full.

Any of the **Manipulate** tools can be selected, either from the
flyout as in Stage 2, or from the palette as in Stage 3. The tool tips for
all the **Manipulate** tools are shown in Fig. 1.23.

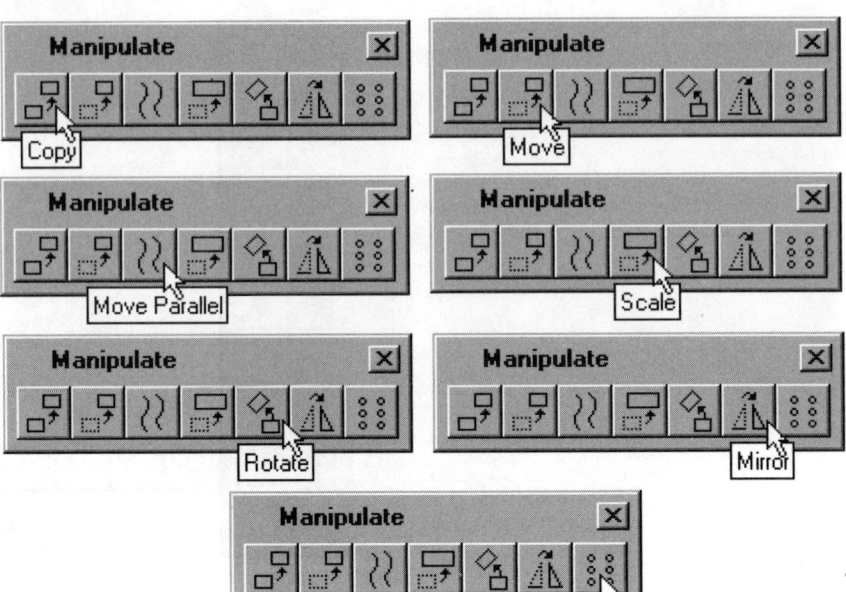

Fig. 1.23 The tool tips of the
Manipulate palette

Notes on tool selection

1. No matter which of the tools are selected, whether from the flyout or from the **Manipulate** palette, the tool icon in the **Main** palette changes to the selected tool icon.
2. When a tool icon is selected, the **Element Selection** dialogue box for that tool appears. Thus, as indicated in Fig. 1.24, when the **Move** tool is selected, the **Move** box replaces the **Element Selection** box. Each tool has its own Element Selection box.

Fig. 1.24 The **Element Selection** box changes to **Move** when the **Move** tool icon is selected

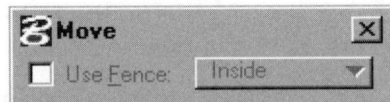

3. There is no need to *drag* a flyout to a new position in order that it appears as a complete palette. Tools can equally well be chosen from the flyout as from a palette.
4. Depending upon whether a Command Window is in operation or not (see page 46), a prompt will appear either in the Command Window or, if the Command Window is not showing, at the bottom left-hand corner of the screen. These prompts inform the operator what his/her next step should be. As an example, Fig. 1.25 shows an element constructed with the **Smart Line** tool moved to another

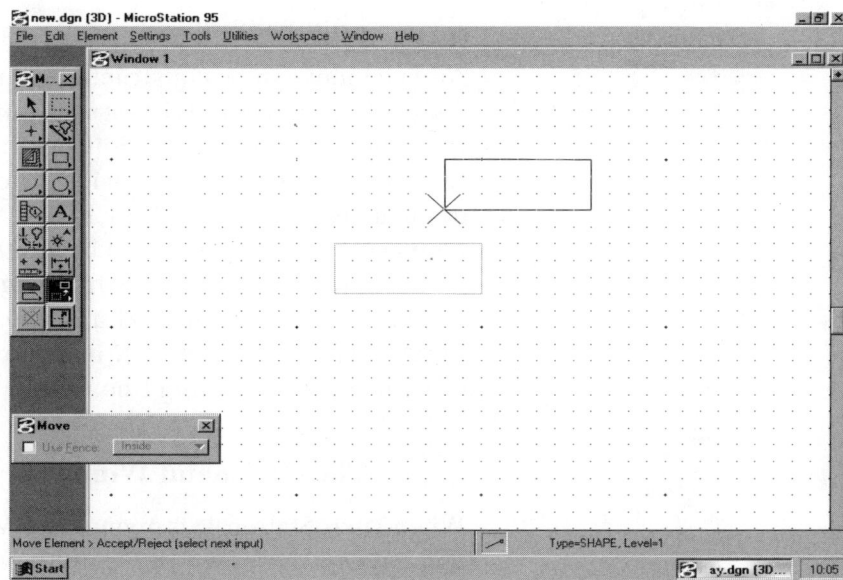

Fig. 1.25 Moving an element
with the **Move** tool

position with the aid of the **Move** tool. The prompts at the bottom
left-hand corner of the screen show in sequence:

Move element
Move element > Identify element
Move element > Accept/Reject (select next input)
    Left-click to **Accept**; *right-click* to **Reject**. If **Accept**, *drag* the
element to its new position (**next input**)
Move element > Identify element

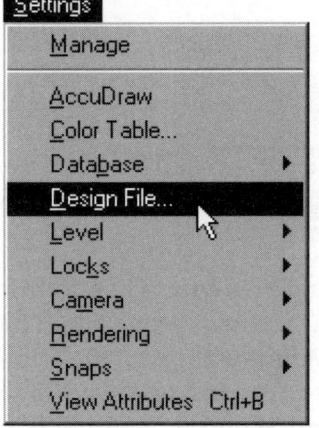

Fig. 1.26 Selecting **Design
File...** from the **Settings** pull-
down menu

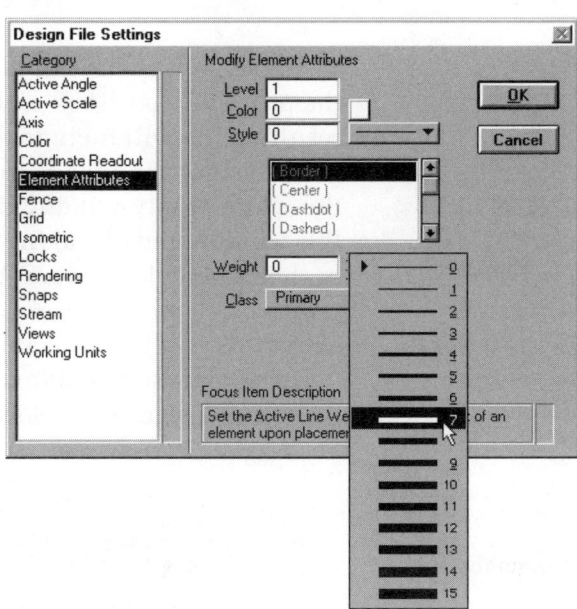

Fig. 1.27 Changing line weight
in the **Design File Settings**
dialogue box

Line weight

Any element can be constructed in any one of 15 line weights. The default line weight is 0. To set a new line weight *left-click* on **Settings** in the menu bar and in the **Settings** pull-down menu which appears (Fig. 1.26) *left-click* on **Design File....** The **Design File Settings** dialogue box appears (Fig. 1.27). In the dialogue box, *left-click* on **Element Attributes** followed by another on the **Weight** box. A pop-up list appears showing the line weights. A *left-click* on the desired weight (in this example **7**) and the line weight is changed to **7**. Finally *left-click* on the **OK** button of the dialogue box. There are other methods of setting line weight, as will be seen in later pages.

The Command Window

When MicroStation 95 is opened, the **MicroStation Manager** dialogue box appears as shown in Fig. 1.10 on page 6. At the bottom of the dialogue box is a set of settings **Workspace**, **Project**, **Interface** and **Style**. A *left-click* on the **Style** box brings down a pop-up list showing both **Status Bar** and **Command Window** (Fig. 1.28).

Fig. 1.28 Selecting **Command Window** from the **Style** pop-up list

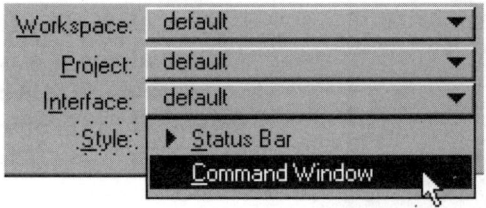

In the pop-up list *left-click* on **Command Window**. Then follow the procedure outlined earlier of making up a **New** design file. The resulting file will include the **Command Window** (Fig. 1.29). If you wish to *enter* commands from the keyboard they can be keyed-in to the white empty window in the **Command Window**. *Left-click* in this window and a blinking cursor appears against which commands or their abbreviations can be *keyed-in*. X,Y coordinate positions of points on elements can also be *keyed-in* at this blinking cursor. More about this in a later chapter (Chapter 4).

The **Command Window** is included in a design file which I have named **aydesign**. The design screen of this file is shown in Fig. 1.30.

Fig. 1.29 The **Command Window**

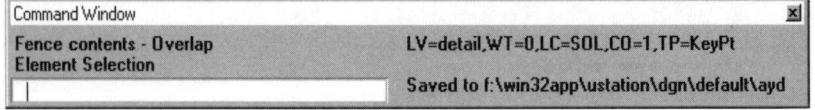

Chapter 3 will contain fuller details about the file **aydesign.dgn**. For the time being we will be working in the design file **ay.dgn** described earlier in this chapter – i.e. without the **Command Window**. The names of the various parts of a design file screen are included in Fig. 1.30.

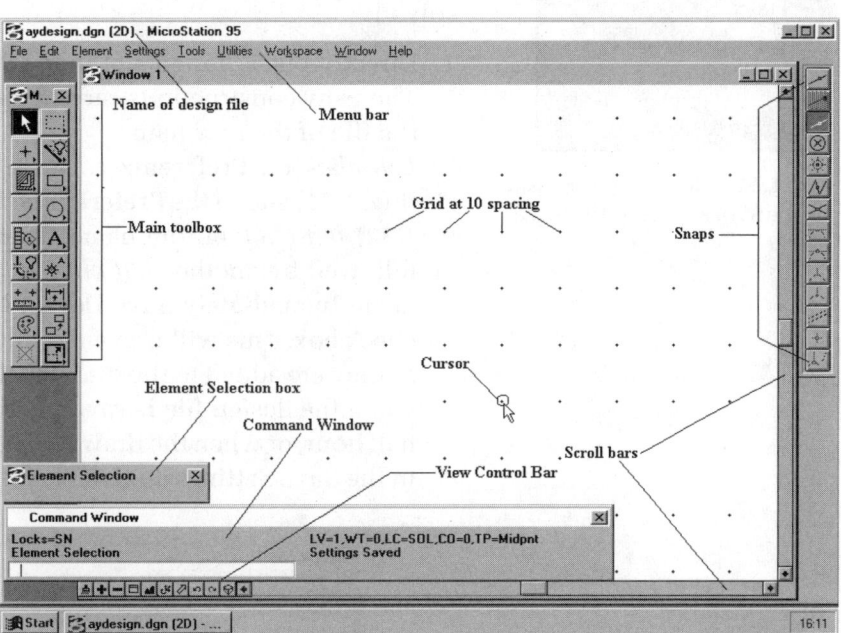

Fig. 1.30 The design file **aydesign** which includes the **Command Window**

Notes on seed files

A number of seed files are included in the MicroStation 95 files. These include seed files for:

> Working in 2D with metres (seed2dm.dgn).
> Working in 3D in metres (seed3dm.dgn).
> Working in 3D in four windows (seedz.dgn).
> Working in 2D in micrometres (schem2d.dgn).
> Working in 3D in micrometres (schem3d.dgn).

Other seed files include those for working in feet, in kilometres, etc.

Seed files 'seed' a new design file by including settings appropriate for the type of drawing in mind – working in 2D or in 3D; working in metres, millimetres, feet, inches, etc.

Saving files

A feature of MicroStation is that any change when working is saved to the file which is open. This saving takes place immediately an

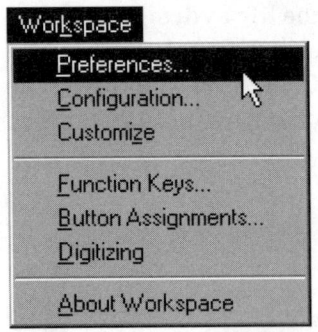

Fig. 1.31 Select **Preferences...** in the **Workspace** pull-down menu

element or other feature is added to a drawing. One of the problems this may cause to a beginner is that when a new session of work is started and one's own design file such as my **ay.dgn** file is opened, all constructions previously carried out in the file will come up on screen. There are two methods by which this problem may be solved:

1. Directly one's design file is loaded, save it to another filename. Then any constructions carried out will automatically be saved to the file of the new name.

2. *Left-click* on **Preferences...** in the **Workspace** pull-down menu (Fig. 1.31) and in the **Preferences** dialogue box which appears (Fig. 1.32) *left-click* on the name **Operation** in the **Category** list box, followed by another *left-click* in the check box to the left of the name **Immediately Save Design Changes** to clear the **X** from the check box. This will prevent additions to a design file being saved as they are added to the drawing. Changes will only then be saved when the design file is saved either at regular intervals, say each half hour, or when the drawing has been completed. Also *left-click* in the **Save Settings on Exit** check box to set it on (**X** in check box).

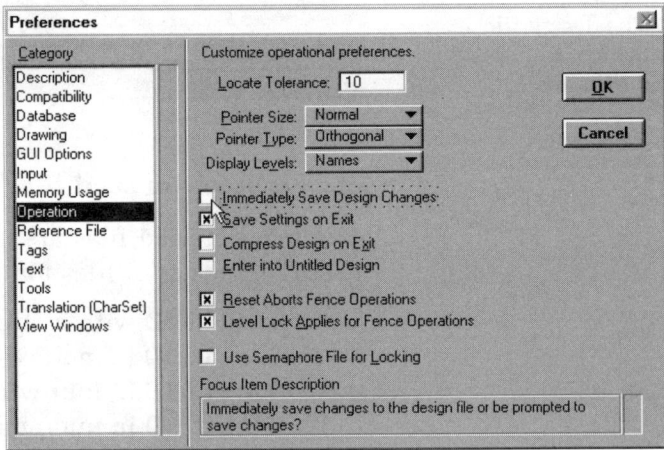

Fig. 1.32 Turning off the check box against **Immediately Save Design Changes**

Note on the saving of design files

No matter which CAD system you are working in, get into the habit of saving your work at regular intervals. If your system crashes for any reason, at least you have saved work up to the last save. Systems may crash for a variety of reasons such as a sudden loss of electrical power, a minor fault in your software (a 'bug'), or a mistake in operating made by the operator.

Pull-down menus in MicroStation 95

Figure 1.33 shows the pull-down menus available from the menu bar in MicroStation 95. It will be seen from the illustration that some command names are 'greyed out'. This is because either there is no drawing on the screen at the time the pull-down menu was selected, or the command has not been set in the design drawing screen.

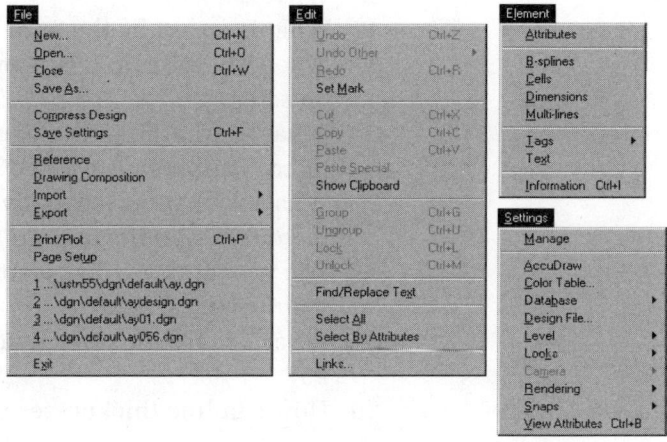

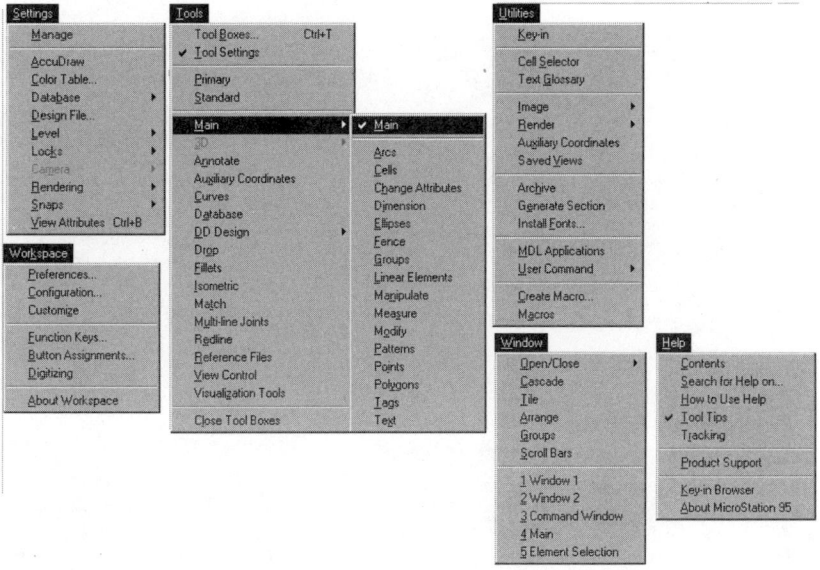

Fig. 1.33 The pull-down menus from MicroStation 95

Questions

The following questions are set here to encourage the reader to revise the contents of the chapter. Most only require a single word or phrase to answer.

1. What is the minimum amount of RAM fitted in a computer before MicroStation 95 will operate?
2. What is meant by the term *cursor*?
3. What is a *flyout*?
4. What is meant by the term *tool tip*?
5. When MicroStation 95 is opened what is the first item to appear on screen?
6. What is the first dialogue box to appear on screen when MicroStation 95 is opened?
7. What to you think is the advantage of having a Command Window in your design file screen?
8. Can you think of a disadvantage of having a Command Window in your design screen?
9. What is a *seed* file and why are seed files important in MicroStation 95?
10. How can line thicknesses be changed in MicroStation 95?

CHAPTER 2

The tool palettes

Descriptions of the tool palettes

Tool palettes are brought to screen from the **Tools** pull-down menu
(Fig. 2.1). In this pull-down menu, if a tool palette is already on
screen, a tick will appear against the tool palette name. Note that the
outward pointing arrow against **Main** in the pull-down menu shows
that a *left-click* on **Main** will bring up a sub-menu with the names of
all the tool palettes held in the **Main** tool palette. Figure 2.1 shows
that the **Linear Elements** palette has been selected from the **Main**
sub-menu. Figure 2.2 shows this palette. This particular palette has
been chosen because it contains the icons of tools very likely to be
used when constructing a drawing in MicroStation.

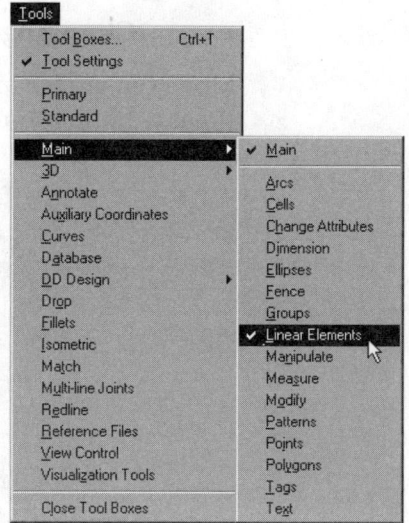

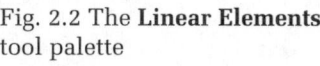

Fig. 2.1 Selecting **Linear
Elements** from the **Main** sub-
menu of **Tools**

Fig. 2.2 The **Linear Elements**
tool palette

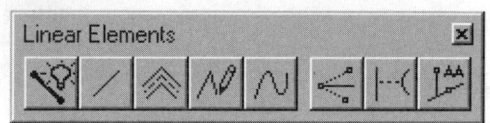

Parts of tool palettes

Palette tool name: The name of the palette shows in the top left-hand corner.

Remove button: The button carrying a cross (**X**) at the top right-hand corner of the palette can be used to remove the palette from the screen. A *left-click* in the button and the palette disappears.

Palette movement: Move the cursor under mouse control into the area of the palette not covered by icons. Hold down the left-hand mouse button and the palette in a *ghosted* form can be *dragged* to another part of the screen (Fig. 2.3). Release the mouse button and the palette reappears in full at its new position.

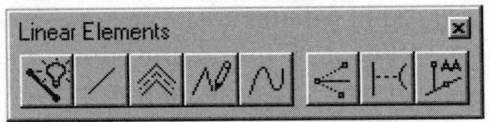

Fig. 2.3 Moving the palette to another part of the screen.

Changing the shape of the palette

Move the cursor under mouse control to any corner of the palette. Press a button and a window *drag* cursor appears at the selected

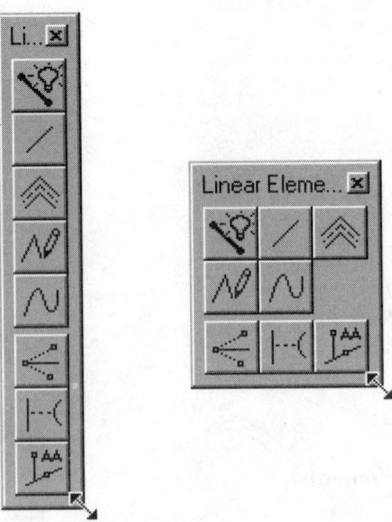

Fig. 2.4 Changing the shape of the palette

corner. The palette can now be *dragged* to a new shape. Figure 2.4 shows a palette which has been changed to a vertical position in this manner, and changed again to a differently shaped rectangle.

The palette at either side of the screen: If the palette is *dragged* to either side of the screen, it loses its name and its **X** button and fits snugly to the side of the **Window 1** window. Figure 2.5 shows the **Main** palette fitted against the left-hand side of the window and the **Linear Elements** palette dragged to the right-hand side of the screen.

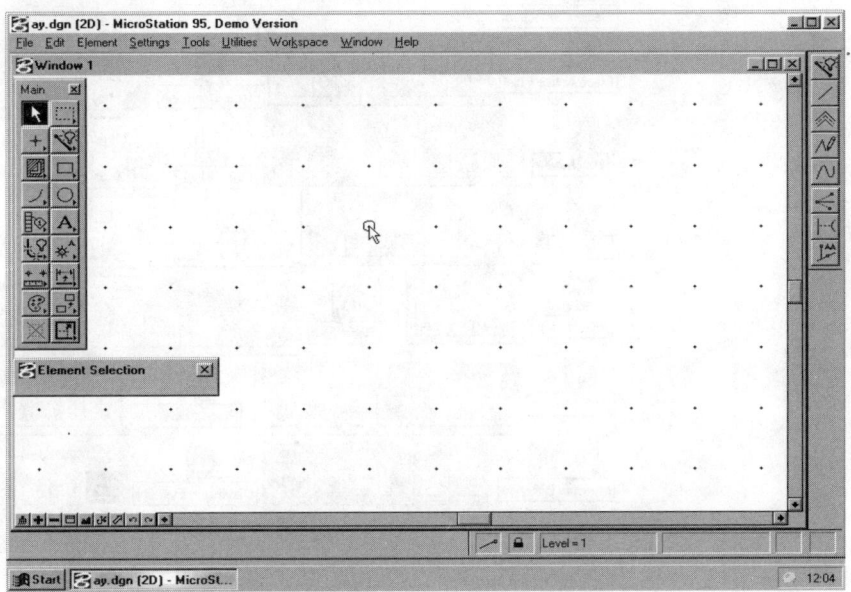

Fig. 2.5 The **Linear Elements** palette moved to the right-hand side of the screen

Flyout: Any tool icon showing a small outward pointing arrow at its bottom right-hand corner, as in Fig. 2.6, will display a **flyout** showing subsidiary tools when the cursor is moved onto the icon and the left-hand mouse button is held down. As explained in Chapter 1, this flyout can be *dragged* from its position to form its own tool palette.

Tool tips: All tool icons from all tool palettes except those on flyouts show a **tool tip** when the cursor under mouse control is moved onto the icon. An example showing the **Place Line** icon and its tool tip are shown in Fig. 2.7.

All tool sub-palettes from the Main tool palette

Figure 2.8 shows all the tool palettes (sub-palettes to the **Main** tool palette) from the **Main** tool palette. The tool tips from the tool icons

Fig. 2.6 The flyout from the
Place Smart Line tool

Fig. 2.7 The **Place Line** tool
icon in the **Linear Elements**
palette showing its tool tip

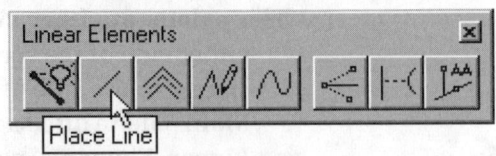

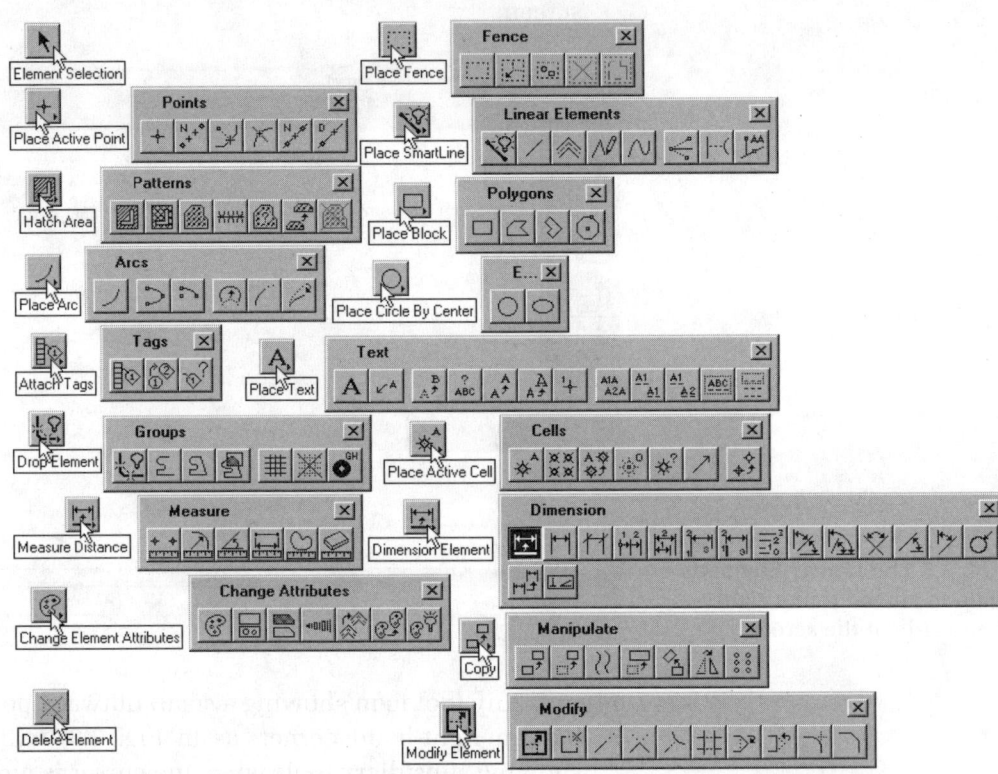

Fig. 2.8 All the tool tips and tool sub-palettes from the **Main** tool palette

from which the sub-palettes are selected by *dragging* their flyouts
are included in this illustration.

Settings in the Design File

Before going on to practise using tools for some simple drawings, it
is suggested that two settings be made as follows:

1. *Left-click* on **Settings** in the menu bar and, in the pull-down menu
   which appears, *left-click* on **Design File...** (Fig. 2.9).

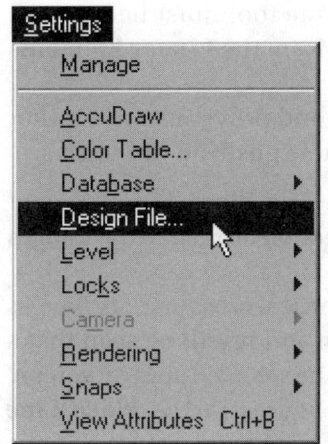

Fig. 2.9 Selecting **Design File...** from the **Settings** pull-down menu

Fig. 2.10 Settings for **Grid** in the **Design File Settings** dialogue box

Fig. 2.11 Settings for **Working Units** in the **Design File Settings** dialogue box

2. In the **Design File Settings** dialogue box which appears, *left-click* on **Grid** and *left-click* again in the check box against **Grid Lock** to set the lock on. A cross (**X**) should appear in the check box showing that the lock is set. See Fig. 2.10.
3. *Left-click* on **Working Units** in the **Design File Settings** box and make settings in the resulting boxes as shown in Fig. 2.11.
4. Save the design screen to a filename on disk. My drawing has been saved as **ay01.dgn** in a directory **c:\ay\design**.

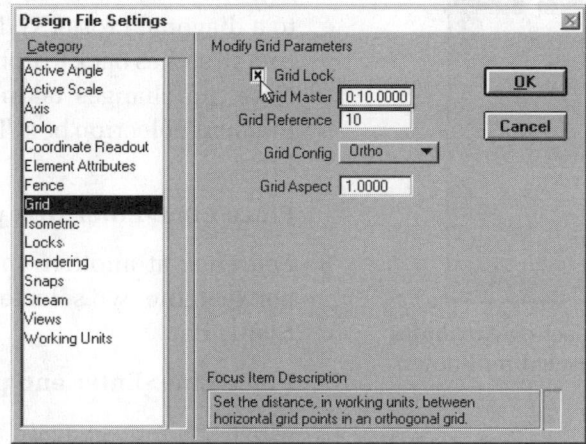

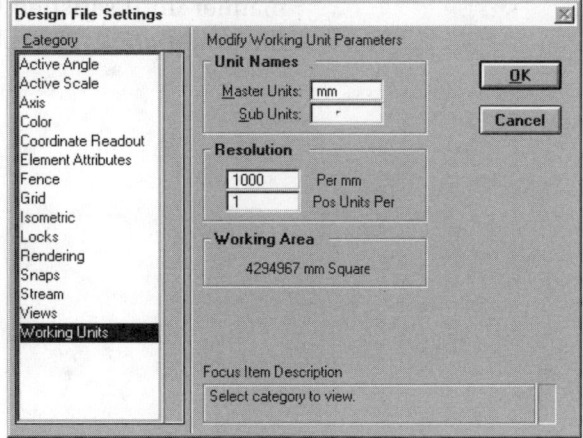

Practise drawing

Now attempt some simple drawings with the **Place Line**, **Place Circle by Center**, **Place Arc** and **Place Regular Polygon** tools. Do not bother about whether the drawings have any meaning or not, the purpose of this practise is to try to get the feel of using those tools which are the most likely to be frequently used for two-dimensional

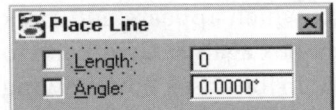

Fig. 2.12 The **Place Line**
Element Selection box

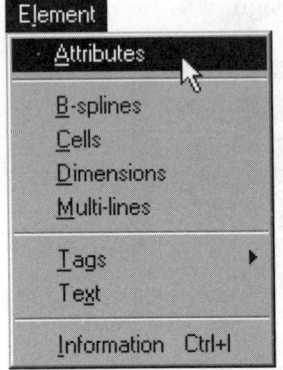

Fig. 2.13 Selecting **Attributes**
from the **Element** pull-down
menu

(2D) drawing. Remember that the **Place Line** tool must be selected
either from the **Place Smart Line** flyout or from the **Linear Elements**
tool palette.

Methods of drawing lines, circles, arcs and polygons are similar.
To draw lines without bothering about their position or lengths:

1. *Left-click* on the **Place Line** tool icon. The **Place Line** Element
   Selection box, replaces the **Element Selection** box. Note the **Length**
   and **Angle** in the selection box (Fig. 2.12).

2. *Left-click* anywhere on the screen. The vertical cross cursor changes
   to a diagonal cross (X). Move the mouse and it will be seen that a
   line stretches back ('rubber-banded') to the selected spot on screen.
   Note the changes taking place in the figures in the **Place Line**
   Element Selection box. The following prompt appears in the Status
   Line:

Place Line>Enter first point

3. *Left-click* at another spot on the screen, a line has been drawn
   between the two selected points. A second prompt appears in the
   Status Bar

Place Line>Enter end point

Move the mouse again and the line is now rubber-banded to the
second selected spot on screen. Continue drawing lines in this
manner until satisfied that you understand how lines are drawn,
then *right-click*. The rubber band is then released from the cursor.

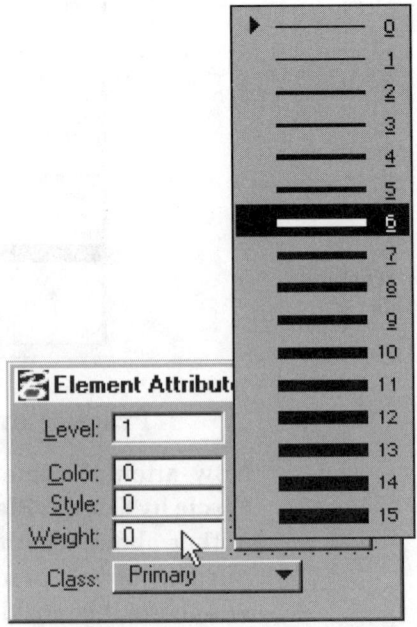

Fig. 2.14 The **Element
Attributes** dialogue box with
the **Weight** pop-up list
showing

4. Now *key-in* some figures into the **Length** and **Angle** boxes of the **Place Line** box – say 20 and 45. When drawing a line now it will be at a fixed length of 20 units (in this drawing this represents 20 mm).

5. When satisfied with the outline you have drawn, *left-click* on **Attributes** in the **Element** pull-down menu (Fig. 2.13). The **Element Attributes** dialogue box appears (Fig. 2.14). *Left-click* on the box to the right of **Weight:** and the line weight pop-up list appears. Select a line weight from the list, in our example this is 6.

6. Construct other outlines with the aid of the **Place Line** tool of line weight 6, then try other line weights selected from the **Element Attributes** dialogue box. Again, do not bother about accuracy or what the shape of the outline is, just try to get the feel of using the **Place Line** tool. But keep an eye on the figures in the **Place Line** Element Selection box.

7. *Left-click* on the **Place Circle by Center** tool icon. The **Place Circle by Center** Element Selection box replaces the **Place Line** box. Two prompts, one after the other in the Status Bar, assist the operator in drawing circles

   Place Circle by Center>Identify Center Point
   Place Circle by Center>Identify Point on Circle

   Draw some circles of various line weights.

8. Now *left-click* on the **Place Arc** tool and practise drawing arcs of various line weight. Watch the Status bar for prompts.

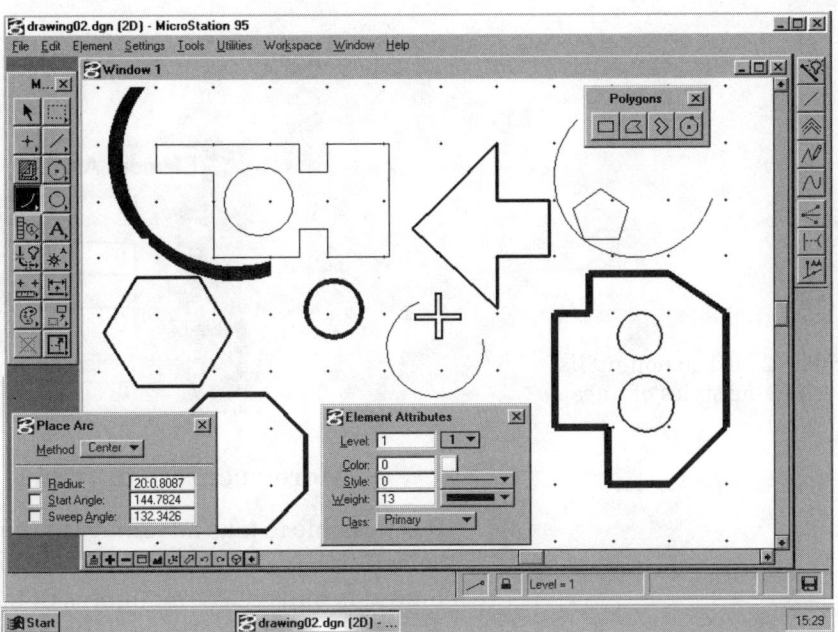

Fig. 2.15 The resulting screen after a practise drawing

9. Finally *left-click on the* **Place Regular Polygon** tool icon and draw 5-, 6- and 8-sided regular polygons (pentagons, hexagons and octagons) of various line weights. Again note prompts in the Status Bar.

The resulting screen should look something like that shown in Fig. 2.15, although your shapes and sizes of circles, arcs and regular polygons are bound to be different to those in that illustration. You may also have different Element Selection boxes on screen.

Note

1. The **Grid Lock** has been set on at 1 unit between locks. This means that whenever you select an end for a line, the selection spot will be at a 1 unit (1 mm) grid lock.
2. The prompts appearing in the Status Bar offer valuable assistance to those new to working in a CAD system.
3. Try drawing elements after *entering* figures such as **Length** and **Angle** into the boxes of the Element Selection dialogue boxes. This is one way in which accurate precise drawings may be constructed.

Line styles

In the **Element Attributes** dialogue box, *left-click* in the window to the right of **Style:**. A pop-up list appears showing the styles of lines available, numbered 1 to 7 (Fig. 2.16). Practise drawing lines of different styles as indicated in Fig. 2.17.

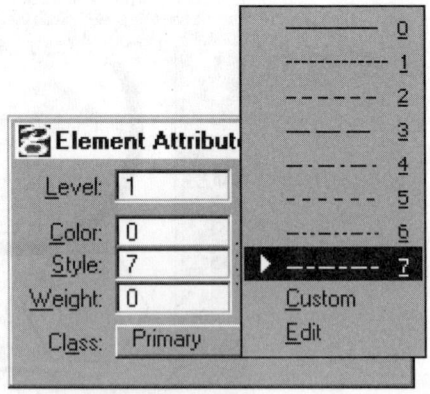

Fig. 2.16 The pop-up list showing styles of lines

More accurate drawing

It is possible to take advantage of the **Length** and **Angle** figures in the selection boxes. When a tool such as **Place Line** is in action, as the mouse is moved, so the figures of length and angle of the line being

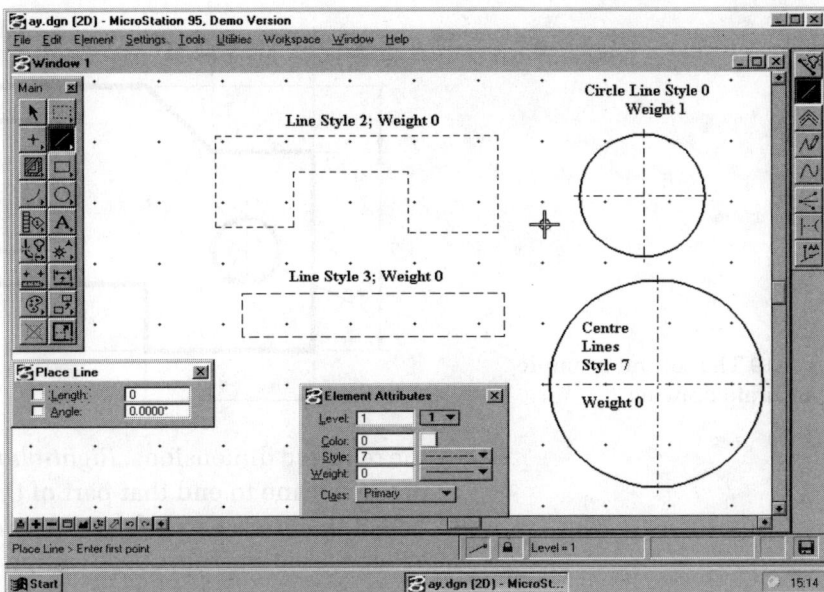

Fig. 2.17 Practise drawing lines of different line styles

drawn are updated in the selection box. Two examples are shown in Figs 2.18 and 2.19. This is not the best method of constructing drawings to accurate sizes, but it is a method which may prove to be of value on occasions. Further information on accurate drawing is given in Chapter 4. It is suggested that you attempt these two examples, but do not attempt to include the dimensions, which are given only for your guidance. Methods of dimensioning are described in Chapter 11.

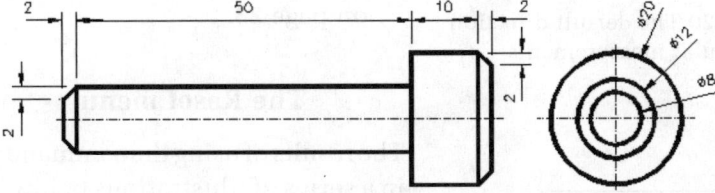

Fig. 2.18 The first example of accurate drawing

To construct drawings such as those shown in the two illustrations:

1. In the **Element Attributes** dialogue box, select the required **Style:** line for the outline (in both examples **0**) and then select the required **Weight:** of line for the outline (in both examples this will be **1**).
2. Select the **Place Line** tool. *Left-click* at a suitable spot on screen and start drawing the outline of any part of the drawing. Watch the **Length:** and **Angle:** figures in the **Place Line** Element Selection box and only *left-click* to end each line when the figures correspond to

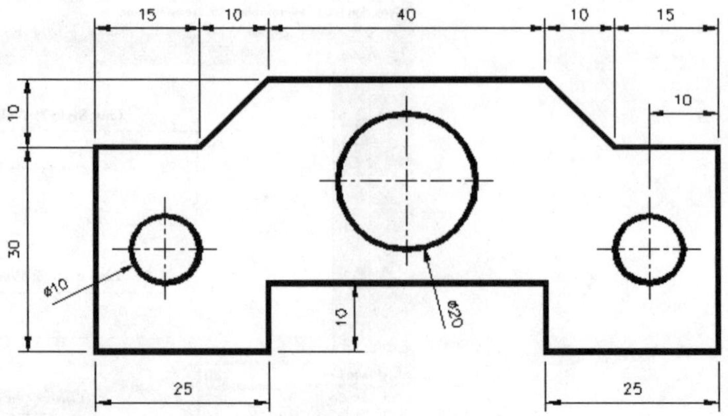

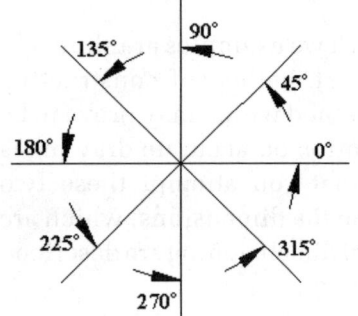

Fig. 2.19 The second example
of accurate drawing

the required dimensions. *Right-click* at the completion of each part
of the outline to end that part of the lines of the outline.

3. Select the **Place Circle by Center** tool and draw the circles.
4. When the outlines have been completed, from the **Element Attributes**
dialogue box, select **Style: 7** and **Weight: 0** and add the centre lines
through the two parts of the drawing with the **Place Line** tool.

Notes

1. By default, angles are measured in degrees, starting with 0° to the
right (east), 90° to the top (north), 180° to the left (west), and 270°
to the bottom (south). See Fig. 2.20. Degrees are therefore measured
in an anti-clockwise (or counter-clockwise) direction from east.
2. In order to have millimetres showing as the first figure in the **Length**
window of the Element Selection boxes, the **Working Units** must
be set in the **Design File Settings** dialogue box as shown in Fig. 2.11
on page 23.

Fig. 2.20 The default direction
of angular measurements

The Reset menu

The results of using the commands in the **Reset** menu are demonstrated
in a series of illustrations below. The original design on which these
illustrations are based is shown in Fig. 2.22. Press and hold down the
Shift key of the keyboard followed by a *right-click*. The **Reset** menu
appears. This menu holds the following commands:

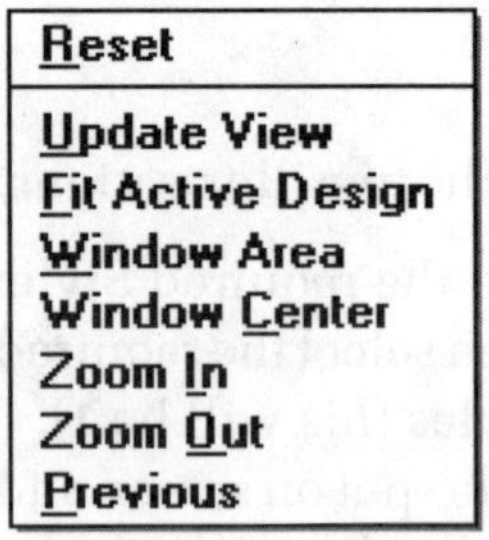

Update View: *Left-click* and the screen regenerates in such a manner
that any partly erased details are brought back in full.
Fit Active Design: *Left-click* and the prompt:

Fit Active Design>Select view

Fig. 2.21 The **Reset** menu
appearing with **Shift**/*right-
click*

appears in the Status Bar. *Left-click* within the area of the view to
be fitted and the view fills the whole drawing area (Fig. 2.23).

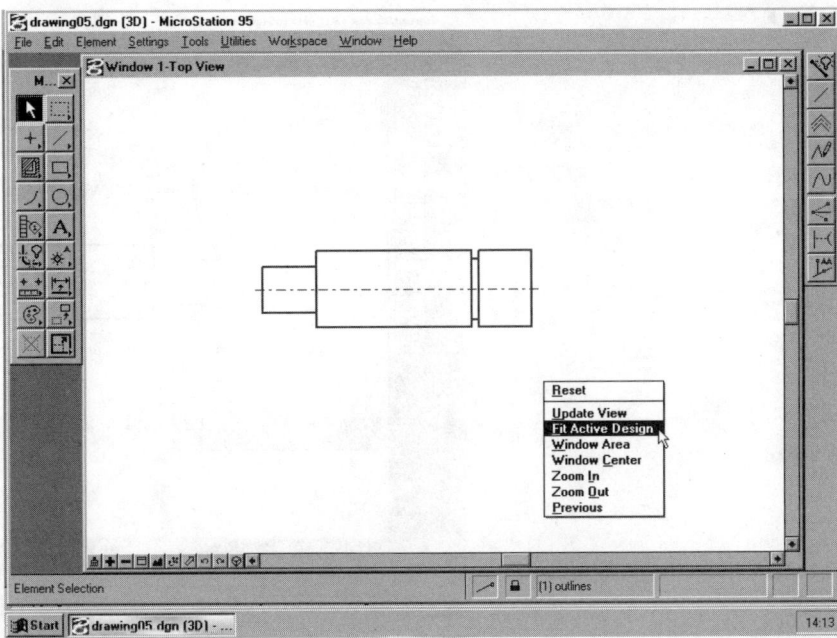

Fig. 2.22 The original design
in the drawing area of a
MicroStation 95 screen

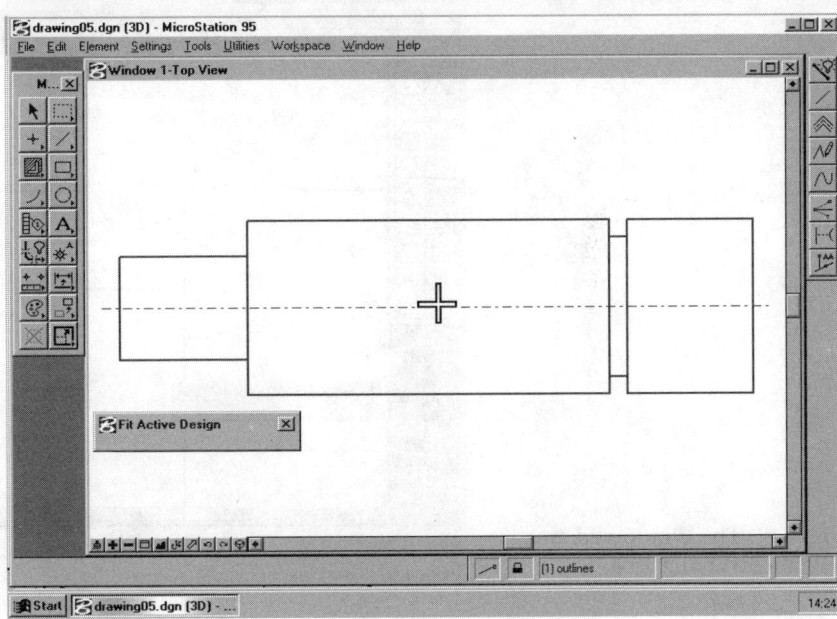

Fig. 2.23 The results of
selecting **Fit Active Design**

Window Area: (Figs 2.24 and 2.25). *Left-click* and the prompt changes:

Window Area>Select window origin

When the origin has been selected, the prompt changes to:

Window Area>Select window corner

When the corner has been selected, the prompt again changes:

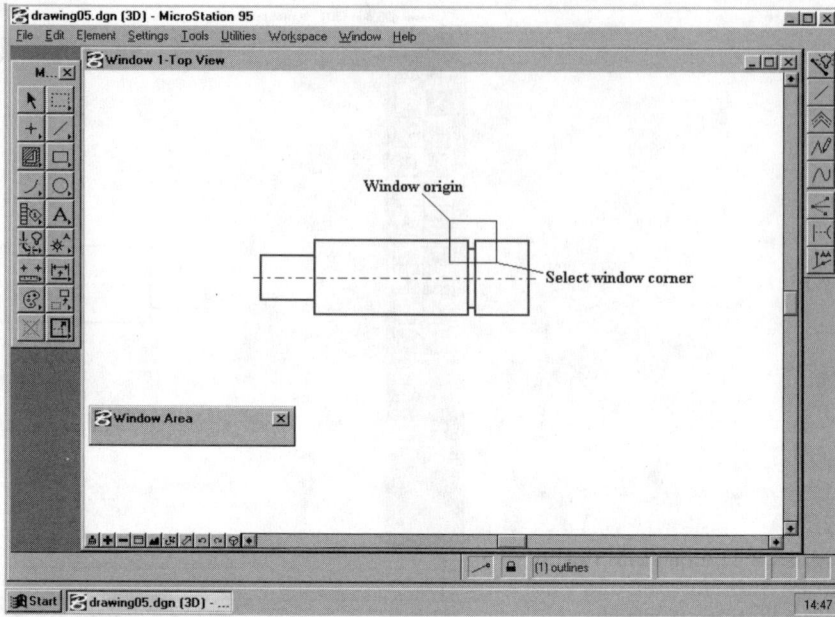

Fig. 2.24 Selecting a **Window Area**

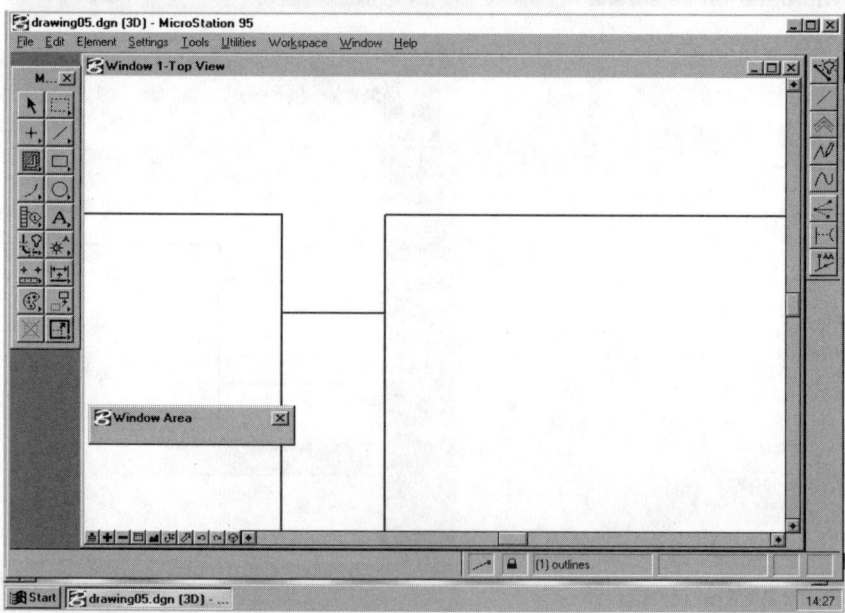

Fig. 2.25 The windowed area fills the drawing area

Window Area>Select view

A *left-click* within the view and the windowed area fills the drawing area.

Zoom Out: *Left-click* on **Zoom Out** results in the prompt:

Zoom Out>Select point to zoom about

Select a point anywhere on screen and the design zooms to a scale of one-half (Scale 1:2).

Zoom In: This has the opposite effect from **Zoom Out** , in that the design is zoomed to a scale of 2:1.

Note

The default zoom in or zoom out scale is 2 – either 2:1 or 1:2 respectively. It will be seen later in this book that, in some circumstances, this zoom scale can be changed. If you zoom in, it is as if you were moving towards the screen, thus the design gets larger. If you zoom out, it is as if you were moving further away from the screen, thus the design becomes smaller.

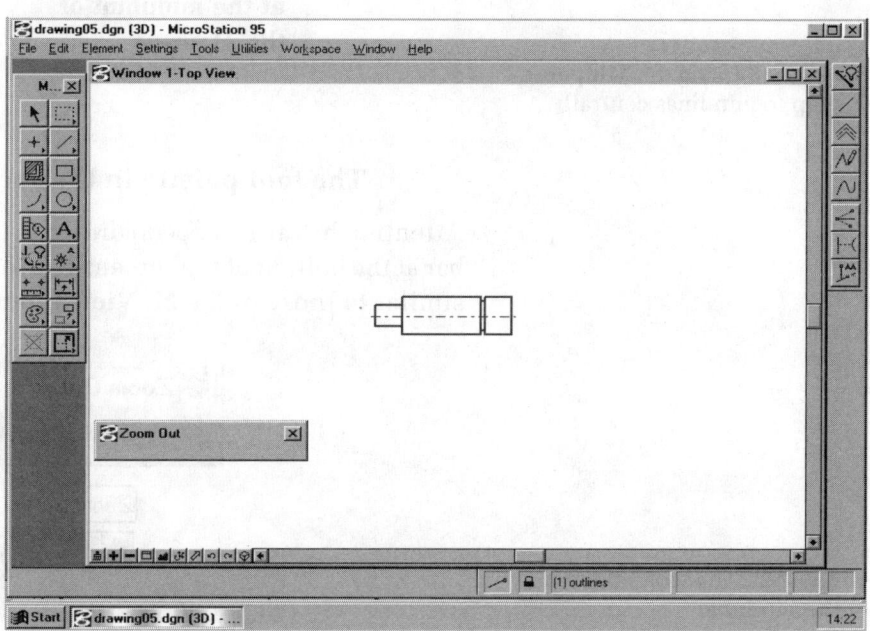

Fig. 2.26 The results of **Zoom Out**

The Button Bar

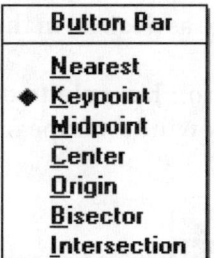

Fig. 2.27 The **Button Bar** menu appearing with a **Shift/** *double-click*

Press the **Shift** key of the keyboard, followed by a *both-click* (both mouse buttons) and the **Button Bar** appears (Fig. 2.27). The **Snap** points displayed in the **Button Bar** allow elements to be placed precisely at positions relative to other elements. Thus a line can be placed starting exactly at the **Midpoint** of another element, by a *left-click* on **Midpoint** in the **Button Bar**, followed by a *both-click* (a tentative point) on the element. This places a vertical cross exactly at the midpoint of the element, to which another element can be attached – for example, another line.

Figure 2.28 shows three lines, one of which has been drawn to the midpoints of the other two, with a fourth line about to be snapped to the third. Other **Button** points can be selected, as can be seen from Fig. 2.28, by using *both-clicks* (tentative points).

The use of snaps from the button bar is another aid to accurate construction in a design.

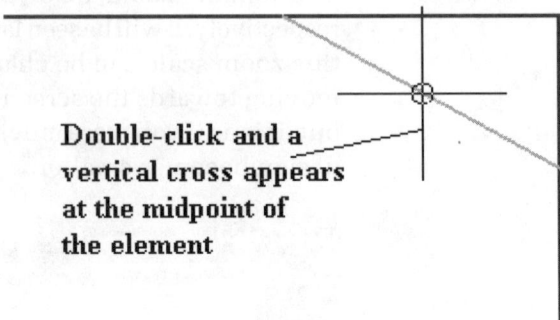

Double-click and a vertical cross appears at the midpoint of the element

Fig. 2.28 Using the **Midpoint** snap to join lines centrally

The tool palette in the scroll bar

Attention has already been drawn to the set of tool icons in the scroll bar at the bottom of the screen. The tools in the palette (Fig. 2.29) are similar to those in the **2D View Control** palette shown in Fig. 2.30.

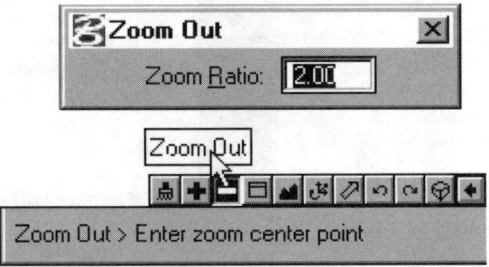

Fig. 2.29 The tool palette in the scroll bar

When a tool is selected from the scroll bar palette, its appropriate Element Selection box comes on to screen. Note that in the case of the **Zoom In** and **Zoom Out** Element Selection boxes the default scale of 2 can be changed by entering another figure as desired in the **Zoom Ratio:** window of the box.

When **Zoom In** is called, whether from the scroll bar palette or from the **2D View Control** palette (Fig. 2.30), a box window appears

Fig. 2.30 The **2D View Control** tool palette

on screen which can be *dragged* under mouse control. It is the area of the drawing on screen within this box window which is zoomed to appear on screen at the **Zoom Ratio** set in the **Zoom In** Element Selection box, usually at the default of **2**.

Questions

1. Why is the **Main** tool palette the one most likely to be always on screen when a design file has been opened?
2. What is the purpose of the button in a tool palette that shows an **X**?
3. What is the difference between a tool palette and a flyout?
4. What is meant by the term *tool tip*?
5. There are two methods by which grid lock is set. Can you describe them?
6. If you wish to draw an element from the end of another element, a snap point can be used. Can you explain how?
7. What is meant by the term *rubber band*?
8. How are line thicknesses changed?
9. If you wish to draw hidden detail lines, how do you proceed to do so?
10. What is the purpose of the **Element Attributes** dialogue box?

Exercises

1. Figure 2.31. With the aid of the **Place Line** tool and with the line style set to 0 and line weight set to 1, construct the four drawings shown in the given illustration to the given dimensions. Do not include any of the dimensions.

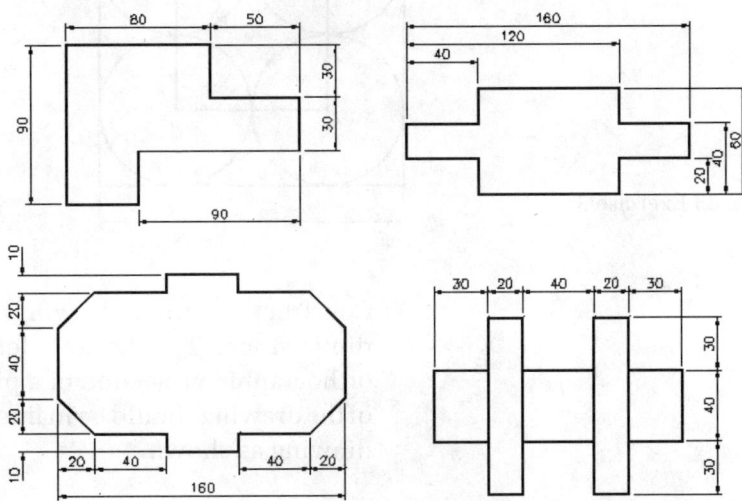

Fig. 2.31 Exercise 1

2. Figure 2.32. Working to the given dimensions construct the four drawings as shown with the aid of the **Place Line**, the **Place Circle by Center** and the **Place Ellipse** tools. Do not include dimensions in your answers.

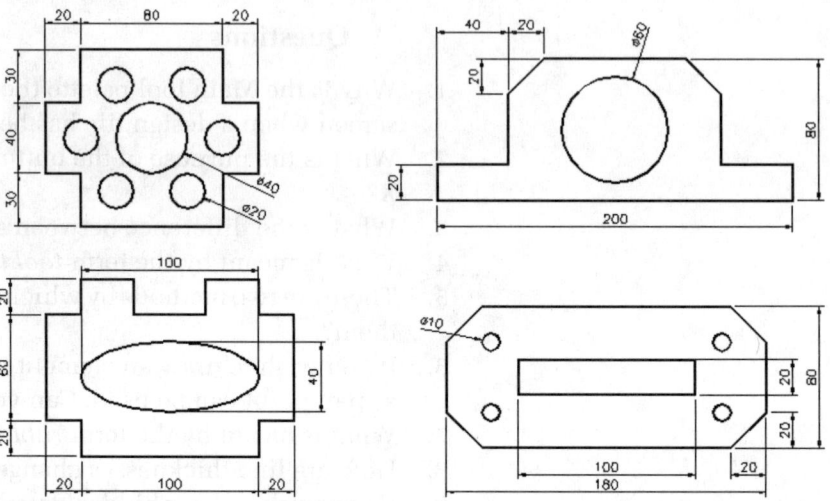

Fig. 2.32 Exercise 2

3. Construct the two figures shown in Fig. 2.33 to the given sizes. Do not include any dimensions.

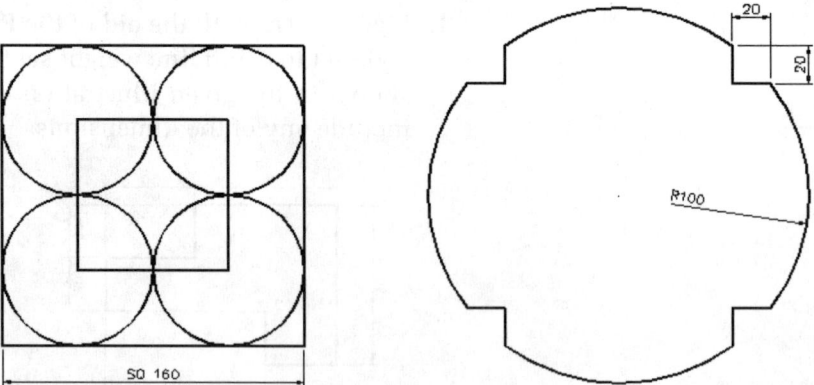

Fig. 2.33 Exercise 3

4. Construct the three drawings of Fig. 2.34 working to the given dimensions. The bottom left-hand drawing is a third-angle orthographic projection of a pin from a machine, so the two parts of the drawing should be in line horizontally. Add the border to that drawing as shown.

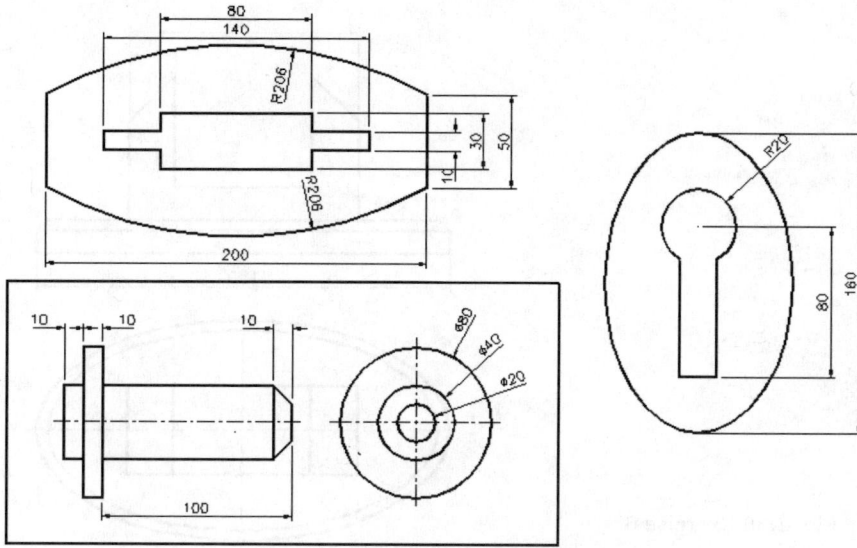

Fig. 2.34 Exercise 4

5. Figure 2.35 is an outline front view of a house. Obviously the given dimensions are of the drawing and not to any sizes the house would be built from. Working to the given sizes, copy the given view.

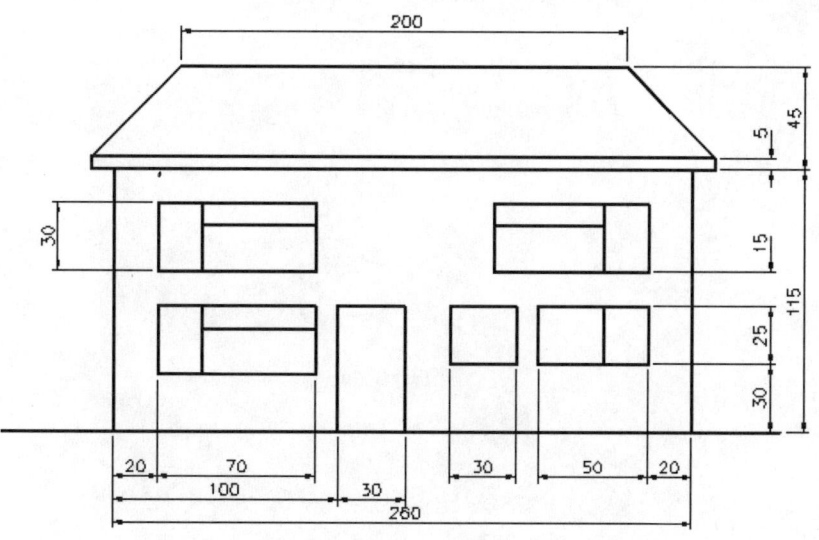

Fig. 2.35 Exercise 5

6. Figure 2.36 is a three-view first-angle orthographic projection of a bracket. Construct the three views to the details given, but do not include the dimensions in your answer.

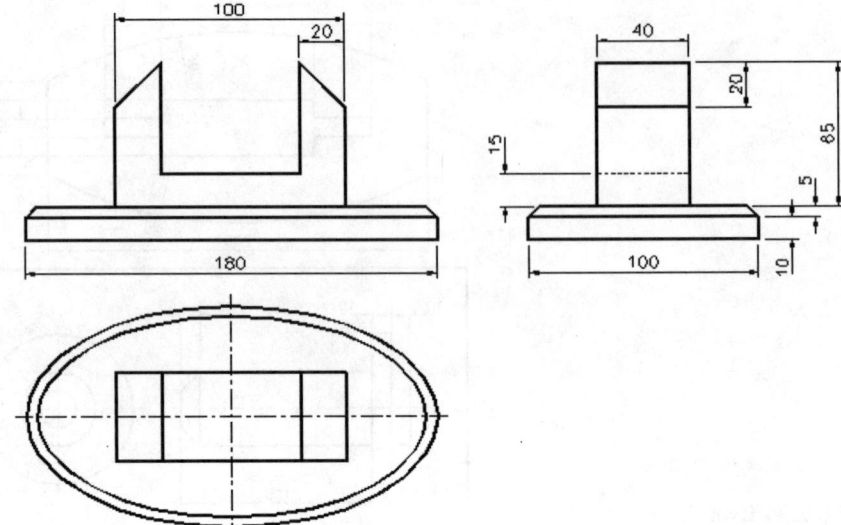

Fig. 2.36 Exercise 6

CHAPTER 3

A prototype design file

Introduction

Most of the drawings contained as illustrations in subsequent chapters are constructed within one of the design files described in this chapter. I have saved the first of these design files on my computer to the filename **aydesign.dgn** – that is my initials (ay) followed by design and the second as **ay01.dgn**. In order to follow the methods of construction described in future pages, it is advisable to construct a similar file of your own. These two files are 3D (three-dimensional) because the final chapters of this book introduce 3D model construction.

You may find settings, other than those given below, to be more suitable for your own methods of construction in MicroStation. If you are at all unsure, it may be best to set up a prototype design file as described below. In any case it is advisable to experiment with a variety of settings to familiarise yourself with the available possibilities.

Fig. 3.1 *Left-click* on the filename **a3form.dgn** in the **MicroStation Manager** dialogue box

Stages in constructing the prototype design files

Stage 1

1. In the **MicroStation Manager** dialogue box, select **Command Window** from the **Style:** box for the **aydesign** file and **Status Bar** for the **ay01** file. Then select the directory **dgn\mechdft** from the directory list. In the file list, *double-click* on the filename **a3form.dgn** (Fig. 3.1). This design file will be the basis for the two prototype files.

2. The **a3form.dgn** design screen appears as shown in Fig. 3.2 (aydesign) or as in Fig. 3.3 (ay01). The drawing shows a border and title block, which we will not be using.

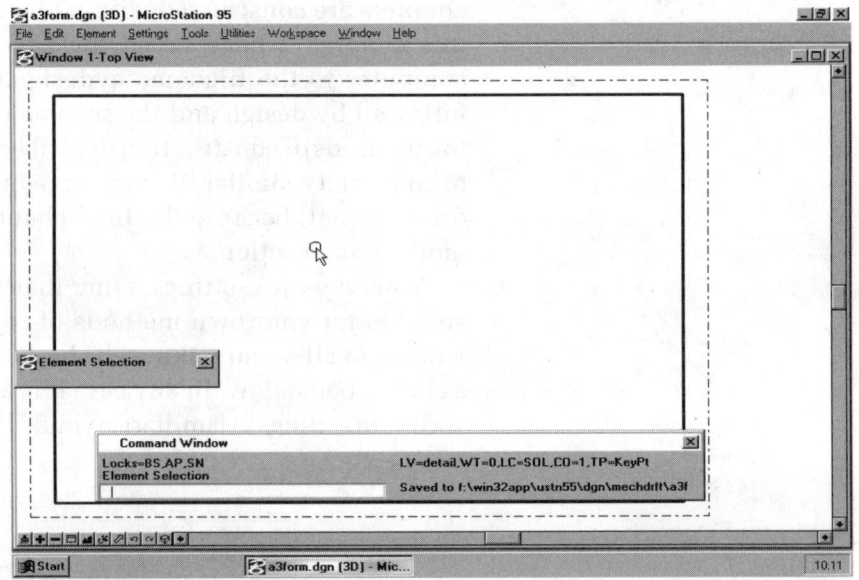

Fig. 3.2 The **a3form.dgn** screen for **aydesign.dgn** as it first appears

Stage 2

1. As a precautionary measure, in the **File** pull-down menu *left-click* on **Save As...** and save the file to the name **aydesign.dgn** as in Fig. 3.4, or to **ay01.dgn**.

2. For either design file, in the **Tools** pull-down menu select **Main** from the **Main** sub-menu (Fig. 3.5).

3. The **Main** tool palette appears on screen (Fig. 3.6).

4. *Left-click* on the **Delete Element** tool icon in the **Main** tool palette (Fig. 3.7). With the tool delete all the borders and all of the title block, resulting in a screen as in Fig. 3.8.

Fig. 3.3 The **a3form.dgn** screen for **ay01.dgn** as it first appears

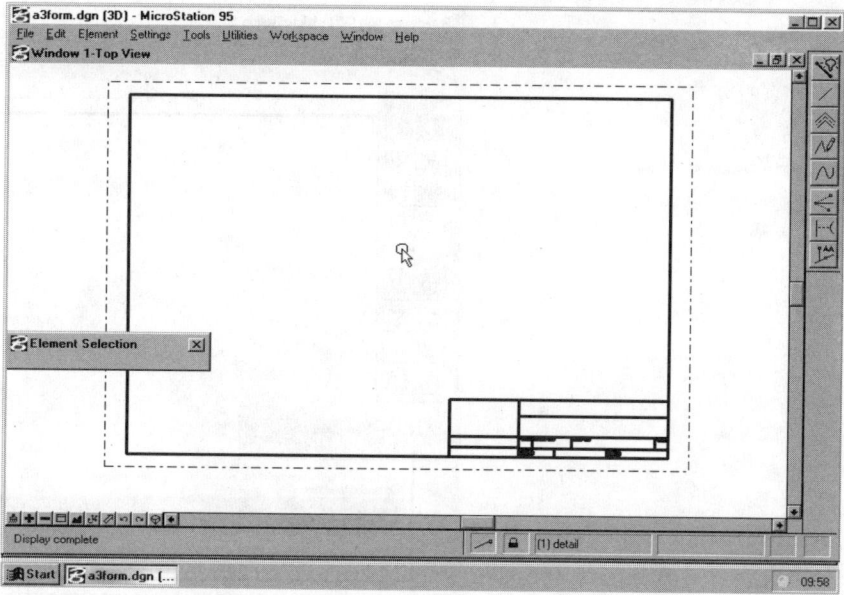

Fig. 3.4 Save the screen to the name **aydesign.dgn** in the **Save Design As** dialogue box

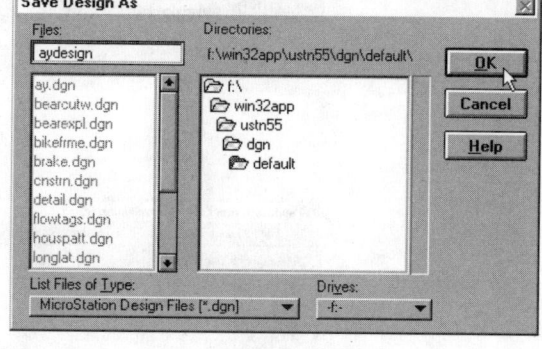

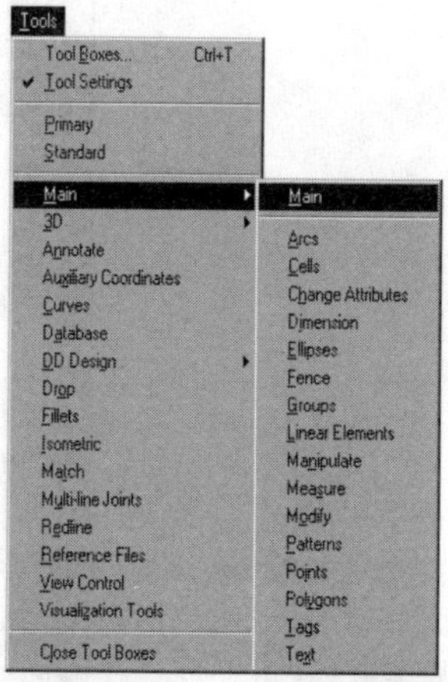

Fig. 3.5 *Left-click* on **Main** in the **Main** sub-menu of the **Tools** pull-down menu

Stage 3

The default cursors for MicroStation 95 when the design file is opened is the Element Selection cursor. When a tool is active, the default cursor will change to one of two: either a small vertical cross – **Normal** cursor (at the start of a tool operation) – or a diagonal cross (as the tool operation proceeds). A **Full View** cursor can be called to screen if desired. Some operators may find this preferable to the default cursors. To set **Full View** cursors:

1. *Left-click* on **Workspace** in the menu bar and in the pull-down menu which appears, *left-click* on **Preferences** (Fig. 3.9).
2. The **Preferences** dialogue box appears (Fig. 3.10).
3. *Left-click* on **Operations** in the dialogue box, followed by a *left-click* on **Full View** in the pop-up list against **Pointer Size** (Fig. 3.10).

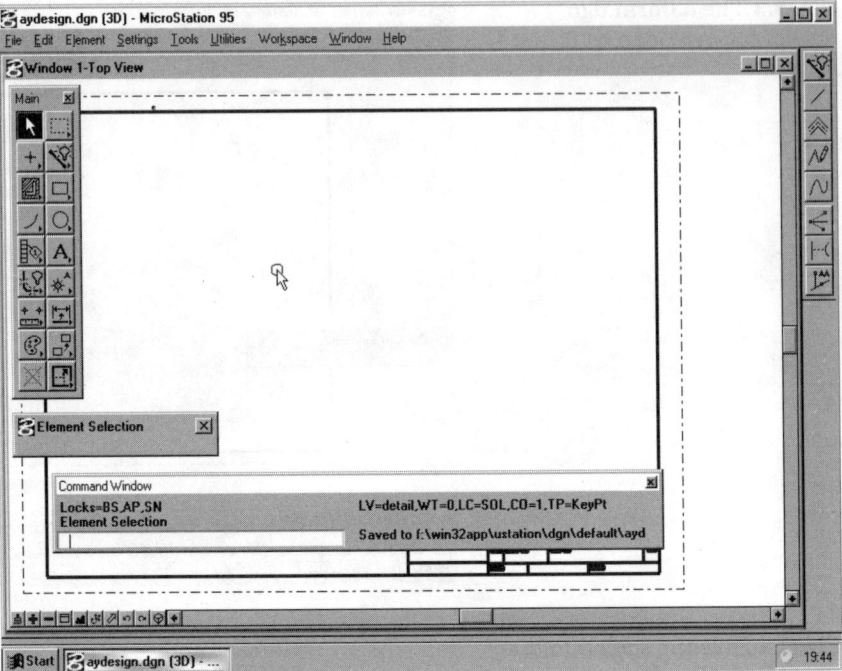

Fig. 3.6 The **Main** tool palette appears at the left-hand side of the screen

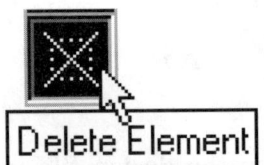

Fig. 3.7 Select the **Delete Element** tool

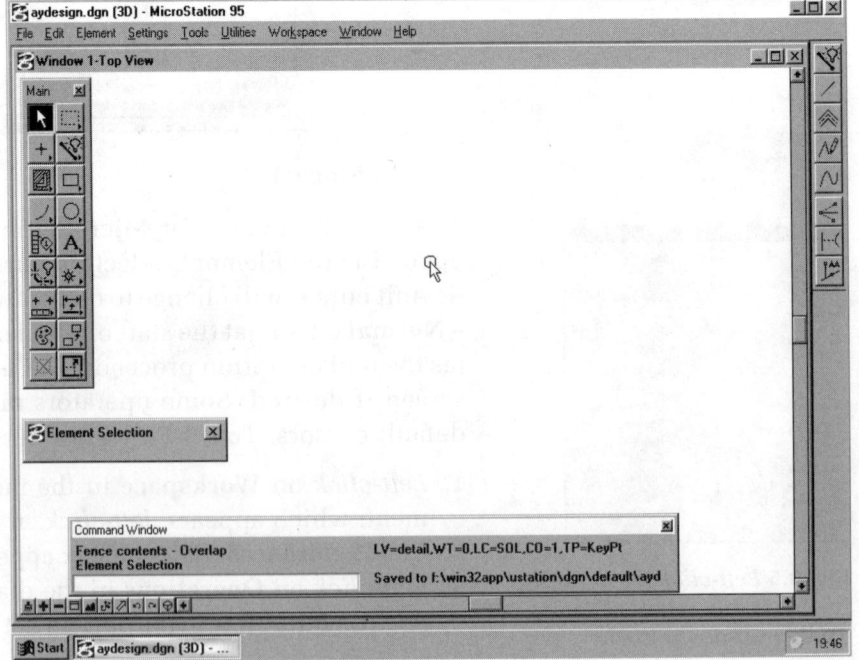

Fig. 3.8 Delete all parts of the borders and title block

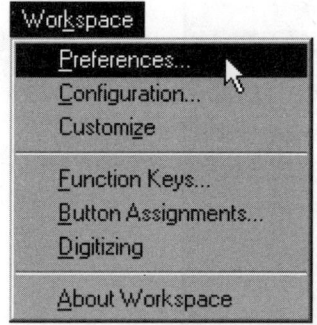

Fig. 3.9 *Left-click* on **Preferences** in the **Workspace** pull-down menu

Fig. 3.10 *Left-click* on **Full View** in the **Pointer Size** pop-up list

Then *left-click* on the **OK** button of the dialogue box. When a tool is selected, the cursor will be a pair of cross hairs, one vertical, the other horizontal, stretching the full height and width of the drawing area.

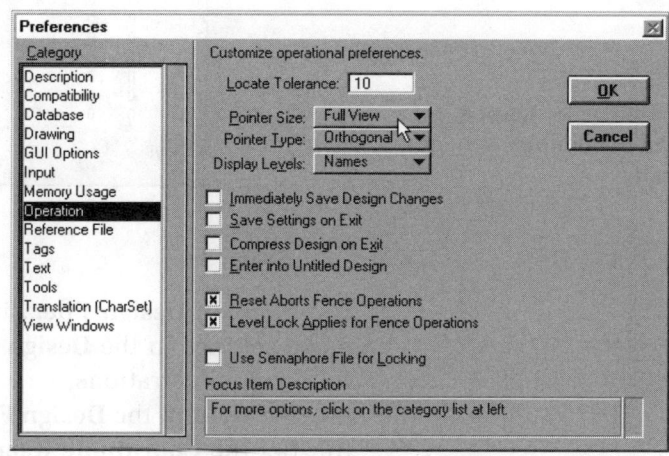

Stage 4

1. *Left-click* on **Symbology...** in the **Settings** pull-down menu (Fig. 3.11).
2. The **Level Symbology** dialogue box appears in which settings can be made for each level (layer) in the design file (Fig. 3.12). In this design file we will only be using one level (**Level 1**) so the **Weight**, **Colour** and **Style** are only set for that level.

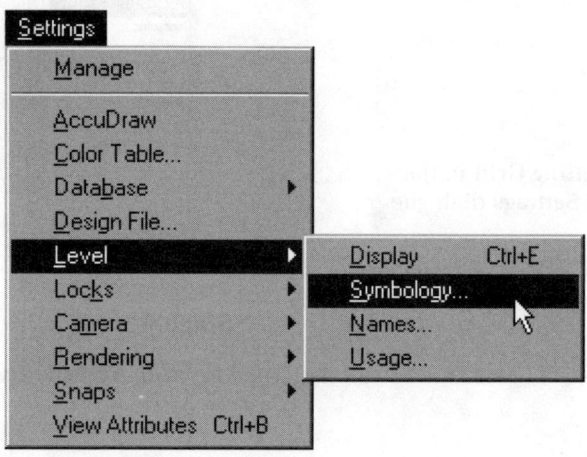

Fig. 3.11 *Left-click* on **Symbology...** in the **Settings** pull-down menu

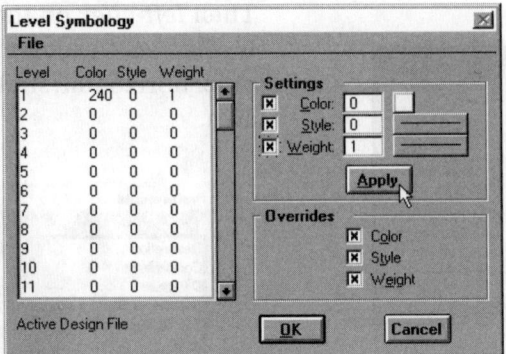

Fig. 3.12 Settings for **Level 1** in the **Level Symbology** dialogue box

Stage 5

1. *Left-click* on **Design File...** in the **Settings** pull-down menu and make settings in the **Design File Settings** dialogue box, as in the following illustrations.

    (a) Set **Grid** in the **Design File Settings** dialogue box (Fig. 3.13)

    (b) Set the **Coordinate Readout** in the **Design Settings** dialogue box as shown in Fig. 3.14. Note once again, no figures after the decimal point.

    (c) Set **Snaps**, as shown in Fig. 3.15.

    (d) Finally check that the **Working Units** are set in the **Design File Settings** dialogue box, as shown in Fig. 3.16.

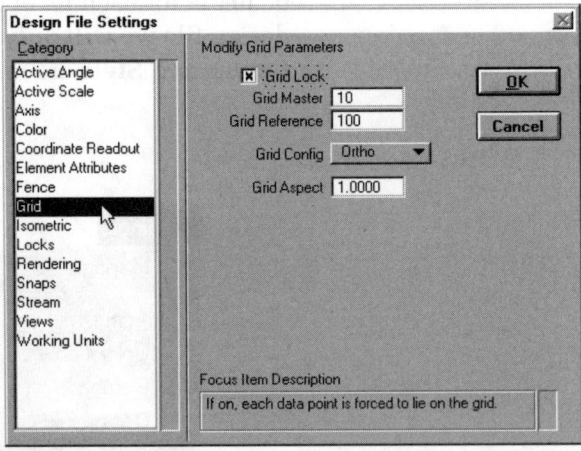

Fig. 3.13 Setting **Grid** in the **Design File Settings** dialogue box

Stage 6

1. *Left-click* on **AccuDraw** from the **Settings** pull-down menu (Fig. 3.17).

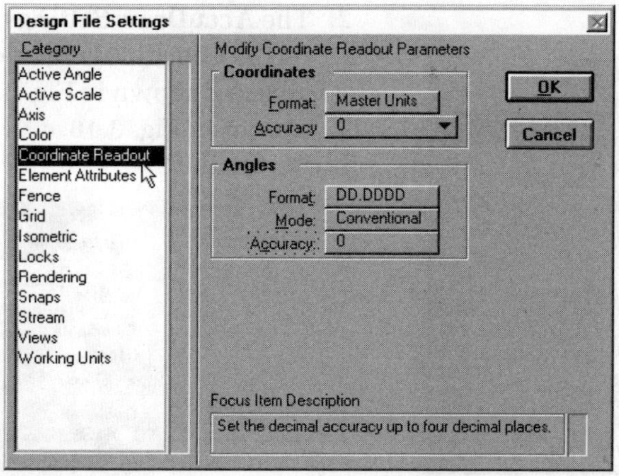

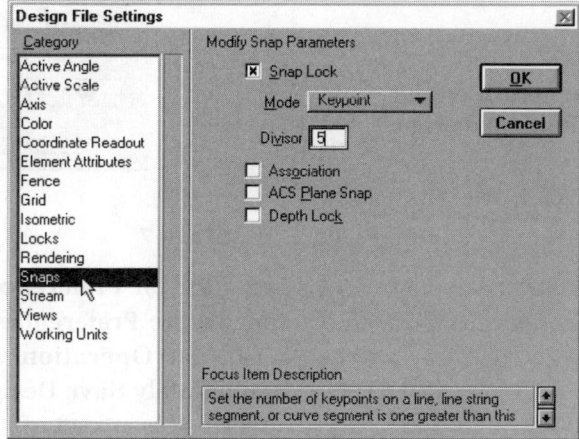

Fig. 3.14 Setting **Coordinate Readout** in the **Design File Settings** dialogue box

Fig. 3.15 Setting **Snaps** in the **Design File Settings** dialogue box

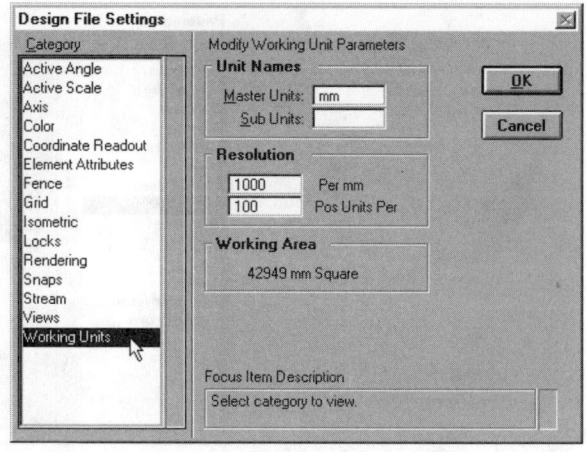

Fig. 3.16 Setting **Working Units** in the **Design File Settings** dialogue box

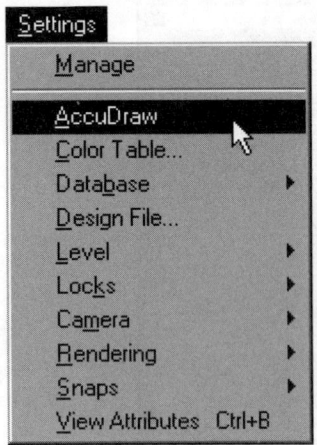

Fig. 3.17 Select **AccuDraw** from the **Settings** pull-down menu

Fig. 3.18 The **AccuDraw** and **Coordinate Readout** dialogue boxes

2. The **AccuDraw Settings** dialogue box appears. In the box, *left-click* on the **Coordinate Readout** button and set the **Coordinate Readout** boxes as shown in Fig. 3.18. For the time being leave the settings as shown in Fig. 3.18.

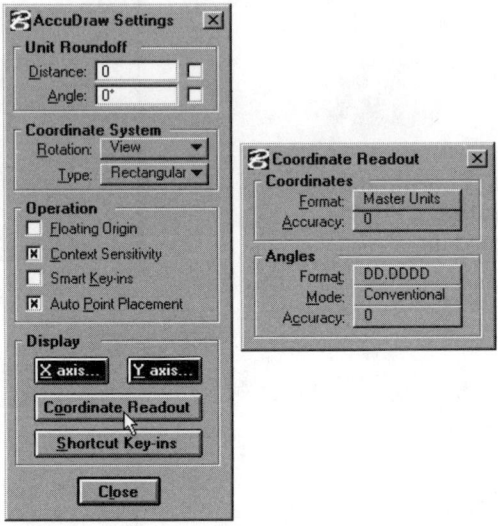

Stage 7

1. *Left-click* on **Preferences...** in the **Workspace** pull-down menu and, in the **Preferences** dialogue box which then appears (Fig. 3.19), set **Operation** as shown. Note in particular that the **Immediately Save Design Changes** and the **Save Settings on Exit** check boxes are set off (no **X**) in the boxes.

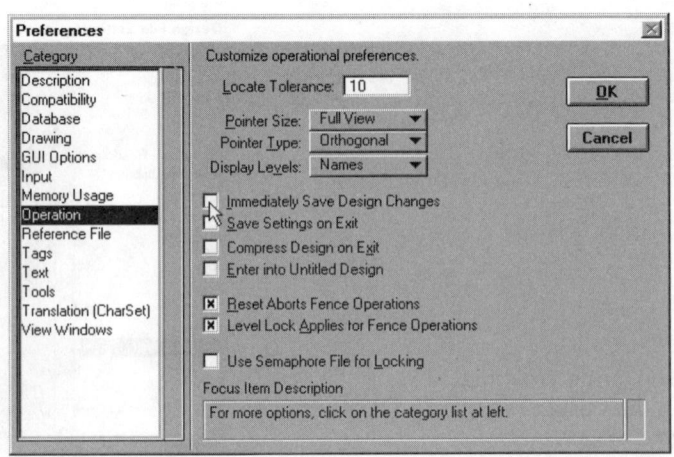

Fig. 3.19 Settings against **Operation** in the **Preferences** dialogue box.

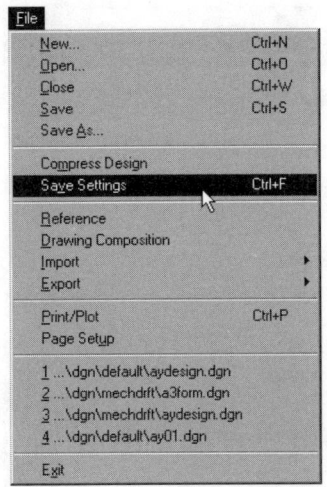

Fig. 3.20 *Left-click* on **Save Settings** in the **File** pull-down menu

Fig. 3.21 *Left-click* on **Save As...** in the **File** pull-down menu

Stage 8

1. *Left-click* on **Save Settings** in the **File** pull-down menu (Fig. 3.20) to ensure that all the settings that have been made are saved with the design file..

2. In the **File** pull-down menu (Fig. 3.21) *left-click* on **Save As...** and save the file to dialogue box by *entering* the name **aydesign** (or **ay01**) in the **File:** box of the **Save Design As** dialogue box, followed by a *left-click* on the **OK** button of the dialogue box. Then save the file to disk with this name (Fig. 3.22).

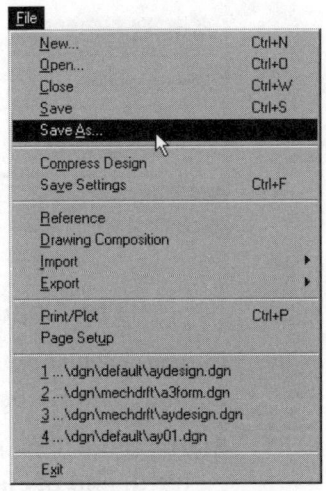

The resulting design file aydesign.dgn

Figure 3.23 shows the resulting design file screen for the **aydesign** file, showing the names of the principal parts of the screen.

Fig. 3.22 In the **Save Design As** dialogue box *enter* the name **aydesign** in the file box

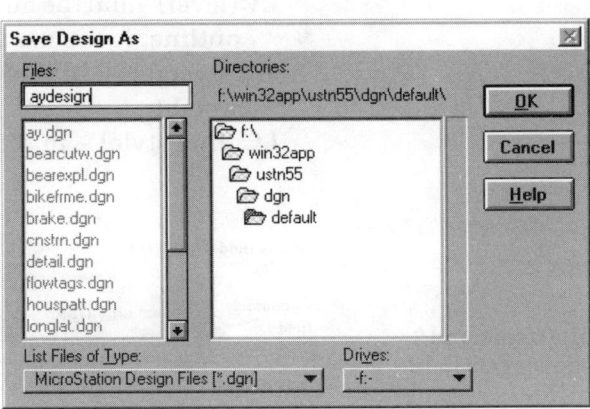

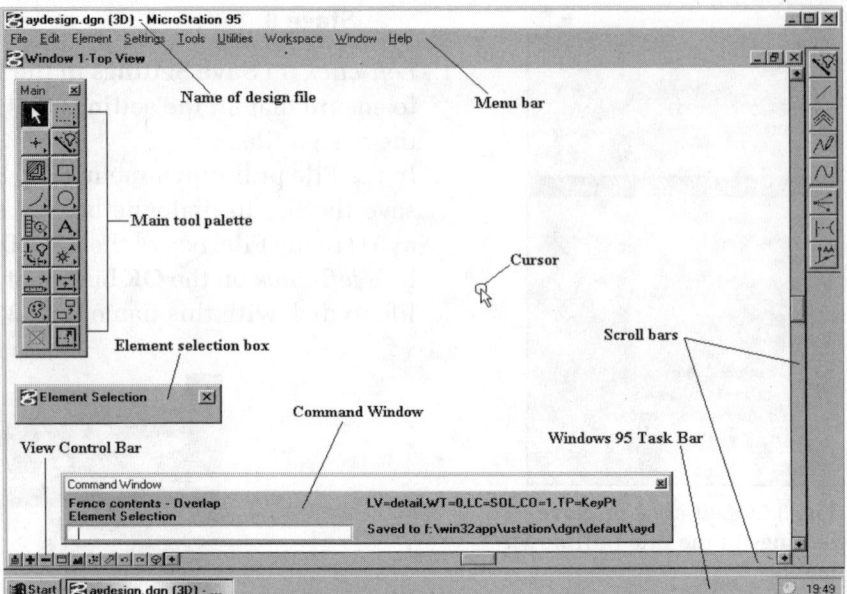

Fig. 3.23 The final design file **aydesign.dgn** with the principal parts named

The Command Window

Figure 3.24 shows the **Command Window** with its parts (fields) named. The fields show the following details:

Status field: This shows the locks in operation. In this example **GR** (grid) and **SN** (snap) locks are set on.

Command field: This displays the names of the current tool in operation. In this example it is the **Place Line** tool.

Key-in field: This is a field in which names of *key-in* commands can be *keyed-in* from the keyboard. Note that this field is only viable if a vertical line cursor is flashing at the left-hand side of the field.

Message field: In this example the following are shown:

> **LV** (level) – and the number or name given to the level, in this case **outline**, is the name given to the current level.
>
> **WT** (weight) – in this example line weight **1** is the current line weight.
>
> **LC** (line style) – in this example **SO**lid is the current line style.

Fig. 3.24 The **Command Window** showing its field names

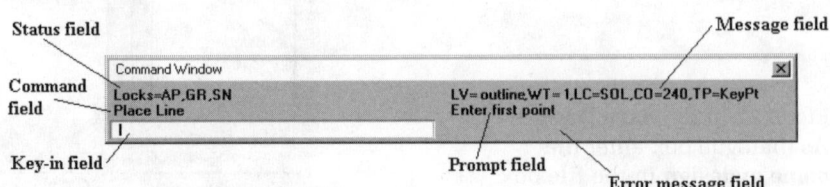

CO (colour) – in this example **240** is the current colour.

TP (tool point) – in this example **Keypoint** is the current tool point.

Prompt field: In this example **Enter first point** is the current prompt for the operator to follow in drawing lines with the **Place Line** tool.

Error field: if the operator makes an error in, say, *entering* an incorrect *key-in* name or abbreviation, a warning message appears in this field.

Note on the Command Window

As can be seen from this example (Fig. 3.24), the **Command Window** shows a large amount of information about the current settings. The operator would be well advised to make sure he/she follows what is stated in the **Command Window** if one is currently in operation.

A Key-in window for the ay01 file

Select **Key-in** from the **Utilities** pull-down menu (Fig. 3.25). The **Key-in** dialogue box appears on screen (Fig. 3.26). Reduce the dialogue box to a *Key-in* window as shown in Fig. 3.26. This window can be dragged into the bottom (or top) of the screen as shown in Fig. 3.26. This provides a **Key-in** field in the Status Bar for the **ay01** prototype design file, as shown in Fig. 3.27.

Fig. 3.25 Select **Key-in** from the **Utilities** pull-down menu

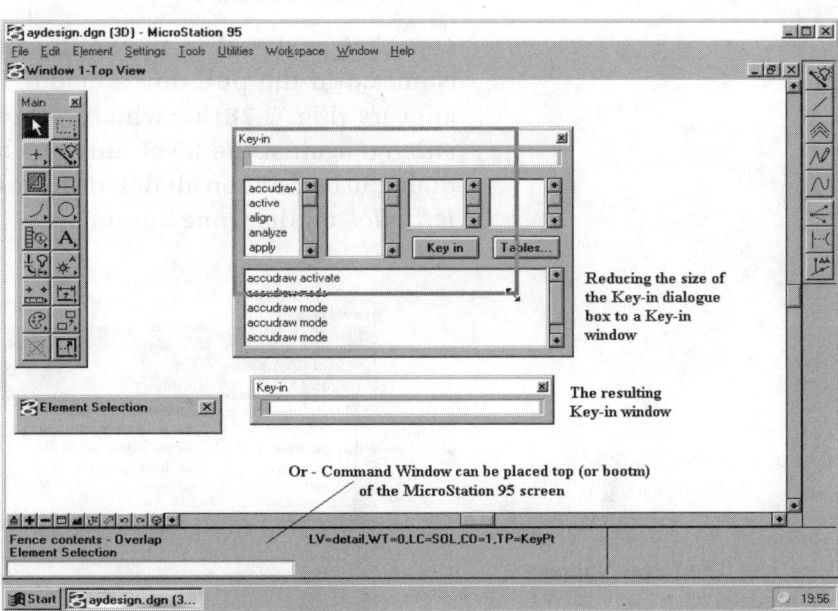

Fig. 3.26 Stages in the fitting of a **Key-in** window in the Status Bar for the **aydesign.dgn** design file

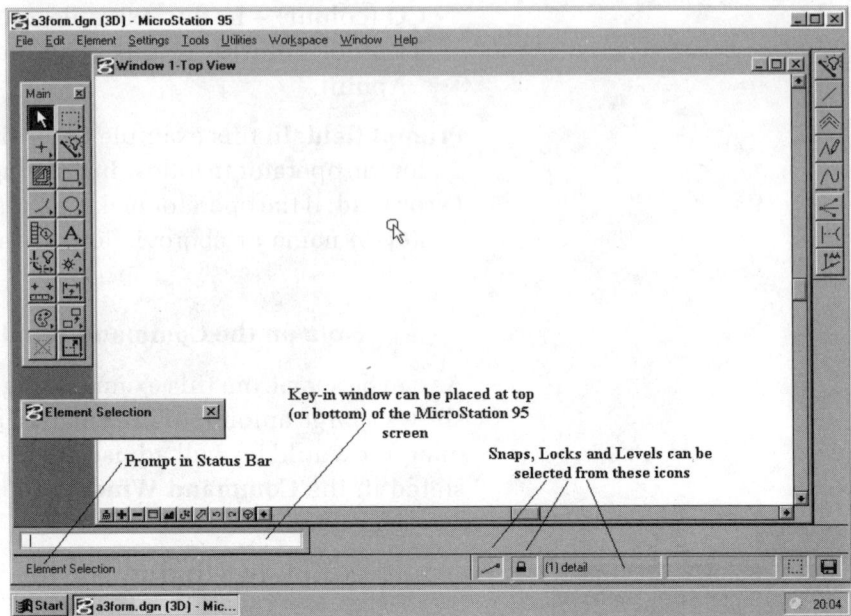

Fig. 3.27 The **ay01.dgn** screen showing the names in the Status Bar

Adding levels to the prototypes

In the prototype file described, only one level has been set – Level 1. That level has been set to use as the level on which outlines are to be drawn at a line weight of 1. Other levels can be set as follows.

Level names

Left-click on **Level** in the **Settings** pull-down menu and again on **Names...** in the pull-down menu. The **Level Names** dialogue box appears (Fig. 3.28) in which names and details of names can be *entered* against the level numbers by using the **Add** button of the dialogue box. When all details have been added in the dialogue box *left-click* on the **Done** button.

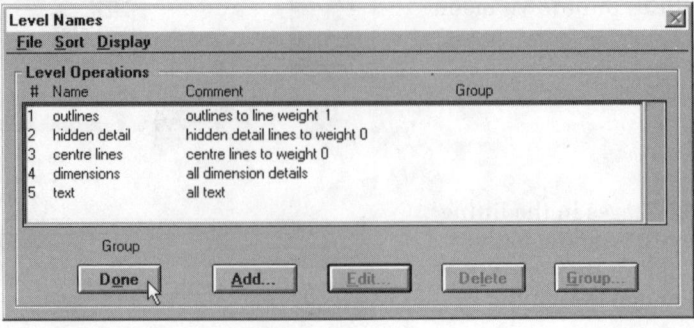

Fig. 3.28 The **Level Names** dialogue box

Level Symbology

In the **Settings** pull-down menu, *left-click* again on **Level** and, in the sub-menu, *left-click* again on **Symbology**. The **Level Symbology** dialogue box appears (Fig. 3.29). In this dialogue box, colours, line weights and style of lines can be set against each of the level numbers.

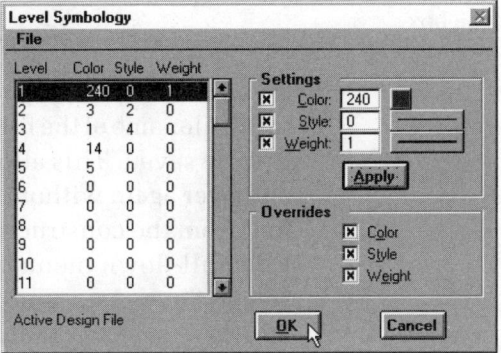

Fig. 3.29 The **Level Symbology** dialogue box

The Element Attributes dialogue box

Left-click on **Attributes** in the **Element** pull-down menu (Fig. 3.30) and the **Element Attributes** dialogue box appears (Fig. 3.31) in which each feature of the elements – colour, line style and line weight – can be attributed to any layer. Note the **Class** pop-up list which contains two classes – **Primary** and **Construction**. We are at the moment only concerned with the **Primary** class of element attributes.

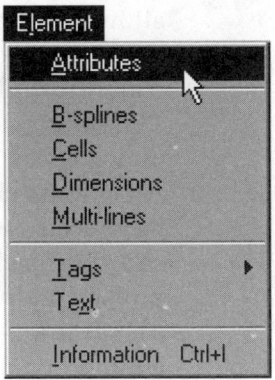

Fig. 3.30 Select **Attributes** from the **Element** dialogue box

Operating note on saving the design screen

Although the **Operation** settings in the **Preferences** dialogue box have been set as shown in Fig. 3.19 on page 44, it is advisable, when

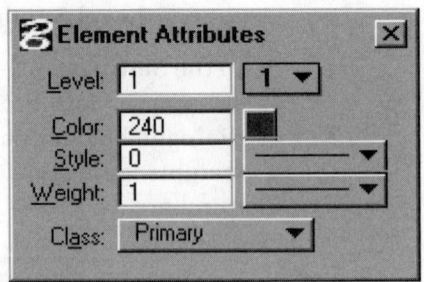

Fig. 3.31 The **Element Attributes** dialogue box

calling one's prototype design file to screen, to immediately save it to the filename of the file to which the drawing about to be constructed is to be saved. This allows the prototype design file to be used over and over again without finding that the file has had elements added to it from the constructions from a previous drawing. Thus open the **File** pull-down menu by a *left-click* on **File** in the menu bar. Then select **Save As...** and when the **Save Design File** dialogue box appears, select a suitable directory and save the screen to the filename of the drawing about to be constructed.

Notes on Settings

1. It will have been noted in working through the details described in this chapter that some settings and preferences have been ignored. This is because the default settings of those that have not been deliberately set, been accepted. However, the reader may wish to change these default settings for his/her own purposes.

2. All the illustrations in this book have been taken from a white background screen. This method has been adopted because it allows illustrations to be more easily followed. The reader may find it easier to work against a black background, as some people find it more restful to the eyes than working against a white background. This setting can be made in **View Windows** option of the **Preferences** dialogue box.

3. All colours chosen for features in the given prototype design file have been 240 (nearly black). This again is because of the ease of showing black on white in a book illustration. The reader may well prefer working in other colours, perhaps with a different colour for each feature – say, one for outline lines, another for hidden detail, another for centre lines, another for dimensions, another for text and so on.

4. If working on a black screen, the default colour (white – number **0**) is preferable for some levels. In fact, when working against a white screen the number **0** colour will be black. You may wish to use

colour **0** as your default colour for some levels, whether working on a white or a black screen. A variety of colours for different levels show up more clearly against a black screen than against a white screen. This will be seen in some of the colour plates (between pages 114 and 115).

Questions

1. What is the purpose of constructing your own prototype design file?
2. Why do you think the borders were deleted from the a3form.dgn file when amending it to my aydesign.dgn file?
3. Can you name the parts of the **Command Window**?
4. How is the **Key-in** dialogue box called to screen?
5. How can a **Key-in** window be placed in the Status Bar?
6. What is the purpose of having a **Key-in** window in the Status Bar?
7. Can you understand why the **Working Units** are set as shown in Fig. 3.16 on page 43?
8. What is the purpose of the **AccuDraw Settings** dialogue box?
9. Why is it necessary to **Save Settings** when constructing a prototype design file?
10. In which dialogue box is it best to set line weights?

CHAPTER 4

Accurate drawing

X,Y coordinates

The sizes of parts of a drawing on the screens of CAD systems are usually based upon Cartesian coordinate geometry. The drawing area of the screen is invisibly divided into a series of equal squares, each 1 unit in width and in height. These unit spaces are measured horizontally in X units and vertically in Y units. This allows any point in the drawing area to be referred to in terms of X in the horizontal direction and Y in the vertical direction in the form **x,y**. Thus, two points x,y=100,100 and x,y=200,100 are 100 units horizontally apart.

The *origin* of the CAD coordinate system is set at x,y=0,0. In MicroStation 95, the origin (x,y=0,0) is usually in the centre of the window on start-up, although it may (or can be) changed from this position. To demonstrate this:

1. *Left-click* on the **Place Line** tool icon.
2. In the **Key-in** field or window *key-in* xy=0,0.

It will then be seen that the starting point of the **Place Line** rubber band is at the centre of the screen, confirming that this is indeed the origin where x,y=0,0.

Positive and negative coordinates

A point on screen lying to the left of the origin 0,0 carries a negative x coordinate; a point below the origin 0,0 carries a negative y coordinate. This means that:

> **+ve x** is to the right of 0,0
> **−ve x** is to the left of 0,0
> **+ve y** is above 0,0
> **−ve y** is below 0,0

To take four examples:

The point x,y=50,50 is 50 units to the right and 50 units above 0,0.

The point x,y=−50,−50 is 50 units to the left and 50 units below 0,0.
The point x,y=−50,50 is 50 units to the left and above 0,0.
The point x,y=50,−50 is 50 units to the right of and below 0,0.

Note

If **Working Units** in the **Design File Settings** dialogue box are set as shown in Fig. 3.16 on page 53, then each coordinate unit can be regarded as being 1 mm in length.

Drawing elements to x,y coordinates

In Chapter 2 we experimented with drawing elements, sizing them on figures in Element Selection boxes such as the **Length** and **Angle** boxes of the **Place Line** Element Selection box. A more accurate method is to *enter* coordinate figures in the **Key-in** field or window in the form **xy=** followed by the figures of the x,y coordinates for the ends, centres, etc., of each part of the element being drawn. Examples of simple drawings involving the use of this method are given below and the reader is advised to copy these drawings.

Example 1 – Place Line

Figure 4.1 shows an outline drawn with the aid of **Place Line**. Note the prompts for **Place Line** appearing in the **Prompt** field of the **Command Window** or in the Status Bar. The drawing was constructed as follows:

1. In the **Key-in** field of the **Command Window** or in the **Key-in** window:

key-in place li *Return*
key-in xy= −200,0 *Return* (Fig. 4.2)

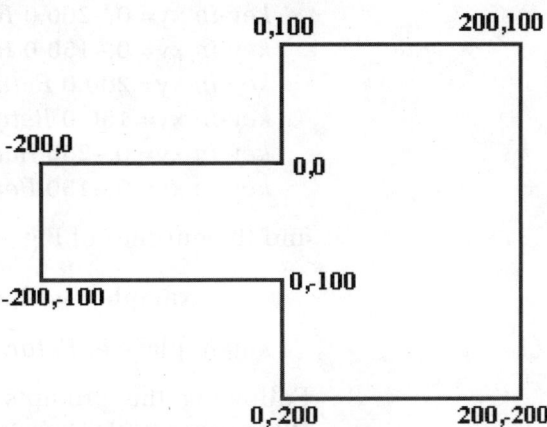

Fig. 4.1 Example 1. The **Place Line** example involving coordinates

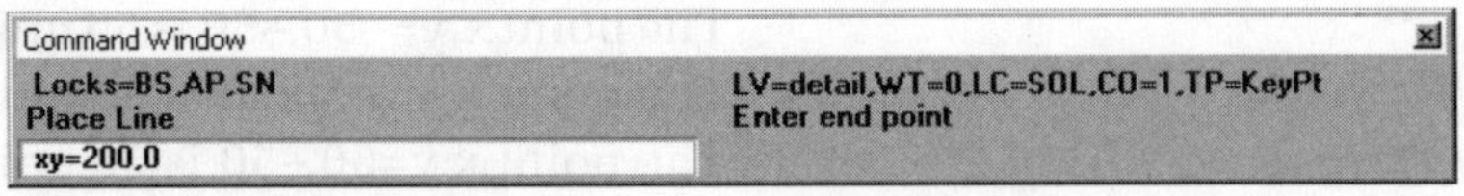

Fig. 4.2 The key-in field of the **Command Window** of the aydesign.dgn design file

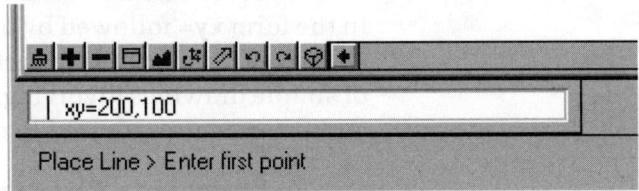

key-in xy= 0,0 *Return*
key-in xy= 0,100 *Return*
key-in xy= 200,100 *Return*
key-in xy= 200,−200 *Return*
key-in xy= 0,−200 *Return*
key-in xy= 0,−100 *Return*
key-in xy= −200,−100 *Return*
key-in xy= −200,0 *Return*

and the outline Fig. 4.1 appears on screen.

Fig. 4.3 The Key-in window of the ay01.dgn design file

Example 2 – Place Circle by Center

key-in place ci *Return*

Following the prompts in the **Prompts** field of the **Command Window**:

key-in xy= 0,0 *Return* (Centre of central circle)
key-in xy= 0,150 *Return* (Point on circumference of circle)
key-in xy= 0,250 *Return* (Centre of upper circle)
key-in xy= 0,150 *Return* (Point on circumference of circle)
key-in xy= 0,−200,0 *Return* (Centre of left-hand circle)
key-in xy= 0,−150,0 *Return* (Point on circumference of circle)
key-in xy= 200,0 *Return* (Centre of right-hand circle)
key-in xy= 150,0 *Return* (Point on circumference of circle)
key-in xy= 0,−250 *Return* (Centre of bottom circle)
key-in xy= 0,−150 *Return* (Point on circumference of circle)

and the outlines of Fig. 4.4 are completed.

Example 3 – Place Ellipse

key-in place el *Return*

Following the prompts in the **Prompts** field of the **Command Window** or in the **Key-in** window:

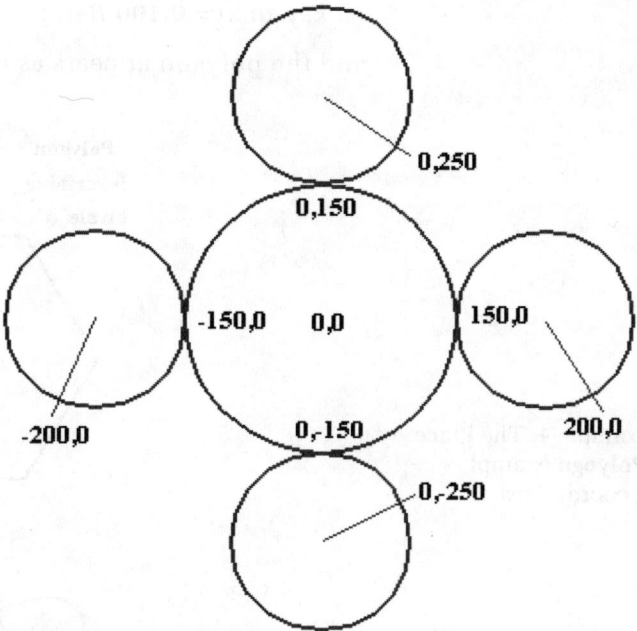

0,250

0,150

-150,0   0,0

150,0

-200,0

0,-150

200,0

0,-250

Fig. 4.4 Example 2. The **Place Circle by Center** example involving coordinates

key-in xy= 50,50 *Return* (Centre of ellipse)
key-in xy= 300,50 *Return* (Right-hand end of axis of ellipse)
key-in xy= 50,150 *Return* (Upper end of axis of ellipse)

and the outline Fig. 4.5 appears.

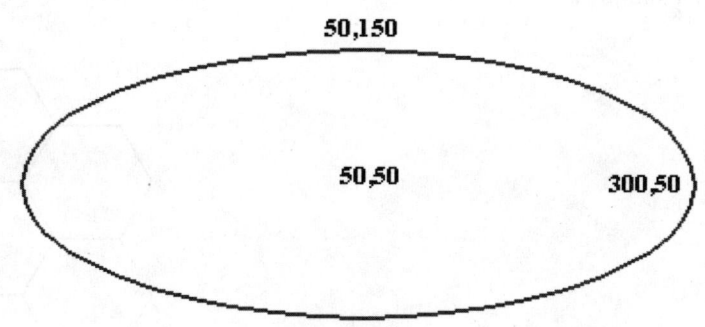

50,150

50,50

300,50

Fig. 4.5 Example 3. The **Place Ellipse** example involving coordinates

Example 4 – Place Regular polygon

key-in place pol *Return*

Following the prompts in the **Prompts** field of the **Command Window**:

key-in xy= 0,0 *Return*

key-in xy= 0,100 *Return*

and the polygon appears as in Fig. 4.6.

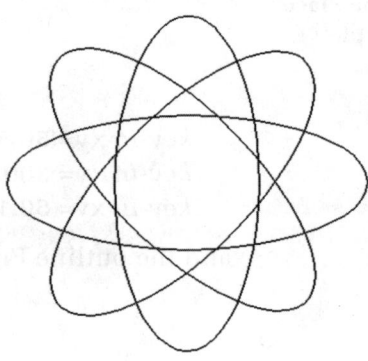

Polygon inscribing circle

0,0

0,-100

Fig. 4.6 Example 4. The **Place Regular Polyogn** example involving coordinates

Fig. 4.7 Example 5

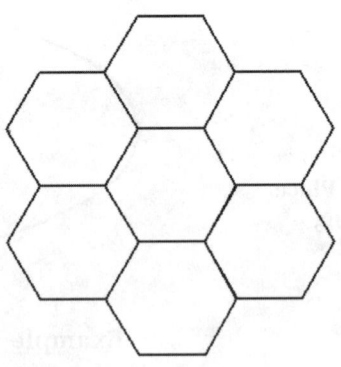

Fig. 4.8 Example 6

Examples 5 and 6

Try constructing the two examples of drawing adjacent, touching elements as shown in Figs 4.7 and 4.8, employing the methods of *keying-in* coordinates. You may find it to be necessary to make rough notes of the necessary coordinate numbers before starting these two examples.

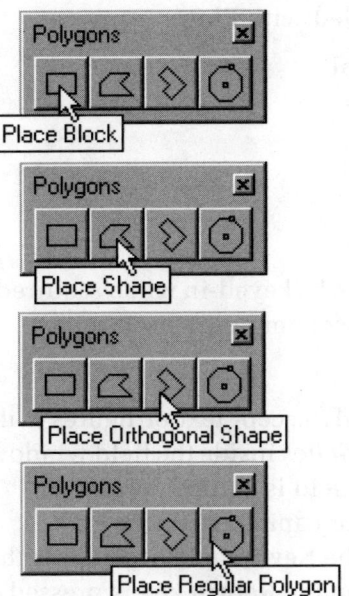

Fig. 4.9 The **Polygon** tool palette

Example 7 – using tools from the Block palette

Figure 4.9 shows the **Polygon** tool palette which displays the icons for the tools **Block**, **Shape**, **Orthogonal Shape** and **Regular Polygon**. Figure 4.10 shows four outlines constructed with the aid of each of the four tools from this palette involving the *keying-in* of coordinates.

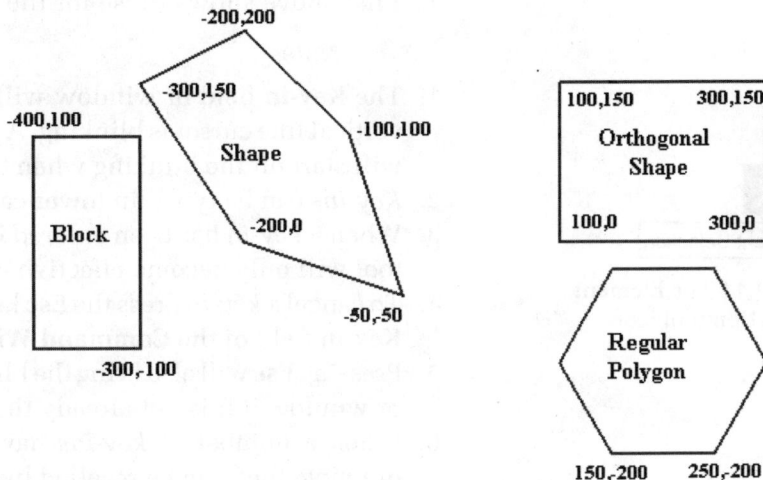

Fig. 4.10 Example 7

Key-in abbreviations

Some operators may prefer to *key-in* into the **Key-in** field or window either the whole tool name or an abbreviation for the tool name rather than selecting from a tool icon. As seen from the above examples, the following *key-in* abbreviations can be used to 'call' tools into action:

place li	for the **Place Line** tool
place ci	for the **Place Circle by Center** tool
place el	for the **Place Ellipse** tool
place pol	for the **Place Regular Polygon** tool

Others which could have been used in conjunction with the **Main** tools are:

place a	for the **Place Arc** tool
place bl	for the **Place Block** tool
place ml	for the **Place Multiline** tool
place sh	for the **Place Shape** tool
place tex	for the **Place Text** tool

and some others which are not preceded with **Place**:

ar   for the **Rectangular Array** tool
cop for the **Copy** tool
mi   for the **Mirror** tool
mov for the **Move** tool
r   for the **Rotate** tool
sc   for the **Scale** tool

There are other abbreviations which can be keyed-in when required. The list above shows those for the most commonly used tools.

Notes

1. The **Key-in** field or window will only accept text or figures if its vertical line cursor is blinking. A *left-click* inside the field window will start off the blinking when the field is empty.
2. *Key-ins* can be typed in lower case or capital letters.
3. When a *key-in* has been *entered* in the **Key-in** field or window the tool will only become effective when the **Return** key is pressed.
4. To cancel a *key-in* press the **Esc** key of the keyboard. This clears the **Key-in** field of the **Command Window**.
5. Pressing **Esc** will also bring the blinking cursor into the **Key-in** field or window if it is not already there.
6. When a number of *key-ins* have been employed to build up a drawing, they can be recalled by pressing the vertical cursor keys of the keyboard. Pressing the up cursor brings the previous key-in into the **Key-in** field and continuously pressing the up cursor will run through all the key-ins previously employed. Similarly pressing the down cursor key brings on the next in a series of key-ins.
7. *Right-click* closes a tool in operation. A *left-click* on the **Element Selection** tool icon (Fig. 4.11) has the same effect.

Fig. 4.11 The **Element Selection** tool icon

Snap points

Another aid to accurate drawing is the use of snap points. These can be selected as follows:

1. From the **Snap Mode** tool palette, which many operators find best fitted to the right-hand side of the screen as a permanent part of their prototype design drawing.
2. By pressing the **Ctrl** and **Shift** keys at the same time with a *both-click* (a tentative point) of the mouse. When a tool is in operation this brings up the **Button Bar** menu shown in Fig. 4.12

When a tool is in operation, a *both-click* brings on a snap point cursor, which snaps to the snap point chosen either from the **Button**

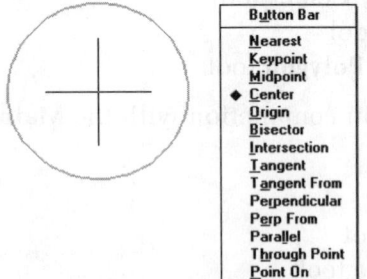

Fig. 4.12 The **Button Bar** menu showing the snap points

Bar menu or from the **Snap Mode** palette. Thus if the **Keypoint** snap is the currently chosen snap point and the *both-click* is near to the end of a line, a snap cursor appears exactly at the end of the line. If the **Midpoint** snap is currently chosen and a *both-click* is made near the centre of a line, the snap cursor appears exactly at the middle of the line. Figure 4.12 shows the snap point appearing at the centre of a circle when the currently chosen snap point is **Center**.

Figure 4.13 shows both the **Button Bar** menu and lines and a circle drawn when some snap points are in action.

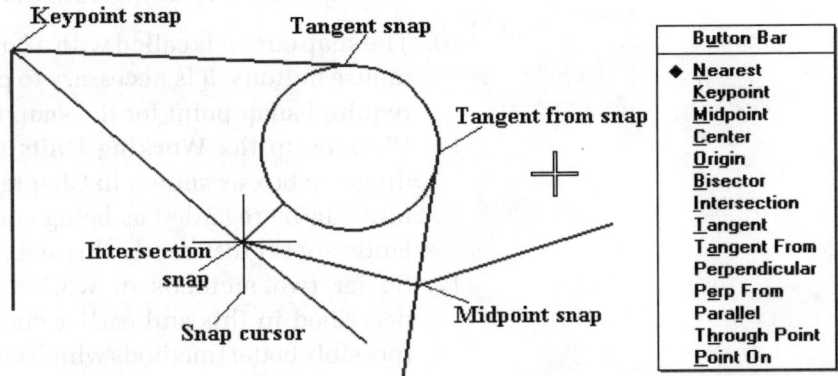

Fig. 4.13 Examples of snap points in use

Note

There are two types of **Button Bar** menu, one which appears with **Ctrl\Shift** *both-click* is carried out with no tool in operation, the other when a tool is in operation. The first contains those snap points most likely to be used. The second contains all available snap points.

Revision

1. If necessary, *left-click* in the **Key-in** field or window to activate the blinking cursor.
2. **Esc** clears the **Key-in** field.
3. Whether a tool is selected from a tool icon in a palette, or its abbreviation *keyed-in* in the **Key-in** field or window, coordinates can be *keyed-in* into the **Key-in** field or window.
4. *Right-click* completes the action of a tool.
5. *Left-click* on the **Element Selection** arrow icon also clears the action of a tool.
6. **Ctrl/Shift**/*both-click* to bring on the **Button Bar** with snaps.
7. Or, call up the **Snap Mode** tool palette from the **Tools** pull-down menu and *drag* it to the right-hand side of the screen.

8. x,y coordinates can only be *keyed-in* in the form, e.g. **xy=100,100**. In this form xy must be followed by the = sign and a comma must be placed between the figures.

9. When working to the method of *keying-in* coordinates, it may be necessary to make calculations of sizes on a scrap of paper, remembering that:

    −ve x is horizontally to the left of 0,0
    +ve x is horizontally to the right of 0,0
    +ve y is vertically up from 0,0
    −ve y is vertically down from 0,0

10. The snap cursor is called with a *both-click* (a tentative point) of the mouse buttons. It is necessary to place the snap cursor near to the required snap point for the snap to be effective.

11. Working to the **Working Units** set in the **Design File Settings** dialogue box as shown in Chapter 3 means that each coordinate unit can be regarded as being equal to 1 millimetre. If **Working Units** are set differently this will not be so.

12. So far two methods of working to accurate sizes have been described in this and earlier chapters. However there are other (possibly better) methods which will be explained in later chapters. For those new to CAD work, it is advisable to attempt working as described in this chapter, in order to familiarise oneself with coordinate units.

Questions

1. What are the lengths in coordinate units between the following x,y points on a CAD screen?

    x,y=200,−50 and x,y=200,280
    x,y=100,−45 and x,y=100,95
    x,y=350,−30 and x,y=350,120
    x,y=−300,−100 and x,y=−500,−100
    x,y=−50,400 and x,y=−50,−20

2. What is meant by the **origin** of a coordinate system?

3. Why is it called the **Cartesian** coordinate system?

4. In the screen as set up as described in Chapter 3, what actual length can each coordinate unit be regarded as?

5. How can a previously entered *key-in* abbreviation be recalled without having to re-enter the *key-in*?

6. If the cursor in the **Key-in** field of the **Command Window** is not blinking, entries cannot be *keyed-in* at the field. How can the field be made ready to receive *key-ins*?

7.   What is a tentative point? What is its purpose?
8.   How can snap points be selected?
9.   What is the snap cursor and how can it be called to the screen?
10. What is the purpose of the **Element Selection** tool?

Exercises

The following exercises are based upon constructions involving the use of *keyed-in* coordinates, working as described in this chapter. When working through these exercises, it is advisable to use both methods of calling tools into action – by a *left-click* on the icon of the required tool or by *keying-in* the abbreviation for the tool in the **Key-in** field or window. It may also be advisable to ensure that the **Snap Mode** tool palette is placed at the right-hand side of the screen to enable snaps to be selected easily. However, try also the methods of bringing the **Button Bar** menu on screen with **Ctrl/Shift/***both-click* because this method may be quicker on occasions.

It is assumed the reader will have already worked through the examples given in Figures 4.1 to 4.10.

You may find it advisable to make sketches on scrap paper of the outlines to be drawn to enable you to calculate the x,y coordinate positions of points in your drawings in answer to these exercises.

Do not attempt to include the dimensions given with the drawings of the exercises. Dimensioning will be dealt with in a later chapter.

If you are not conversant with the principles of orthographic projection for Exercises 9 and 10, just copy the given views. Orthographic projection is an important form of technical drawing and the basis of this method of drawing will be explained later in Chapter 10.

1.   Figure 4.14 is a view of a shaped plate made from steel with a number of holes cut through. Construct the given view to the details given.

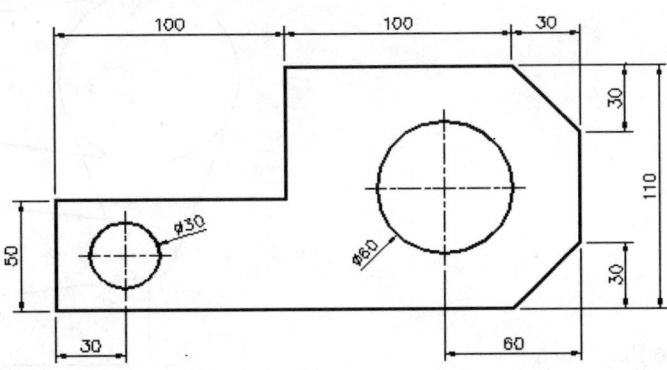

Fig. 4.14 Exercise 1

2.   The top left drawing of Fig. 4.15 consists of three regular hexagons (6-sided) all drawn on the same centre and all the same size. Construct the given drawing to the sizes given.

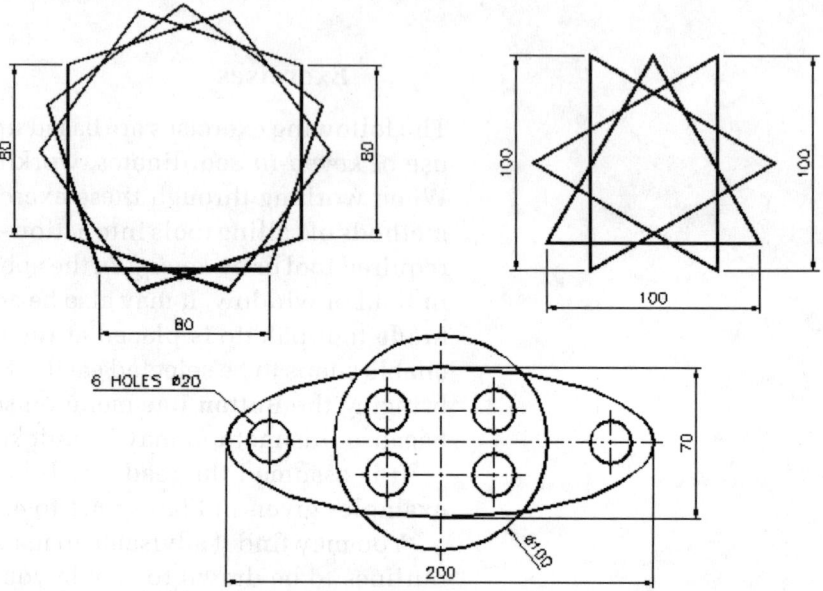

Fig. 4.15 Exercises 2, 3 and 4

3.   The top right drawing of Fig. 4.14 consists of three equilateral triangles of the same size and drawn about the same central point. Construct the given drawing to the dimensions shown.

4.   The bottom drawing of Fig. 4.15 shows several circles and an ellipse. Working to the given dimensions make a copy of the drawing.

5.   Figure 4.16 shows an arrangement of lines and circles in which all lines are tangential to the circles which they are touching. Construct an accurate, correct size drawing of Fig. 4.16.

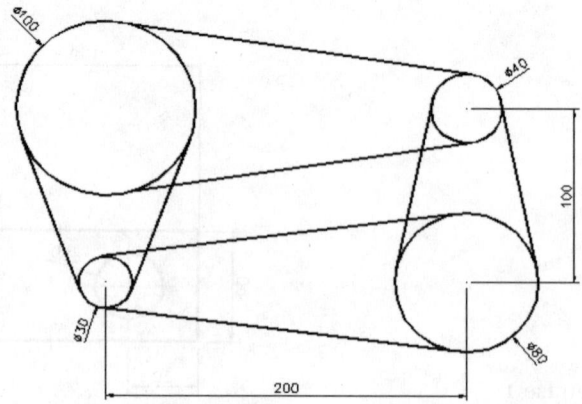

Fig. 4.16 Exercise 5

6.   The top left-hand drawing of Fig. 4.17 shows a shaped sheet with a triangular and two circular holes cut through. Make an accurately sized drawing of the sheet.

7.   The top right-hand drawing of Fig. 4.17 shows a shaped plate in which a hole has been cut with its boundaries 10 mm in from each edge. Make an accurate drawing of the plate.

8.   The two lower drawings of Fig. 4.17 show shapes drawn with the aid of the **Place Ellipse**, **Place Arc** and **Place Line** tools. No dimensions are given and the answer should be to sizes of the reader's own discretion. Make copies of the two outlines.

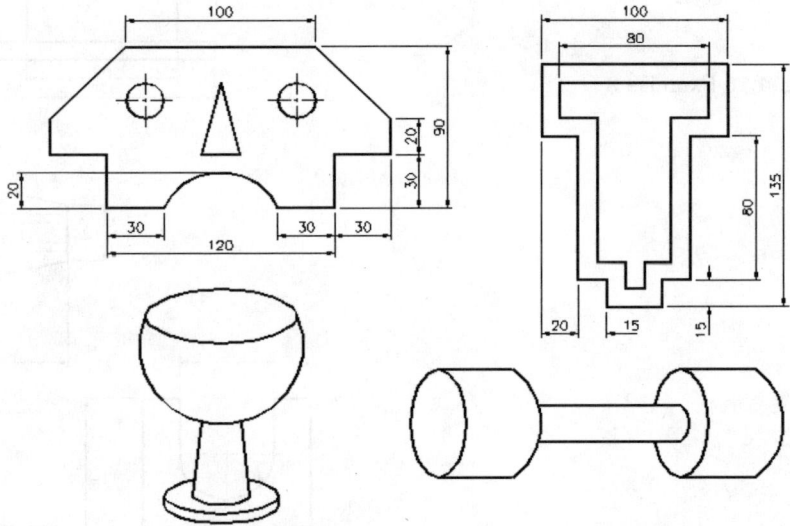

Fig. 4.17 Exercises 6, 7 and 8

9.   Figure 4.18 is a three-view third-angle orthographic projection of a simple bearing bracket. Working to the dimensions given make an accurate drawing of the three views.

10.   Figure 4.19 is a third-angle orthographic projection of a bracket. Make an accurate copy of the bracket to the dimensions given.

11.   Figure 4.20 is a view of a wheel hub cover from a motor car drawn to a small scale. Figure 4.21 shows the shapes upon which the view was drawn. Make an accurate drawing of the cover to the given sizes.

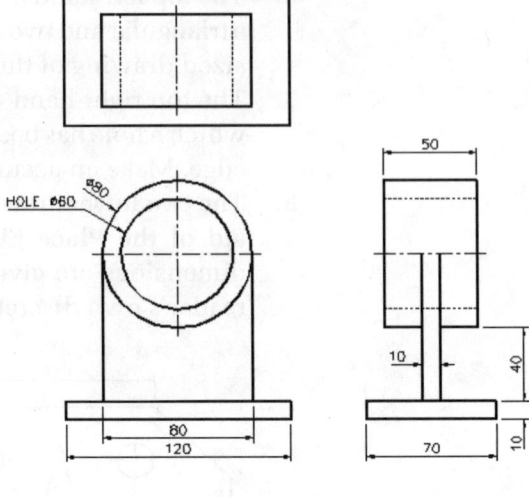

Fig. 4.18 Exercise 9

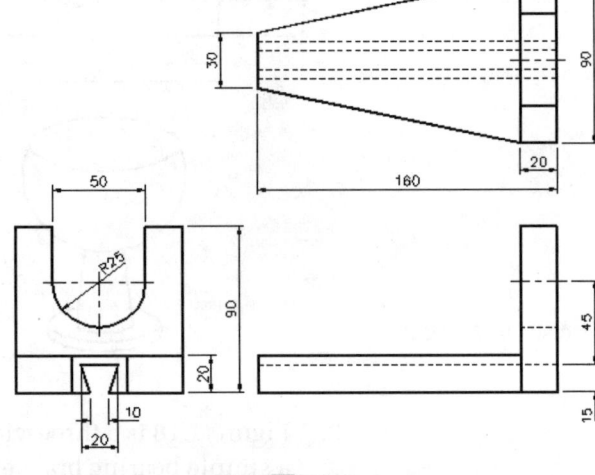

Fig. 4.19 Exercise 10

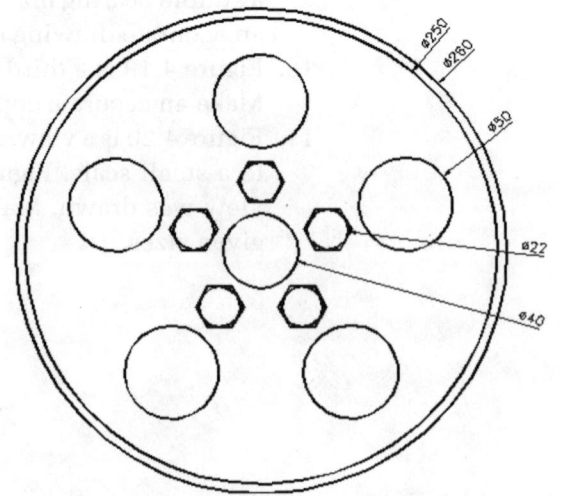

Fig. 4.20 Exercise 11

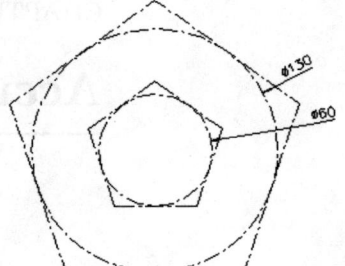

Fig. 4.21 Sizes for Exercise 11

AccuDraw

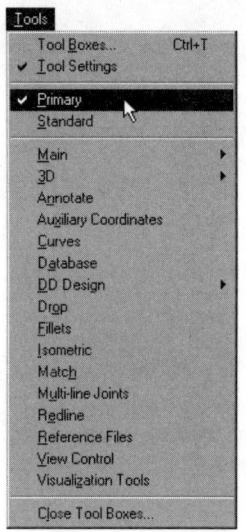

Fig. 5.1 Select **Primary** from the **Tools** pull-down menu

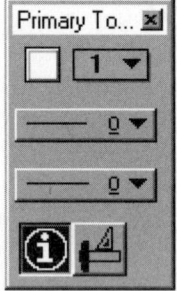

Fig. 5.2 The **Primary Tools** tool palette

Fig. 5.3 A *left-click* on the icon brings the **AccuDraw** coordinates window on screen

Preparing the screen for AccuDraw

AccuDraw is a MicroStation 95 system by which drawings can be easily, speedily and accurately constructed. Although it is not essential to prepare the MicroStation 95 screen especially to work with AccuDraw, doing so enables work to begin with AccuDraw without further settings. It is therefore suggested that the ay01.dgn prototype drawing file be further refined to include both the **Primary Tools** tool palette and the **AccuDraw** window in the Status Bar of the screen and then saving the resulting screen as either ay01.dgn or ay02.dgn (or your own initials).

These two items are added to the screen as follows:

1. *Left-click* on **Primary** in the **Tools** pull-down menu (Fig. 5.1). The **Primary Tools** tool palette appears (Fig. 5.2).
2. *Drag* the tool palette into the Status Bar. It will fit in just below the **View Control Bar**.
3. *Left-click* on the **AccuDraw** icon and the **AccuDraw** coordinates window appears on screen (Fig. 5.3). The window shows the position of the cursor in X, Y and Z coordinate units. We only require the X,Y coordinates at the moment. If working in a 2D screen the **AccuDraw** window will only show X and Y coordinates. However, remember we will be working in 3D (with X, Y and Z coordinates) in the final chapters of this book.

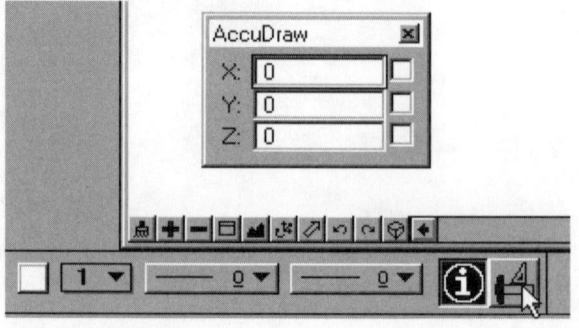

4. Now *drag* the coordinates window into the Status Bar. The screen now appears as in Fig. 5.4.

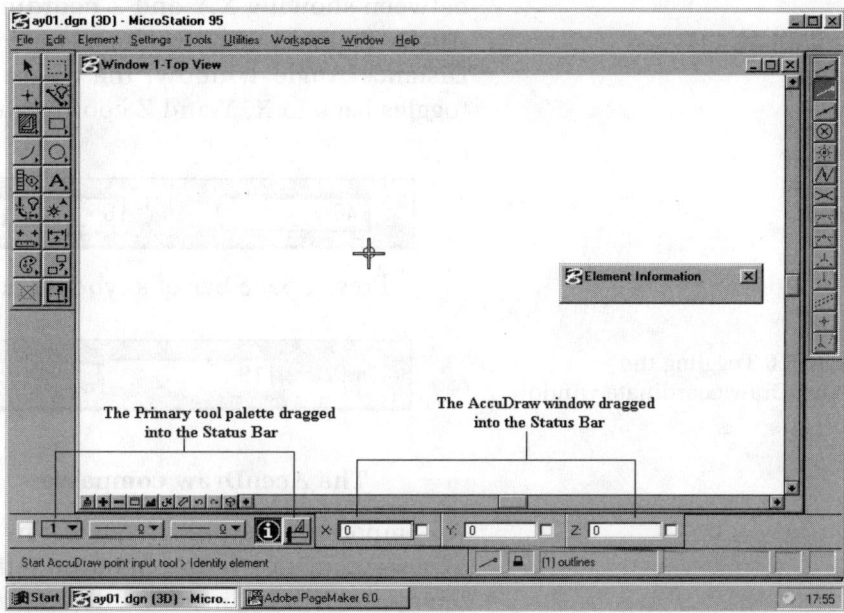

Fig. 5.4 The screen showing both the **Primary Tools** palette and the coordinates window in the Status Bar

The Primary Tools palette

There are six icons in the **Primary Tools** palette (See Fig. 5.5). From left to right these show:

Active Color: A *left-click* brings up a colour dialogue box from which any available colour can be selected.

Active Level: A *left-click* brings up a dialogue box showing all 64 available levels with the active one highlighted against a circular background.

Active Line Style: A *left-click* brings up the line style palette, from which the line style can be changed for that currently in use.

Active Line Weight: A *left-click* brings up the line weight palette.

Analyse Element: A *left-click* on any element on screen and details of the element appear in the Status Bar.

Start AccuDraw: This brings up the coordinates window if it is not already on screen and starts AccuDraw functioning.

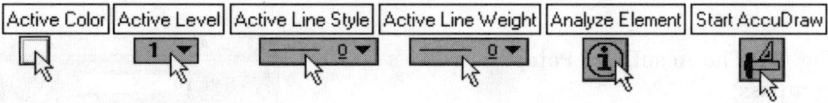

Fig. 5.5 The names of the icons in the **Primary Tools** palette

Switching between coordinates and angles

Pressing the keyboard **Space** bar toggles the coordinate window between showing X,Y and Z coordinates to showing **Distance** and **Angle**. Figure 5.6 shows the change which occurs. If, while in the Distance/Angle window, the **Space** bar is pressed, the window toggles back to X, Y and Z coordinates.

Press Space bar of keyboard and the window changes

Fig. 5.6 Toggling the AccuDraw coordinate window

The AccuDraw compasses

An important feature of AccuDraw is the AccuDraw 'compass'. When AccuDraw is in operation, either a **Rectangular** or a **Polar** 'compass' will be in action, depending upon whether elements are at right angles to a previous element, or angular to it. The type of compass is reflected in the changes to the AccuDraw window in the Status Bar when the **Space** bar is used to toggle between the coordinate and Distance/Angle windows. The **Rectangular** compass shows with the coordinate window and the **Polar** compass with the Distance/Angle window. See Figs 5.7 and 5.8. Note that the heavier arms of the compasses are facing to the +ve X and +ve Y directions as elements are constructed with the aid of AccuDraw.

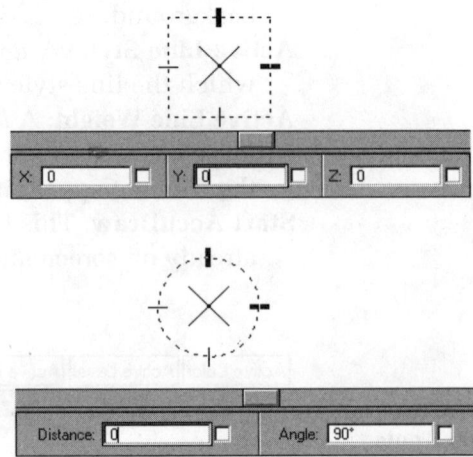

Fig. 5.7 The AccuDraw **Rectangular** compass

Fig. 5.8 The AccuDraw **Polar** compass

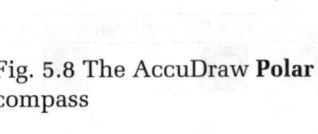

Examples of the use of AccuDraw

Example 1 – Fig. 5.11

The outline Fig. 5.11 was constructed as follows:

1. *Left-click* on **AccuDraw** in the **Settings** pull-down menu (Fig. 5.9) and in the **AccuDraw Settings** dialogue box which then appears (Fig. 5.10). Make sure that **Context Sensitivity** is off (no **X** in its check box).

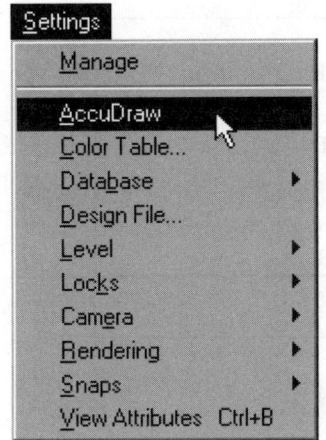

Fig. 5.9 Select **AccuDraw** from the **Settings** pull-down menu

Fig. 5.10 Make sure that the **Context Sensitivity** check box is set off

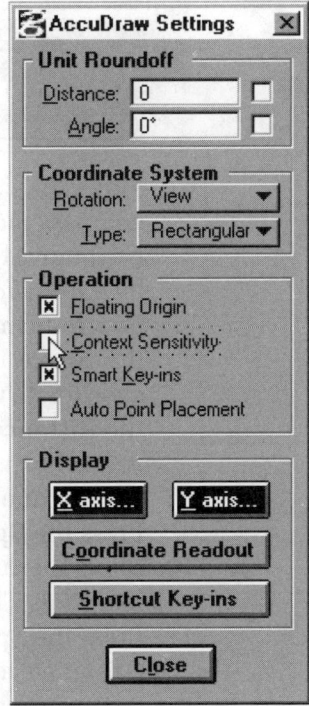

2. *Left-click* on the **Start AccuDraw** icon in the **Primary Tool** palette in the Status Bar to start AccuDraw functioning. The AccuDraw coordinate window appears in the Status Bar – or on screen if it has not previously been *dragged* into the Status Bar.
3. *Left-click* on the **Smart Line** tool icon to make it active.
4. *Left-click* at **A** (Fig. 5.11). The **Rectangular** compass appears at **A**.
5. Move the cursor under mouse control to the right – along the X axis. Note that the **X** box in the coordinate window shows the distance as the mouse is moved. *Enter* 100, then *left-click*. There is no need to *left-click* in the coordinate window. AccuDraw starts the line cursor blinking in the **X** box of the coordinate window showing that it is ready to have figures *entered*. The compass moves to **B**.

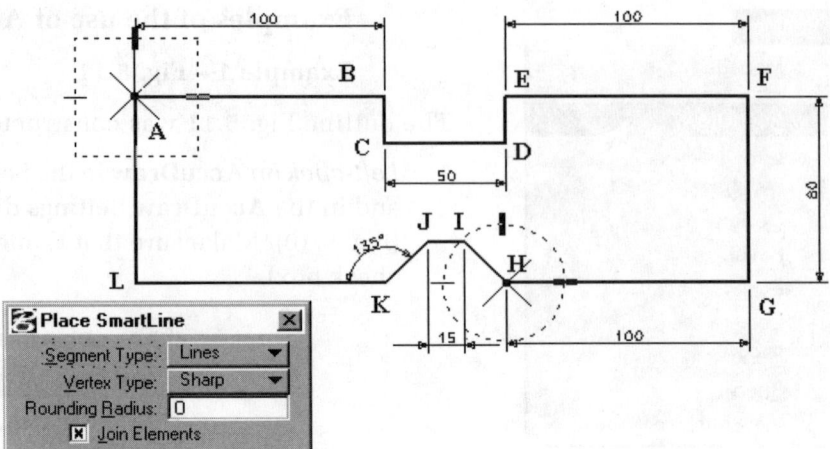

Fig. 5.11 Example 1. Using
AccuDraw

6.   Move the cursor along the Y axis. *Enter* 15, then *left-click*. The compass moves to **C**.
7.   Now move the cursor in the X axis direction and *enter* 50 followed by a *left-click*. The compass moves to **D**.
8.   Continue in this manner until the compass reaches **H**. Then press the **Space** bar. The compass changes to a **Polar** type and the coordinate window changes to a Distance/Angle type. *Enter* 25 in the **Distance** box. Press the **Tab** key of the keyboard to make the Angle box active. *Enter* the angle 45. *Left-click* in the screen and the 45° line to **I** appears.
9.   Press the **Space** bar and the **Rectangular** compass reappears.
10.   Move the cursor towards the corner **J** and *enter* 15, followed by a *left-click*. The compass moves to **J**.
11.   Press the **Space** bar to reactivate the **Polar** compass and *enter* 25 (Distance) and 45 (Angle), followed by a *left-click* on screen. The compass moves to **K**.
12.   Press the **Space** bar to bring back the **Rectangular** compass to the X,Y axes.
13.   Now complete the outline back to **A**. A *right-click* closes the action of **Smart Line**.

Notes on AccuDraw

1.   If **Context Sensitivity** is active, the compasses will rotate as the angle of the next element is changed. It is as well to experiment with this facility by turning **Context Sensitivity** on, then drawing some outlines. For the examples given here it has been turned off.
2.   If you no longer wish to work with AccuDraw, press the **Q** key of the keyboard with the cursor placed in the AccuDraw window and the coordinate window disappears from the Status Line – or from screen if not in the Status Line. A *left-click* on the **Start AccuDraw**

icon reactivates AccuDraw and the coordinate window reappears in the Status Bar.

3. Pressing the **Tab** key or the vertical cursor keys of the keyboard toggles between the X, Y and Z boxes of the AccuDraw coordinate window.

4. When working in a 2D screen, only the X and Y coordinates show in the AccuDraw coordinate window. However, remember that we will be dealing with the third coordinate, Z, when 3D drawing is introduced in the final chapters.

5. If no tool is active, when the cursor is moved around the screen under mouse control, the AccuDraw coordinate window shows the true positions on the screen in terms of x,y coordinates as the movement takes place. When the AccuDraw compass is in operation the coordinates shown in the coordinate window are in relation to the position of the centre of the compass at the last entered point, which then assumes the origin point when the check box of the **Context Sensitivity** box in the **AccuDraw Settings** dialogue box is empty (off).

Example 2 – Fig. 5.12

This example is included to indicate that most tools in the MicroStation 95 set will use AccuDraw if it is active.

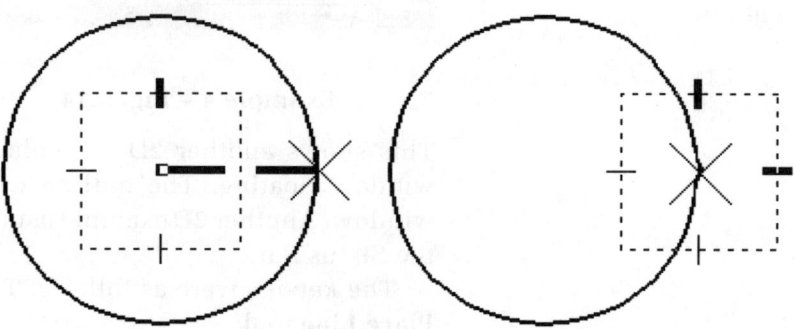

Fig. 5.12 Example 2. Using **AccuDraw**

Example 3 – Fig. 5.13

In this example the **Key-in** window has been *dragged* into the Status Bar and the **AccuDraw** coordinates window is left on screen. This example is showing a 2D (two-dimensional) screen, so only the X and Y coordinates are showing in the coordinates window. The active tool is **Smart Line** and the start point of an outline has been *keyed-in* to the **Key-in** window. This example is included because occasions may arise when it is easier to *key-in* a coordinate than to use other methods, such as relying upon moving the cursor until the coordinate window shows the required coordinate position.

This example also shows a grid at 10 unit (mm) intervals with Grid Lock. Irrespective of Grid or Grid Lock, AccuDraw positions override Grid Lock.

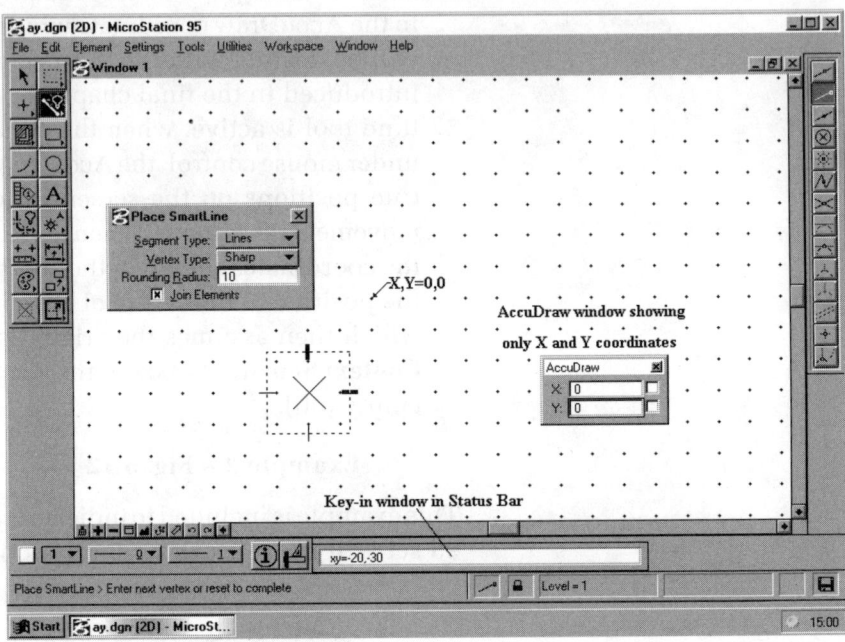

Fig. 5.13 Example 3. Using
AccuDraw

Example 4 – Fig. 5.14

This shows another 2D example with the AccuDraw coordinate window floating. The outline was constructed with the **Key-in** window. Another 2D example using the **Key-in** window stationed in the Status Bar.

The *key-ins* were as follows. To start off the outline, select the **Place Line** tool:

> **Place Line >Start point:** *key-in* xy=50,50
> Followed by using AccuDraw to complete the outline.

To place left-hand circle:

> **Place Circle by Center > Center point:** *key-in* xy=30,20
> **Place Circle by Center > Point on circle:** *key-in* xy=40,20

To place right-hand circle:

> **Place Circle by Center > Center point:** *key-in* xy=20,20
> **Place Circle by Center > Point on circle:** *key-in* xy=25,20

You may find it instructive to work through this example on screen. It can be worked on either a 2D or a 3D screen.

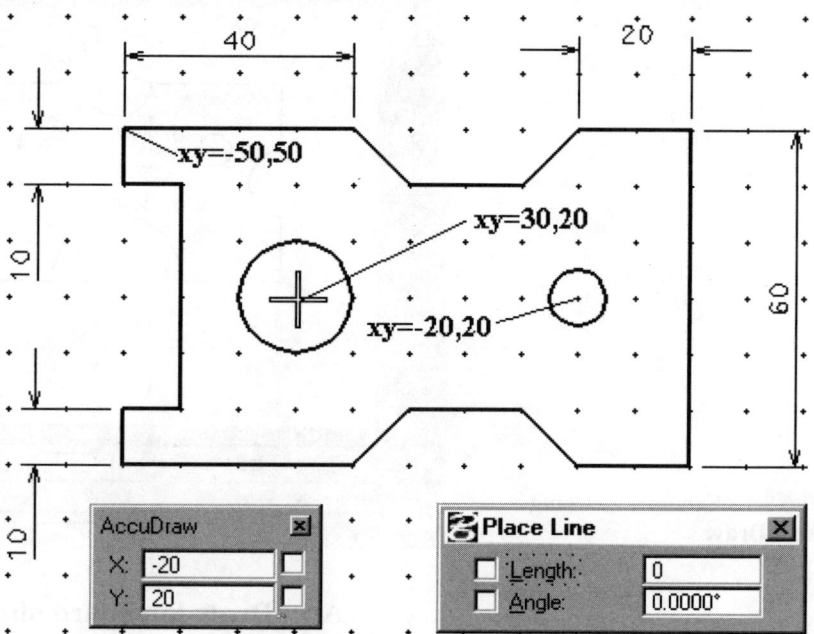

Fig. 5.14 Example 4. Using **AccuDraw**.

Example 5 – Fig. 5.15

In this example the **Key-in** window has been *dragged* into just below the Menu bar. The **Primary Tools** palette is in the Status Bar as is also the 3D AccuDraw coordinate window.

To construct the outline the position of the top left-hand corner of the outline was *keyed-in*, as were the centres of the circles.

Points on the circles to determine their radius were also *keyed-in*.

Other positions such as the lines and arcs were constructed from AccuDraw settings in the AccuDraw coordinate window.

It will be noted that the screen coordinate origin where x,y is 0,0 is shown in this example. This is included in the illustration to show why the centre of the upper left-hand lower left-hand circle was *keyed-in* as −10,10 and that of the lower of the two circles *keyed-in* as −10,−10.

This example is constructed in a 3D screen – the AccuDraw coordinate window shows X, Y and Z coordinate boxes, but only the X and Y coordinates are in use because the drawing is a 2D one.

You may care to attempt this example, using either a 2D or a 3D screen.

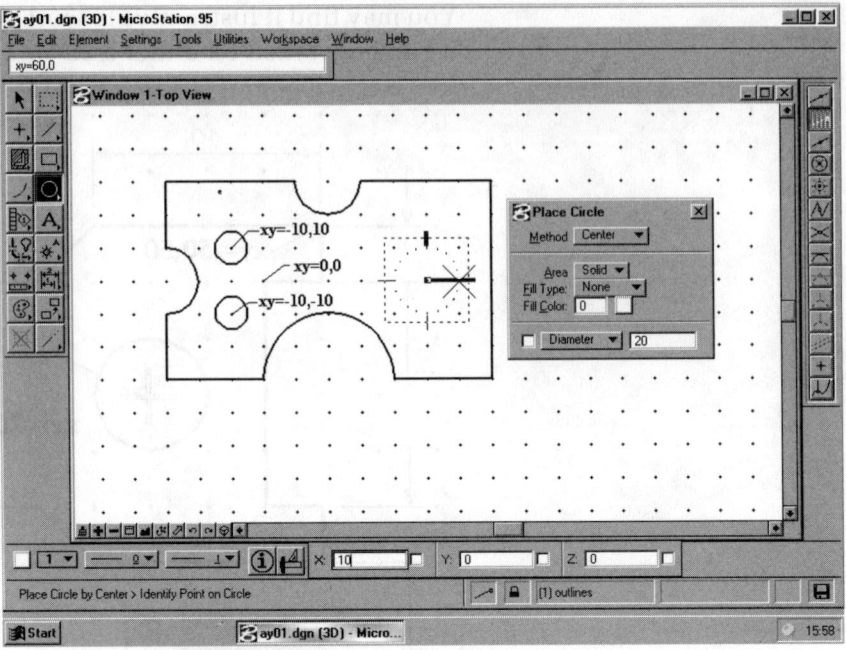

Fig. 5.15 Example 5. Using
AccuDraw

AccuDraw keyboard shortcuts

There are several keyboard shortcuts available when using AccuDraw, some of which are not included here. Those that will be of interest to readers of this book are shown below.

Coordinate window smart locks

When in the AccuDraw coordinate window, press the **X** key of the keyboard and the number in the **X** coordinate box locks – its check box automatically shows an **X**. See Fig. 5.16.

When in the AccuDraw coordinate window, press the **Y** key of the keyboard and the number in the **Y** coordinate box locks – its check box automatically shows an **X**.

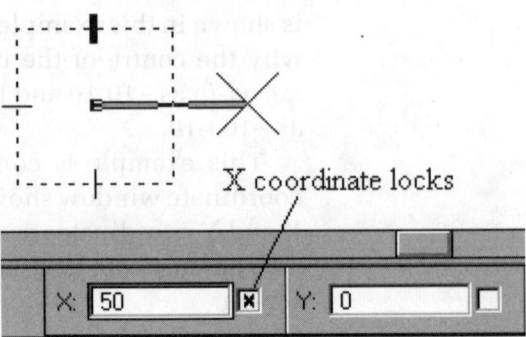

Fig. 5.16 Press the **X** key and
the X locks

When in the AccuDraw Distance/Angle window, press the **D** key of the keyboard and the number in the Distance box locks – its check box automatically shows an **X**. See Fig. 5.17.

When in the AccuDraw Distance/Angle window, press the **A** key of the keyboard and the number in the Angle box locks – its check box automatically shows an **X**.

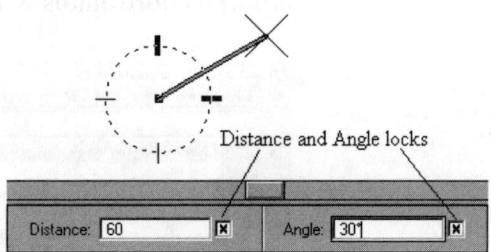

Fig. 5.17 Press the **D** key and the Distance locks. Press **A** and the Angle locks

The AccuDraw shortcuts dialogue box

Place the cursor within the AccuDraw coordinate window and press the **?** key of the keyboard. The **AccuDraw Shortcuts** dialogue box appears (Fig. 5.18). If you scroll the list in this dialogue box you will see all of the AccuDraw keyboard shortcuts.

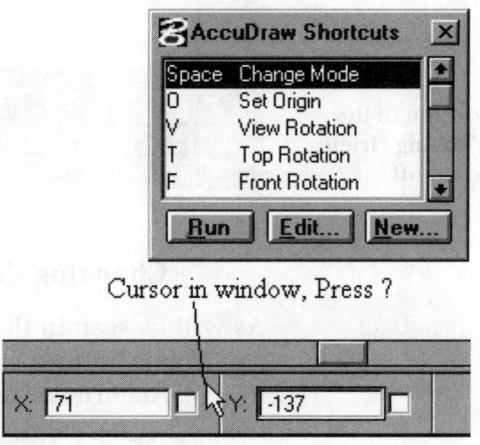

Fig. 5.18 Place the cursor in the AccuDraw coordinate window and press the **?** key and the **AccuDraw Shortcuts** dialogue box shows

Forcing AccuDraw to X or Y axes

When a line is being drawn with AccuDraw active, pressing the **Return** key forces the line towards whichever is the nearer axis – **X** or **Y**. Press the **Return** key to release the lock on the axis position.

Non-floating Origin

Left-click in the **Floating Origin** check box to turn the facility off – see Fig. 5.9 on page 69. The AccuDraw compass will then stay at the true coordinate of the screen – i.e. where x,y = 0,0. Figure 5.19 shows the compass at the screen origin – with the check box set off (no **X**).

Even though AccuDraw is active, constructions will show away from the origin set compass. This facility allows the operator to check where the true origin is and *key-in* coordinates in relation to the true origin. The compass does not follow the positions of the *entered* coordinates when the **Floating Origin** facility is turned off.

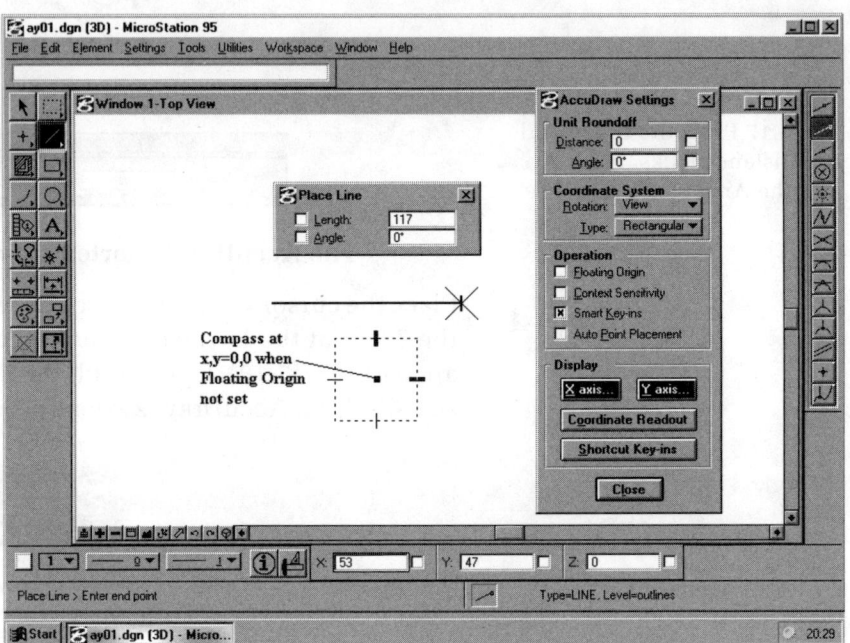

Fig. 5.19 The position of the compass with **Floating Origin** check box switched off

Changing the colour of axes in the compass

As will be seen in the **AccuDraw Settings** dialogue box, the **X axis** and **Y axis** buttons show the colour of the axes as they will appear in the AccuDraw compasses. These colours can be changed if wished. A *left-click* on either button brings the **Modify Axis Color** dialogue box on screen (Fig. 5.20); the colour of the chosen axis can be modified either by changing the **RGB** sliders to obtain a different colour or by selection of a colour name in the **Named Colors** list box of the dialogue box. After selection, a *left-click* on the **OK** button of the dialogue box and the selected axis button will change colour.

The colours in the compasses (either **Rectangular** or **Polar**) are of value when **Context Sensitivity** is on, because as the compass rotates in line with the last element, the directions of both axes rotate and with colours it is easier to identify which axis is **X** and which is **Y**.

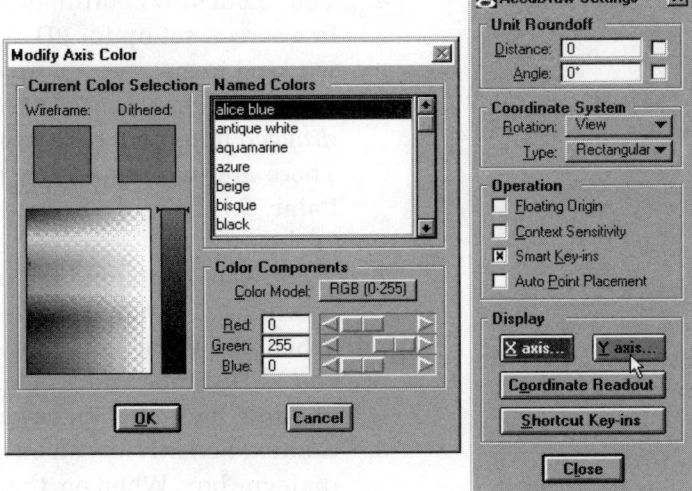

Fig. 5.20 Changing the colour of the **X axis** or **Y axis** colours in the AccuDraw compass

Revision notes on AccuDraw

1. *Drag* the **Primary Tools** palette into the Status Bar, although it can be *dragged* to left, right or top if wished. See Fig. 5.21.
2. **Color**, **Level**, **Line Style**, **Line Weight** and **Start AccuDraw** can be selected from the **Primary Tools** palette.
3. The AccuDraw coordinates window is called to screen with a *left-click* on the **Start AccuDraw** icon in the **Primary Tools** palette. This also starts the action of AccuDraw.

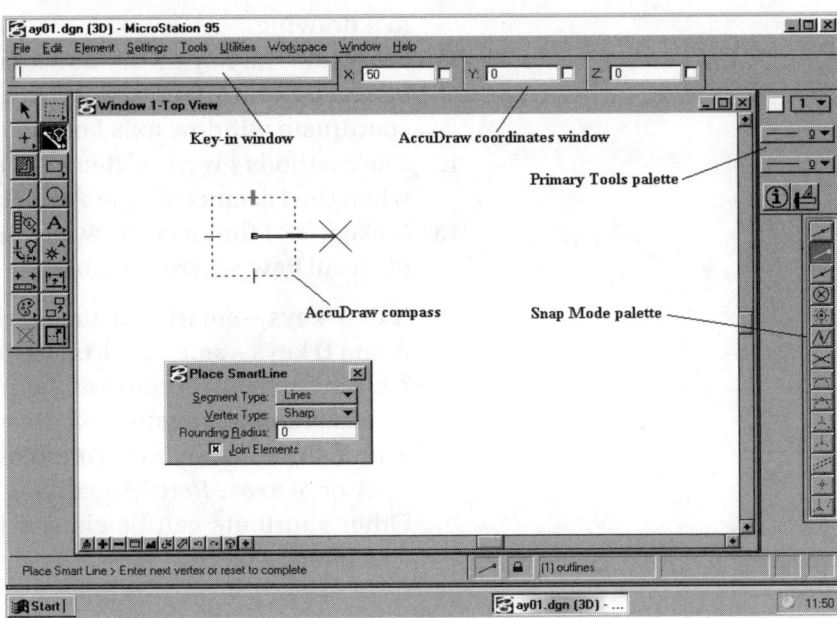

Figf. 5.21 Different positions for the **Primary Tools** palette and AccuDraw window

4. The AccuDraw coordinate box will show X and Y when working in a screen set up for 2D. X, Y and Z will show in the box when working in a screen set up for 3D.

5. The AccuDraw can either be left to float on screen or can be *dragged* to bottom or to top. See Fig. 5.21.

6. There are two types of AccuDraw compass – **Rectangular** and **Polar**. To change from one to the other, press the **Space** bar of the keyboard.

7. When the **Rectangular** compass is in action, the AccuDraw coordinates window shows X, Y (and when in 3D, Z) axis figures. When the **Polar** compass is in action the AccuDraw window shows **Distance** and **Angle**. To toggle between the two types of window press the **Space** bar.

8. **Context Sensitivity** can be set on or off in the **AccuDraw Settings** dialogue box. When on, the AccuDraw compass axes rotate in line with the last element drawn. When off the compass axes always line up with the true X and Y axes (and in 3D work with the Z axis).

9. To toggle between X and Y boxes or between Distance and Angle boxes of the AccuDraw coordinate window, press the **Tab** key of the keyboard (often marked with two opposite-facing arrows) or the up or down cursor keys.

10. Coordinate X or Y figures can be *entered* to the respective coordinate window X or Y boxes by just *entering* the figures at the keyboard for whichever of the boxes shows a vertical line cursor. The figures will automatically appear in the box. A *left-click* on screen confirms the position of the end point of the element being added to a drawing.

11. Press the **Tab** key or the down facing cursor arrow key to move between X and Y (and also Z if in use), when *entering* figures to the coordinate window axis boxes.

12. The methods given in items 10 and 11 above can also be used when the Distance/Angle AccuDraw window is in operation.

13. Make use of the AccuDraw keyboard shortcuts to control the use of AccuDraw where possible:

    X or **Y** keys – smart lock on coordinate window X and Y boxes.
    A and **D** keys – smart lock on Distance and Angle window boxes.
    ? with cursor in AccuDraw window – to bring up **AccuDraw Shortcuts** dialogue box.
    X or **Y** followed by *Return* forces line being drawn towards the X or Y axes. *Return* again and the lock is released.
    Other shortcuts can be chosen from the **AccuDraw Shortcuts** dialogue box.

14. Use the **Key-in** window or the coordinate window to *key-in* x,y start points of lines, circles, arcs and other elements when working in AccuDraw.

Questions

1. Why can constructions be drawn faster in AccuDraw yet as accurately as methods of drawing given in earlier chapters?
2. What are the differences between design screens shown in this chapter to those shown in earlier chapters?
3. What is the purpose of the **Primary Tools** tool palette?
4. Which design screen do you think you will be working in when using MicroStation 95? Can you explain why you have made this choice?
5. Can the AccuDraw coordinate window be parked in the right-hand side of the screen?
6. Can the **Primary Tools** palette be parked on the left-hand side of the screen?
7. How does one switch between the **Rectangular** compass and the **Polar** compass when using AccuDraw?
8. What else happens when you switch between the rectangular and the polar compasses?
9. Have you tried using AccuDraw with the **Floating Origin** option set off in the **AccuDraw Settings** box?
10. Why do the two axes in the compasses carry different colours?

Exercises

The drawings for the exercises given below carry dimensions. At this stage it is advisable not to include dimensions in the answers to the exercises. Dimensioning of drawings in MicroStation 95 will be described in Chapter 11.

Some of the drawings below are orthographic projections. Do not bother if you do not understand the basis of orthographic projection because a short explanation of the theory underlying orthographic projection will be given in Chapter 10.

1. Figure 5.22 is a simple line logo of the initials of my name. Working to approximately the same dimensions, construct a similar logo using the initials of your own name.
2. Make an accurate copy of the arrow shown in Fig. 5.23 working to the given dimensions.
3. Figure 5.24 is a front view and end view in orthographic projection of a wall holder into which a circular rod end is to be fitted. Construct an accurate copy of the two views to the given sizes.

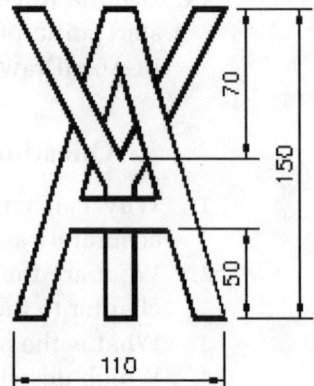

Fig. 5.22 Exercise 1

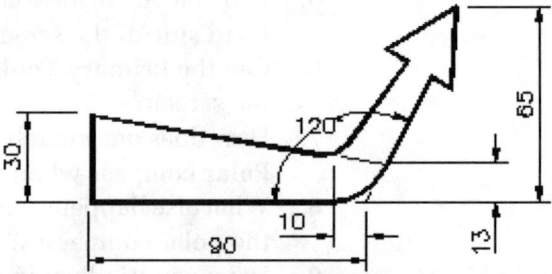

Fig. 5.23 Exercise 2

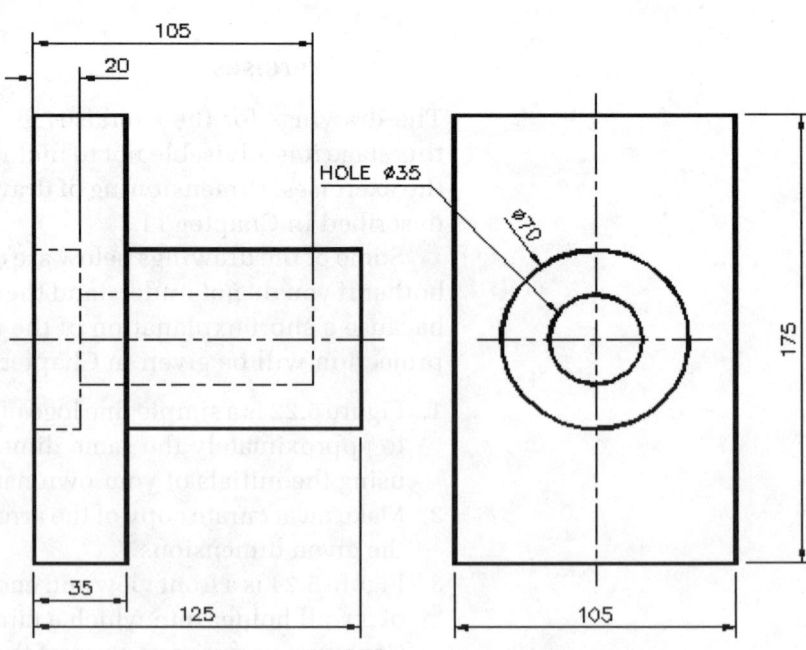

Fig. 5.24 Exercise 3

4. Figure 5.25 is a view of a seat belt adjusting plate. Construct an accurate copy of the plate to the given dimensions.

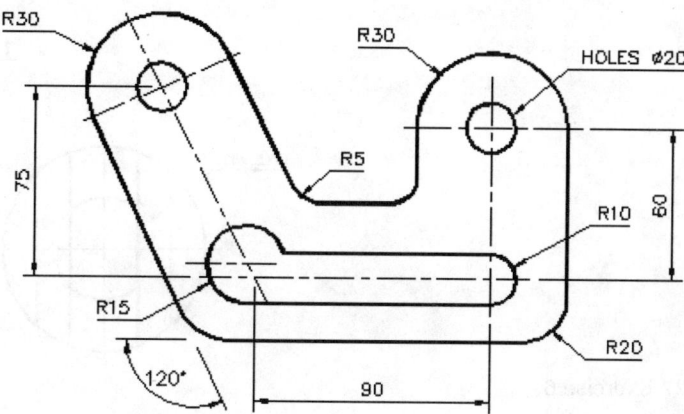

Fig. 5.25 Exercise 4

5. A three-view third-angle orthographic projection of an adjusting slide for a grinding machine is shown in Fig. 5.26.
   Construct an accurate copy of the given views to the sizes shown with the projection.

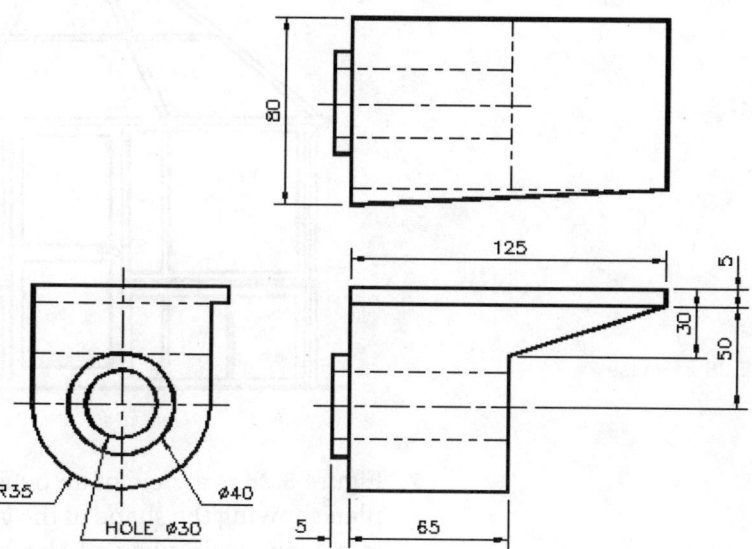

Fig. 5.26 Exercise 5

6. Make an accurate copy of the three-view projection of a coupling device given in Fig. 5.27.

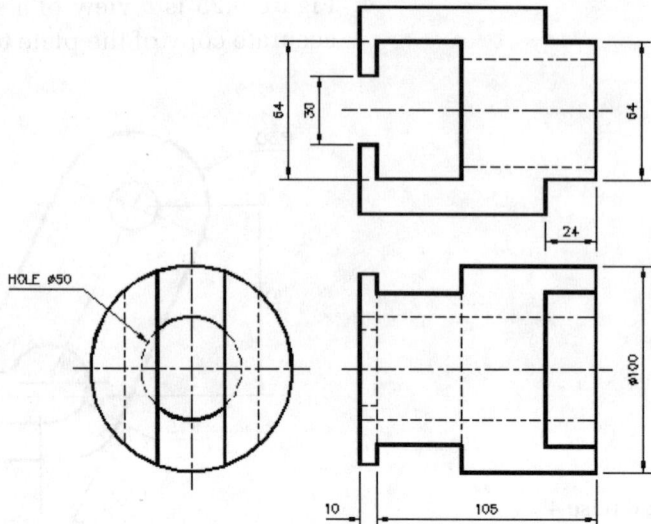

Fig. 5.27 Exercise 6

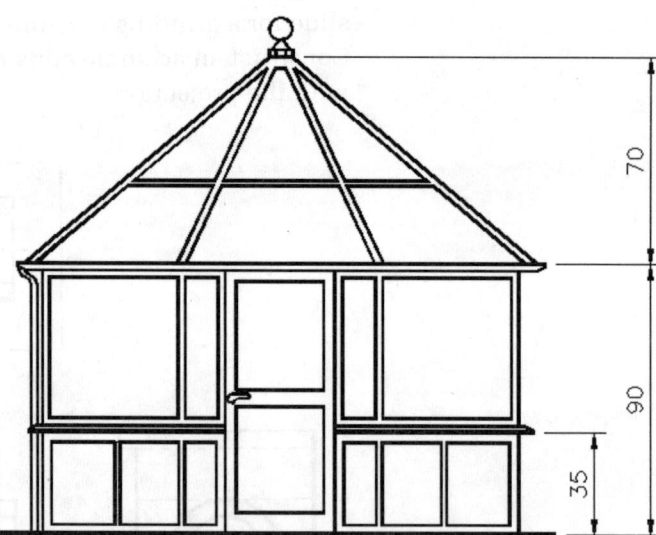

Fig. 5.28 Exercise 7

7. Figure 5.28 is a view of an octagonal greenhouse. Figure 5.29 is a plan showing the shape of the greenhouse from above. Figure 5.30 is a large scale view of the boss at the top of the roof of the greenhouse.

    Working as near as you can to the given dimensions, make an accurate copy of the given front view, Fig. 5.28. Dimensions not given are left to your judgement.

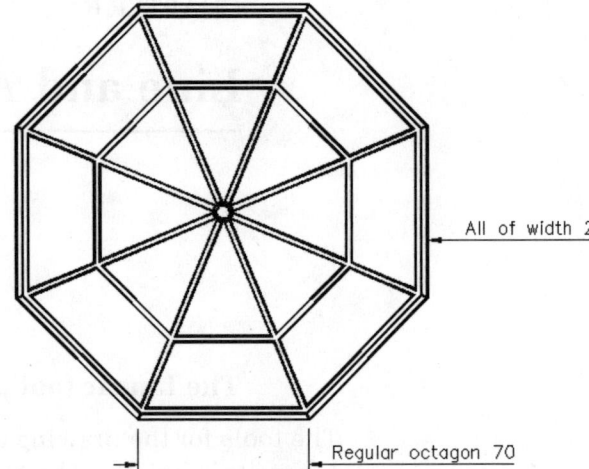

Fig. 5.29 Plan view for
Exercise 7

All of width 2

Regular octagon 70

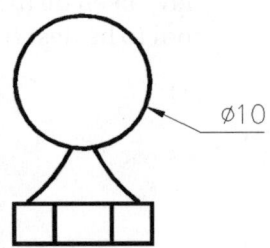

Fig. 5.30 Sizes of the boss on
top of the roof of the
greenhouse

Ø10

8. Figure 5.31 shows a view of a rotating arm and slider from a
temperature-controlling device.

Construct an accurate copy of the given view, using your own
judgement about sizes not shown in the drawing. Use **Rounding
Radius** set to 5 with **Vertex Type** set to **Rounded** in the **Smart Line**
Element Selection box to obtain the 5 mm fillets.

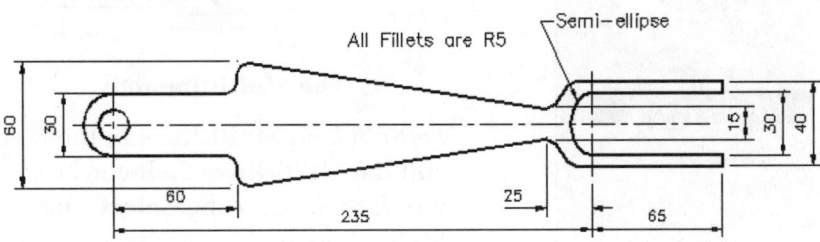

All Fillets are R5

Semi-ellipse

Fig. 5.31 Exercise 8

CHAPTER 6

Line and Arc tools

The Linear tool palette

The tools for the drawing of different types of lines are held in the **Linear** tool palette. The tool tips of all the tools in this palette are shown in Fig. 6.1. The two tools **Place Smart Line** and **Place Line** have been dealt with to some extent in previous chapters, so the first tool to be described in this chapter will be the **Place Multi-line** tool.

Fig. 6.1 The tool tips of the tools in the **Linear** tool palette

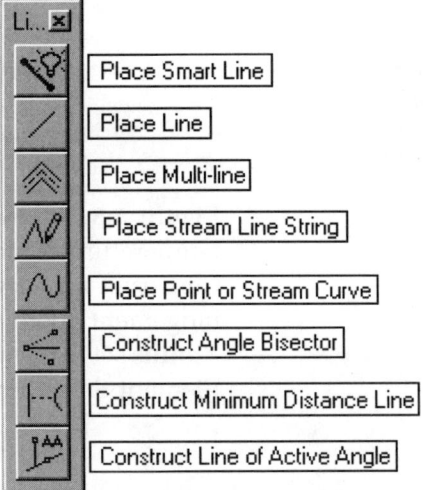

The Multi-line tool

Left-click on **Multi-lines** in the **Element** pull-down menu (Fig. 6.2) and the **Multi-lines** dialogue box appears (Fig. 6.3). In the dialogue box *left-click* on the **Select Line Style** button and the **Select Line Style** dialogue box appears (also in Fig. 6.3).

As an example of the use of these dialogue boxes, *left-click* on **Rail Road** in the list box of **Select Line Style**. Then *left-click* on the **Multi-lines** style tool icon in the **Linear** tool palette. The **Place**

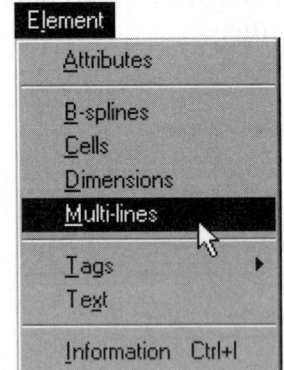

Fig. 6.2 Selecting **Multi-lines** from the **Element** pull-down menu

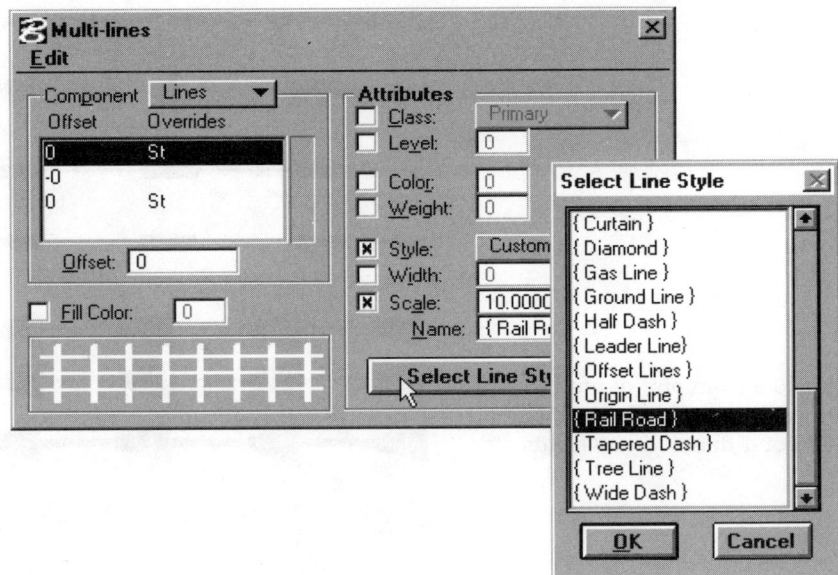

Fig. 6.3 The **Multi-lines** and
Select Line Style dialogue
boxes

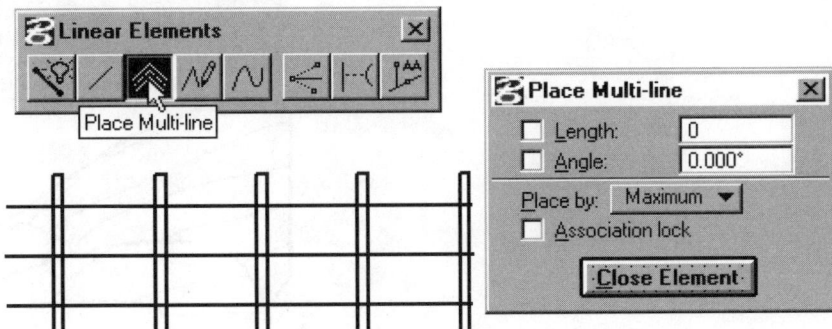

Fig. 6.4 An example of placing
a multi-line

Multi-line Element Selection box appears. Following the prompts in
the Status Bar, draw a multi-line of style **Rail Road** (Fig. 6.4).

Other multi-lines of different styles are shown in Fig. 6.5. These
examples show different line weights and scales. The scale of a
multi-line is set in the **Scale** box of the **Multi-lines** dialogue box. The
line weight is set from the line weight icon in the **Primary Tools**
palette.

The Place Stream Line String and Stream Curve Tools

Figure 6.6 is an example of a freehand illustration in which the
wings were drawn with the freehand drawing tool **Place Stream
Line String** and the **Place Point or Stream Curve** tool. The first of
these tools allows freehand lines to be speedily drawn – *left-click* to
commence drawing, draw the shape by *dragging* movements of the

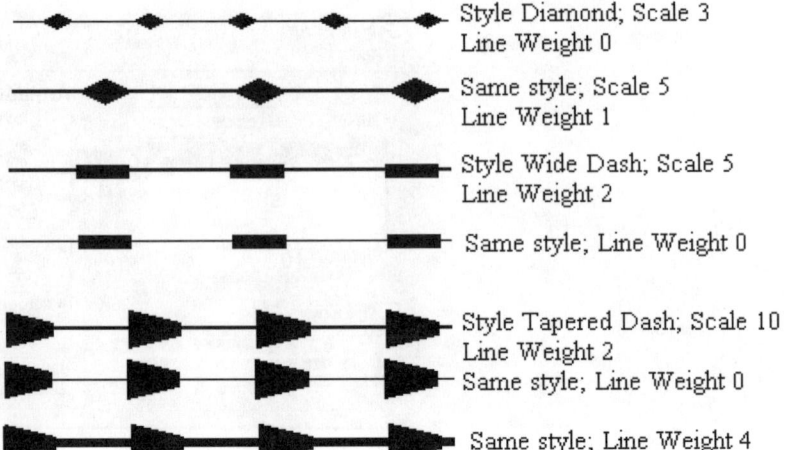

Fig. 6.5 Examples of multi-lines drawn to different scales and of different line weights

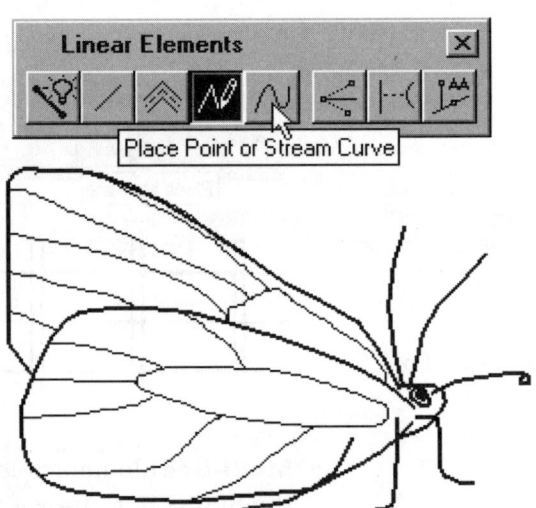

Fig. 6.6 A freehand drawing constructed with the two tools shown with the illustration

mouse. When the shape has been completed, *right-click*. The second of the tools allows curves to be drawn from a point. *Left-click* to start the curve at a point, *drag* the curve in the required direction and *left-click* again to continue drawing the curve. The given illustration, Fig. 6.6, was drawn by movement of a mouse as a digitiser, but a pencil type stylus used as a drawing tool would probably be a better drawing digitiser for this type of freehand drawing. The inner shapes of the wings were drawn with the **Place Stream Line String** tool with the outlines of the wings and of the head drawn with the **Place Point or Stream Curve** tool.

The Construct Angle Bisector tool

This tool will precisely bisect the angle between two lines, When the tool is selected, the following prompts appear in the Status Bar, one after the other as the required points are selected:

Construct Angle Bisector > Enter endpoint of angle leg
Construct Angle Bisector > Enter angle vertex
Construct Angle Bisector > Enter endpoint of angle leg

The angle bisector then appears in the line weight currently employed after each of the points has been selected in turn. Figure 6.7 shows an example of the use of the tool.

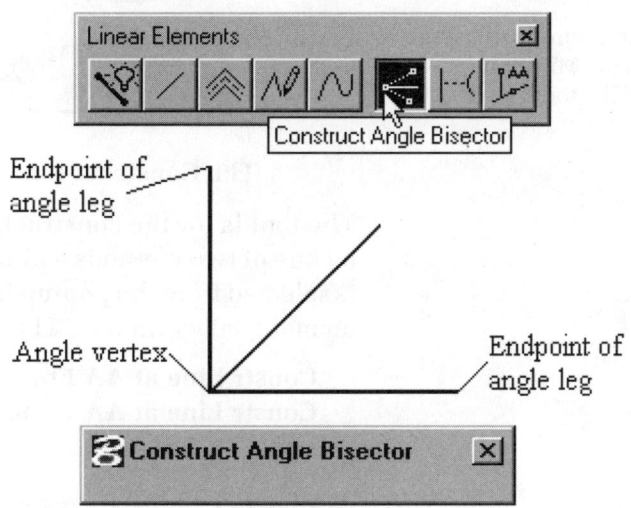

Fig. 6.7 An example of the action of the **Construct Angle Bisector** tool

The Construct Minimum Distance line tool

This tool is used in relation to the prompts appearing in the Status Bar as follows:

Construct minimum distance line > Identify element: *left-click* on first element
Construct minimum distance line > Accept, Identify 2nd element: *left-click* on second element
Construct minimum distance line > Accept, Initiate min dist calculation: *left-click* and the minimum distance line appears and a statement such as **Dist = 28 mm** also appears in the Status Bar.

Figure 6.8 is an example showing the minimum distance line between a circle and an arc.

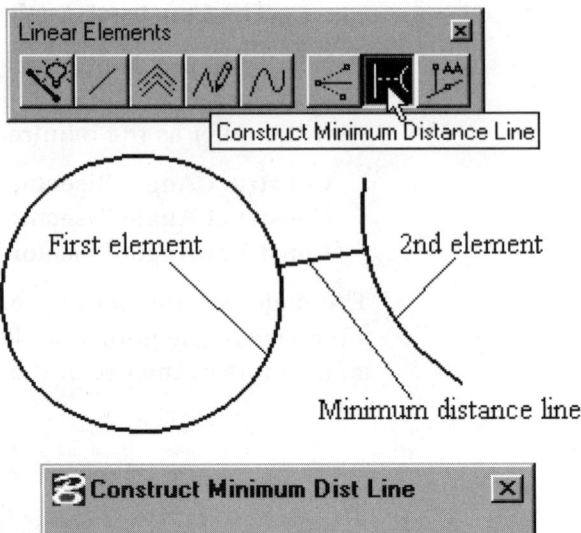

Fig. 6.8 An example of using the **Construct Minimum Distance Line** tool

The Construct Line of Active Angle tool

The tool is for the construction of a line at an angle to another line by one of two methods – either **From Point** or **To Point**. The method is selected from the pop-up list of the **Construct Line of Active Angle** element selection box. The prompts in the Status Bar are either:

> **Constr Line at AA From Point > Identify element**
> **Constr Line at AA From Point > Enter endpoint**

or:

> **Constr Line at AA To Point > Select line segment**
> **Constr Line at AA To Point > Enter endpoint**

Figure 6.9 gives two examples – the left-hand drawing being a line at 45° from a point selected on the element, the right-hand drawing showing a line at 45° to a point from the endpoint of the angle line to the element.

The Arcs tool palette

Tools for the drawing of arcs are held in the **Arcs** tool palette. The tool tips for all the tools in this palette are shown in Fig. 6.10.

The Place Arc tool

It must be remembered when using the **Place Arc** tool that the drawing of arcs follows the default angular rule of being constructed anti-clockwise (counter-clockwise). When the **Place Arc** tool is

Fig. 6.9 Two examples of using the **Construct Line of Active Angle** tool

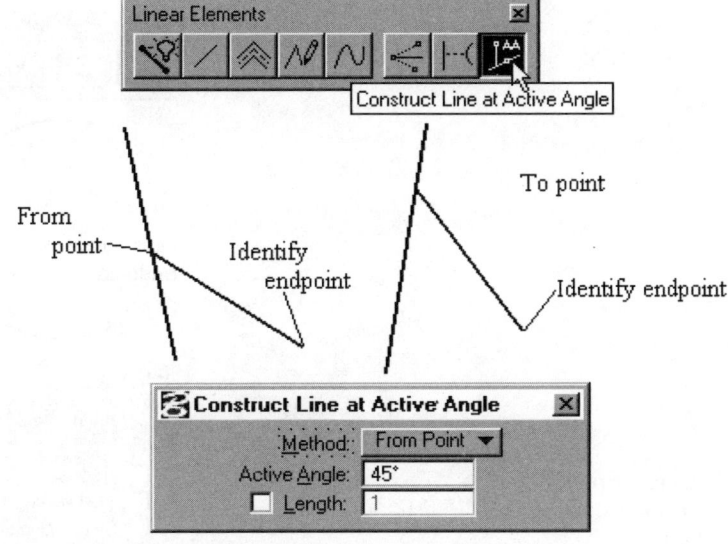

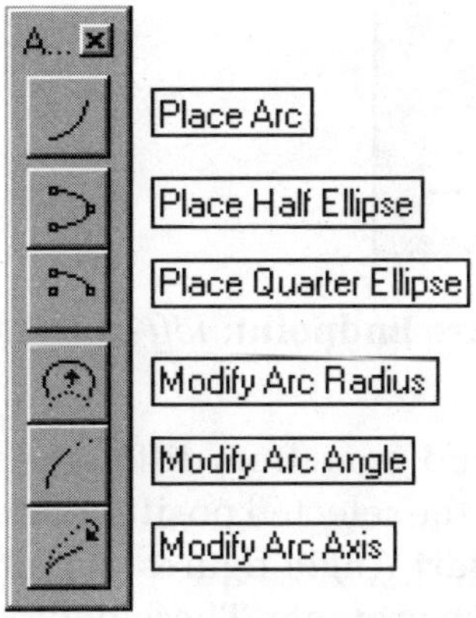

Fig. 6.10 The **Arcs** tool palette

selected, the **Place Arc** Element Selection box shows that either of two methods are available. *Left-click* on the **Method** button in the Element Selection box and a pop-up list which then appears gives a choice between **Center** and **Edge** (Fig. 6.11). Each of these selections has its own prompts appearing in the Status Bar.

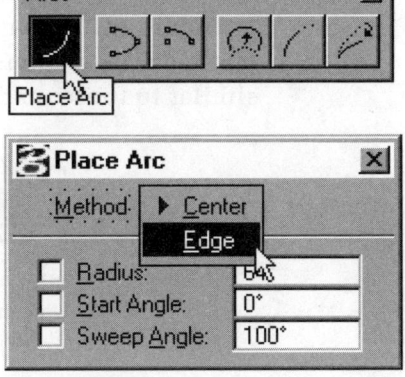

Fig. 6.11 The **Method** pop-up list in the Element Selection box

Figure 6.12 shows the results of constructing an arc using the **Edge** method. The prompts and responses will be:

Place Arc by Edge > Identify First Arc Endpoint: *left-click* at the first point on the arc – or – *key-in* an x,y coordinate. A square identification spot appears at the selected point.

Place Arc by Edge > Identify Point on Arc Radius: *left-click* at a second point on the arc – or – *key-in* an x,y coordinate.

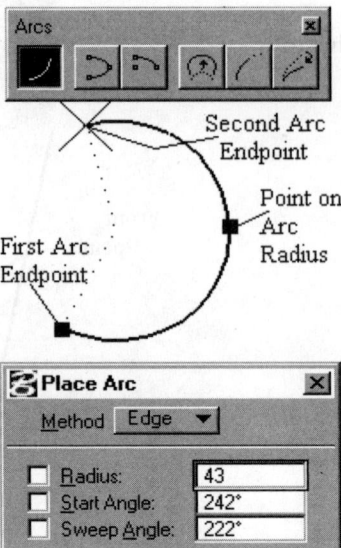

Fig. 6.12 An example of constructing an arc using the **Edge** method

Place Arc by Edge > Identify Second Arc Endpoint: *left-click* at the endpoint of the arc.

When drawing an arc by the **Center** method, apart from differences in the prompts appearing at the Status Bar, the selected positions are reflected in changes in the **Radius** and **Start Angle** figures, which become locked as responses are made to the prompts. These figures are not locked when the **Edge** method is used.

Figure 6.13 is an example of drawing an arc using the **Center** method. The responses to the three prompts in the dialogue box are similar to those made when using the **Edge** method.

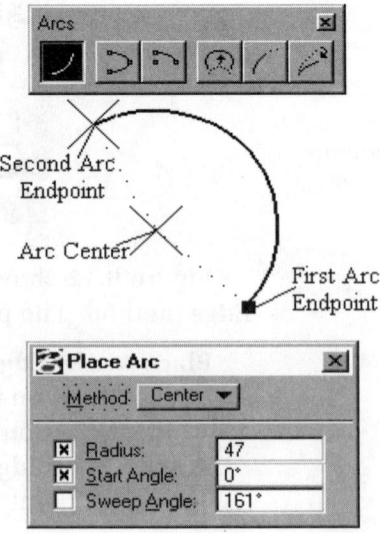

Fig. 6.13 An example of constructing an arc using the **Center** method

The Place Half Ellipse and Place Quarter Ellipse tools

Three points, either selected with a *left-click* on points on the screen or by *keying-in* coordinates, are required when using either of these tools. See Fig. 6.14. Prompts appear in the Status Bar. For the **Place Half Ellipse** tool:

One point of axis; Any point on the ellipse; Other end of axis

For the **Place Quarter Ellipse** tool:

Enter one end of ellipse quadrant; Point on axis; Endpoint

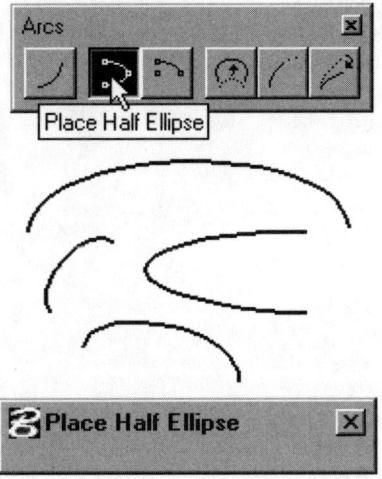

Fig. 6.14 An example of using the **Place Half Ellipse** tool

The Modify Arc Radius, Modify Arc Angle and Modify Arc Axis tools

These three tools all bring up similar prompts in the Status Bar. For the **Modify Arc Radius** tool:

Modify Arc Radius > Identify element
Modify Arc Radius > Select next input

For the **Modify Arc Angle** tool:

Modify Arc Angle > Identify element
Modify Arc Angle > Select next input

For the **Modify Arc Axis** tool:

Modify Arc Axis > Identify element
Modify Arc Axis > Select next input

In each case the **next input** is either by a *left-click* at a selected point on screen or by the *keying-in* of coordinates. See Figs 6.15 and 6.16.

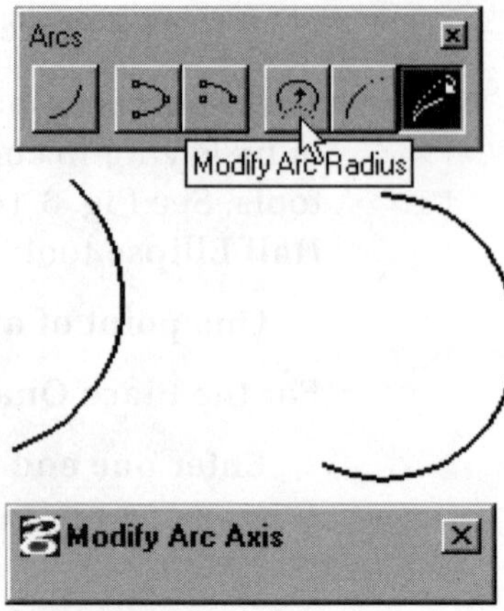

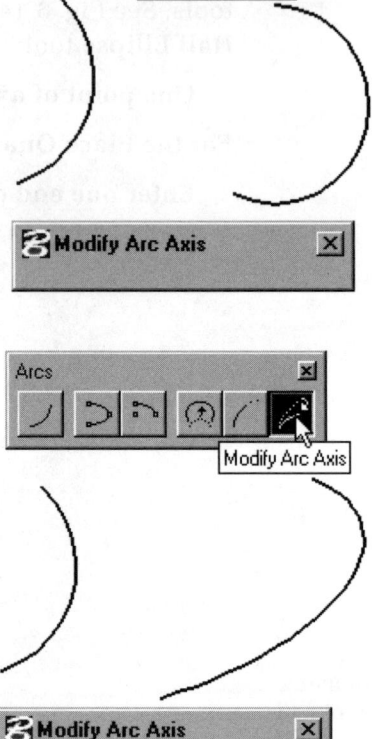

Fig. 6.15 An example of the use of the **Modify Arc Radius** tool

Fig. 6.16 An example of the use of the **Modify Arc Axis** tool

Selecting tool by icons or key-ins and shortcuts

As will have already been noted tools can either be called into action by the selection of tool icons from tool palettes or from flyouts or by the *keying-in* of tool name abbreviations. In practice, most operators will develop a style of working of their own choice which will most likely be to select most tools from tool icons, but by *keying-in* others. Most operators, as skill develops by practice, will find their own best (probably speediest for them) method of working.

There are also some keyboard shortcuts enabling dialogue boxes to be called to screen or commands to be executed and it is sometimes quicker to use these shortcuts than to select the box name for the menu bar. Examples are:

Ctrl+O **Open Drawing File** dialogue box
Ctrl+S saves the current design file
Ctrl+F saves Settings
Ctrl+P **Plot** dialogue box

Ctrl+Z undo
Ctrl+R redo
Ctrl+E **View Levels** dialogue box
Ctrl+B **View Attributes** dialogue box

Of these the shortcuts most likely to be used are **Ctrl+Z** for undo and **Ctrl+R** for redo.

Undo

Undo is selected either by using **Ctrl+Z**, by selection from the **Edit** menu, or by *keying-in* undo in the **Key-in** window. This causes the last element to be added to a drawing to be deleted from the drawing. This means that if a mistake is made it can immediately be undone by using one of the methods of calling **Undo**. If **Undo** is called again the previously placed element is undone and so on right back to the first element to be added to the design file drawing in the current drawing session.

Note that when selecting **Undo Other** there are two choices, as shown in Fig. 6.17 – **All** or **To Mark**. A mark can be set at any time during a drawing session, either by selecting **Set Mark** from the **Edit** pull-down menu , or by *keying-in* mark at the **Key-in Window**. Once a mark has been set in this way, only elements added after the mark can be acted upon by **Undo**. However if **All** is selected from **Undo Other**, then everything will be undone, but not before a *left-click on* the **OK** button of the Alert box shown in Fig. 6.18. The Alert comes on to screen for obvious reasons – you may find details undone which you did not wish to be undone, so use this **All** option with care.

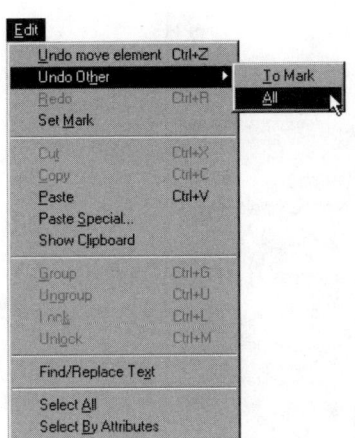

Fig. 6.17 Selecting **Undo All** from the **Edit** pull-down menu

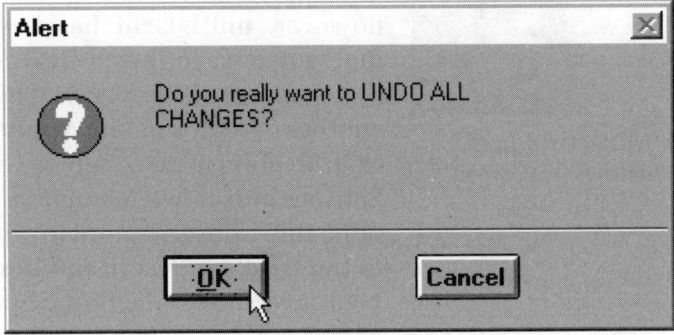

Fig. 6.18 The **Undo All** Alert box

Redo

Redo is called either by a *left-click* on **Redo** in the **Edit** pull-down menu, or by *keying-in* redo in the **Key-in** Window. Like undo, redo redoes the last element undone and repeated use of redo redoes everything that has been undone. **Redo** will also bring back details undone to **To Mark** or to **All**. Thus errors in using any of the **Undo** options can be rectified with **Redo**.

Grid

Grid points have been shown in several illustrations in previous chapters. The settings for grid spacing is carried out in the **Design**

Fig. 6.19 Setting **Grid** in the **View Attributes** dialogue box

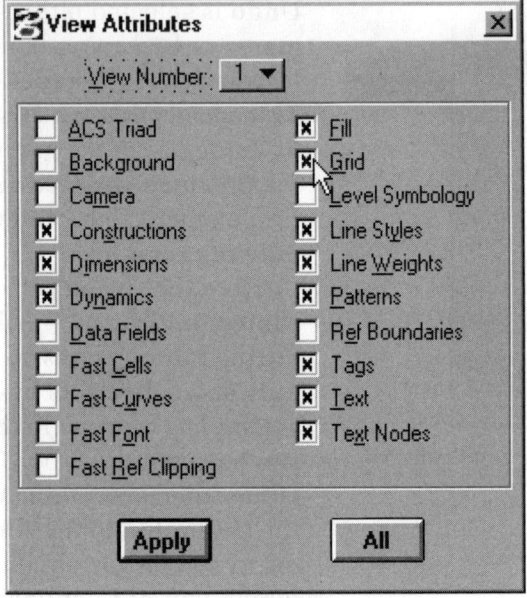

Fig. 6.20 Setting **Grid Lock** from the **Settings** pull-down menu

File Settings dialogue box, called from the **Settings** pull-down menu as described in Chapter 3 (page 42). Grid points will not show, however, until **Grid** has been checked in the **View Attributes** dialogue box, followed by a *left-click* on the **Apply** button of the dialogue box (Fig. 6.19). The grid points will not appear until another *left-click* on the **Apply** button. If you wish to lock the cursor to grid points, then Select **Grid** from the **Lock** sub-menu of the **Settings** pull-down menu (Fig. 6.20). When grid is locked, the cursor will jump from grid point to grid point at set grid distances according to the **Grid** settings in the **Design File Settings** dialogue box. **Grid Lock** overrides selection of points from *left-clicks* on screen, the cursor locking to the nearest grid point. However, with *keyed-in* coordinates or when using AccuDraw **Grid Lock** is ignored.

Fig. 6.21 The **Fence** flyout

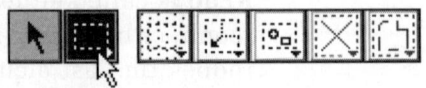

The Fence tool palette

Left-click on the **Place Fence** tool icon and the **Fence** flyout appears (Fig. 6.20). The names of the tools in this palette are shown in Fig. 6.22.

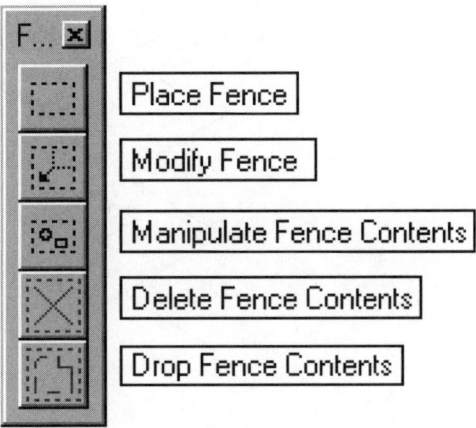

Fig. 6.22 The tools in the **Fence** tool palette

The Place Fence tool

When the tool is selected the Status Bar shows the prompt:

Place Fence Block > Enter first point.

When the first point has been selected, the prompt changes to:

Place Fence Block > Enter opposite corner.

When both points have been selected a ghosted fence appears on screen. To remove the fence, *left-click* on the **Place Fence** tool icon again and the fence disappears from screen.

The shape of the fence can be changed with the **Modify Fence** tool. *Left-click* on a part of the fence and the **Modify Fence** tool will allow the fence outline to be *dragged* to a new shape.

Details of the **Manipulate Fence Contents** will be described in Chapter 7.

When a fence has been placed around a set of elements, and the **Delete Fence Contents** tool is selected, a *left-click* on any point in the fence outline deletes all of the elements within the fence. When the deletion has occurred, a *left-click* on the **Place Fence** tool icon deletes the fence itself.

Levels

The setting of levels (layers) has already been described in Chapter 3. But what is a level? Figure 6.23 shows in diagrammatic form the

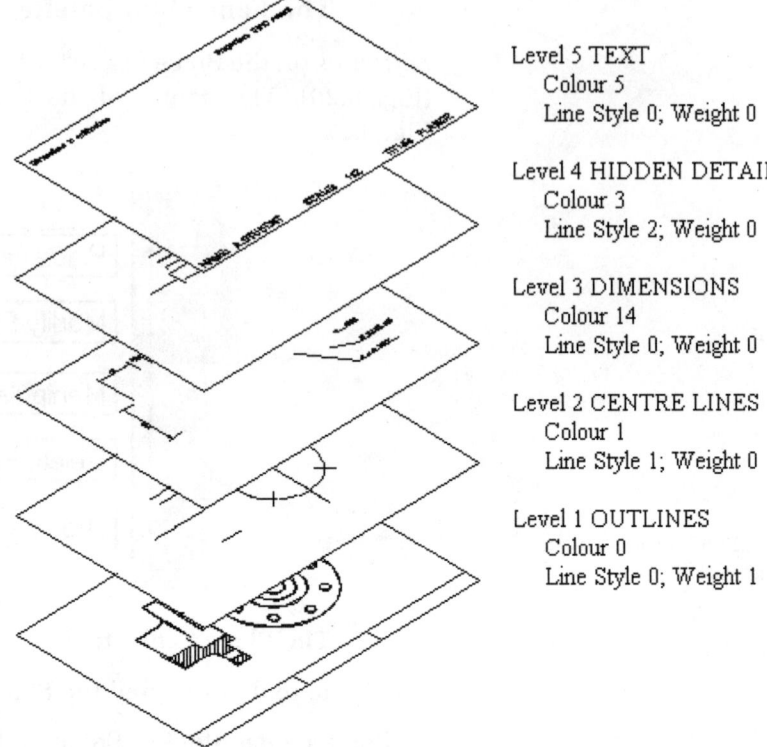

Level 5 TEXT
    Colour 5
    Line Style 0; Weight 0

Level 4 HIDDEN DETAIL
    Colour 3
    Line Style 2; Weight 0

Level 3 DIMENSIONS
    Colour 14
    Line Style 0; Weight 0

Level 2 CENTRE LINES
    Colour 1
    Line Style 1; Weight 0

Level 1 OUTLINES
    Colour 0
    Line Style 0; Weight 1

Fig. 6.23 A pictorial view of
levels in a drawing as if they
were tracings

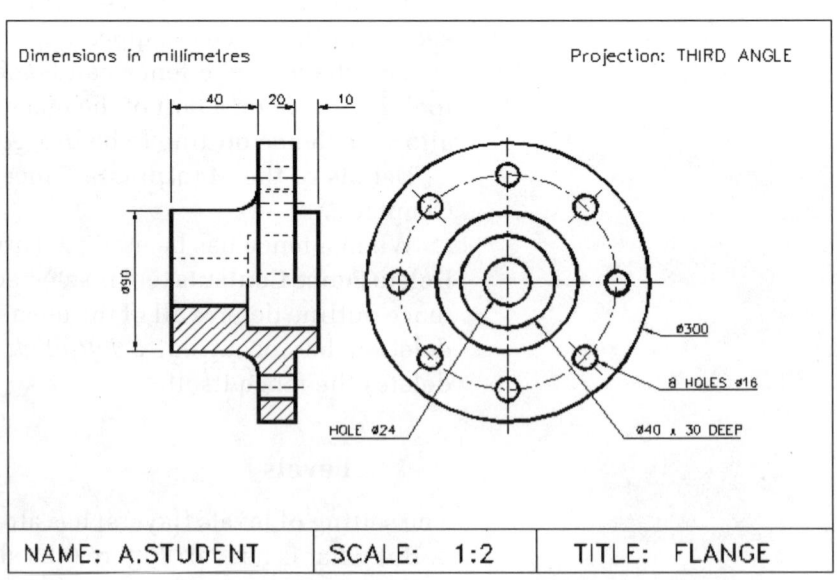

Fig. 6.24 The drawing upon
which Fig. 6.23 is based

levels on which the engineering drawing in Fig. 6.24 was constructed. Each level can be regarded as if it were a tracing on each of which only the details, such as those shown in Fig. 6.23, are constructed. Like a set of tracings, when laid one on top of the other, the tracings (levels) form a complete drawing. Each level can have its own line style and weight and colour. An example of levels of different line styles, weights and colours was given in Chapter 3.

In order that the colours, line style and weight can become active when a level is chosen, the **Level Symbology** item in the **View Attributes** dialogue box must be set on (**X** in check box against the item). See Fig. 6.25.

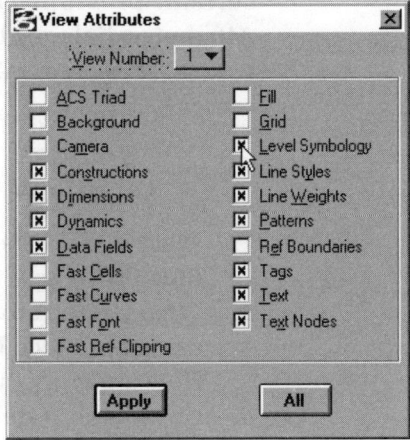

Fig. 6.25 The check box against **Level Symbology** in **View Attributes** must be set on

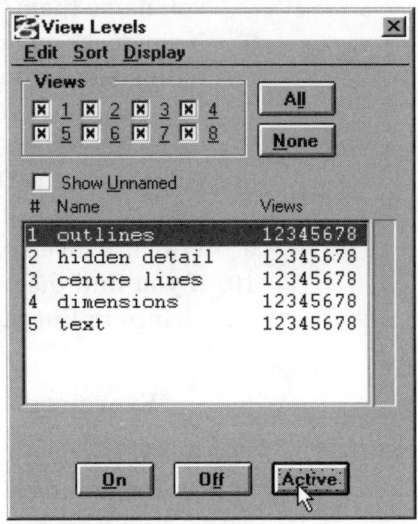

Fig. 6.26 Levels can be set **On**, **Off** or **Active** in the **View Levels** dialogue box

Levels can be turned **On**, **Off** and/or made **Active** in the **View Levels** dialogue box, which is called to screen either from **Display** in the **Level** sub-menu of the **Settings** pull-down menu, or with the **Ctrl+E** keyboard shortcut. See Fig. 6.26.

If a level is switched **Off** its contents do not show on screen. This can have two advantages:

1. The screen is less encumbered with detail if the drawing is a complicated one.
2. Further constructions will be faster without the detail on the level which has been turned **Off**.

Note that when a level has been made **Active** its name is highlighted in the **View Levels** dialogue box (Fig. 6.26). The **Active** level is the current level on which constructions can take place. When a level is current, providing **Level Symbology** is checked on in the **View Attributes** dialogue box, the colour, line style and weight will be the colour, style and weight in which constructions will be drawn on screen.

Questions

1. What is the difference in the results from using the **Place Stream Line String** tool and the **Place Point or Stream Curve** tool?
2. What are the advantages of using the **Place Smart Line** tool over using the **Place Line** tool? Are there any disadvantages?
3. How are multi-lines selected?
4. How is the style of multi-line changed?
5. There are two methods for drawing an arc in MicroStation 95. Can you name them?
6. If you make an error in drawing an arc by drawing it to the wrong radius, how would you correct the error?
7. What is the advantage of using the **Delete Fence Contents** over using the **Delete** tool?
8. After using the **Delete Fence Contents** tool, the fence remains on screen. How is it deleted?
9. Why use levels?
10. If you find that a change of level does not produce an expected change in line style or weight, what have you forgotten to do?

Exercises

The exercises below are intended to be worked with either the aid of **AccuDraw** and using the AccuDraw coordinate window to achieve accuracy, or by *keying-in* coordinates in the **Key-in** window. The constructions will be more accurate if you also take advantage of the snaps from the **Snap Mode** palette.

Do not include any dimensions in your answers to these exercises.

1. Figure 6.27 shows four drawings constructed with the aid of the **Multi-lines** tool. Working to any convenient sizes, copy the four given drawings.

2. Figure 6.28 is a frame for a folder cover. Using the **Place Smart Line** and **Multi-lines** tools, copy the given drawing using any suitable sizes.

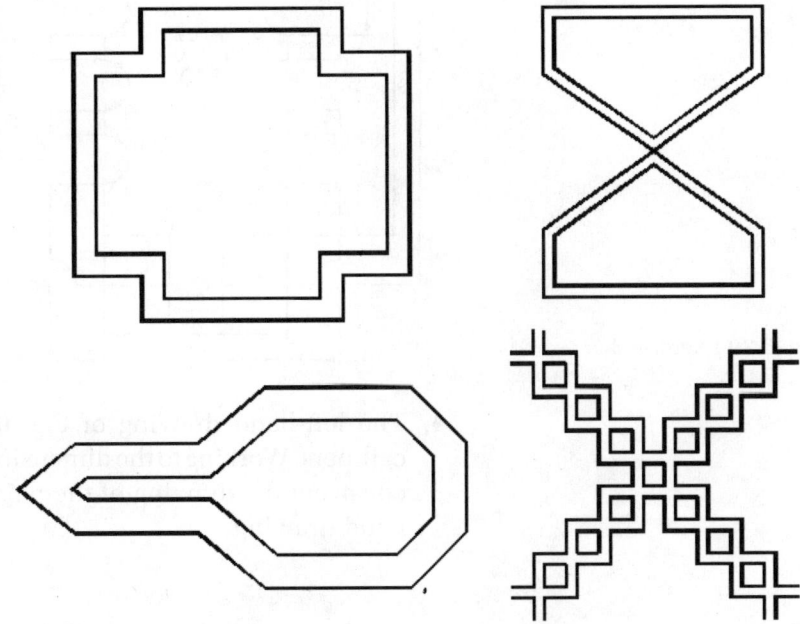

Fig. 6.27 Exercise 1

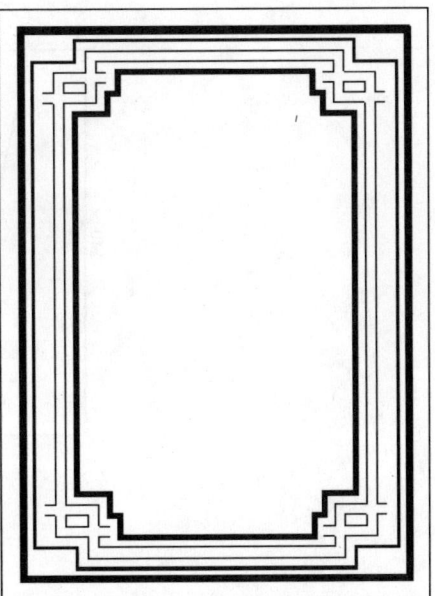

Fig. 6.28 Exercise 2

3. Working to the dimensions given in the left-hand drawing of Fig. 6.29, construct the right-hand drawing.

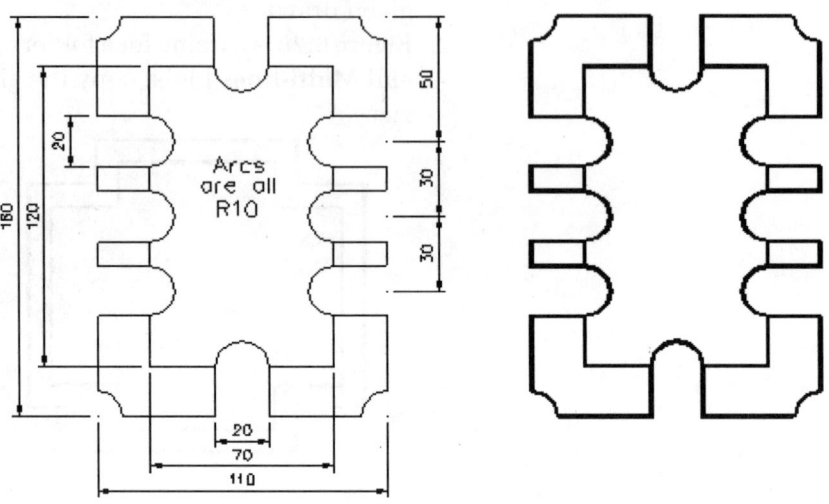

Fig. 6.29 Exercise 3

4. The left-hand drawing of Fig. 6.30 shows one leg of a pair of callipers. Working to the dimensions given in the left-hand drawing, construct the drawing of the pair of callipers shown in the right-hand drawing.

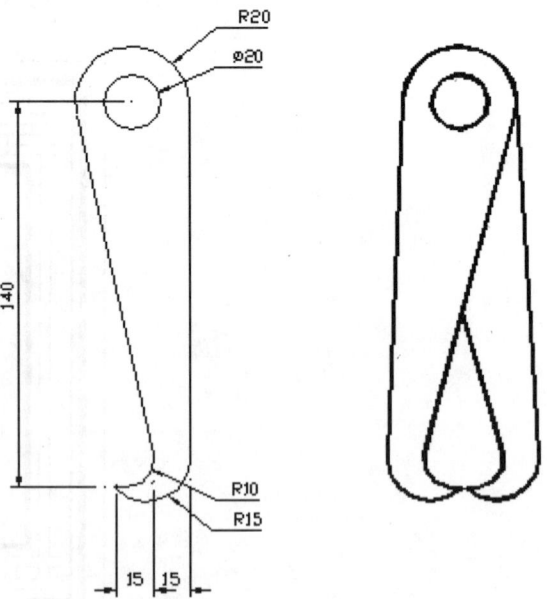

Fig. 6.30 Exercise 4

5. Figure 6.31 is a view of the foot of a column. The curves of the moulding are all quarter-ellipses. Working to the sizes given with the drawing, make an accurate copy of the foot.

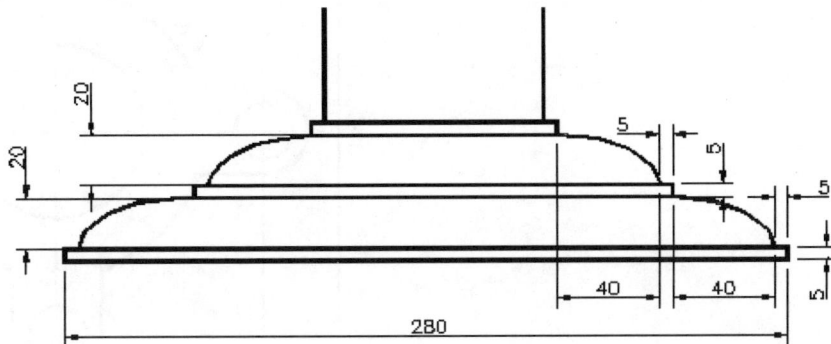

Fig. 6.31 Exercise 5

6. Figure 6.32 shows a plan view of an elliptical tab clip. Working to the given dimensions make an accurate drawing of the given plan view.

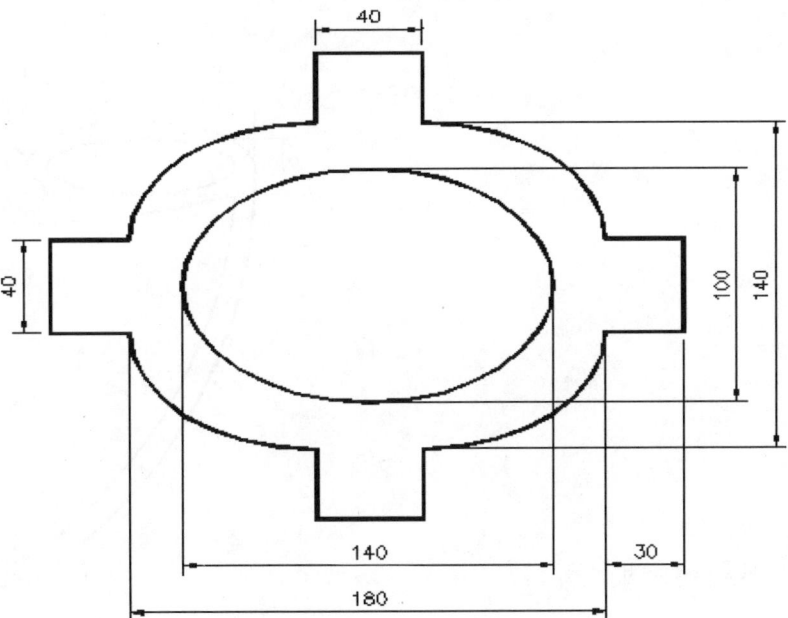

Fig. 6.32 Exercise 6

7. Figure 6.33 is a plan view of another clip, this one constructed from a series of circles and arcs. Working to the given dimensions, make an accurate copy of the given tab clip.

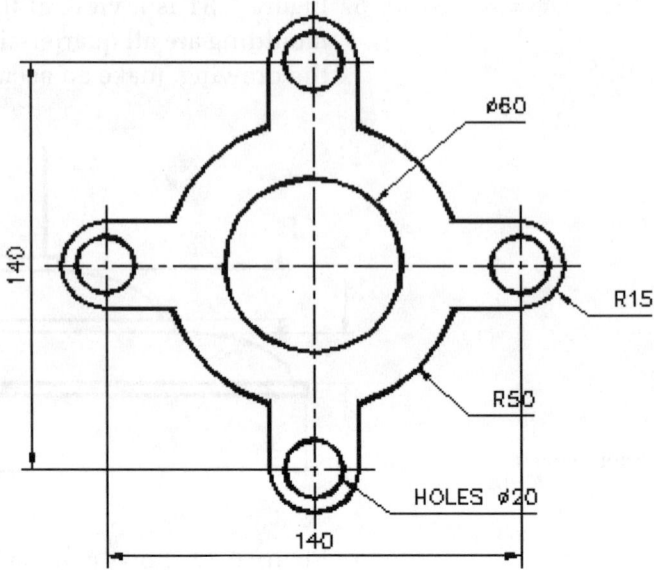

Fig,. 6.33 Exercise 7

8. Working to the dimensions given with the drawing, make an accurate copy of Fig. 6.34.

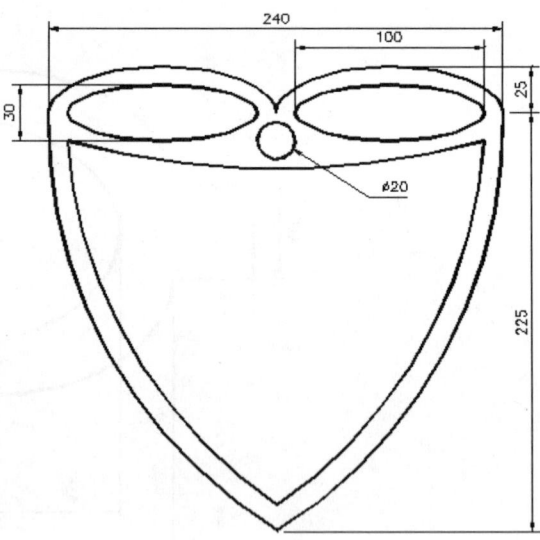

Fig. 6.34 Exercise 8

CHAPTER 7

The Manipulate tools

The tools associated with Manipulate

As the name implies, the tools held in the **Manipulate** palette are for manipulating elements in a drawing. In some manipulation examples, it may be necessary to use tools from the **Fence** tool palette and/or the **Groups** tool palette. Figure 7.1 shows the flyout from a *left-click* on the **Copy** tool icon in the **Main** palette and Fig. 7.2 all the tool tips of the tools in the resulting **Manipulate** palette when it has been dragged from the flyout.

Figure 7.3 shows the tool tip from the **Place Fence** icon in the **Main** palette and Fig. 7.4 the flyout from the **Fence** icon. Figure 7.5

Fig. 7.1 The flyout from the **Copy** tool icon in the **Main** tool palette

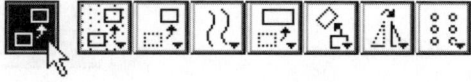

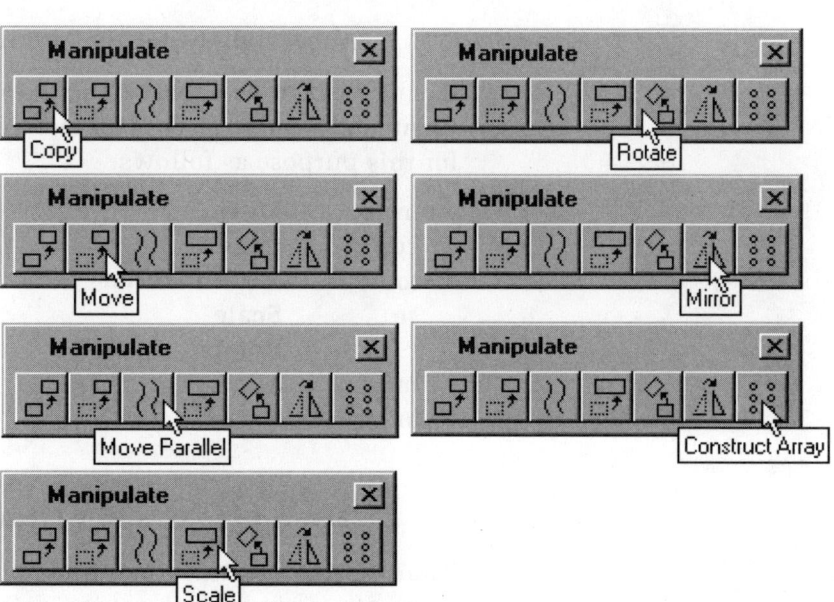

Fig. 7.2 All tool tips of the tools in the **Manipulate** tool palette

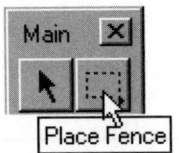

Fig. 7.3 The **Place Fence** tool tip

shows the **Fence** tool palette, with one tool tip, that of the **Manipulate Fence Contents** tool, which will be used during an example in this chapter.

Figure 7.6 shows the flyout from the **Group** icon in **Main** and Fig. 7.7 the **Add to Graphic Group** icon from the resulting **Group** tool palette.

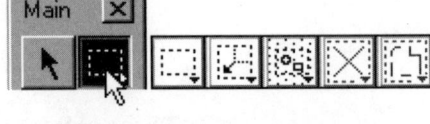

Fig. 7.4 The **Fence** flyout

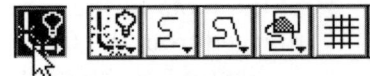

Fig. 7.5 The **Manipulate Fence Contents** tool tip

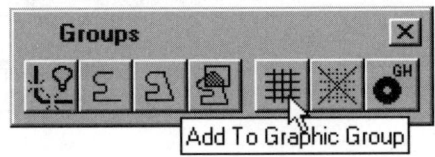

Fig. 7.6 The **Group** flyout

Fig. 7.7 The **Add to Graphic Group** tool tip

Abbreviations for the Manipulate tools

If you wish to use abbreviations to *key-in* tool commands at the **Command Window**, each of the tools in **Manipulate** has an abbreviation for this purpose as follows:

mov	**Move**
cop	**Copy**
mov pa	**Move Parallel**
sc	**Scale**
r	**Rotate**
mi	**Mirror**
ar	**Array**

The Add to Graphic Group tool

The **Manipulate** tools manipulate elements in a drawing – e.g. elements can be moved, copied, rotated, etc. If several elements are

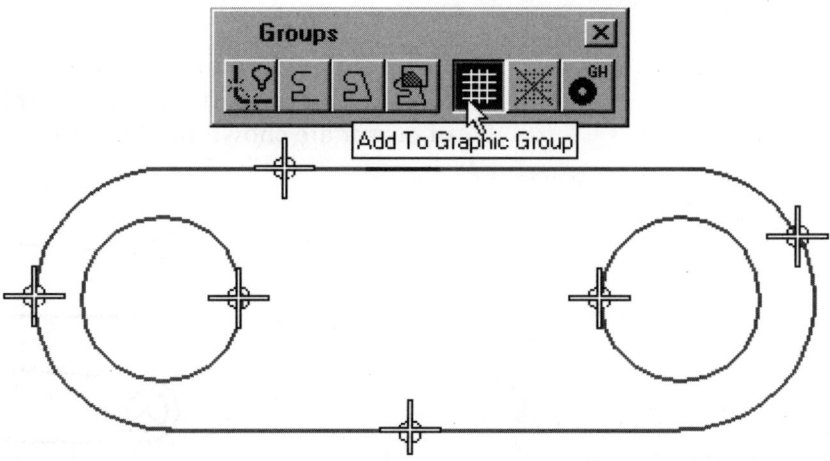

Fig. 7.8 Grouping a set of elements

placed in a **Group** they can be manipulated as if they were a single element. Figure 7.8 shows an example of several elements – lines, circles and arcs – grouped together with the aid of the **Add to Graphic Group** tool. Before grouping a set of elements of this type, make sure the **Graphic Group** lock is set (Fig. 7.9). Then:

1. *Left-click* on the **Add to Graphic Group** tool icon. Following the prompts in the **Prompt** field of the **Command Window**, *left-click* on each element in turn as indicated in Fig. 7.8, finishing with a *left-click* after the selection of the last element.
2. The group can now be acted upon by a **Manipulate** tool as a single element.

The Move tool

Move – Example 1

Figure 7.10 shows the moving of a single element (a circle) from one end of a drawing to the other end. The procedure is:

1. *Left-click* on the **Move** tool to make it active.
2. Following the prompts in the **Prompt** field of the **Command Window**:

   Identify element: Identify the circle by a *left-click* at its centre (upper drawing of Fig. 7.10).
   Select next input: *Drag* the circle by its centre to its new position (lower drawing of Fig. 7.10). *Left-click* to fix the position. *Right-click* to complete the use of the **Move** tool.

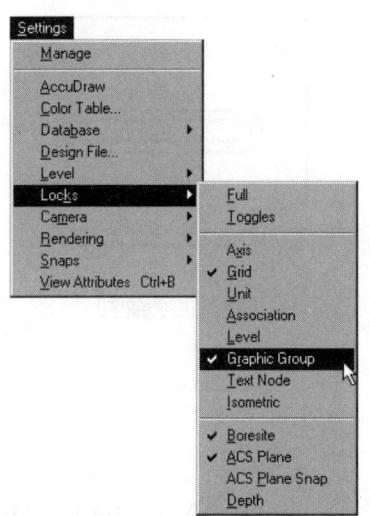

Fig. 7.9 Setting the **Graphic Group** lock on

Note

Unless full view cursors are in operation, the cursor changes from a cross with a small circle at its centre to a diagonal cross. Both types of cursor are shown in Fig. 7.10.

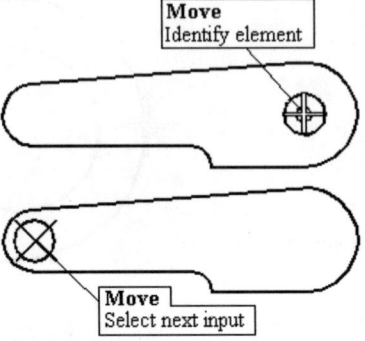

Fig. 7.10 **Move** – Example 1

Move – Example 2

If several elements are to be moved as a group, they must first be grouped together by selecting the **Add to Graphics Group** tool, followed by a *left-click* on each element in turn, finishing with a final *left-click* when the last element has been selected. Figure 7.11 shows the cursors as each element is selected (left-hand drawing) and the cursor when the **Select next input** position is selected.

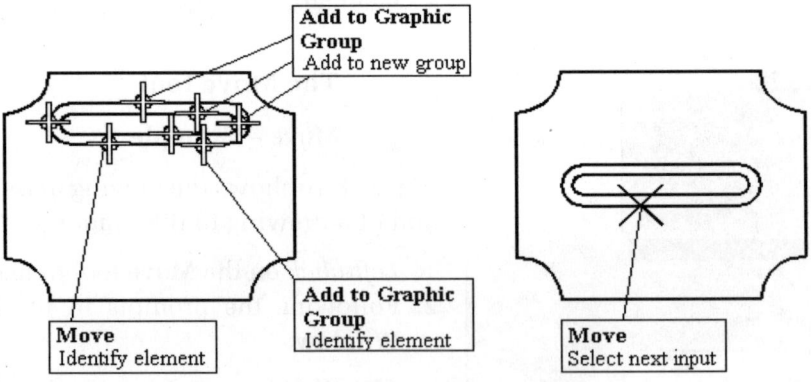

Fig. 7.11 **Move** – Example 2

The Copy tool

Copy – Example 1

The same procedure is followed as when using the **Move** tool. Two elements are shown as being copied as separate elements – in this example – a square **Block** and a circle.

1. *Left-click* on the **Copy** tool to make it active.
2. Following the prompts in the **Prompt** field of the **Command Window**:

   Define origin: Identify elements in turn by a *left-click* at their centre (left-hand drawing of Fig. 7.12).

   Define distance: *Drag* the selected element by its centre to its new position (right-hand drawing of Fig. 7.12). *Left-click* followed by *right-click*.

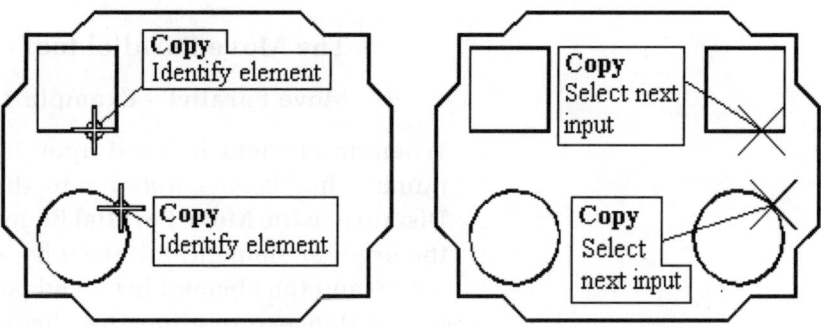

Fig. 7.12 **Copy** – Example 1

Copy – Example 2

In Fig. 7.13 two elements have been copied to several new positions. The two elements – a circle and a regular polygon (hexagon) were first placed in a fence by calling the **Fence** tool, forming a fence around the two elements as shown, then calling the **Manipulate Fence Contents** tool. A *left-click* either on the fence or anywhere within the fence, allows its contents to be *dragged* to new positions. Note that the prompts will show **Copy Fence Contents**.

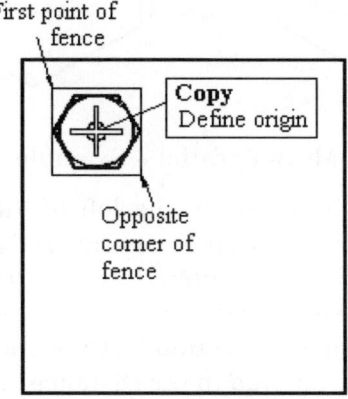
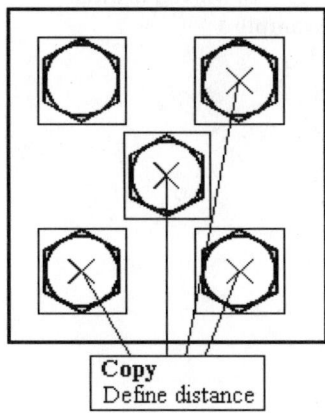

Fig. 7.13 **Copy** – Example 2

Notes

1. When using the **Copy** tool as many copies can be made as required. Each *left-click* fixes the copy in its new position, a second *left-click* fixes the second copy in place and so on. A final *right-click* finishes the sequence of copying.
2. Note the difference between using a **Fence** tool and **Manipulate Fence Contents** tool. **Fence** only places a fence around the required elements. **Manipulate Fence Contents** is for copying the elements within the fence placed in position with the **Fence** tool.

The Move Parallel tool

Move Parallel – Example 1

When an element is acted upon by the **Move Parallel** tool and a number has been *entered* into the numbers box to the right of **Distance** in the **Move Parallel** Element Selection box, a *left-click* on the original element, followed by another *left-click* to confirm the action and the element is moved parallel to the original element by that distance providing the check box to the left of **Distance** is checked with an **X**. Figure 7.14 shows the action of the tool when the distance 10 has been *entered*, with the check box active. In this first example the **Make Copy** check box is not active (no **X**). Left-hand drawing – original. Right-hand drawing – result.

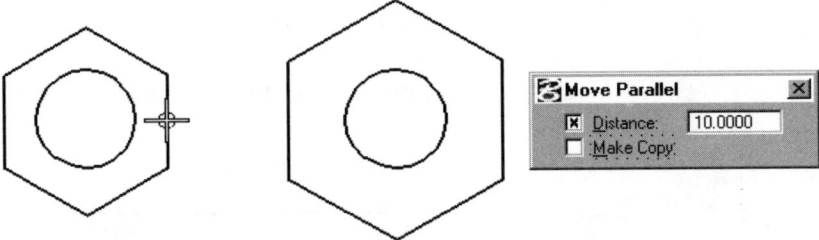

Fig. 7.14 **Move Parallel** – Example 1

Move Parallel – Example 2

If the check box to the left of **Make Copy** in the **Move Parallel** Element Selection box is checked (**X** present), then a copy is made at the distance *entered* in the **Distance** box, leaving the original element in position. In the example in Fig. 7.15, both check boxes in the Element Selection box are checked and a copy is made at the distance *entered* in the **Distance** box. Left-hand drawing – original. Right-hand drawing – result.

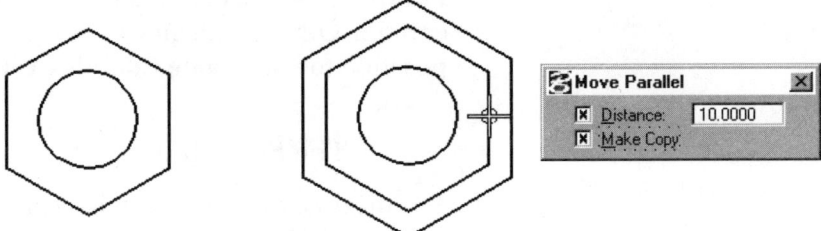

Fig. 7.15 **Move Parallel –**
Example 2

Move Parallel – Example 3

Draw any type of element as shown in Fig. 7.16. Set the check boxes on. *Left-click* in the boxes toggles either on (**X**) or off (no cross). *Entering* a suitable number in the **Distance** box and *left-click* on each element in turn to produce parallel copies. Once a copy has been made, a *left-click* on the copy will produce another. Copies will continue to be made until a *right-click* completes the tool action. Note the difference between the action of **Move Parallel** on a **Smart Line**, in which all parts of the line are treated as a single element, to the action on a **Line**, in which each part of the line is an element in its own right.

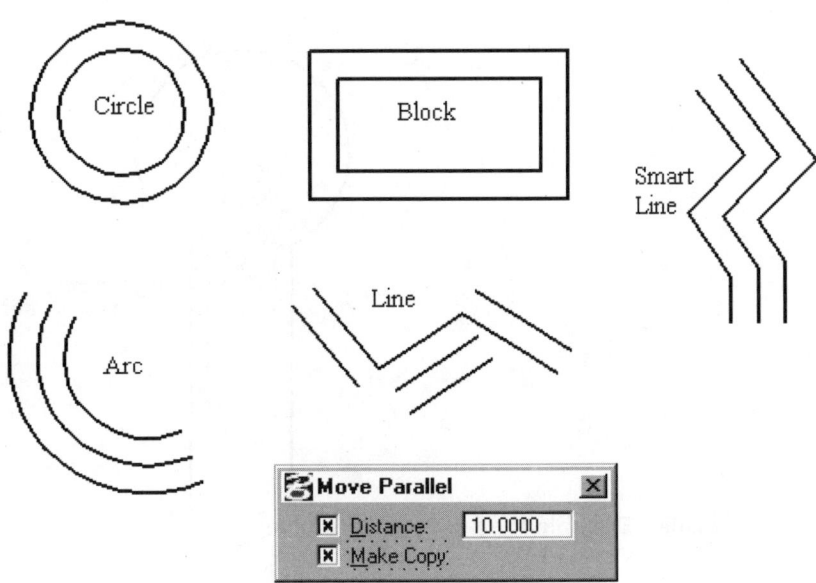

Fig. 7.16 **Move Parallel –**
Example 3

Note

Move Parallel will only act upon elements and not on a group. If a set of elements has been grouped with the aid of the **Add to Graphic Group** tool, a *left-click on* any one of its elements when **Move**

Parallel is active only results in that element being either moved or copied. Other elements in the group are unchanged. It may be possible to use **Create Complex Chain** instead.

The Scale tool

The original drawing (usually a group) can be scaled up or down, in proportion to its original shape or distorted in all directions. Four examples are given below.

Scale – Example 1

Figure 7.17 shows both the original group in ghosted form (prior to finalising the scaling with a *right-click*) and the scaled-up group. The **Method** selected has been **Active Scale** and the number 1.5 has been *entered* in the **Scale** boxes of the **Scale** Element Selection box. The operating prompts are **Identify element**, and when the element (in this example a group) has been selected with a *left-click*, the prompt changes to **Enter origin point**. A *left-click* brings the element up to the required scale and a *right-click* confirms. In this example the **Make Copy** check box is unchecked, so the original will disappear when the scaling has taken place.

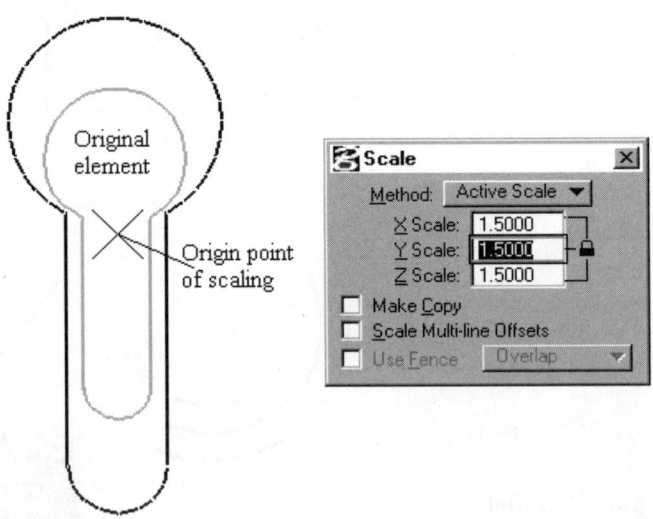

Fig. 7.17 **Scale** – Example 1

Scale – Example 2

This example (Fig. 7.18) is similar to the first example, except that a copy has been made, with the **Origin point** of the scaled-up copy selected to the right of the original element.

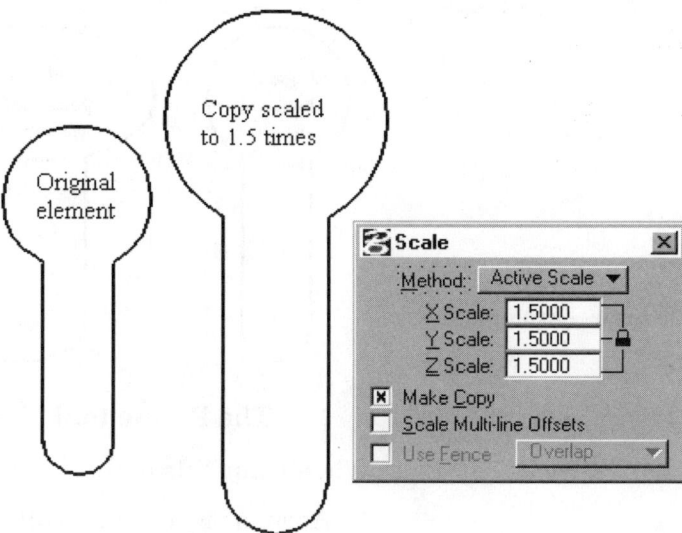

Fig. 7.18 **Scale** – Example 2

Scale – Example 3

In this example (Fig. 7.19) the scaling has been made down (to 0.8 of the size of the original element). A copy has also been requested – **Make Copy** box checked.

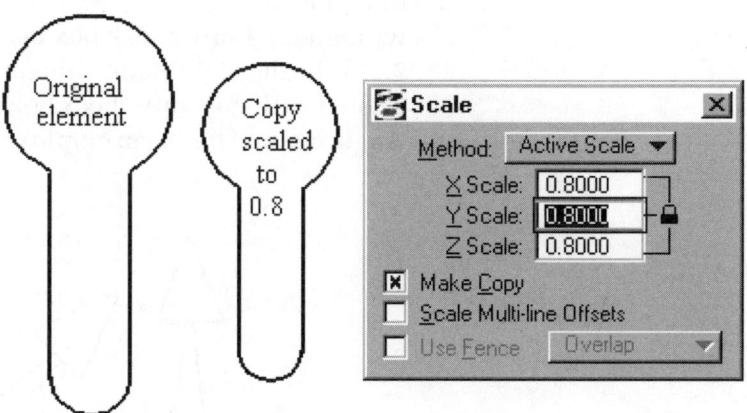

Fig. 7.19 **Scale** – Example 3

Scale – Example 4

Figure 7.20 shows the scaling effect when the **3 points** method is selected from the pop-up list and the **Proportional** check box is unchecked. Three points have been selected in this example in such a manner that the lack of proportion between the X and Y axes shows clearly.

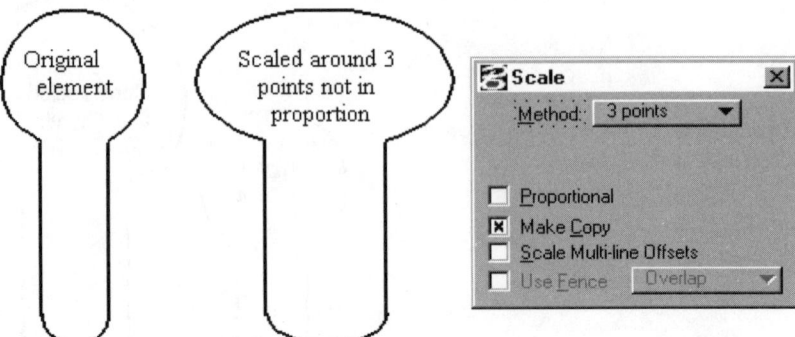

Fig. 7.20 **Scale** – Example 4

The Rotate tool

When using this tool two features must be borne in mind.

1. Angular movements in MicroStation are, by default, anti-clockwise (counter-clockwise).
2. The tool **Rotate** will act upon either single elements or on groups.

Rotate – Example 1

Enter an angular number in the angle box, in this example this is 45°. A copy can be made of the rotation or not, as desired. This example shows both possibilities. From the original drawing (left-hand drawing of Fig. 7.21), the group has been rotated through 45° without the **Copy** check box being checked (central drawing of Fig. 7.21). In the right-hand drawing of Fig. 7.21, the group has been rotated with the **Copy** check box checked. In this example the **Active Angle** method has been employed. A *left-click* on the button marked

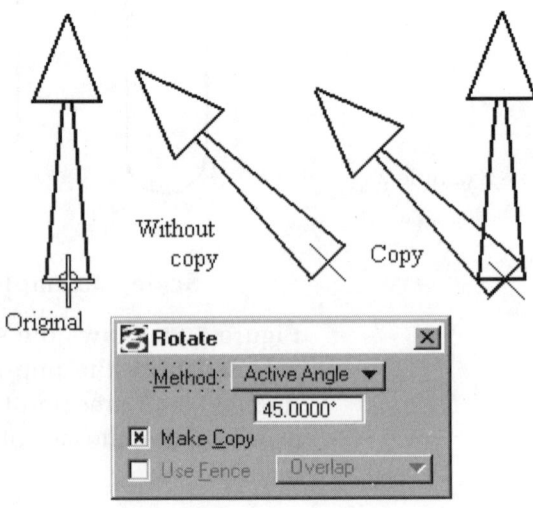

Fig. 7.21 **Rotate** – Example 1

Active Angle brings down a small pop-up list from which one of three methods can be selected.

Rotate – Example 2

In this example (Fig. 7.22) the **2 points** method has been selected from the pop-up list. After selecting the group (*left-click* on its outline), two points are selected about which the rotation takes place. A *left-click* confirms and a *right-click* finishes the action of the tool. Note that in this example no angle is *entered* because the rotation is under the movement of the mouse around the two selected points. Figure 7.22 shows the 'ghosted' original prior to confirmation of position with a *right-click*.

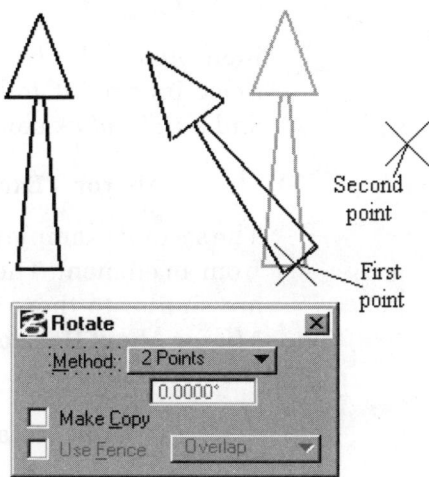

Fig. 7.22 **Rotate** – Example 2

The Mirror tool

A mirror image of an element is made with the aid of this tool. The image can be made either horizontally, vertically or at any angle by mirroring around a line. The three examples which follow show each of these options and in each example a copy has been made of the mirrored element – **Make Copy** has been set in the **Mirror** Element Selection box. All three cases also show the mirroring of a graphic group.

Mirror – Example 1

Figure 7.23 shows a graphic group mirrored vertically. When the **Vertical** option is chosen from the pop-up menu, **Mirror About Vertical** appears in the **Command Window**, together with the prompt **Identify element**. When the element (in this case a group) has been

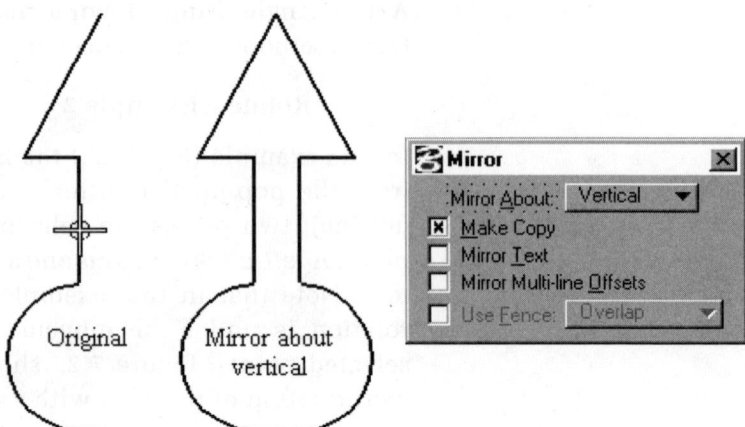

Fig. 7.23 **Mirror (Vertical)** –
Example 1

identified with a *left-click*, the prompt changes to **Select new input**. Selecting a point, followed by a *left-click,* brings up the mirror image and a *right-click* confirms if it is in the required position.

Mirror – Example 2

The second example (Fig. 7.24) shows a horizontally mirrored image from an element. The prompts appearing in the **Command Window** are similar to those as in the vertical example above, except that **Mirror About Horizontal** shows that the mirroring will take place in the horizontal line.

Mirror – Example 3

In this example (Fig. 7.25) the mirroring has taken place around a line already drawn on screen. Again the prompts are similar, except that two prompts **1st point on mirror line** and **2nd point on mirror**

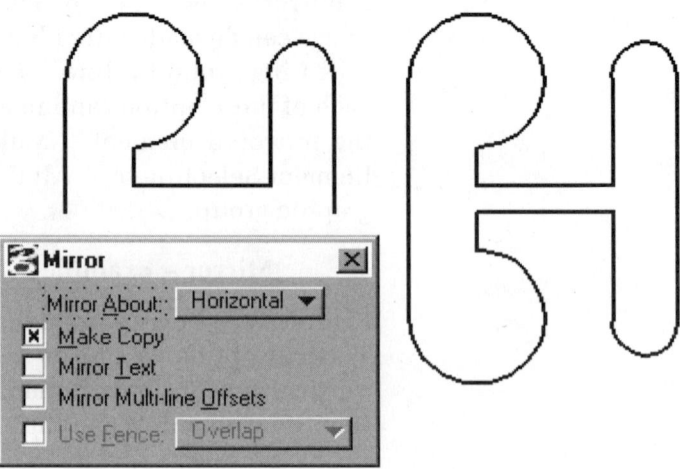

Fig. 7.24 **Mirror (Horizontal)** –
Example 2

Plate I A three-view orthographic projection of a pillar support stand constructed against a black screen

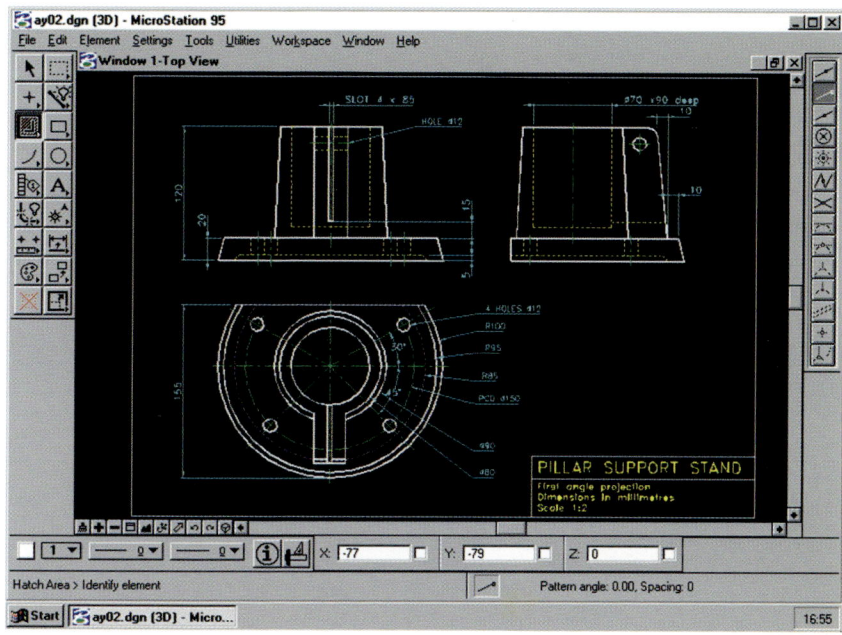

Plate II Two views in orthographic projection of a four-bedroom house design

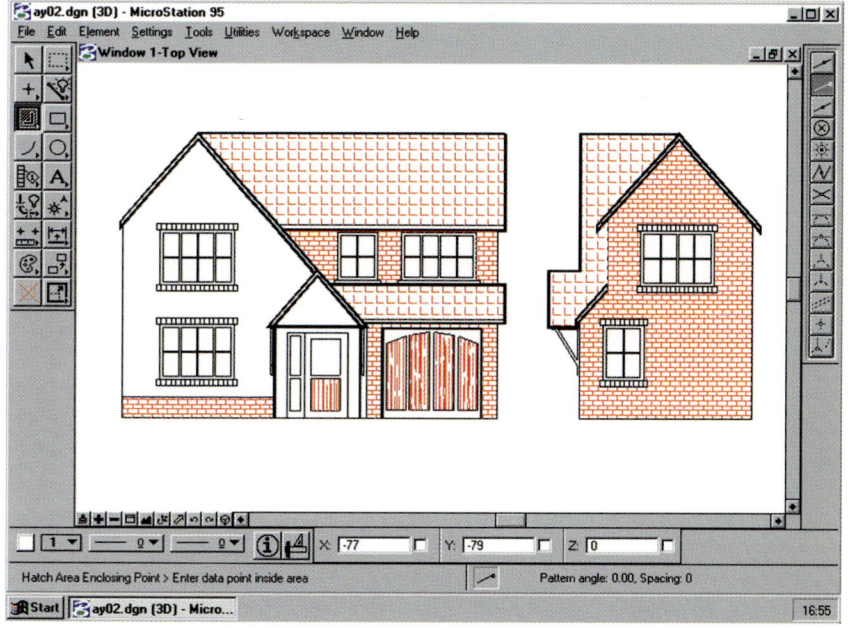

Plate III   A three-view
orthographic projection of
a hanger roller bracket
constructed against a
white screen

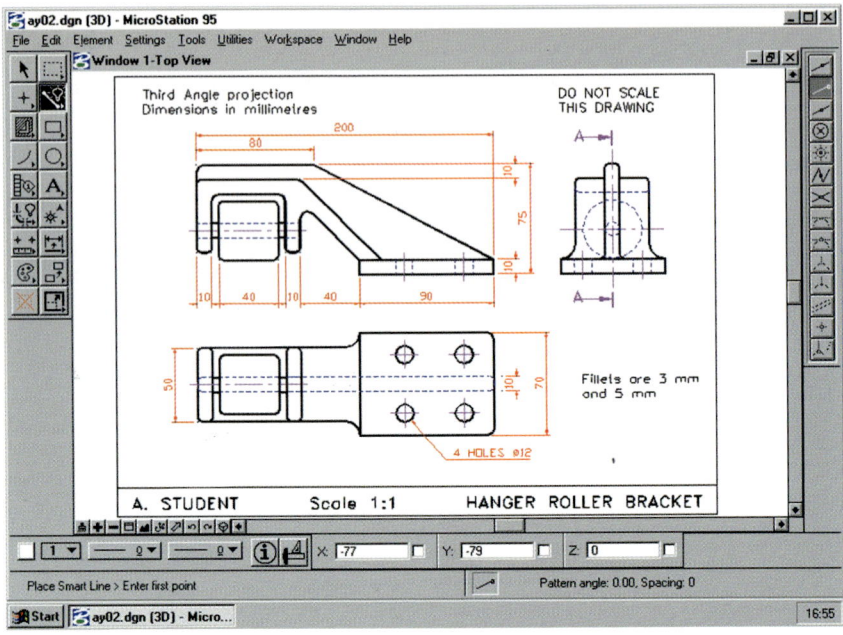

Plate IV   An end view of
a design for a restaurant
extension to a small hotel

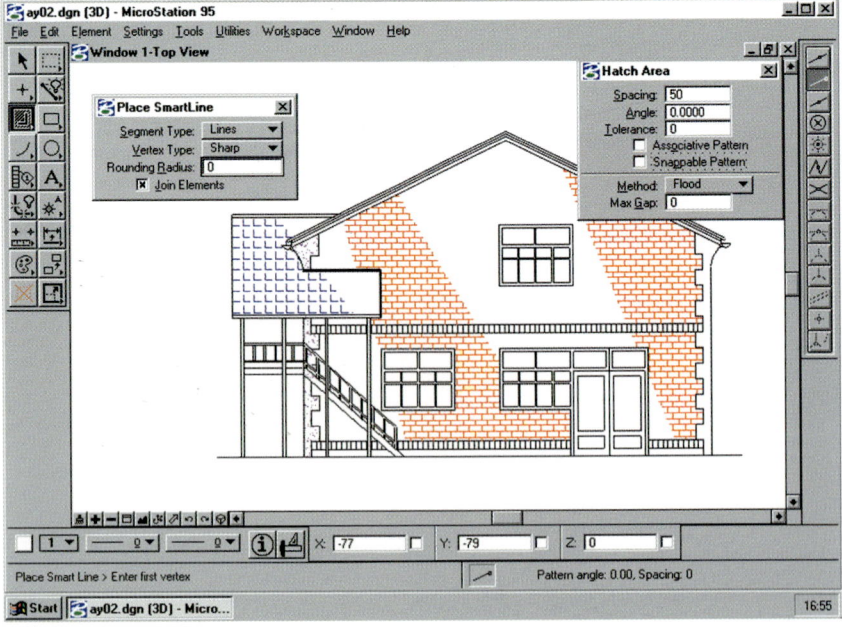

Plate V A design for a
conservatory to be built in
the back garden of a large
house

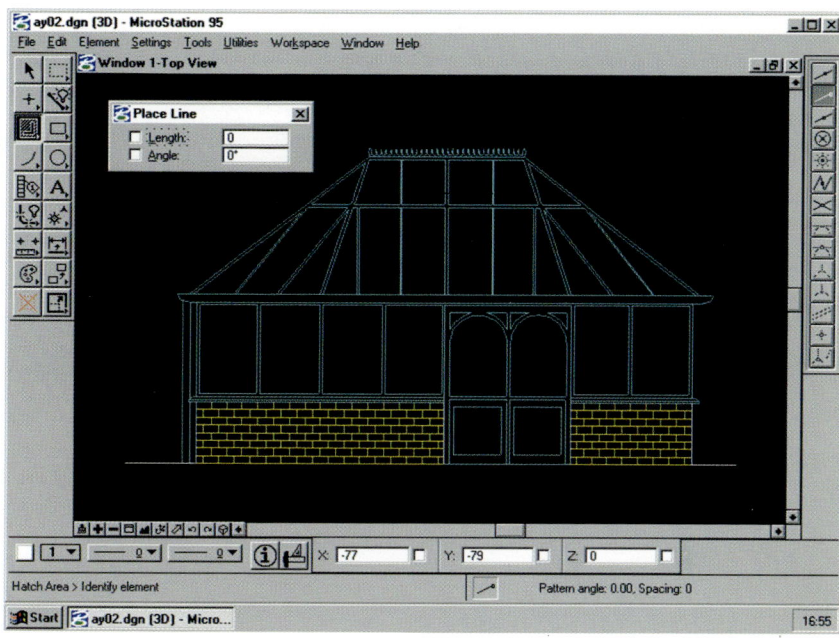

Plate VI A single element
of a repeating pattern
intended for printing on
cloth

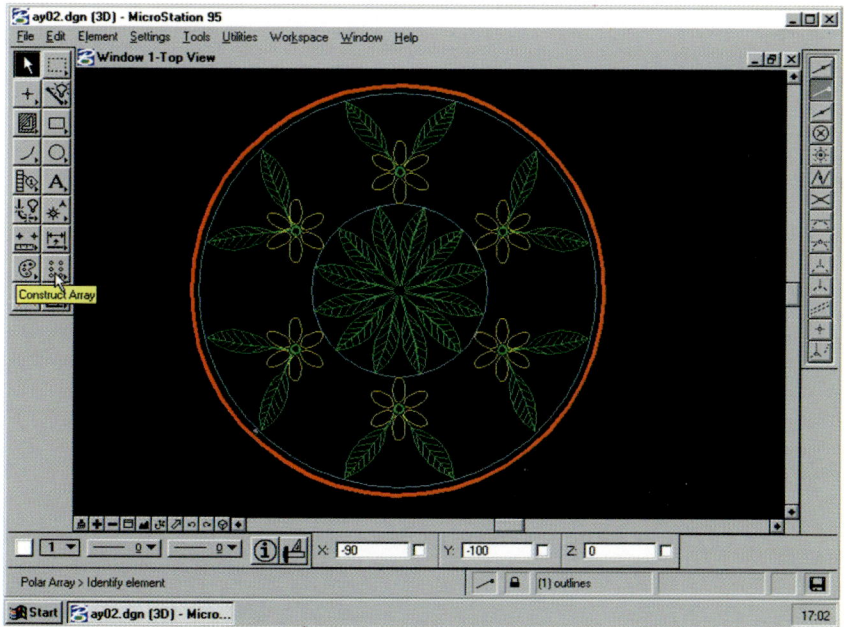

Plate VII A three-view
third-angle orthographic
projection of a stand
constructed on five levels

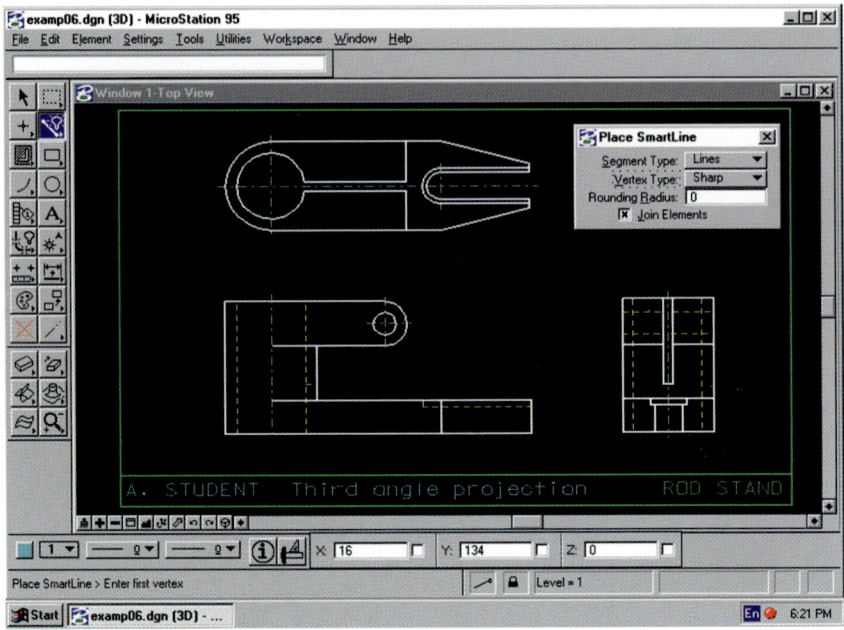

Plate VIII A four-window
screen showing a 3D
model and including a
rendering of the model in
the **Isometric View**
window

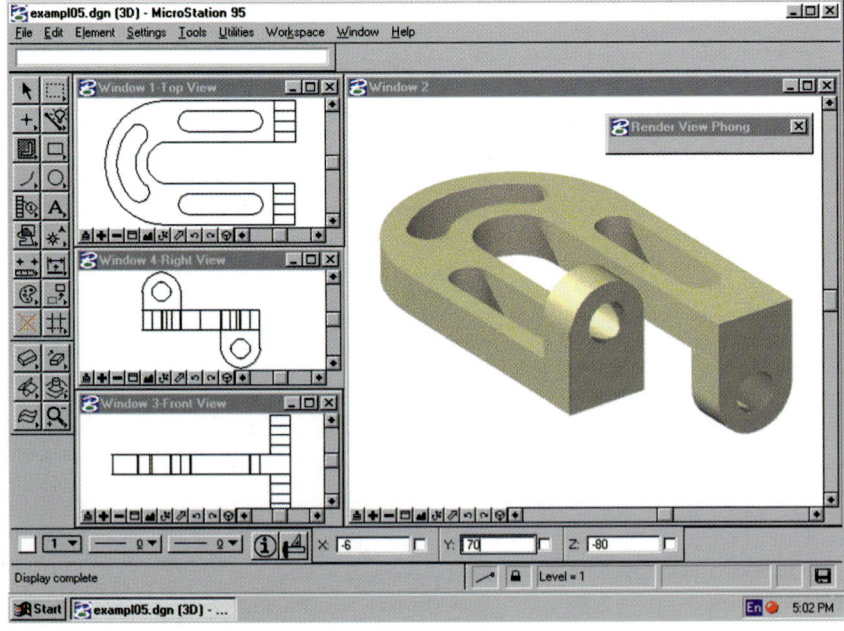

Plate IX A rendering of
the 3D model from Plate
VII in a full-screen
window

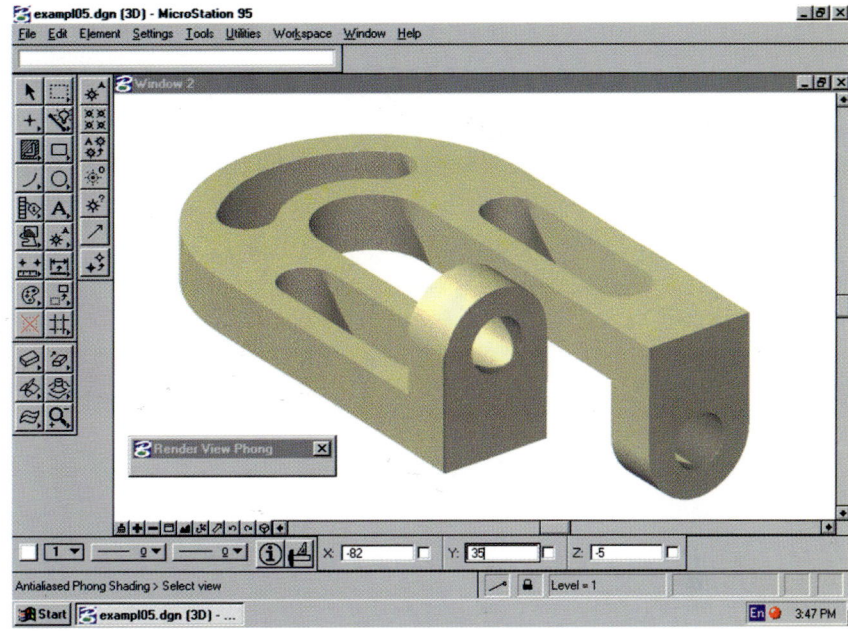

Plate X The 3D model
from Plate VIII showing
Global Lighting selected
from the **Settings** pull-
down menus

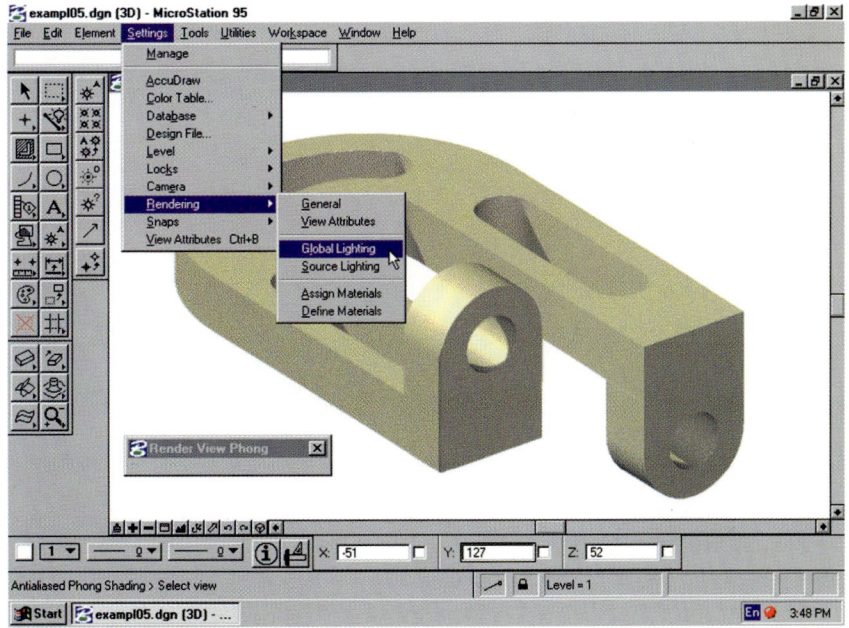

Plate XI A two-window screen showing a 3D model with a rendering in the **Isometric View** window

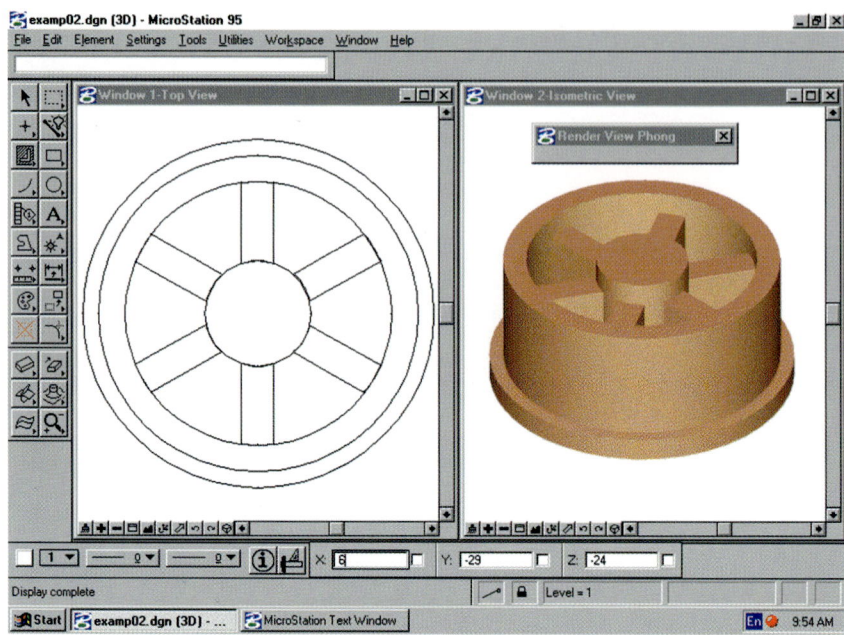

Plate XII A three-window screen for a 3D model of a metal flask with an outlet pipe, including a rendering

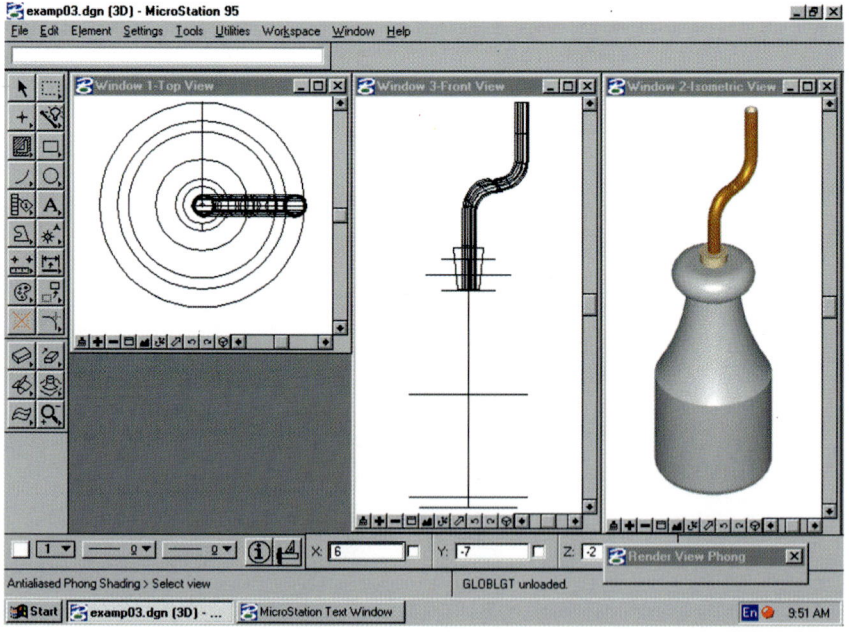

Plate XIII A three-view 2D orthographic projection of the 3D model shown in Plates XV and XVI

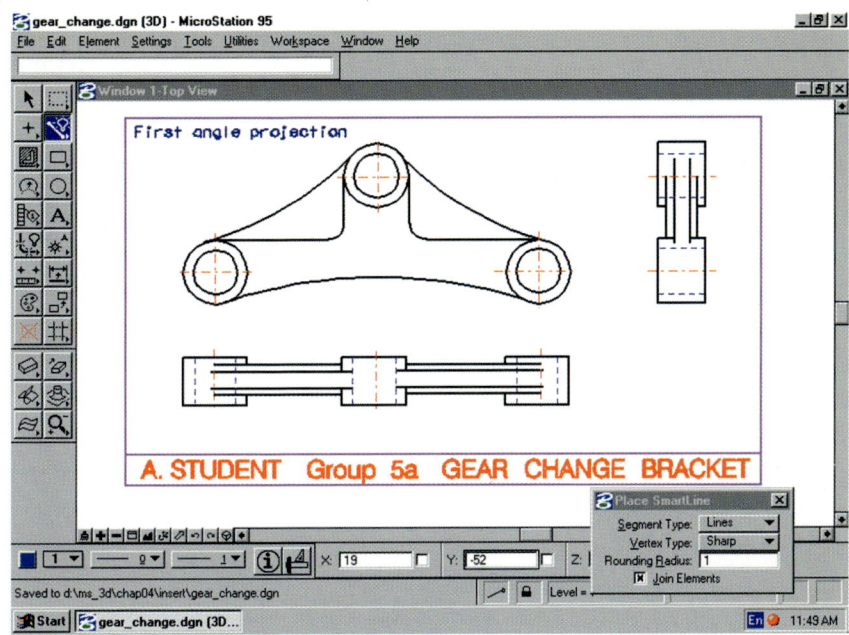

Plate XIV The same 2D views as in Plate XIII with the **Save Design As** dialogue box open

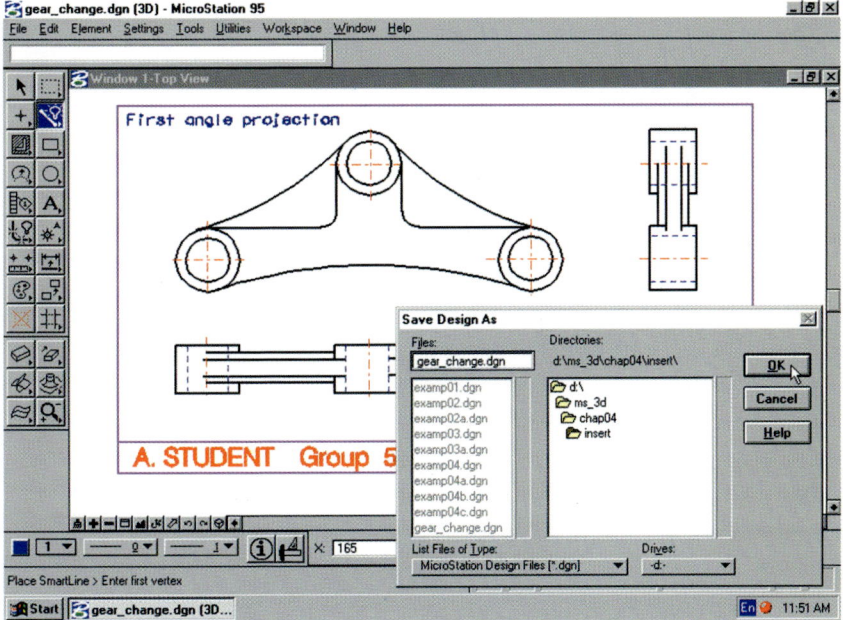

Plate XV   A three-window screen of the gear change bracket shown in Plates XIII and XIV with a rendering in the **Isometric View** window

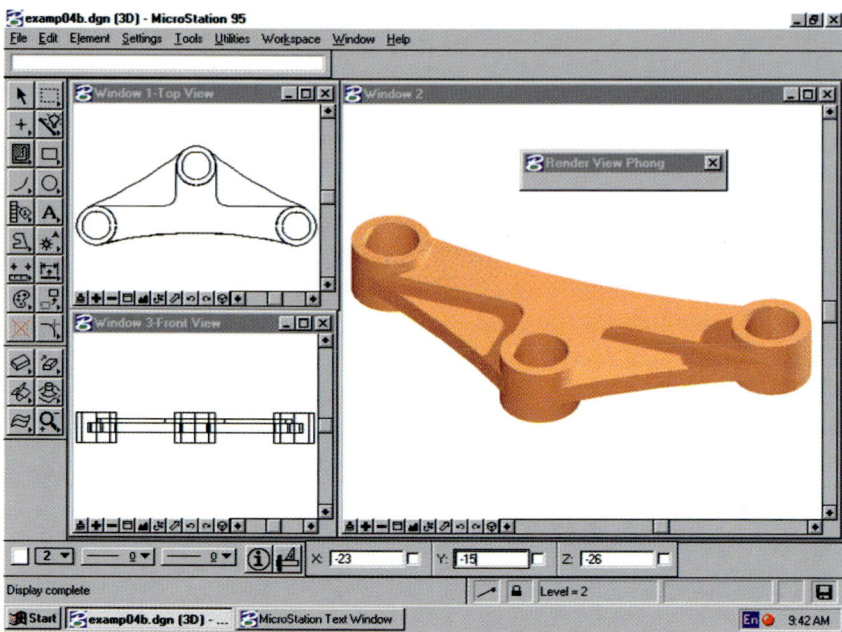

Plate XVI   The same 3D model as in Plate XV with part of the **Global Lighting** dialogue box showing

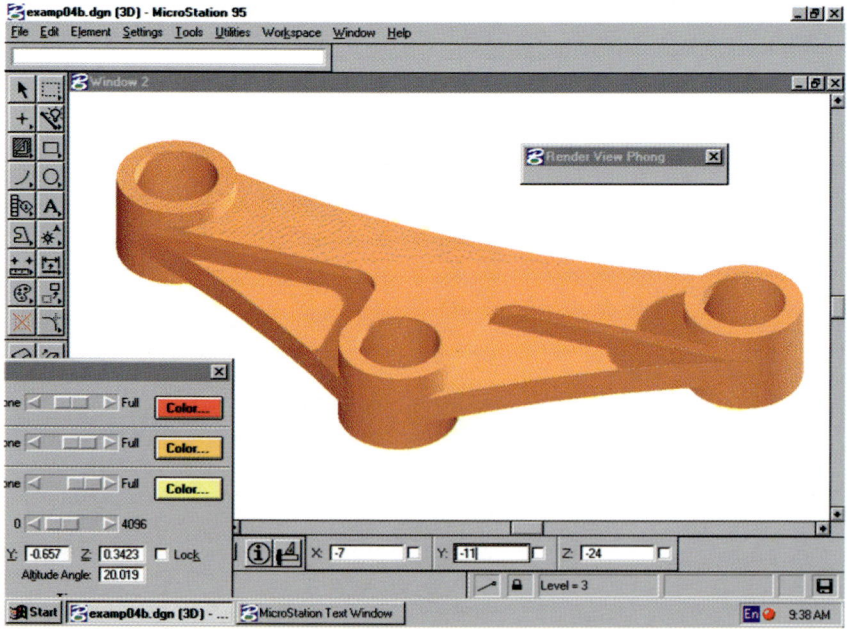

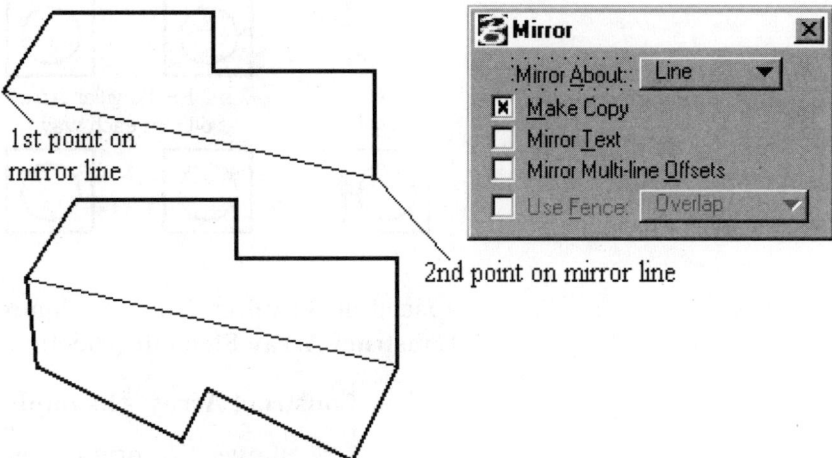

Fig. 7.25 **Mirror (Line)** –
Example 3

line asked for the mirroring points to be selected. Use snaps to
position the line ends.

Note

Make full use of **snaps** (*both-clicks* or tentative points) when selecting
points around which the mirror image is to be developed. Failure to
do so may result in unexpected results.

The Construct Array tool

Arrays can be **Rectangular** or **Polar**. If rectangular, the elements in
an array are arranged in horizontal **Rows** and vertical **Columns**. The
spacing between elements in the rows and columns are the distances
horizontally and vertically between identical points on each element.
Because of this, care must be taken when *entering* the numbers in the
Row Spacing and **Column Spacing** boxes of the **Construct Array**
Element Selection box.

In **Polar Arrays**, the elements are arranged around a central point
– the pole of the array. Any number of elements can be arranged in
the array and the spacing between each is determined by the degree
figures *entered* in the **Active Angle** box of the Element Selection box.
The individual elements in a polar array can be rotated towards the
pole or not as required.

Construct Array – Example 1

Figure 7.26 shows the original group (left-hand drawing) from
which a **Rectangular Array** (right-hand drawing) has been developed,
composed of 2 rows and 2 columns with rows and columns both

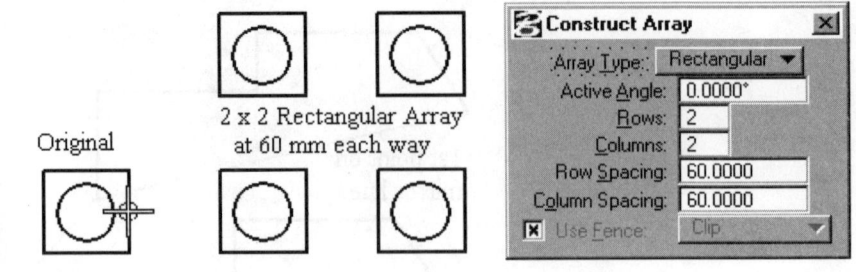

Fig. 7.26 **Construct Array**
(**Rectangular**) – Example 1

spaced at 60 units. Note the figures *entered* in the boxes of the **Construct Array** Element Selection box.

Construct Array – Example 2

Figure 7.27 shows the original group (left-hand drawing) from which a **Polar Array** (right-hand drawing), consisting of 8 copies 45° apart, is arrayed around a central point. Again note the numbers *enter* in the various boxes of the **Construct Array** Element Selection dialogue box.

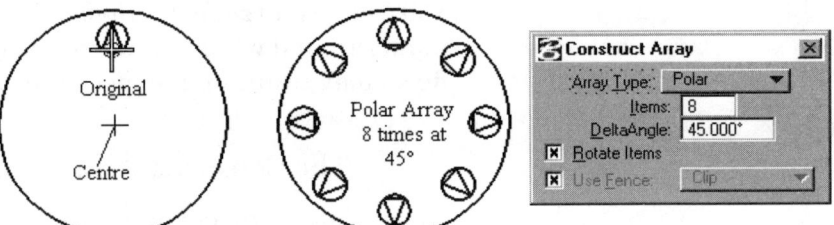

Fig. 7.27 **Construct Array**
(**Polar**) – Example 2

Construct Array – Example 3

Another **Polar Array** is shown in Fig. 7.28, this time consisting of 4 arrayed elements at angle of 30°. Note the numbers in the boxes of the dialogue box and that the elements have been rotated as they are arrayed.

Questions

1. Can you name all the tools in the **Manipulate** tool palette?
2. What is the purpose of the tool **Manipulate Fence Contents**?
3. How is a group formed from a number of separate elements?
4. Can you list all the *key-in* abbreviations for the **Manipulate** tools?
5. When selecting an element for manipulation can you write down the sequence of mouse *clicks* from start to finish in the use of the tools?

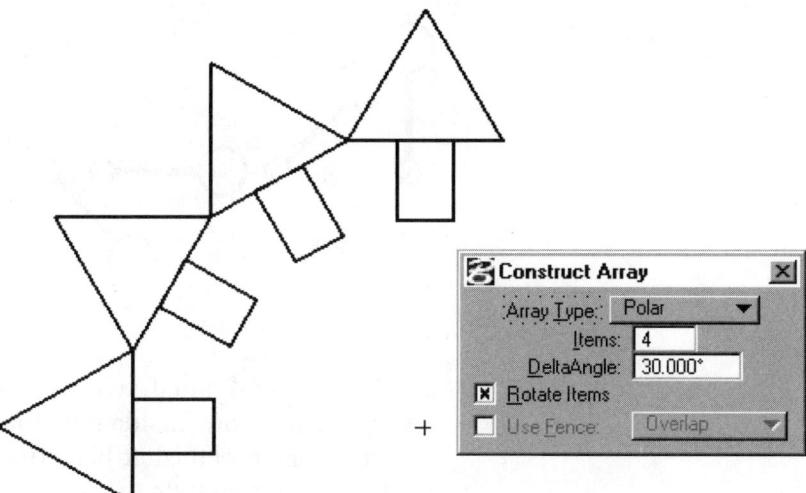

Fig. 7.28 **Construct Array –** Example 3

6. If you wish to make several copies of an element, how do you proceed? In what way is making several copies different from making a single copy?

7. When using **Move Parallel** how can the original element be left in the drawing as well as the parallel element?

8. What is the difference between a **Rectangular Array** and a **Polar Array**?

9. Can an element be mirrored so as to produce an image at an angle to the original element? If so how?

10. What happens if the **Proportional** box is not checked when using **Scale** through 3 points?

Exercises

When constructing drawings in answer to the following exercises, do not attempt to include any of the dimensions given with the exercise drawings. However, do attempt to construct your answers to the given sizes where dimensions are included. Where exercise drawings are not dimensioned, use your own judgement about suitable sizes.

1. Figure 7.29 shows a series of similar elements rotated around a pivot point. Construct the elements as shown in the left-hand drawing to any suitable sizes. Group the elements. With the aid of the **Copy** tool copy the group 7 times and with **Rotate** rotate each copy as shown.

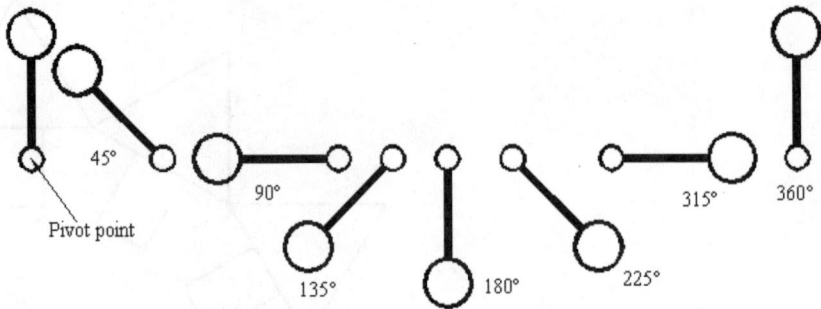

Fig. 7.29 Exercise 1

2. The top left-hand drawing of Fig. 7.30 shows a dimensioned pair
    of outlines, one inside the other. Construct drawings as follows:
    (a) Construct the left-hand drawing to the given dimensions, but
         do not include the dimensions.
    (b) With **Copy** make three copies of the original drawing.
    (c) With the aid of **Scale** make scale copies of either parts of the
         drawings or the whole drawing as indicated in Fig. 7.30.

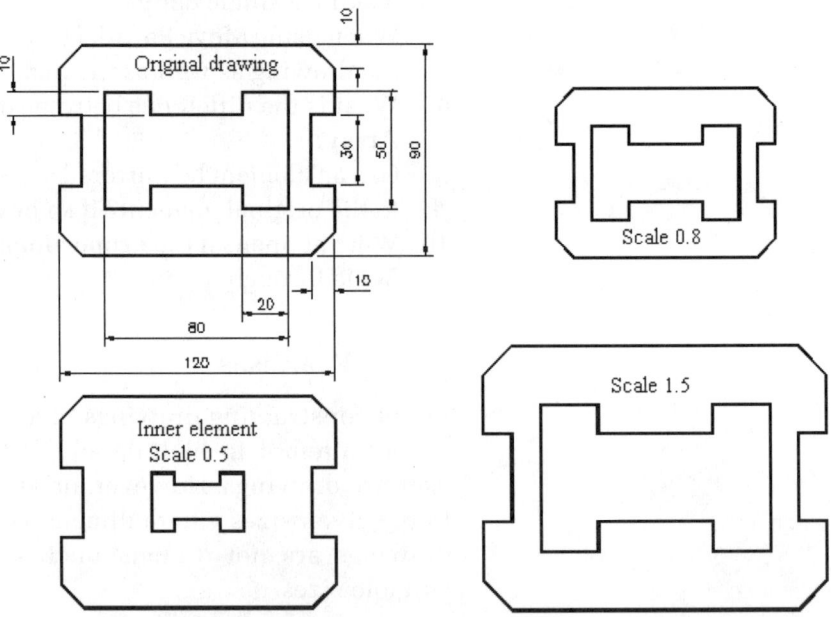

Fig. 7.30 Exercise 2

3. The upper left-hand drawing of Fig. 7.31 shows an outline which
    has first been grouped with the aid of **Add to Graphic Group** and
    then had a copy made with **Move Parallel**. The right-hand upper
    drawing shows the left-hand drawing after using the **Mirror** tool.
    Construct the given drawings.
        The left-hand drawing of the lower set of three drawings of Fig.
    7.31 shows a similar set of outlines formed with **Line**, **Arc** and

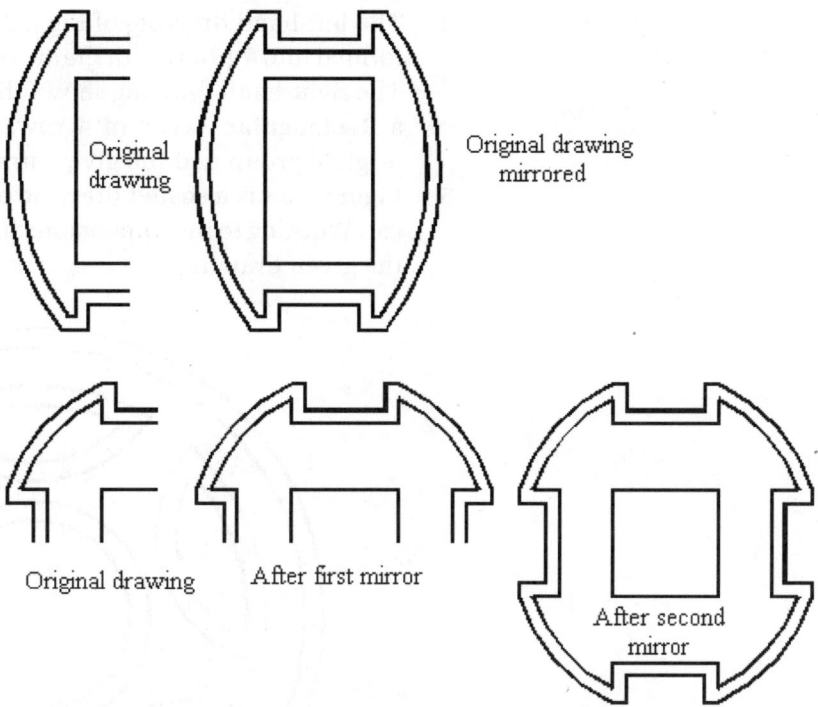

Fig. 7.31 Exercise 3

Move Parallel. This left-hand drawing has then been acted upon by **Mirror** (**vertical**), then the mirrored pair have again been acted upon by **Mirror**, but this time with the **Horizontal** option active. Construct the given drawings.

Note that in each case the elements to be mirrored must be formed into a graphic group with the **Add to Graphic Group** tool.

Original graphic group. Width 2

Array - 4 rows; 5 columns

Fig. 7.32 Exercise 4

4. The left-hand drawing of Fig. 7.32 shows a circle and a hexagon formed into a group with the aid of the **Add to Graphic Group** tool. The right-hand drawing shows the grouped elements formed into a **Rectangular Array** of 4 rows and 5 columns. Construct the original group and the given array.

5. Figure 7.33 is a scaled drawing of a hub wheel cap from a motor car. Working to the dimensions included with Fig. 7.33, construct the given drawing.

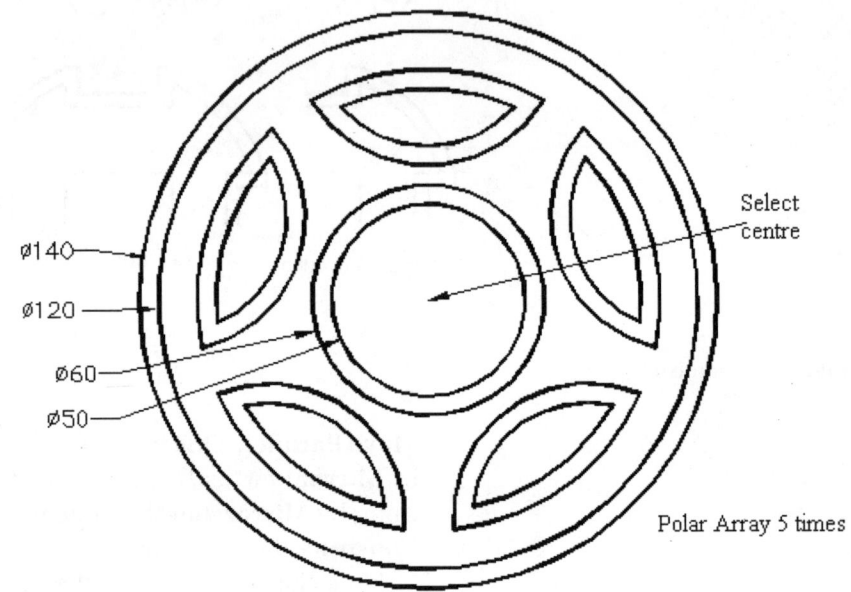

Fig. 7.33 Exercise 5

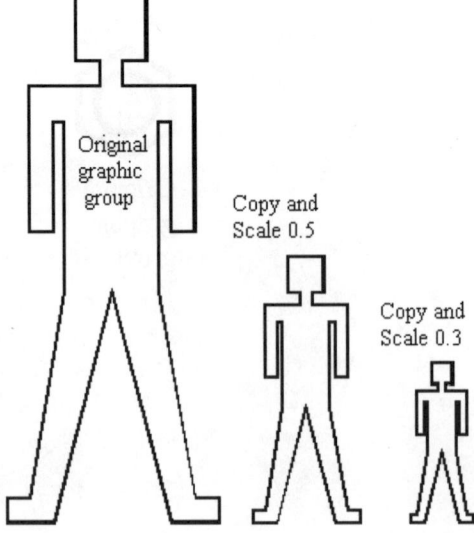

Fig. 7.34 Exercise 6

6.   Construct the left-hand part of Fig. 7.34 to any suitable dimensions, then copy the drawing twice with **Copy** and **Scale** the copies as shown.

7.   Figure 7.35 shows three **Rectangular Arrays**. Each is based upon an original group shown, in each case, to the left of the arrays. Construct the three arrays, working to any suitable sizes.

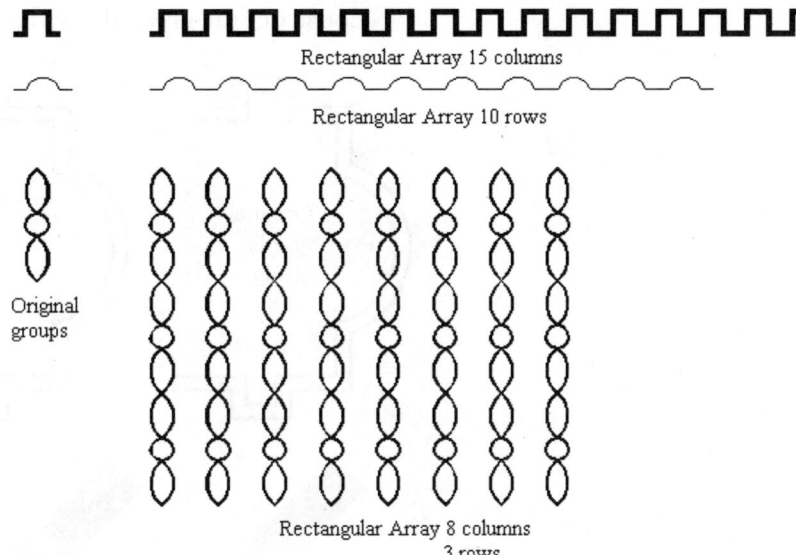

Fig. 7.35 Exercise 7

8.   The left-hand drawing of Fig. 7.36 shows the dimensioned outline of the group of elements for the **Polar Array** shown in the right-hand drawing. The array consists of 24 copies of the original. Working to the given dimensions, construct the array.

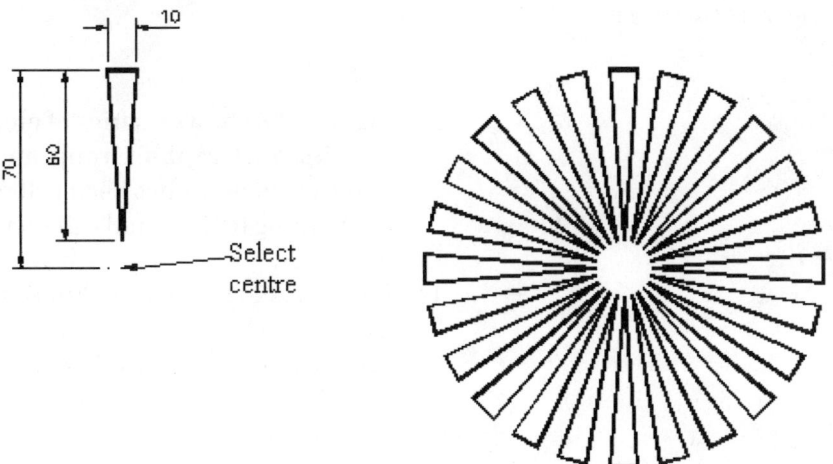

Fig. 7.36 Exercise 8

9. Figure 7.37 shows two sets of drawings. The upper pair show outlines constructed with **Line**, **Arc** and **Move Parallel**. The right-hand drawing shows the outlines then acted upon with the **Mirror** tool.

   The lower pair of drawings of Fig. 7.37 show a **Line** of weight 15 drawn at an angle of 45°. The line is then acted upon by **Construct Array**.

   Construct the given drawings.

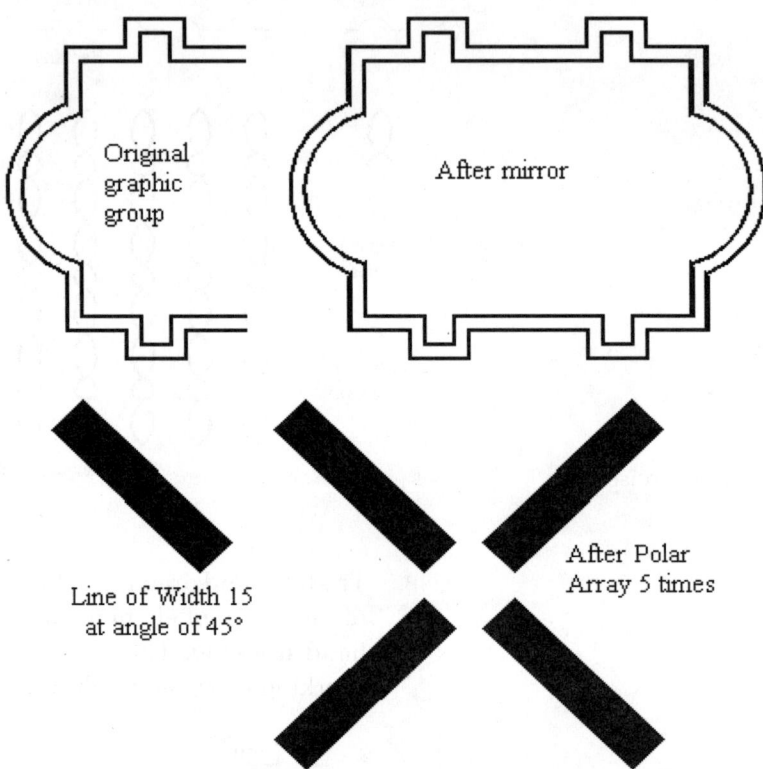

Fig. 7.37 Exercise 9

10. Figure 7.38 shows a series of elements – a **Line**, a **Block** , a **Circle**, an **Ellipse**, a **Graphic Group**, an **Arc** and a **Regular Polygon**. Each of these elements has been acted upon by the **Move Parallel** tool.

    Working to the details given with Fig. 7.38, construct the given drawings.

11. Figure 7.39 shows scaled drawings of the front and the rear of a garden gate constructed from wooden slats. Working to the dimensions given with Fig. 7.39, construct the two views.

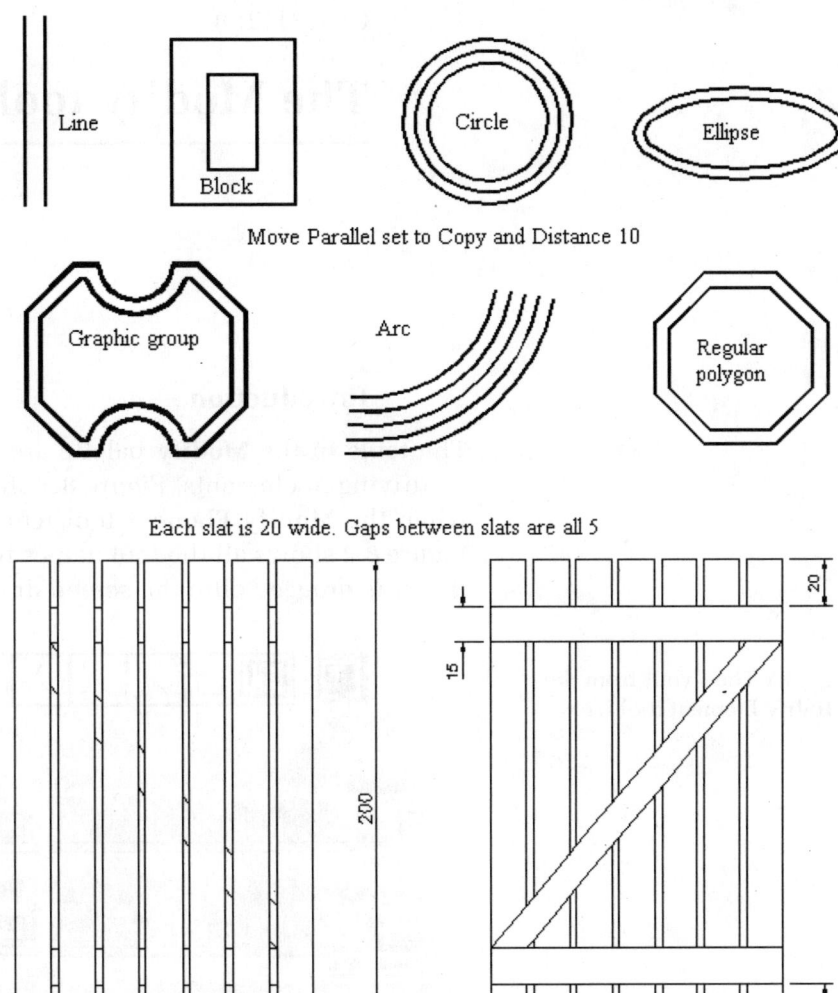

Move Parallel set to Copy and Distance 10

Fig. 7.38 Exercise 10

Each slat is 20 wide. Gaps between slats are all 5

Fig. 7.39 Exercise 11

View looking at front of gate   View looking at rear of gate

CHAPTER 8

The Modify tools

Introduction

The tools in the **Modify** palette are, as the name implies, for the modifying of elements. Figure 8.1 shows the flyout which appears when the **Modify Element** tool icon is selected with a *left-click*. Figure 8.2 shows all the tool names in the **Modify** palette when the flyout is *dragged* onto the screen drawing area.

Fig. 8.1 The flyout from the **Modify Element** tool icon

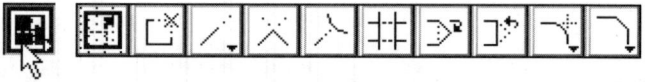

Fig. 8.2 The names of the tools in the **Modify** tool palette

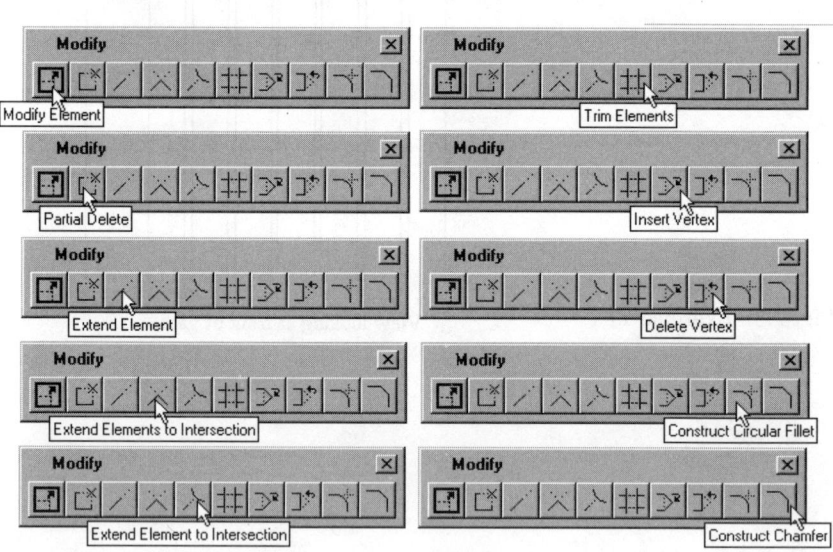

The Modify Element tool

There are three options available when using this tool – these are chosen from the **Vertex Type** pop-up list. Figures 8.3 to 8.6 give simple examples of each of these options when modifying a block.

1. **Sharp** option: Fig. 8.3. In the **Vertex Type** pop-up list select **Sharp** and *left-click* in the check box against **Orthogonal** to set that option on (**X** in check box). Move the cursor onto one corner of the block and the block can be *dragged* to a new shape, retaining its orthogonal form (all right angles retained).

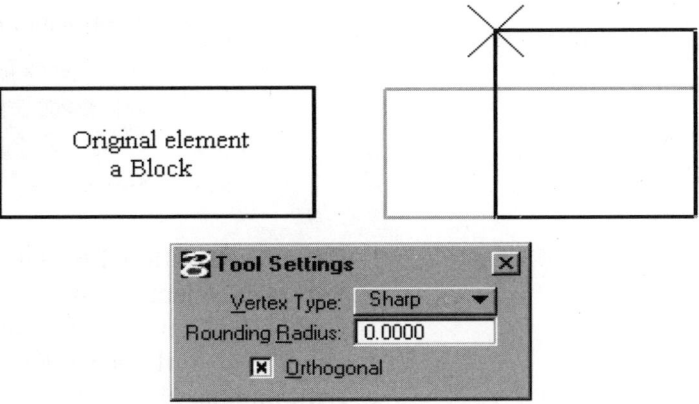

Fig. 8.3 **Sharp** option, with **Orthogonal** set

Figure 8.4 shows the same block modified when the **Orthogonal** check box is not set – the right angles of the block are not retained under the modification. Note that in both these **Sharp** examples, **Rounding Radius** is zero.

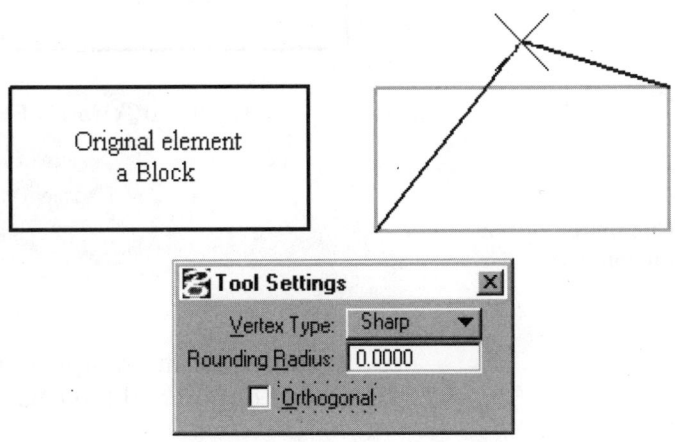

Fig. 8.4 **Sharp** option, with **Orthogonal** not set

2. **Rounded** option: Fig. 8.5 shows the modification which takes place when the **Rounded** option is chosen, with **Orthogonal** check box set. The corner nearest the cursor point is rounded (filleted) to the radius *keyed-in* to the **Rounding Radius** box.

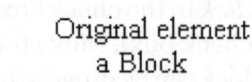

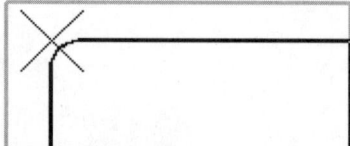

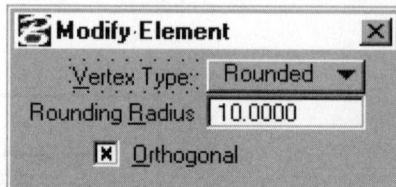

Fig. 8.5 **Rounded** option, with
Orthogonal set

3. **Chamfered** option: Fig. 8.6 shows the result when the **Chamfered** option is selected from the **Vertex Style** pop-up list and with **Orthogonal** set on. The corner nearest the modifying cursor is chamfered to the sizes *keyed-in* to the **Chamfer Offset** box. The right-angular shape of the original block is unchanged.

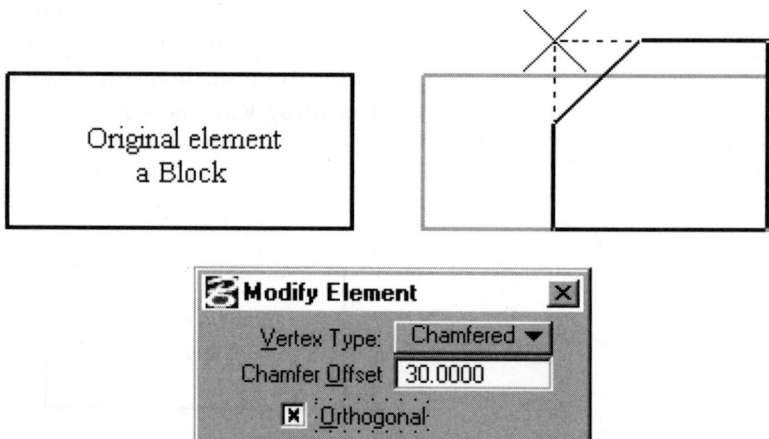

Fig. 8.6 **Chamfered** option,
with **Orthogonal** set

Figure 8.7 is an example of repeated modification using both the **Rounded** option and the **Chamfered** option.

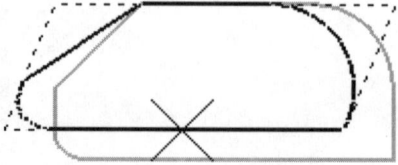

Fig. 8.7 Repeated modification
using both **Rounded** and
Chamfered options

The Partial Delete tool

Figure 8.8 shows the action of **Partial Delete** on three elements – a circle, an ellipse and a line. The procedure for using the tool involves three *left-clicks*:

1. First *left-click* – on the element to select it – the element changes to a ghosted form.
2. Second *left-click* – selects the beginning of the partial delete. Note that in the case of a circle, the partial deletion will be in the default anti-clockwise (counter-clockwise) direction. This does not apply to other elements such as an ellipse.
3. Third *left-click* – select the end of the partial delete and *left-click* to complete the deletion. The element returns from its ghosted form.

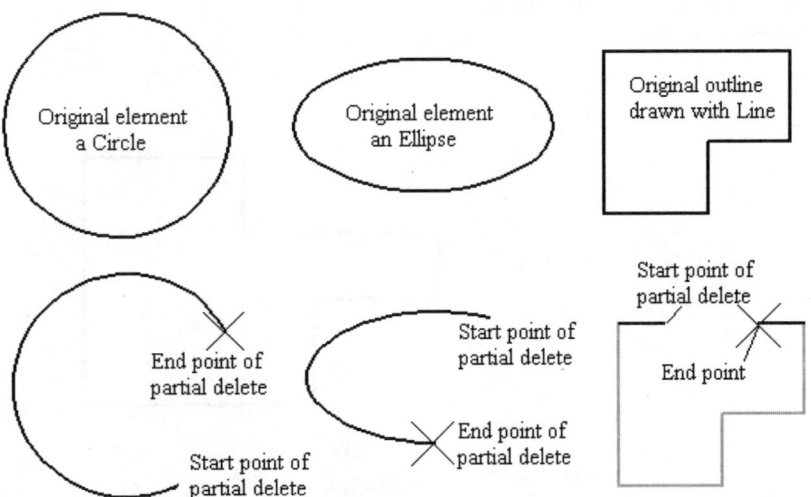

Fig. 8.8 The action of the **Partial Delete** tool

The Extend Element tool

Figures 8.9 and 8.10 indicate the results of using this tool, Fig. 8.9 when no number is *entered* in the **Distance** box of the Element Selection dialogue box and Fig. 8.10 when a number is *entered* in the box.

No number in **Distance** box – the element is extended by *dragging*.
Number in **Distance** box – the element automatically extends by the *entered* distance nearest to the point selected on the element to start off the action of the tool.

Note that when the **Extend Element** tool is called, the Element Selection box is named **Extend Line** and the tool will only act on lines.

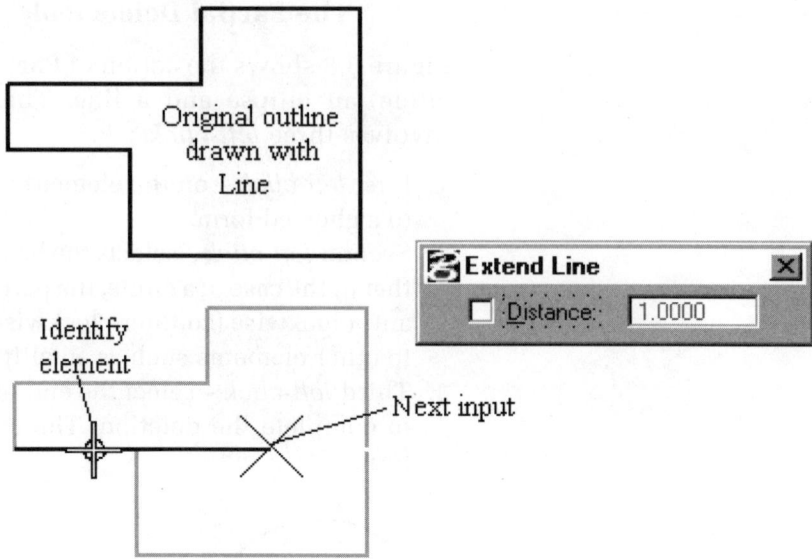

Fig. 8.9 *Dragging* when **Extend Element** is in use

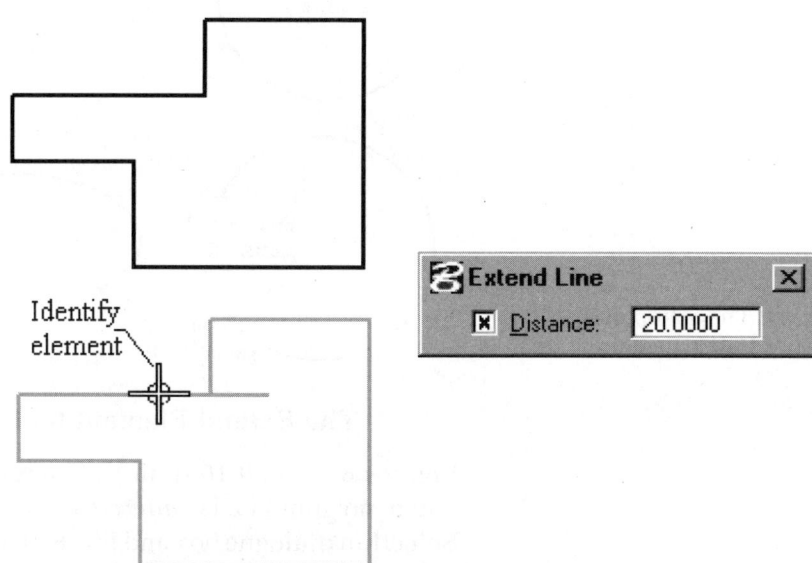

Fig. 8.10 The action of the **Extend Element** tool when a **Distance** number if *entered*

The Extend Elements to Intersection tool

The action of this tool is shown in three examples in Fig. 8.11. When two elements are selected with *left-clicks* they automatically form an intersection. Parts of the elements outside the intersection point are automatically deleted.

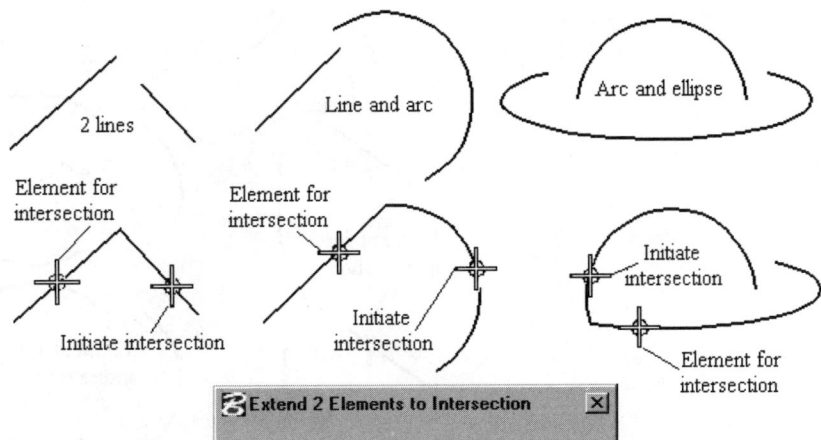

Fig. 8.11 The action of the **Extend Elements to Intersection** tool

The Extend Element to Intersection tool

The action of this tool is similar to that of the **Extend Elements to Intersection** tool, the difference lying in the fact that only one element is extended to intersect with a second and no deletion of parts outside the intersecting point take place. See Fig. 8.12. Three prompts will be seen in the **Prompt** field of the **Command Window**;

> **Select first element for intersection:** *left-click* on element
> **Select element for intersection:** *left-click* on element
> **Initiate intersection:** *left-click* and intersection occurs.

> *Note*

If the second element is not long enough to itself extend to the point of intersection when using the tool, the selected element extends to what would have been the point at which both elements would have intersected had the second been long enough. This is demonstrated in the left-hand pair of drawings in Fig. 8.12.

The Trim Elements tool

Figure 8.13 shows examples of the use of this tool. Two prompts will be seen in the **Prompts** field of the **Command Window**:

> **Select Cutting Element:** *left-click* on the element which is used to cut off the trimmed element(s).
> **Identify Trim Elements:** *left-click* on element, or on elements one after the other. Then *right-click* to finish with the tool, or to start trimming other parts of a drawing.

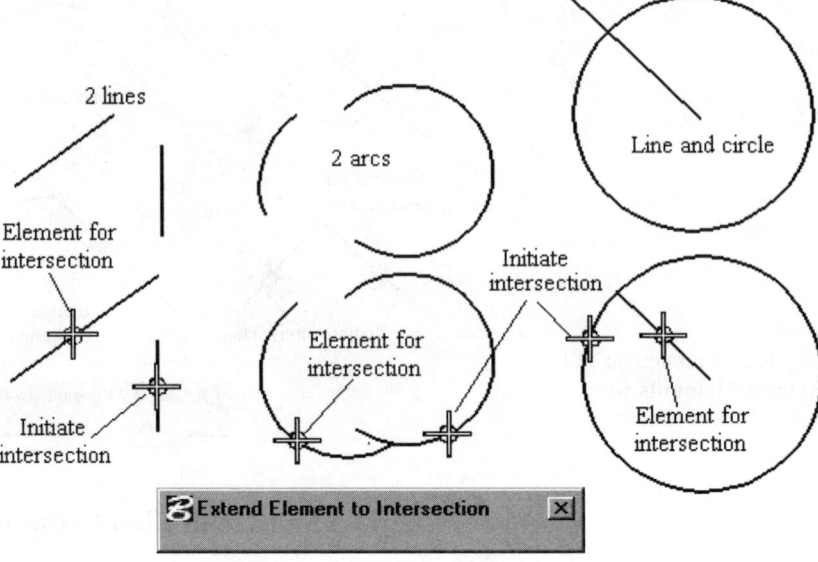

Fig. 8.12 The action of the **Extend Element to Intersection** tool

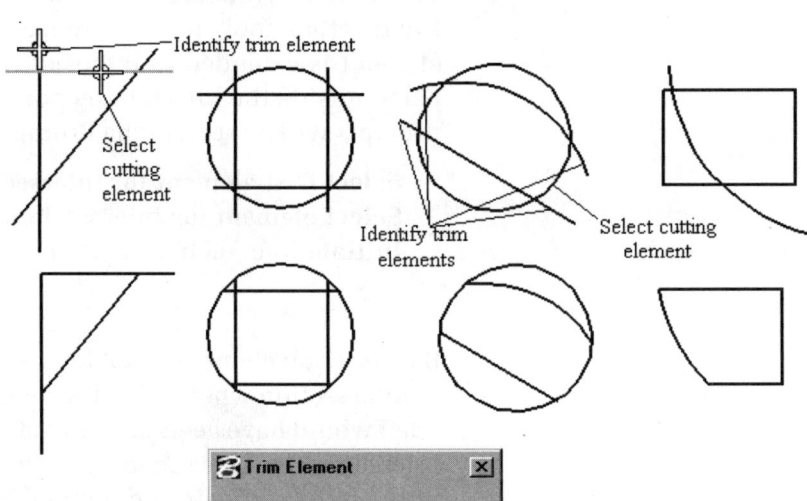

Fig. 8.13 The action of the **Trim Elements** tool

Trim Elements is a tool which most operators will be using frequently.

The Insert Vertex tool

A vertex can be inserted in any element other than circles and ellipses. With its use the tool can be used to change the shape of an element by inserting a vertex and then *dragging* the vertex to another position. Figure 8.14 shows examples of the use of the tool.

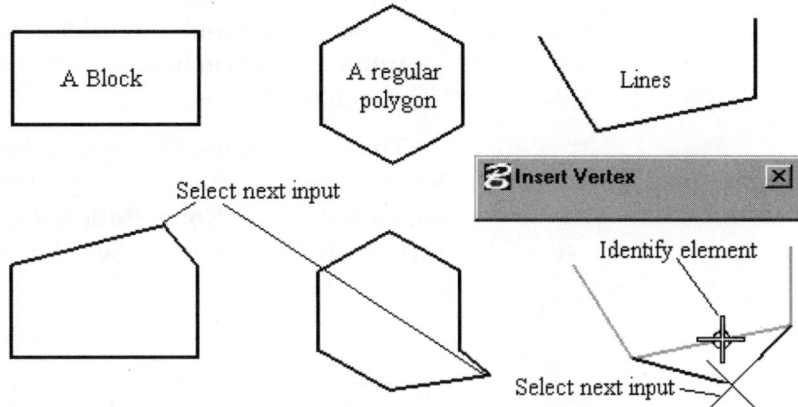

Fig. 8.14 Examples of the use of **Insert Vertex**

The Delete Vertex tool

This tool is used to delete inserted vertices and so undo the effect of changing the shape of an element by using the **Insert Vertex** tool. Figure 8.15 shows the changes made to elements in Fig. 8.14 being undone with the tool.

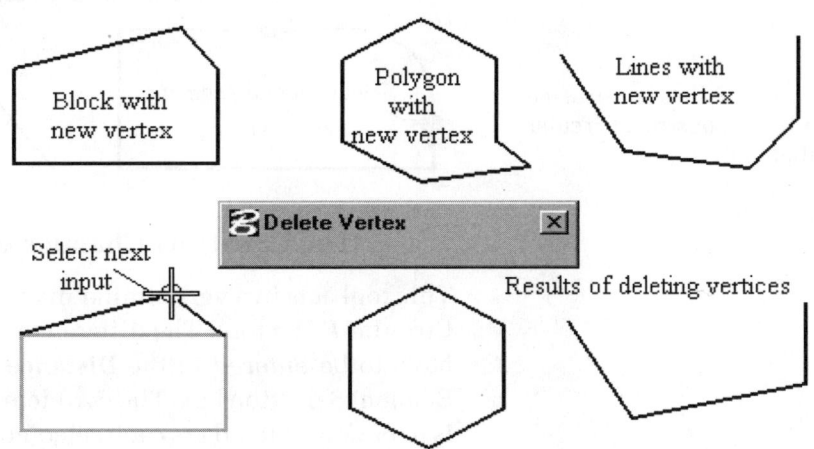

Fig. 8.15 Undoing the action of **Insert vertex** with **Delete Vertex**

The Construct Circular Fillet tool

Figure 8.16 shows three examples of adding fillets between elements – in a block, between lines and between an arc and a line. Fillets can be added between any of the elements in MicroStation 95.

The three prompts in the **Prompt** field of the **Command Window** for this tool are:

Select first segment: *left-click* on the first of the two elements between which the fillet is to be constructed.

Select second segment: *left-click* on the second of the two elements between which the fillet is to be constructed.

Initiate construction: *left-click* and the fillet is added between the two elements.

The radius of the fillet depends upon the number *entered* in the **Radius** box. A *left-click* on the **Truncate** button and a pop-up list appears showing **None**, **Both** or **First**. In the examples given in Fig. 8.16 the **Both** option has been selected from the pop-up list.

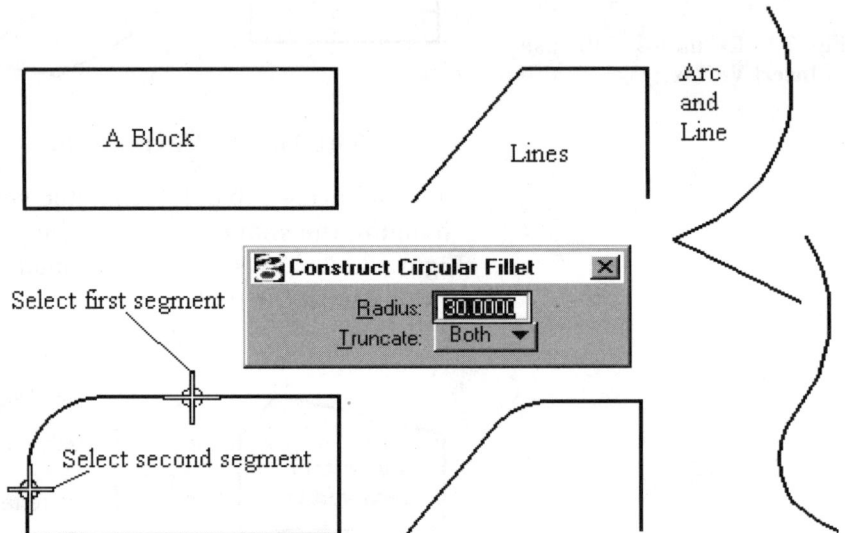

Fig. 8.16 **Fillets** constructed with the **Construct Circular Fillet** tool

The Construct Chamfer tool

This tool acts in a very similar manner to the action of the **Construct Circular Fillet** tool. The difference lies in the fact that two numbers have to be *entered* in the **Distance 1** and **Distance 2** boxes of the Element Selection box. The two elements between which the chamfer is to be constructed are each selected with *left-click* and another *left-click* confirms the addition of the chamfer. Truncation is automatic of those parts of the element outside the chamfer line. Figure 8.17 shows three examples of chamfers being added between elements or parts of elements – in a block, between lines and in a regular polygon.

Some abbreviations

If you wish to *key-in* abbreviations for the **Modify** tool in the **Command Window** *key-in* field, here are some which can be used:

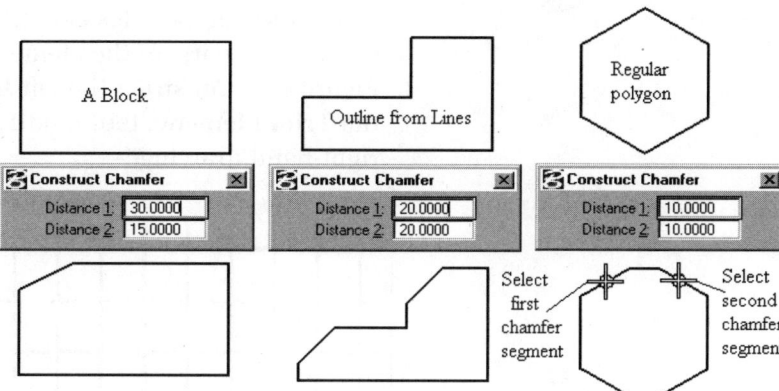

Fig. 8.17 The action of the
Construct Chamfer tool

mo	**Modify Element**
ex	**Extend Element**
ext el	**Extend Element to Intersection**
tri	**Trim Elements**
ins	**Insert Vertex**
del ver	**Delete Vertex**
fill	**Construct Circular Fillet**
cham	**Construct Chamfer**

Questions

1. What is the difference in the actions between the two tools **Extend Elements to Intersection** and **Extend Element to Intersection**?
2. What is the difference, when using the **Construct Circular Fillet** tool, between fillets constructed when the **Truncate** option is **Both** and when it is **First**?
3. Can a circle be modified with the aid of **Modify Element**?
4. Can a fillet be constructed between a circle and a line?
5. Can a fillet be constructed between an arc and a circle?
6. What is meant by the setting **Orthogonal** in connection with the **Modify Element** tool?
7. What rule governs the deletion of part of a circle?
8. Can an arc be extended with the aid of **Extend Element**?
9. What is the purpose of the **Insert Vertex** tool?
10. Can any element be trimmed with **Trim Elements**?

Exercises

1. Draw lines, arcs, circles and ellipses at random and attempt to add fillets and chamfers between the elements you have drawn.

2. Draw lines, arc, circles and ellipses at random, but crossing each other. Trim parts of the elements you have drawn.

3. Figure 8.18 Construct the left-hand drawing as shown, then using the **Trim Elements** tool modify your drawing as indicated by the right-hand drawing.

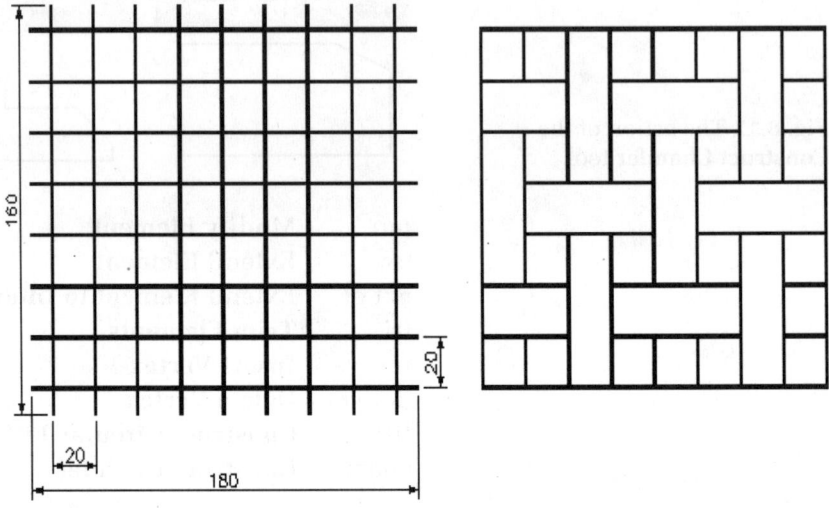

Fig. 8.18 Exercise 3

4. In Fig. 8.19 the upper row of illustrations show three drawings made up from various elements. Working to any convenient sizes, copy the three drawings, then trim off parts of the drawings to produce results as shown in the lower three drawings.

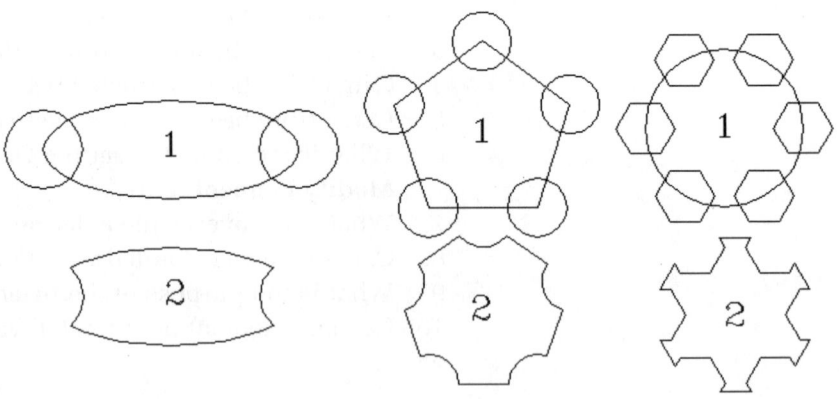

Fig. 8.19 Exercise 4

5. From the constructions shown in the upper drawing of Fig. 8.20, produce the lower of the two drawings.

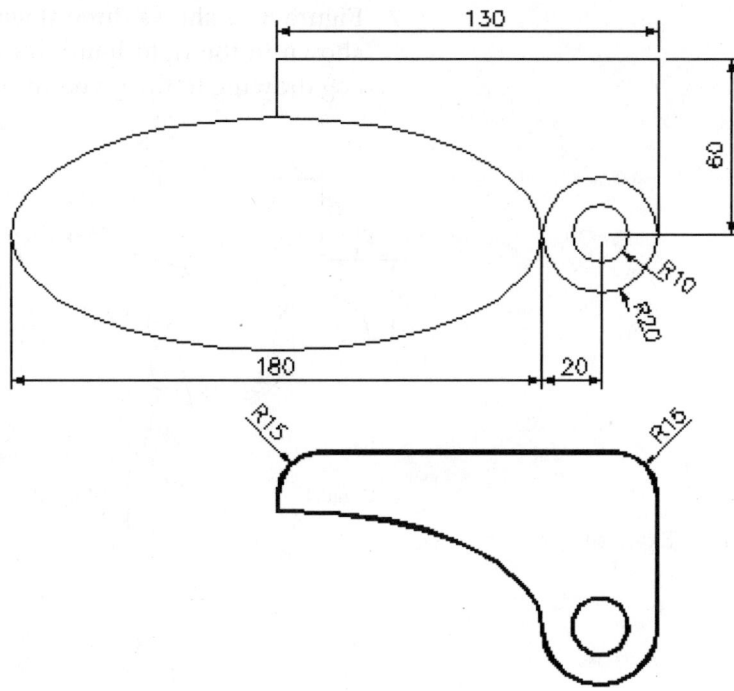

Fig. 8.20 Exercise 5

6. Construct the view of the front of a greenhouse as shown in Fig. 8.21.

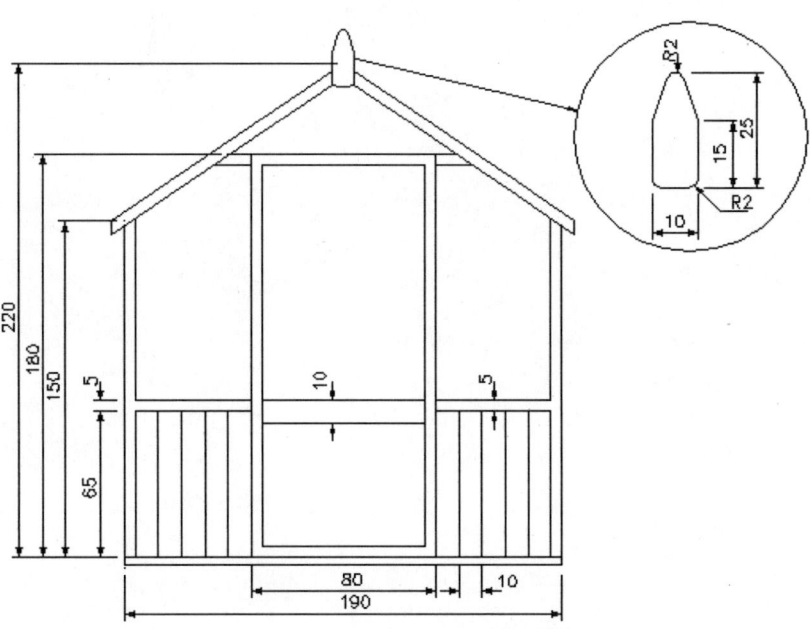

Fig. 8.21 Exercise 6

7. Figure 8.22 shows three stages in the drawing of a ratchet cog, as shown in the right-hand drawing (Stage 3). Construct the ratchet cog drawing to the given information.

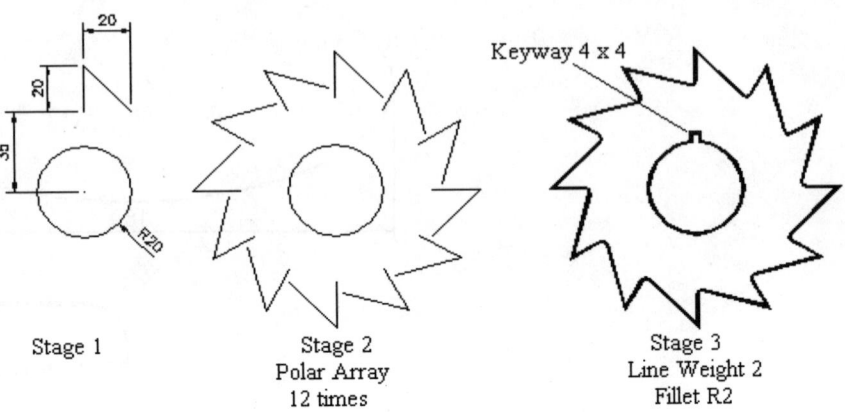

Stage 1

Stage 2
Polar Array
12 times

Keyway 4 x 4

Stage 3
Line Weight 2
Fillet R2

Fig. 8.22 Exercise 7

CHAPTER 9

The Text tools

Introduction

The adding of text within drawings is an important part of the
production of technical drawings. MicroStation 95 has a number of
tools for adding and amending text. Because this book is intended
for those learning how to use the software package, those text tools
dealing with data will not be discussed.

The flyout resulting from a *left-click* on the **Place Text** icon in the
Main palette is shown in Fig. 9.1 and the **Text** palette in Fig. 9.2. It
will be seen that the palette is made up of three sections, the left-
hand one containing two tools, the centre one with five tools and the
right-hand one another five tools. It is the tools in this right-hand
part of the tool palette which will not be described in this book. This
is why the tool tips from the right-hand section of the palette are not
included in Fig. 9.2.

Fig. 9.1 The flyout from the
Place Text tool icon

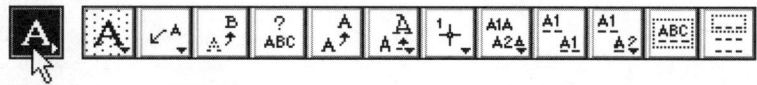

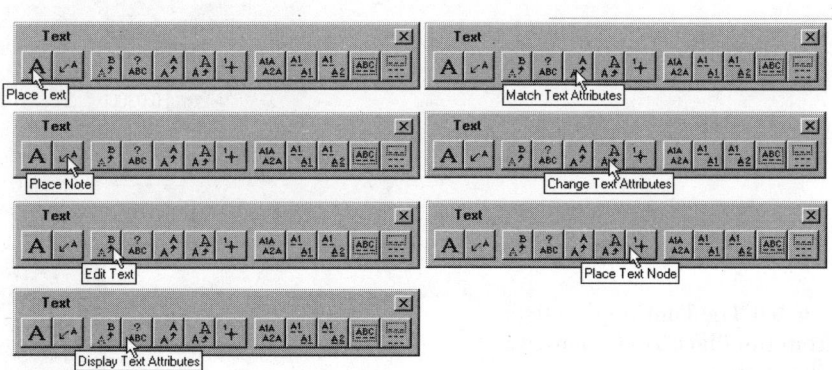

Fig. 9.2 The tool tips of the
Text tool in the left and centre
sections of the palette

The Place Text Element Selection box

A *left-click* on the **Place Text** icon brings the **Place Text** Element Selection dialogue box to screen. The dialogue box contains three buttons, a *left-click* on any of which brings down a pop-up list. Figure 9.3 shows the list resulting from a *left-click* on the **Method** button. Figure 9.4 shows the pop-up list from a *left-click* on the **Font** button. Figure 9.5 shows the pop-up list from a *left-click* on the **Justification** button.

These lists show the controls for the method, the type of font and the positioning of the text to be added to a drawing. Taking the **Font**

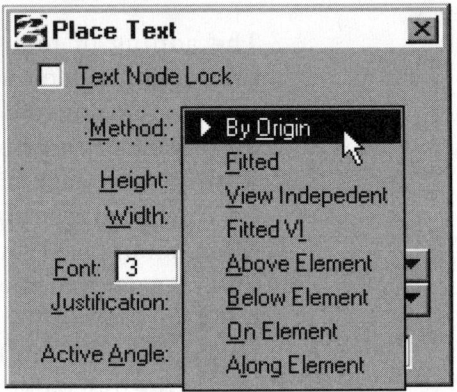

Fig. 9.3 The **Method** pop-up list from the **Place Text** Element Selection box

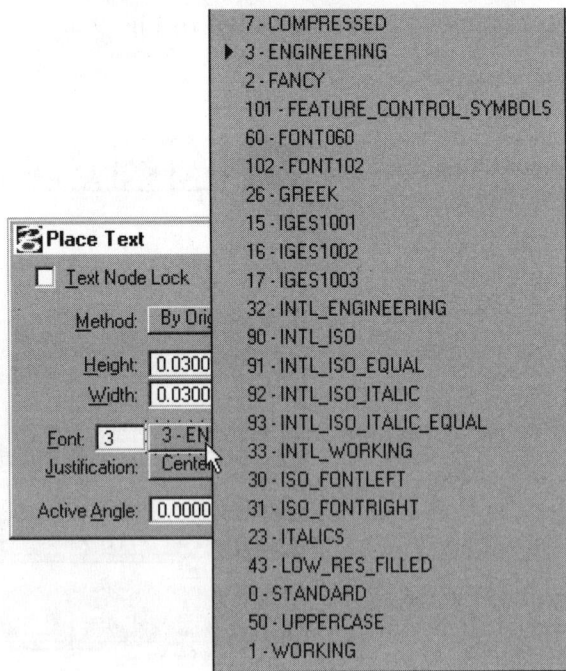

Fig. 9.4 The **Font** pop-up list from the **Place Text** Element Selection box

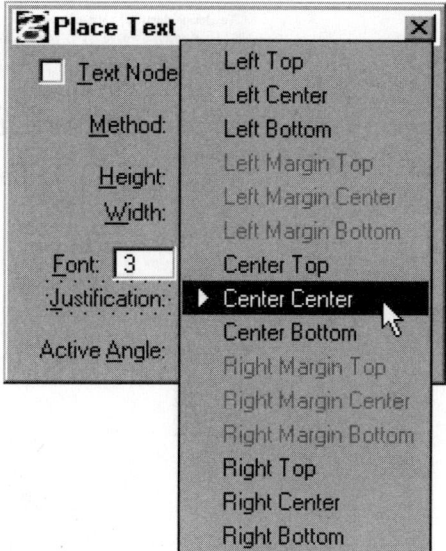

Fig. 9.5 The **Justification** pop-up list from the **Place Text** Element Selection box

list first, Fig. 9.6 shows screens containing a variety of types of font selected from the **Font** pop-up list, with sizes and angles *entered* in the **Height**, **Width** and **Active Angle** boxes of the **Place Text** Element Selection dialogue box.

Notes

1. All the text shown in Fig. 9.6 has been added to the drawing with the lock icon seen to the right of the **Height** and **Width** boxes in the

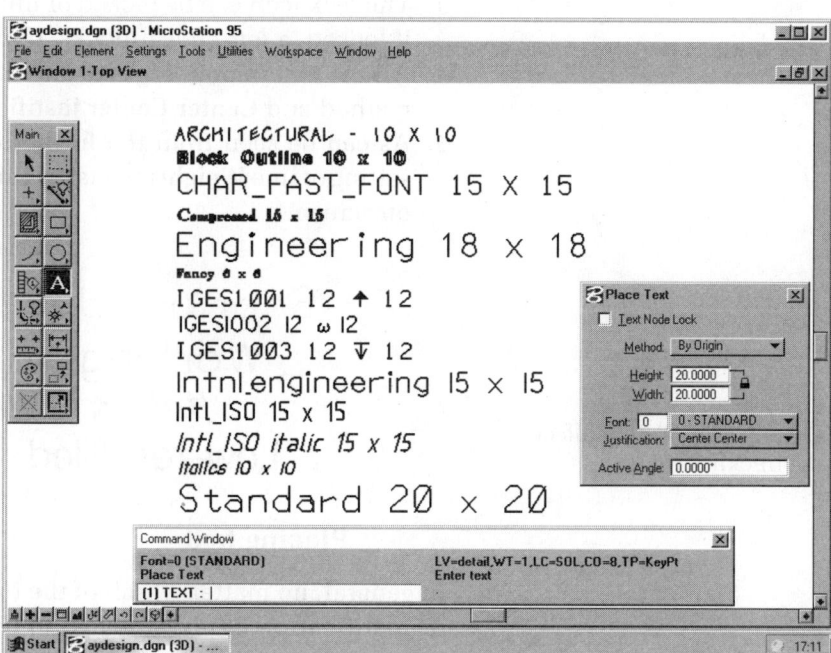

Fig. 9.6 Examples of different fonts at various heights.

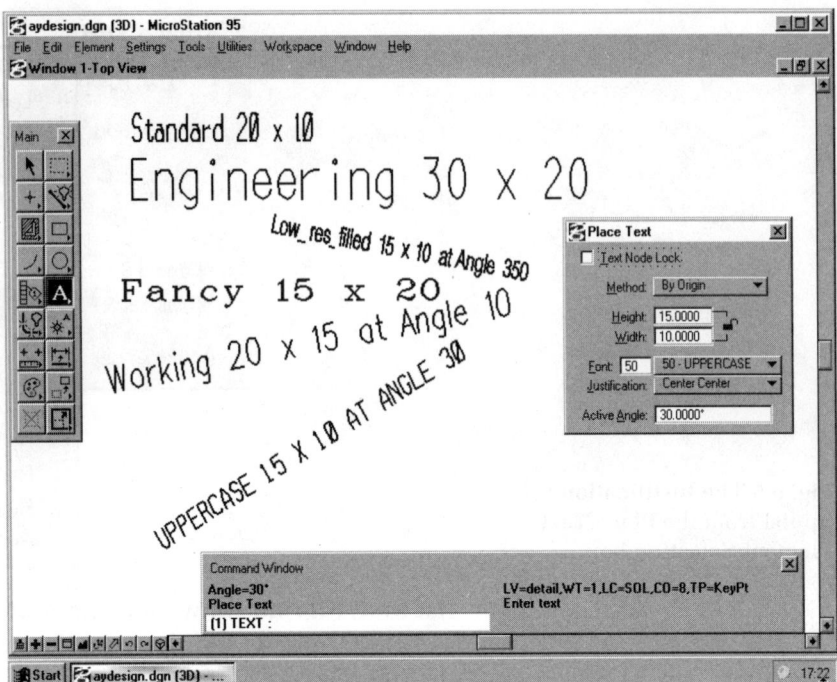

Fig. 9.7 Examples of different fonts at various heights, widths and angles

Place Text Element Selection dialogue box shown as locked. This automatically forces the height and width sizes to the same figures.

2. In Fig. 9.7 the lock icon is unlocked (open). This allows text to be *entered* with widths of a different size to height.

3. The lock icon can be locked or unlocked by *left-clicks* on the icon. If locked, a *left-click* unlocks. If unlocked, a *left-click* locks.

4. All the text in both Figs 9.6 and 9.7 were positioned by **By Origin** method and **Center Center** justification.

5. As can be seen from the further examples given in Fig. 9.8, the setting of line **Weight** affects the thickness of the parts of text placed on screen.

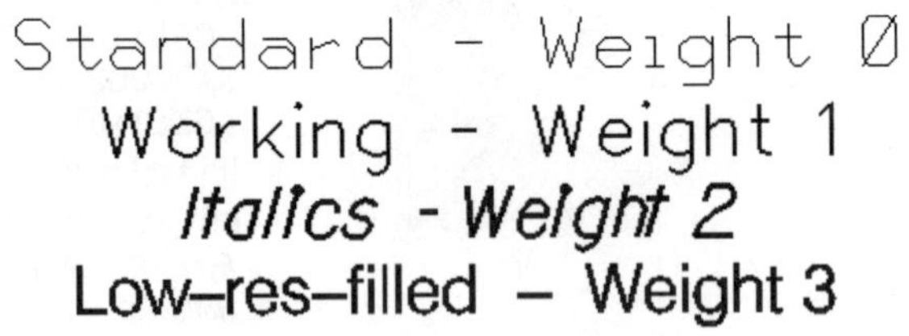

Standard – Weight 0

Working – Weight 1

Italics - Weight 2

Low–res–filled – Weight 3

Fig. 9.8 Line **Weight** affects the thickness of text

Placing text

In general, no matter which of the options is chosen for the **Method** or **Justification** of text, the text to be added to a drawing must first be *entered* in the **Text Editor**, which appears when the tool is selected. When satisfied that the text is correct, the *entered* text can be *dragged* into position where it is to be placed. A *left-click* positions the text and another *right-click* confirms the position. The screen cursors will appear at the position in the text as set in the **Justification** options. In the given example (Fig. 9.9), the **Justification** is **Center Center** so the cursor will appear centrally along and centrally vertically in the text as it is *dragged* into position. The cursor disappears at the *right-click*. Note that the example given in Fig. 9.9 is for the sake of illustrating the method, because once the text appears in the drawing area of the screen, it will not also appear in the **Text Editor**.

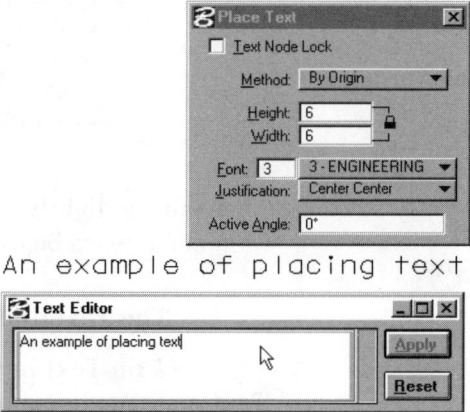

Fig. 9.9 *Keying-in* and positioning text

Other text settings

View Attributes

Left-click on **Settings** in the menu bar and again on **View Attributes** in the resulting pull-down menu. The **View Attributes** dialogue box (Fig. 9.10) includes several features which can affect text:

Line Weights: If checked (**X** in check box) then the setting of the **Line Weight** affects text. Text will appear on screen at the thickness set by weight. If the check box does not carry an **X** then text will be drawn at the default line weight of **0**.

Text: If the check box against this feature is empty, text will not show on screen. If showing an **X** then text will appear. This may be of value when a great deal of text is on screen. Text takes time to appear and is somewhat memory hungry. Releasing it from the screen after it has been placed, by unchecking this check box, will

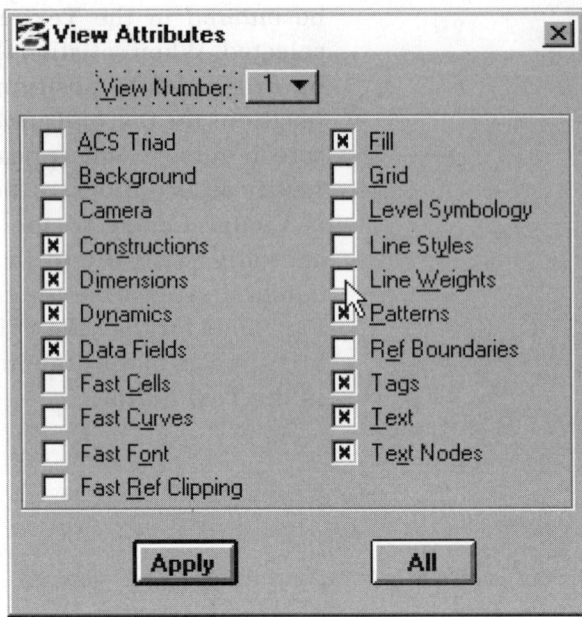

Fig. 9.10 The **View Attributes** dialogue box

make for slightly faster working for the remainder of the drawing. It can always be called back by checking the **Text** check box.

The Text dialogue box

Left-click on **Text** in the **Element** pull-down menu (Fig. 9.11). The **Text** dialogue box appears (Fig. 9.12). Many settings for text can be made in this dialogue box:

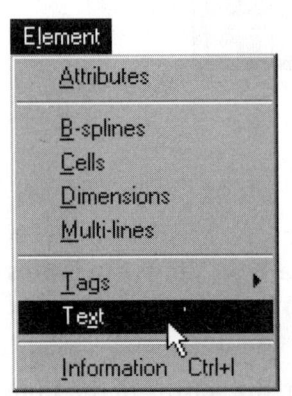

Fig. 9.11 Select **Text** from the **Element** pull-down menu

Left-click on the **View** button and the **Fonts** dialogue box appears. Select the font which you wish to examine from the list and a complete alphabet and figures showing the font members will appear in the **Fonts** box.

Height, **Width** and **Angle** can be set in the box.

Line Spacing can be set if a number of lines of text are to be included.

Justification: Two boxes show the position of the cursor whatever justification is selected. The position is set according to justification seen by *left-clicks* buttons below the two boxes. Pop-up lists show the various possibilities.

Slant: The slope or slant of letters in text can be set at an angle *keyed-in* to the **Slope** box.

Fractions can be included by checking the check box against the word.

Underline: If this check box is checked, then text will be underlined.

Vertical Text: With this check box active (**X** in box) text will be placed vertically instead of horizontally.

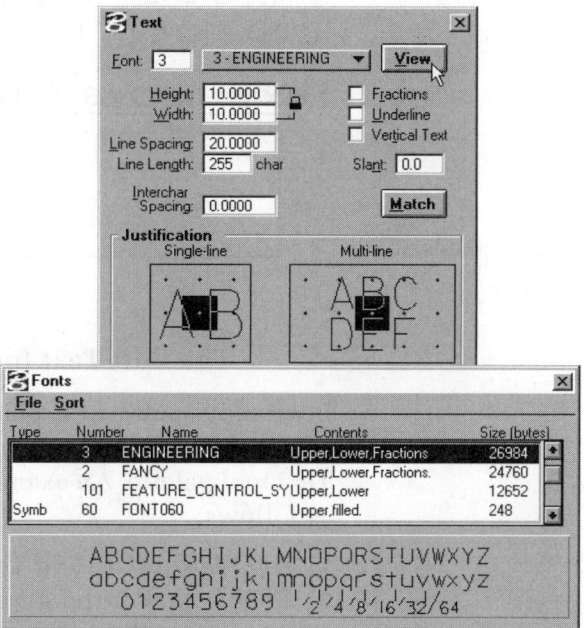

Fig. 9.12 The **Text** dialogue box with **Fonts** showing

Method

Only three methods, as selected from the **Method** pop-up list of the **Place Text** Element Selection box, will be shown here. Others are left to the reader to experiment with.

By Origin: This has already been shown in the examples in Figs 9.6 and 9.7.

Fitted Text: Another method of justifying is shown in Fig. 9.13, in which the **Place Fitted Text** justification is employed. The options for this form of justification requests two positions – **Position text**, followed by **Endpoint of text**. As the end point is selected, so the text adjusts in height and width to fit between the two points, no matter what **Height** and **Width** is set for the text. Thus, as can be seen from the **Place Text** Element Selection box in Fig. 9.13, the two sets of **Place Fitted Text** have been placed with the same height and width, yet differ considerably in height and width because the text has been fitted between the two selected points.

Above Element: Figure 9.13 also shows text placed above an element – in this example a block. Similar placements are **Below Element**, **On Element**, **Along Element**.

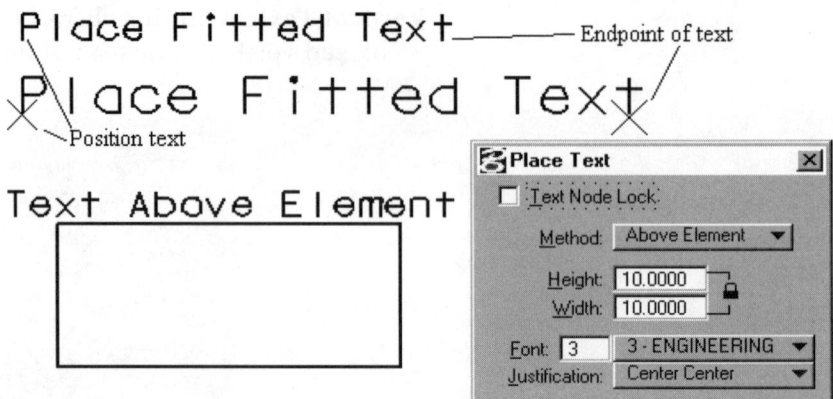

Fig. 9.13 Several **Methods** of placing text

The Edit Text tool

If wrongly spelt text is placed in the drawing area of the screen, the errors can be edited out with the aid of the **Edit Text** tool from the **Text** tool palette. An example is given in Fig. 9.14. The procedure is as follows:

1. *Left-click* on the **Edit Text** tool icon to make the tool active.
2. *Double-click* on the offending text. The text ghosts and automatically appears as wrongly spelt in the **Text Editor**.
3. Edit out the offending parts of the text, with the aid of the cursor keys (those showing up, down, left and right arrows), the backspace key and the **Delete** key, replacing wrong text with the correct text.
4. When the editing is complete press the **Apply** button in the **Text Editor**. The corrected text appears in place of the incorrect text.

The method of editing will be the same as that carried out in any text editing program, such as when misspelling occurs in a word processing package:

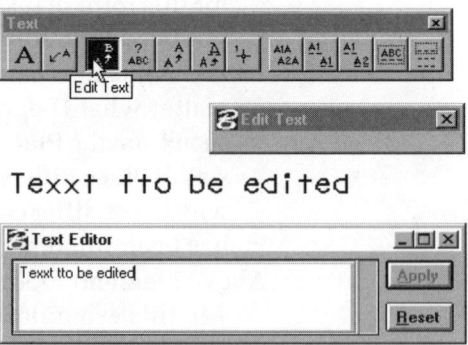

Fig. 9.14 An example of using the **Edit Text** tool

The Display Text Attributes tool

Left-click on the **Display Text Attributes** tool and again on the text the attributes of which the operator wishes to know. This example shows text with the **Command Window** active. The text ghosts and the attributes appear in the **Message** field of the **Command Window** in the form:

TH=10 Text Height = 10
TW=10 Text Width = 10
LV=1 Level = 1
FT=3 Font = 3 (Engineering)

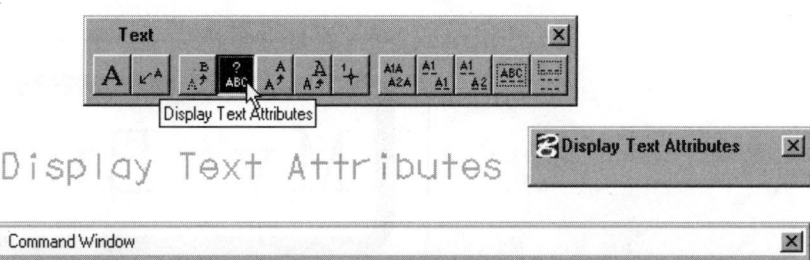

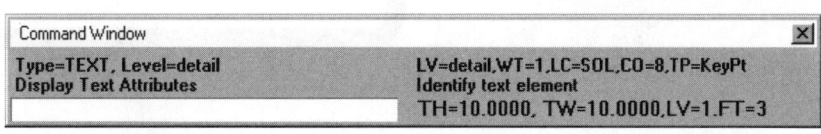

Fig. 9.15 An Example of using the **Display Text Attributes** tool

Note

There is much more to placing text in drawings in MicroStation 95 than has been described in this chapter. However, sufficient information has been given to enable the reader to place text as required in most circumstances that may arise. Further experimentation with placing text is advised.

Questions

1. How does an operator select the font for text being placed?
2. Can you explain the difference between **Method** and **Justification** as selected from the **Place Text** Element Selection box?
3. What is the purpose of the lock icon showing to the right of the **Style** and **Weight** boxes in the **Place Text** Element Selection box?
4. How can the slope of text be changed?
5. How does the **Line Weight** setting affect text as seen on screen?
6. From which dialogue box can one examine the font being selected for text?
7. If a mistake is made in text already placed on screen, which tool is used to amend the mistake?

8.   What is the sequence of mouse *clicks* when editing text which contains mistakes?
9.   What is the purpose of the **Display Text Attributes** tool?
10.   What is meant when the following appears in the Message field of the Command Window:

TH=20,TW=15,LV=1,FT=43?

Exercises

1.   Construct a simple house sign such as that shown in Fig. 9.16, using any suitable outlines and text font.

Fig. 9.16 Exercise 1

2.   Figure 9.17 shows the name of the software used throughout this book placed in an elliptical frame. Using the same wording construct a similarly framed **MicroStation 95**.

Fig. 9.17 Exercise 2

3.   Figure 9.18 shows an invoice sheet constructed with the aid of MicroStation 95. Make a copy of the invoice using any suitable fonts.

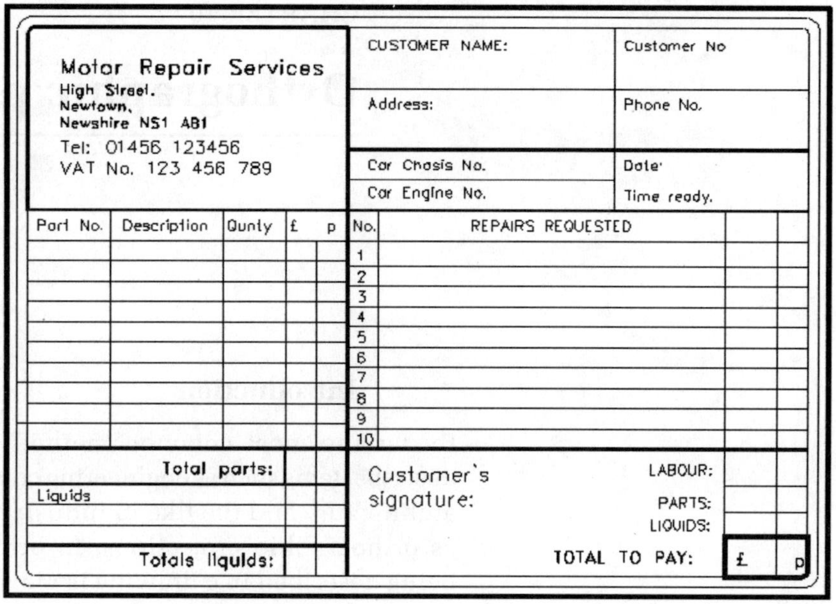

Fig. 9.18 Exercise 3

CHAPTER 10

Orthographic projection

Introduction

By far the most common method of technical drawing used to describe items such as engineering components, assemblies, buildings, architecture and the like in industry is in the form of a type known as orthographic projections. In orthographic projection, the item being described in a drawing is viewed from various directions and the views so obtained are then placed in line with each other – usually either vertically and/or horizontally. On occasions views are obtained from angles other than vertically or horizontally, but the principles involved are the same anyway.

The theory underlying orthographic projection is based upon two planes – a Vertical Plane and a Horizontal Plane, intersecting each other at right angles (or orthogonally) as shown in Fig. 10.1. These two planes form four angles, referred to as the first, second, third and fourth angles. In technical drawing only the first and third of these angles are of any value in the production of orthographic projections.

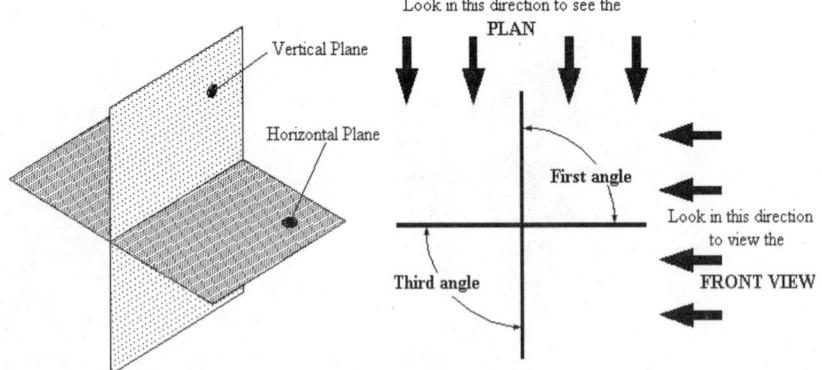

Fig. 10.1 The Horizontal and Vertical Planes upon which the theory of orthographic projection is based

First angle orthographic projection

When constructing an orthographic drawing, the planes are invisible
and are not usually shown in the drawing. In general, there can be
only one Horizontal Plane, but any number of Vertical Planes can be
added to the set of planes as required. Figure 10.2 shows how an item
to be drawn is placed in the area formed by a Horizontal Plane and
two Vertical Planes in the first angle. This illustration also shows the
direction of viewing and the three views – front view, plan and end
view – cast upon the three planes. Note that perspective is ignored
and the viewing is as if carried out with all the viewing 'rays' parallel
to each other.

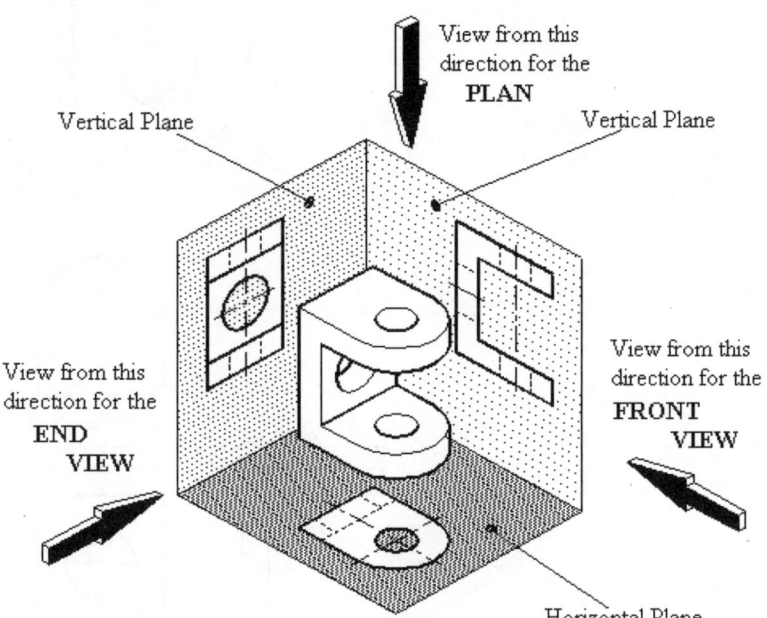

Fig. 10.2 An item placed in
three planes in the First Angle

The planes are then imagined as being rotated through 90° so as
to lie all in the same plane, as indicated in Fig. 10.3.

The basic theory can be extended to any number of views. In Fig.
10.4, six views have been obtained by inserting suitably placed
Vertical Planes and then rotating them to lie on the same plane with
the Horizontal Plane. Although it is not good practice to name the
views, they have been named in Fig. 10.4 to show the reader how the
views were obtained.

Note the symbol for first angle projection in the bottom right-
hand corner of Fig. 10.4. The symbol is itself a first angle projection
of a truncated cone.

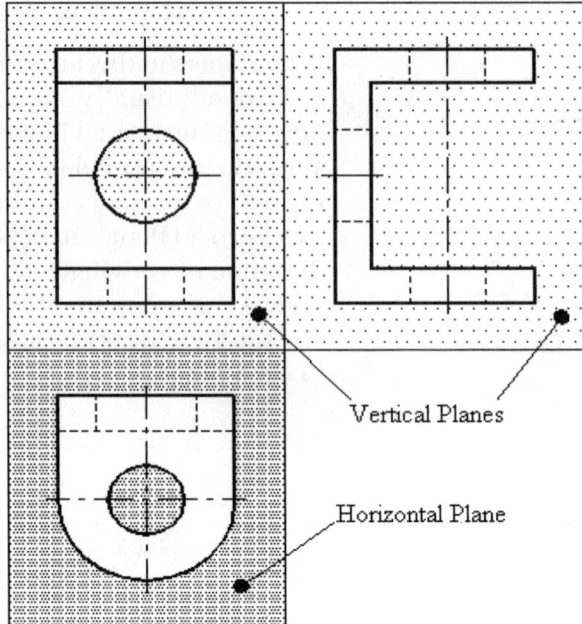

Fig. 10.3 The planes rotated through 90° so as to lie all in the same plane

Vertical Planes

Horizontal Plane

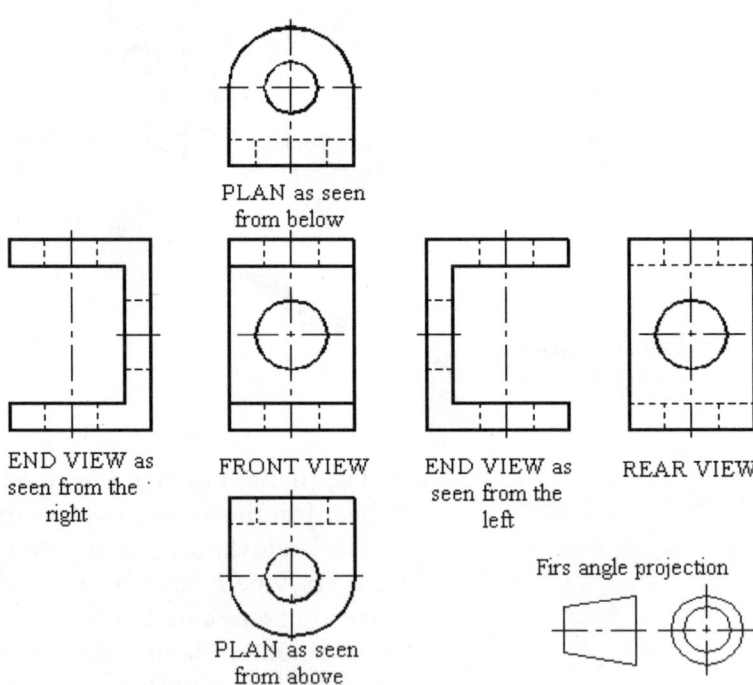

PLAN as seen from below

END VIEW as seen from the right

FRONT VIEW

END VIEW as seen from the left

REAR VIEW

Firs angle projection

PLAN as seen from above

Fig. 10.4 Six views in first angle orthographic projection

Third angle orthographic projection

Figures 10.5 to 10.7 show the same principles applied to third angle orthographic projection. Note again the symbol for third angle

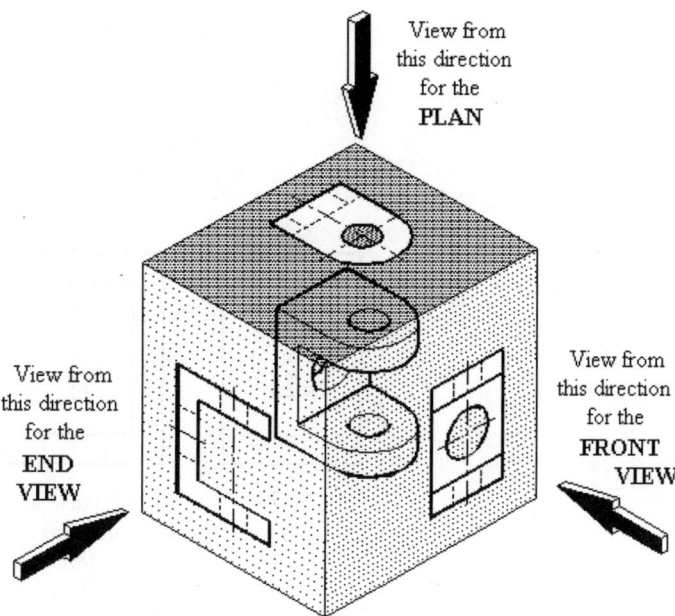

Fig. 10.5 An item placed in three planes in the third angle

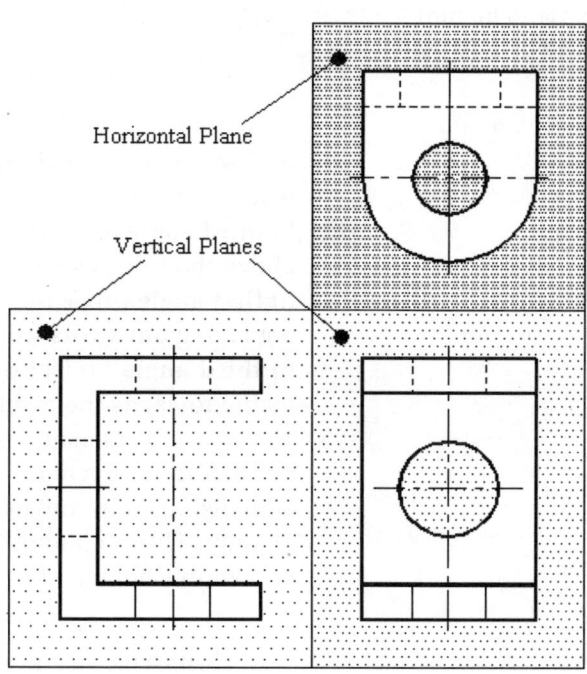

Fig. 10.6 The planes rotated through 90° so as to all lie in the same plane

projection in the bottom left-hand corner of Fig. 10.7 – itself a third angle projection of a truncated cone.

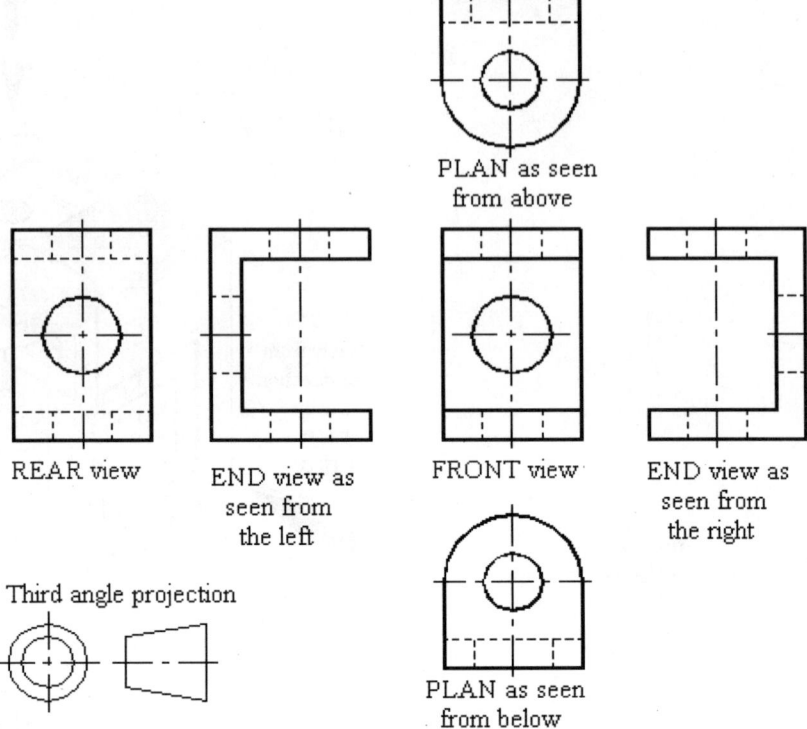

PLAN as seen
from above

REAR view

END view as
seen from
the left

FRONT view

END view as
seen from
the right

Third angle projection

PLAN as seen
from below

Fig. 10.7 Six views in third
angle orthographic projection

Notes

1. In **first angle** projection, the plan as viewed from above is placed **below** the front view.
2. In **third angle** projection, the plan as viewed from above is placed **above** the front view.
3. In **first angle** projection, end views are placed so that their fronts are facing **outwards** from the front view.
4. In **third angle** projection, end views are placed with their fronts facing **towards** the front view.
5. Views can be named, e.g., as front view, end view, etc., but this is not a normal practice.
6. Dimensions have not been included in any of the drawings in this chapter. The methods of including dimensions in a drawing will be shown in Chapter 11.

Constructing an orthographic drawing

The various stages for a method of constructing a third angle orthographic projection of the engineering component illustrated in the previous illustrations is now given:

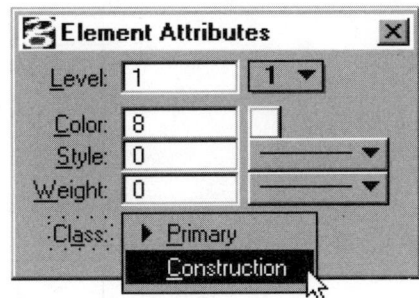

Fig. 10.8 Stage 1. The **Element Attributes** dialogue box showing **Construction Style** being selected

Stage 1: In the **Element** pull-down menu, select **Element Attributes** and in the **Element Attributes** dialogue box, set **Weight** to **0**. Then *left-click* on the **Class** pop-up list and select **Construction** (Fig. 10.8).

Stage 2: From the **Settings** pull-down menu, select **View Attributes** (Fig. 10.9). The **View Attributes** dialogue box appears. Make sure that the check box against **Constructions** is checked (**X** in box). See Fig. 10.10.

Stage 3: Draw the construction lines as shown in Fig. 10.11 on which the three views of the orthographic projection will be based.

Stage 4: In the **Element Attributes** dialogue box, set **Weight** to **1** and **Class** to **Primary**. Add the outlines of the three views as shown in Fig. 10.12.

Stage 5: In the **View Attributes** dialogue box, *left-click* in the **Constructions** check box to turn that facility off. The construction

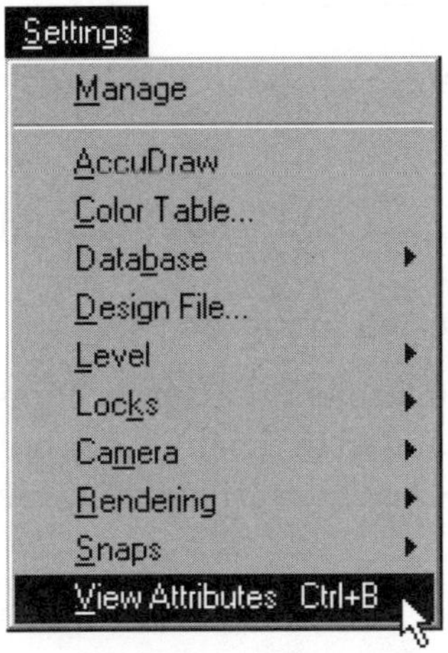

Fig. 10.9 Selecting **View Attributes** from the **Settings** pull-down menu

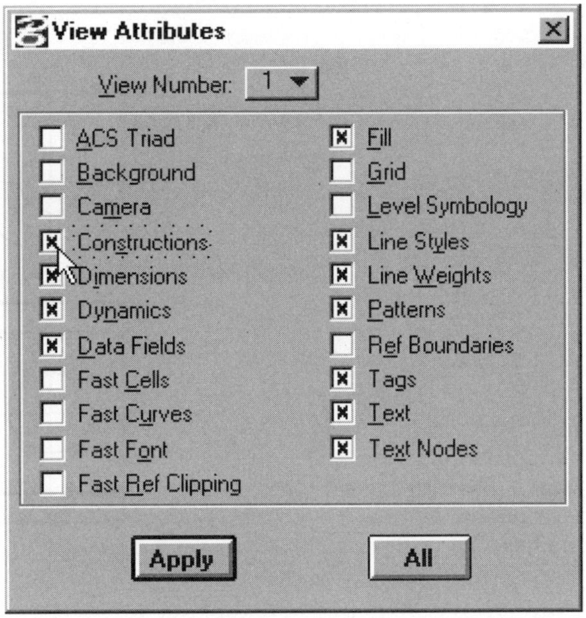

Fig. 10.10 Stage 2. Setting **Constructions** in the **View Attributes** dialogue box

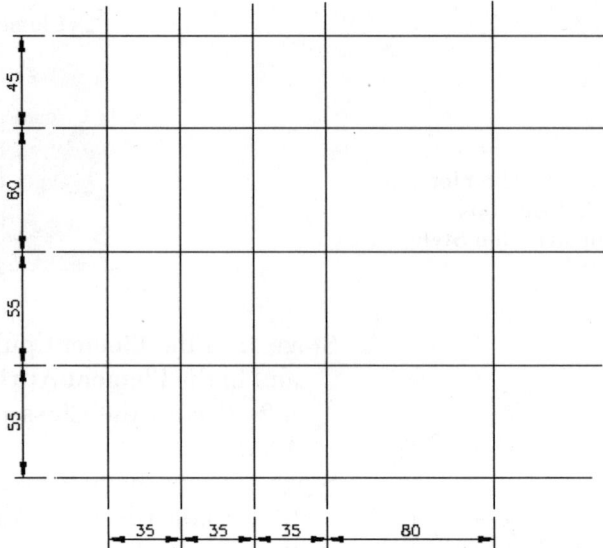

Fig. 10.11 Stage 3. Construction lines forming basis of the orthographic projection

lines disappear from the drawing (Fig. 10.13). Add centre lines and hidden detail lines as shown.

Stage 6: Add a border and title box as indicated in Fig. 10.14.

The three-view third angle orthographic projection is now completed. Dimensions would normally be included in the drawing, but as methods of dimensioning have not as yet been described, they are not added to this example.

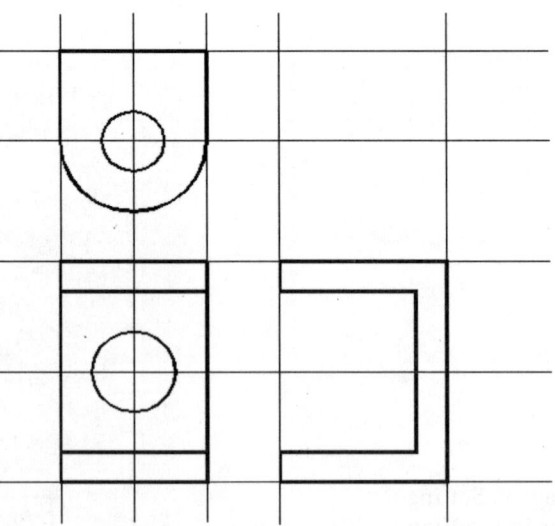

Fig. 10.12 Stage 4. Construct the three views on the construction lines

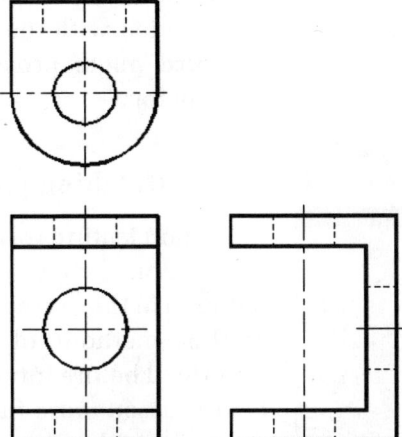

Fig. 10.13 Stage 5. Turn off **Constructions**. The construction lines disappear

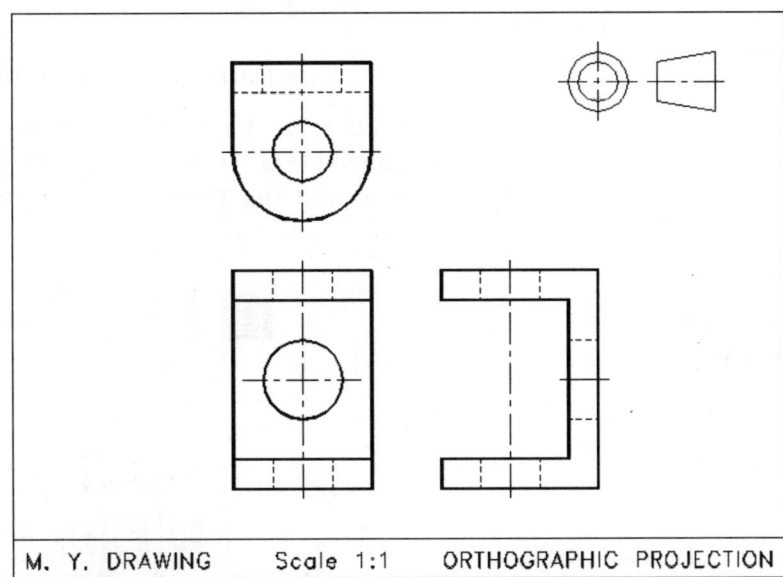

M. Y. DRAWING   Scale 1:1   ORTHOGRAPHIC PROJECTION

Fig. 10.14 Stage 6. The completed drawing

Notes

1. In the example given above, construction lines were used to ensure that views were in line with each other and that overall sizes for the views were easily found. However, some operators may feel that the use of construction lines is unnecessary.

2. When **Constructions** is turned off in the **View Attributes** dialogue box (no **X** in box) construction lines neither show on screen nor print.

3. If **Axis** is set on in the **Locks** sub-menu of the **Settings** pull-down menu (Fig. 10.15), all lines can only be drawn vertically and horizontally.

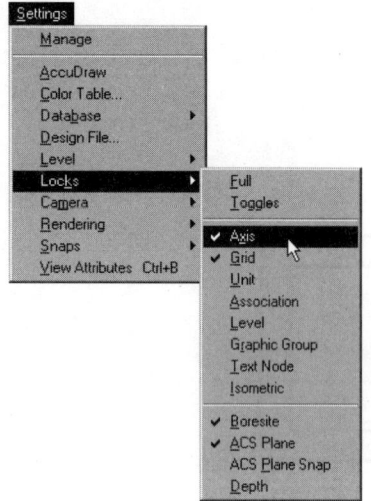

Fig. 10.15 Setting **Axis Lock** in the **Settings** pull-down menu

4. In the example given above the symbol for projection has been included with the drawing. If this is not included, the statement **Third angle projection** should be printed somewhere on the drawing.

Hatching patterns with the Hatch Area tool

Important features of orthographic projections, not so far mentioned, are sectional views. Most sectional views carry hatching lines or patterns in those areas of the view which show cut surfaces. Because of this, methods of adding hatch patterns to views need to be described before introducing sectional views. Pattern hatching will be discussed more fully in Chapter 12. For the time being only the methods of hatching of parts of sectional views in engineering drawings will be described.

The Patterns tool palette

Left-click on the **Hatch Area** tool icon and the **Pattern** flyout is produced (Fig. 10.16). *Drag* the flyout into the drawing area of the screen and the flyout changes to the **Patterns** tool palette (Fig. 10.17).

Fig. 10.16 The flyout from the **Hatch Area** tool icon

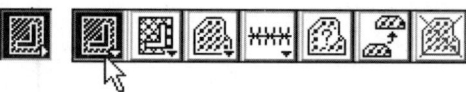

Fig. 10.17 The **Patterns** tool palette

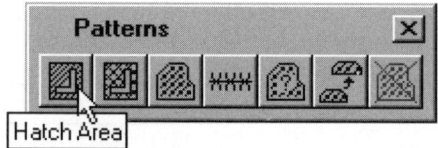

Left-click on the **Hatch Area** icon and the **Hatch Area** Elements Selection box appears (Fig. 10.18). *Left-click* again in the pop-up list to the right of **Method** and the pop-up list shows the available methods of adding patterns to a drawing. Figure 10.19 shows three of the methods available for the hatching of areas with lines 3 units apart and at an angle of 45°.

The three methods shown in Fig. 10.19 are:

Flood (top left-hand drawing): When **Flood** is selected a *left-click* inside any enclosed area fills that area with the selected pattern.

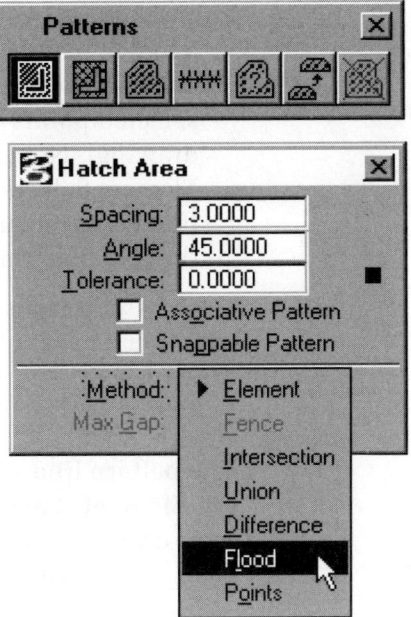

Fig. 10.18 The **Hatch Area**
Elements Selection

Element (top right-hand drawing): When **Element** is chosen, a *left click* on any element, such as a block, circle or ellipse causes the element to fill with the hatch pattern.

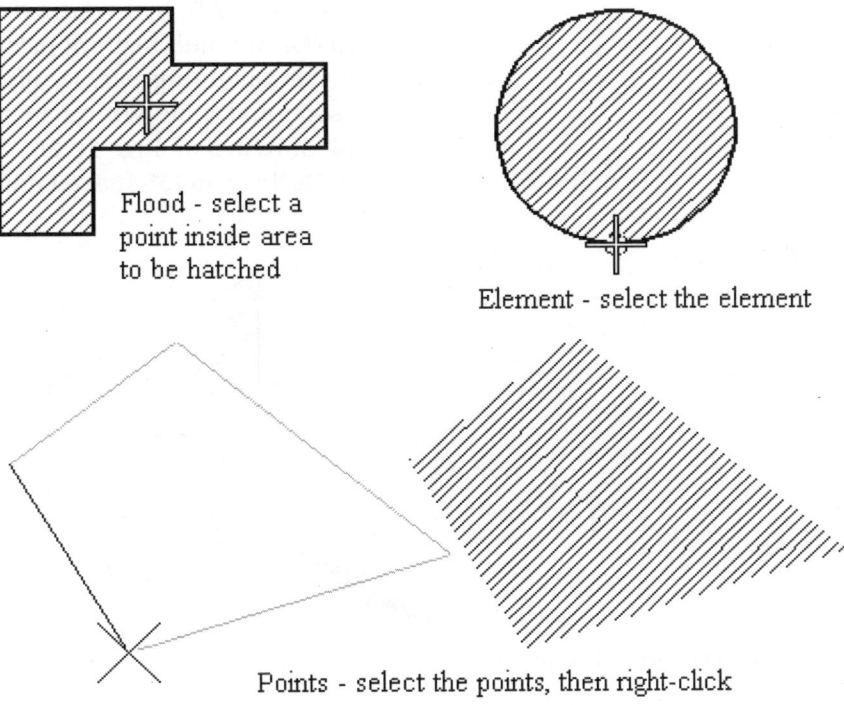

Fig. 10.19 Three methods of
hatching

Points (bottom two drawings): *Left-clicks* at points on the screen cause a line to be rubber-banded between all the points as shown in the left-hand bottom drawing. A *right-click* causes the area within the selected points to fill with the chosen pattern (right-hand bottom drawing). Note that if the **Associative Pattern** check box of the Element Selection box is active (**X** in box), then the lines formed by the points remain on screen. If the check box is empty (no **X**) then the line does not appear with the hatching pattern.

For the purposes of this chapter, these three **Methods** should enable hatching of the majority of sectional views in engineering drawings.

Note

The pattern line weight is dependant upon the setting of **Weight** in the **Element Attribute** box. The three hatch patterns of Fig. 10.19 were drawn with the line weight set at 0, although the outlines have been drawn with the line weight set to 1.

Sectional views

Imagine the object being cut by a plane – horizontal, vertical or at any angle – cutting through the object being drawn. An example is shown in Fig. 10.20 in which the left-hand drawing shows the object has been cut centrally by a vertical plane. When viewed from the direction as shown and the front part of the object discarded, the cut surface of the remaining part is regarded as a sectional view. The resulting sectional view within its vertical plane is shown in the right-hand drawing of Fig. 10.20. Note that all cut surfaces are hatched with lines at 45° spaced equally across the cut surface.

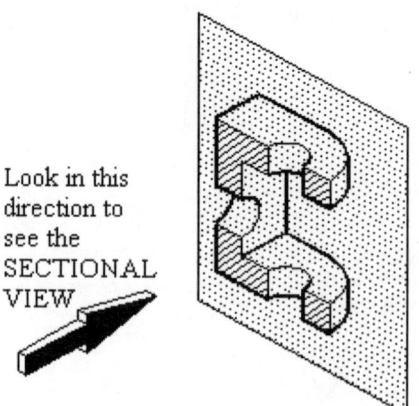

Look in this direction to see the SECTIONAL VIEW

Fig. 10.20 The theory behind sectional views

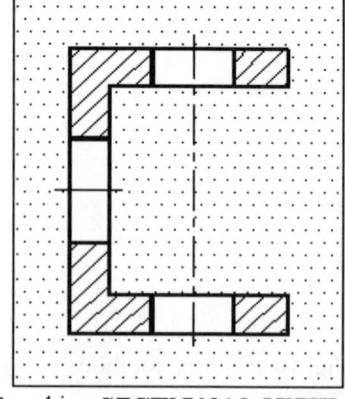

Resulting SECTIONAL VIEW

General principles

Figure 10.21 shows the general principles when hatching an engineering drawing. The given illustration is a two-view third angle orthographic projection, one of the views being a sectional view on the cutting plane A–A. Note the following:

The cutting plane A–A: This is a centre line ending in thick lines against which arrows point in the direction of viewing.

The hatching: Normally this consists of lines at angles of 45° or 315°, at a spacing of 3 (or 4). Small areas may occasionally have spacing of 2.

Webs, spindles, shafts, nuts, bolts, washers, etc., are shown as outside views. They are not hatched.

Section label: The sectional view carries a label A–A, indicating it is the result of the section cut made along the section line A–A.

Features beyond the cutting plane are included in the sectional view.

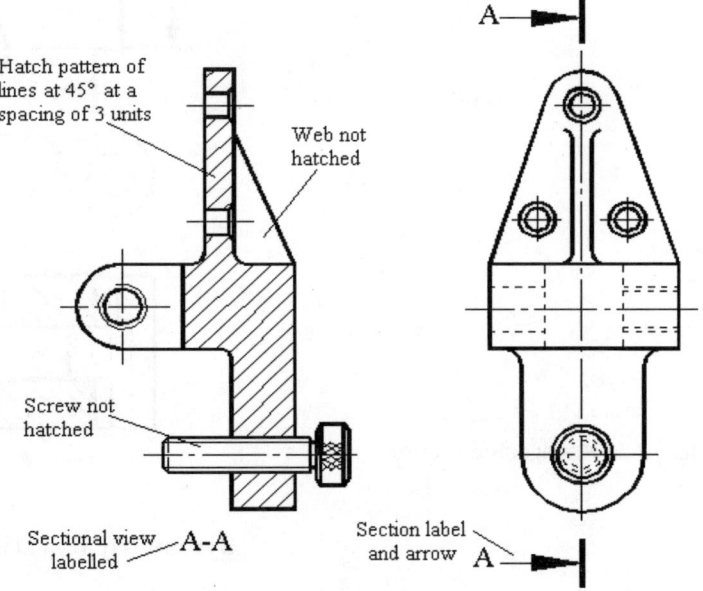

Fig. 10.21 The general principles when drawing sectional views

Half sections

In a view which is symmetrical around a centre line, it is sometimes possible to draw a half section instead of a full section to obtain full details about the shape of the item. Figure 10.22 shows a half section.

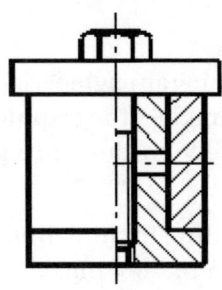

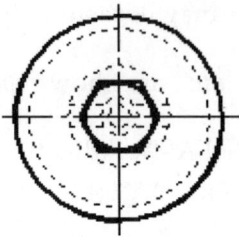

Fig. 10.22 A half section

Note

1. *No hidden detail*: There is no need for hidden detail in a half section, because it is assumed that the part not sectioned is symmetrical with the part which is.
2. *No need for section plane line*: It is obvious where the plane should be.

Fig. 10.22 shows another common feature of sectional view hatching. Adjacent touching areas within a section are hatched at opposite angles.

Section on staggered section plane

When it is convenient to show a sectional view in two (or more) parallel section planes, it may be possible to draw a staggered sectional view as illustrated in Fig. 10.23. Note that the change of direction in the section plane line has thick lines between its two parts.

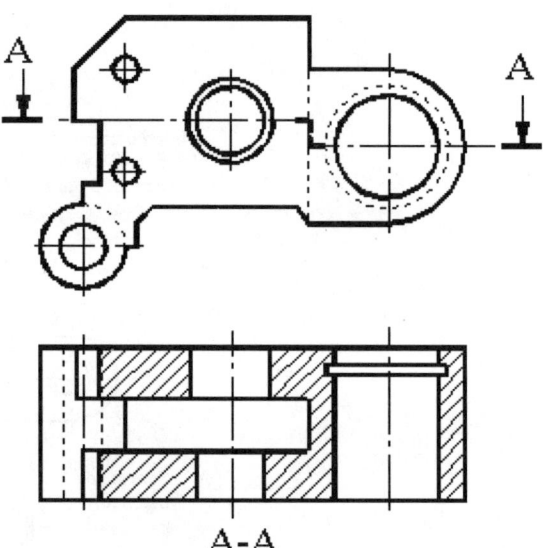

Fig. 10.23 A staggered section

A-A

Symmetrical section

Figure 10.24 shows a sectional view of a part which is symmetrical around its central axis. Note the thick parallel lines indicating the lines of symmetry.

Types of lines in engineering drawing

The reader will have seen that a number of different types of lines are used in technical drawings, particularly in engineering drawings.

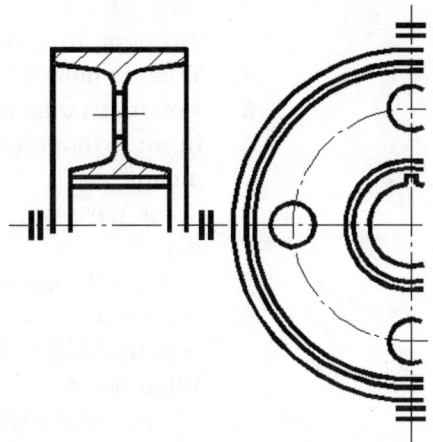

Fig. 10.24 a symmetrical
section

Those types of lines in most common use in engineering drawings
are illustrated in Fig. 10.25.

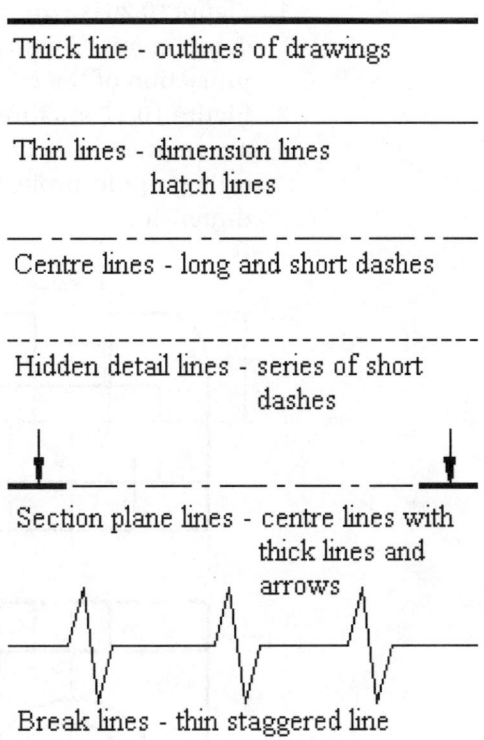

Fig. 10.25 Types of lines used
in engineering drawings

Questions

1. Why is the name *orthographic* given to this form of projection?
2. Can you describe the differences between first angle orthographic
   projection and third angle orthographic projection?

3. Why should **Lock Axis** be a useful tool when constructing orthographic projections?
4. What is meant by the term *sectional view*?
5. You may come across the term *elevation* when referring to views in an orthographic projection. Can you explain what the term means?
6. Some parts of sectional views are not normally hatched. Which parts?
7. What is the advantage of a half section over a full sectional view?
8. Why is it important that users of CAD understand the methods of constructing orthographic projections?
9. What is a *centre line*?
10. What is the difference between an outline and a line used for dimensions?

Exercises

1. Figure 10.26 is a first angle orthographic projection of an engineering component. Construct a three-view third angle orthographic projection of the component. Do not include any dimensions.
2. Figure 10.27 is a three-view third angle orthographic projection of an engineering component. Construct a three-view first angle orthographic projection of the component. Do not include any dimensions.

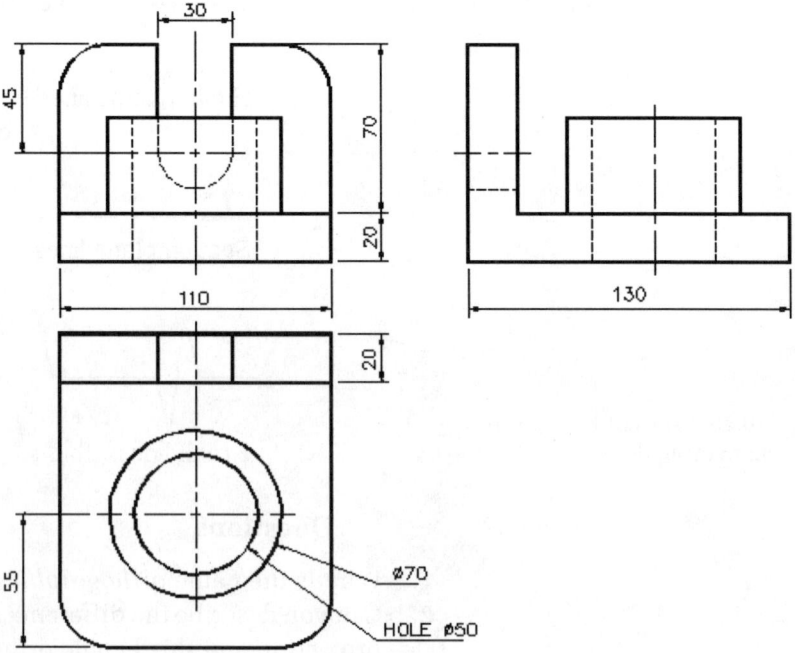

Fig. 10.26 Exercise 1

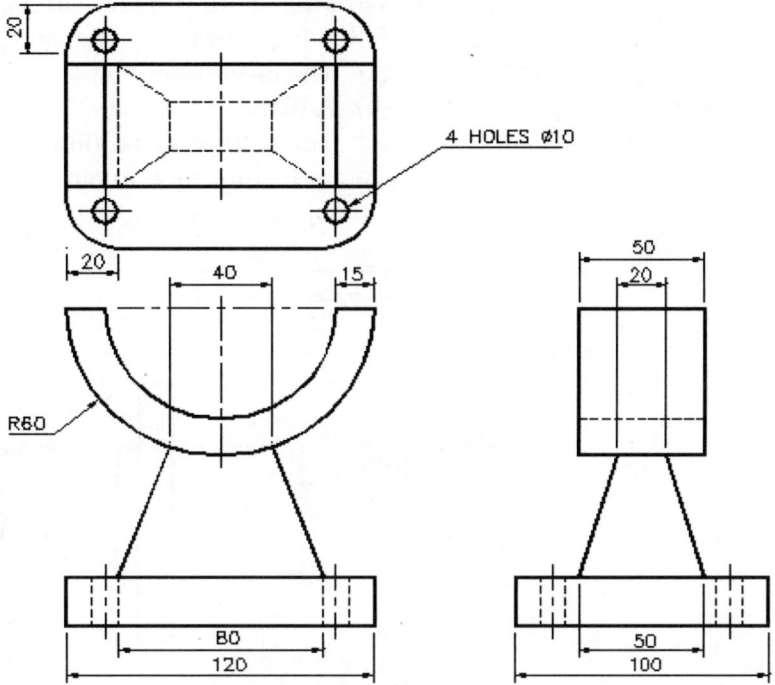

Fig. 10.27 Exercise 2

3. Working in first angle orthographic projection, construct the following views of the component shown in Fig. 10.28: A front view as given, a plan as given, the sectional end view A–A. Do not include dimensions in your drawing.

THIRD ANGLE PROJECTION

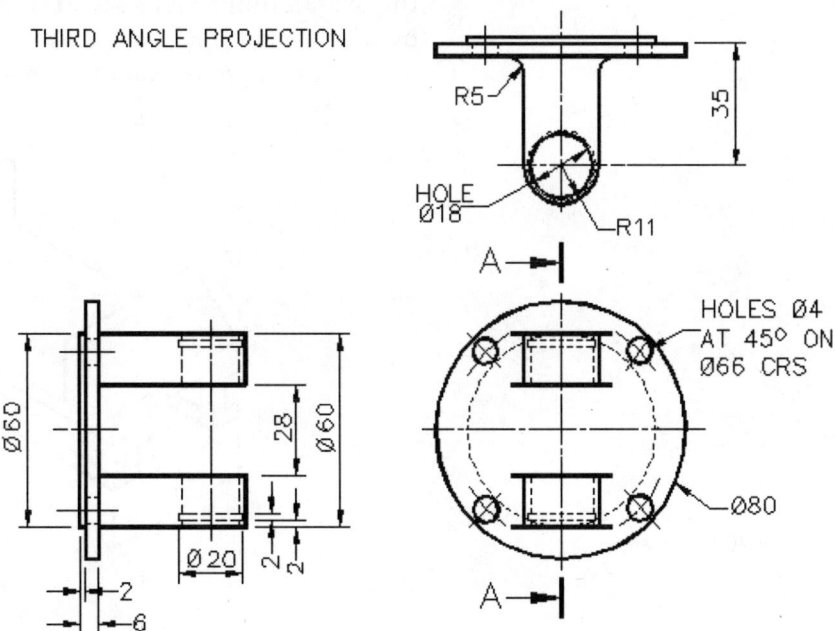

Fig. 10.28 Exercise 3

4. Working in first angle orthographic projection, construct the following views of the flange shown in Fig. 10.29:
   (a) The given front view.
   (b) A plan.
   (c) The sectional end view B–B.
   Do not include any dimensions with your drawing, but include a suitable border and title block.

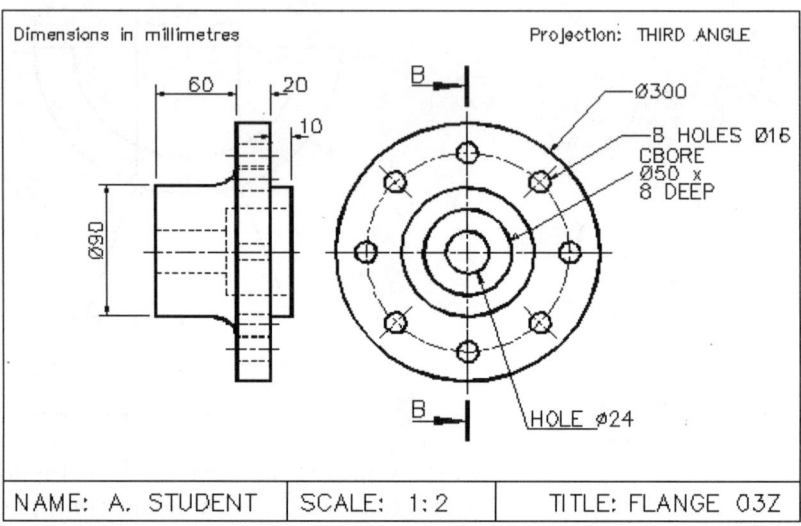

Fig. 10.29 Exercise 4

5. Figure 10.30 is an isometric drawing of a slide. Basing the sizes on the overall dimensions given with the drawing and making your own judgement about other sizes, construct a three-view first angle orthographic projection of the slide.

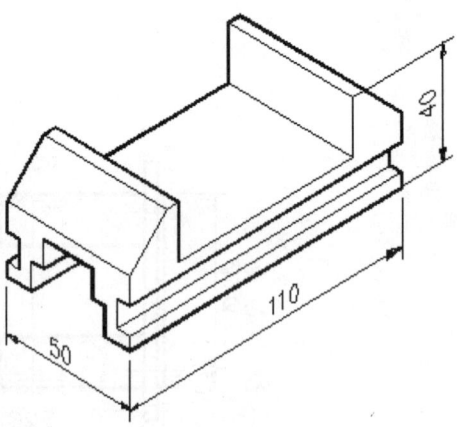

Fig. 10.30 Exercise 5

6. Construct a third angle orthographic projection drawing of the component shown in Fig. 10.31. Use your own judgement about sizes not shown in the given drawing.

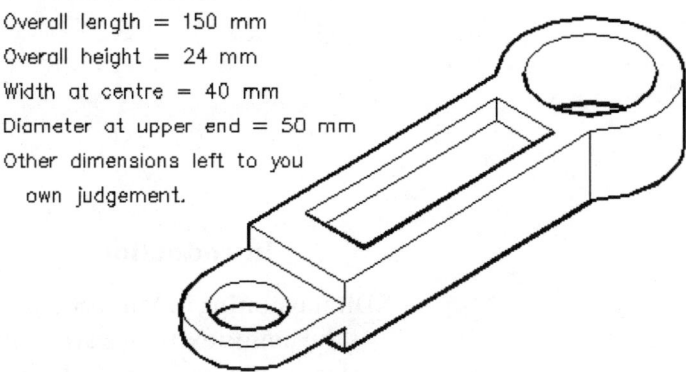

Overall length = 150 mm
Overall height = 24 mm
Width at centre = 40 mm
Diameter at upper end = 50 mm
Other dimensions left to you
  own judgement.

Fig. 10.31 Exercise 6

7. Construct a three-view third angle orthographic projection of the component given in the drawing Fig. 10.32. Do not include any dimensions. One of your views should be a sectional view.

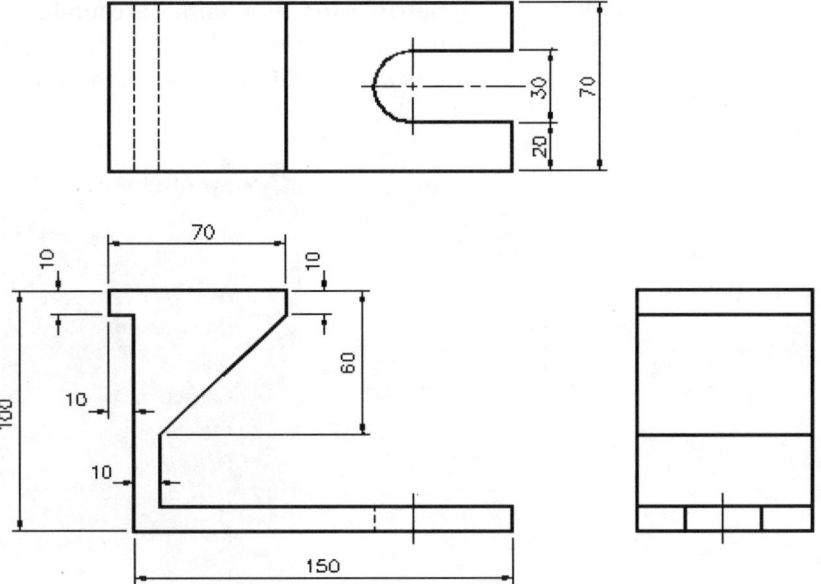

Fig. 10.32 Exercise 7

CHAPTER 11

Dimensioning

Introduction

Dimensioning in MicroStation 95 can be a complex business. Because of the complexity, we are only concerned here in this book with the most common forms of including dimensions in a mechanical engineering drawing. More complex forms of dimensioning are available as you become more proficient in the use of MicroStation 95.

Dimension settings

Settings for dimensions are made in the **Dimension Settings** dialogue box, but before using that dialogue box, first ensure that the check box against **Dimensions** in the **View Attributes** dialogue box is set on

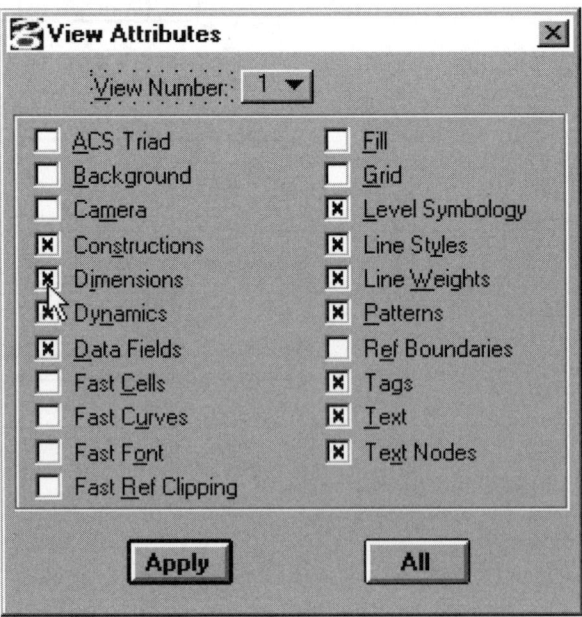

Fig. 11.1 Check that the **Dimensions** and **Level Symbology** check boxes are set on

(**X** in check box). Because we will also be using levels and dimensions that are to be placed on level 4, the check box against **Level Symbology** should also be on. See Fig. 11.1. A *left-click* on the **Apply** button ensures the attributes are applied to the current design file.

View Attributes is called to screen by selecting **View Attributes** from the **Settings** pull-down menu, or with the shortcut **Ctrl+B**.

The **Dimension Settings** dialogue box is called to screen by selecting **Dimensions** from the **Element** pull-down menu. When making settings in this dialogue box, it must be remembered that some of the sizes are dependent upon the height of the **Text** setting. In our settings, text is to be set at a height of 4, so other settings such as arrow heads (terminators) are set as a decimal of that figure.

Not all of the settings in the dialogue box will be relevant to the methods of dimensioning described in the following pages. We will only be concerned with settings for **Dimension Lines**, **Extension Lines**, **Terminators** (arrows, etc.), **Text** and **Units**.

Dimension Lines

Figure 11.2 shows the settings for dimension lines. *Left-click* on **Dimension Lines** in the dialogue box. The check box against **Level** should be on (**X** in check box). The level number (**4**) should be entered in the level number box. **Color** is set at **1** (blue), line **Style** and line **Weight** are both set at **0**.

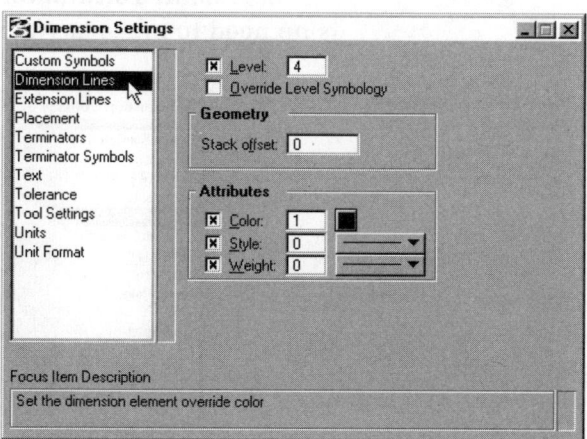

Fig. 11.2 The **Dimension Lines** settings in **Dimension Settings**

Extension Lines

Left-click on **Extension Lines** in the dialogue box and make settings as shown in Fig. 11.3. Note that the **Offset** and **Extension** figures are 0.75, which as a decimal of the text height of 4 mm, makes these two

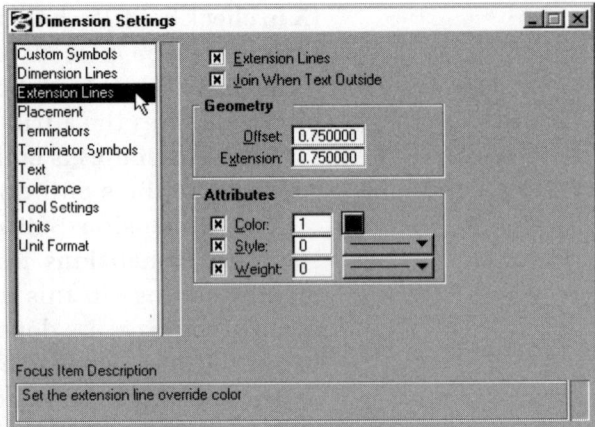

Fig. 11.3 The **Extension Lines** settings in **Dimension Settings**

settings each 3 mm. **Color** is again **1** (blue) and line **Style** and line **Weight** are both set to **0**.

Terminators

Setting for the arrow heads are shown in Fig. 11.4. *Left-click* on **Terminators** in the dialogue box and the settings for arrow heads (etc.) appear. In our case, the length of the arrow head is based upon the text height, so arrow head length at 1.0 is 4 mm long with a width of 2 mm. Again **Color**, **Style** and **Weight** are set to **1**, **0** and **0** respectively.

The default **Terminator Symbols** are used in our work, so there is no need to make any change in the settings in this case.

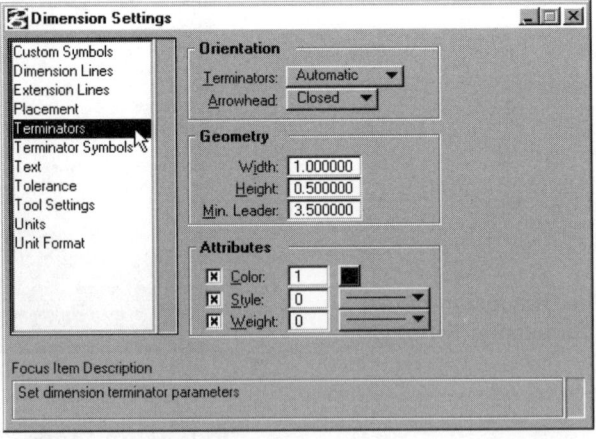

Fig. 11.4 The **Terminators** settings in **Dimension Settings**

Text

The **Text** settings in the dialogue box are shown in Fig. 11.5. *Left-click* on **Text** and make settings as shown: **Orientation – Above**;

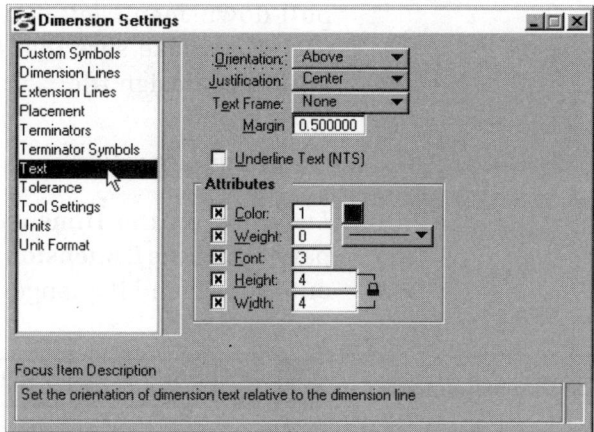

Fig. 11.5 The **Text** settings in
Dimension Settings

Justification – Center; Text Frame – None. Color and **Weight** as
before. The **Font** is **3** (Engineering font) with a **Height** and **Width** of
4.

We are not dealing with **Tolerance** for the time being, so will
make no settings for this form of dimensioning. See later – page 173.
Neither will we be making settings for **Tool Settings**.

Units

Units are set as indicated in Fig. 11.6. The **Format** is **Mechanical**.
The units are **Metric** with an **Accuracy** of **0** (no decimal points after
the dimension figures). The **Scale Factor** is **1**, but if working to other
scales this may need to be changed. No other settings are made for
units.

This completes our settings for dimensions in the **Dimension
Settings** dialogue box. *Left-click* on the **X** at the top right-hand corner
of the box to release the dialogue box from screen and in the **File**

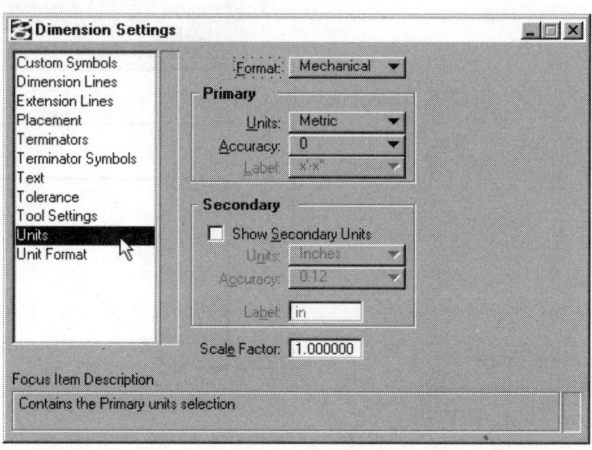

Fig. 11.6 The **Units** settings in
Dimension Settings

pull-down menu *left-click* on **Save Settings,** or use the shortcut **Ctrl+F** to make sure that the settings just made are saved to your prototype design file.

The Dimension tool palette

Left-click on the **Dimension Element** tool icon in the **Main** tool palette and the **Dimension** flyout appears (Fig. 11.7). *Drag* the flyout onto screen and it changes to the **Dimension** tool palette (Fig. 11.8).

Fig. 11.7 The **Dimension** tool flyout

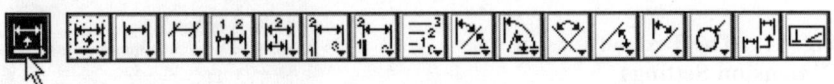

Fig. 11.8 The **Dimension** tool palette

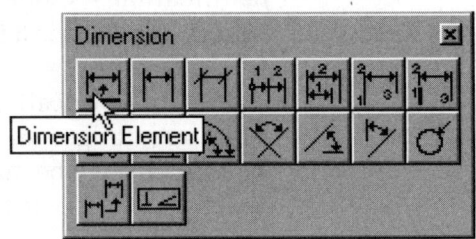

The Dimension Element tool

When the **Dimension Element** tool is selected, its Element Selection box appears, in which a *left-click* on the **Alignment** button, causes

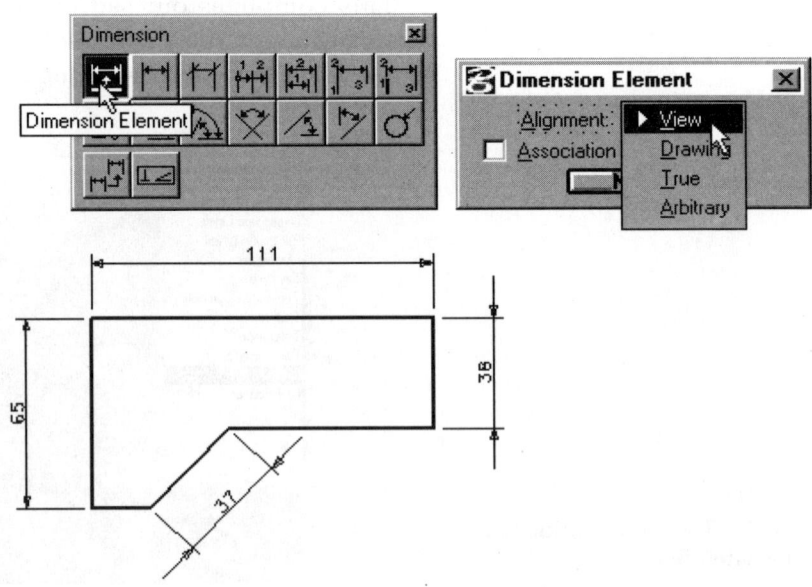

Fig. 11.9 Placing **True** alignment dimensions with the **Dimension Element** tool

a pop-up list to appear allowing a choice from four forms of alignment – **View**, **Drawing**, **True** and **Arbitrary**. Figure 11.9 shows the dimensions resulting from **True** alignment. The dimensions were placed on the drawing by:

1. *Left-click* on the element to be dimensioned. The dimension appears.
2. *Drag* dimension to its required position and *left-click*. The dimension is placed. The result is shown in Fig. 11.9.

Figure 11.10 shows the dimensions resulting from the **View** alignment. The dimensions become aligned with the view rather than with the element.

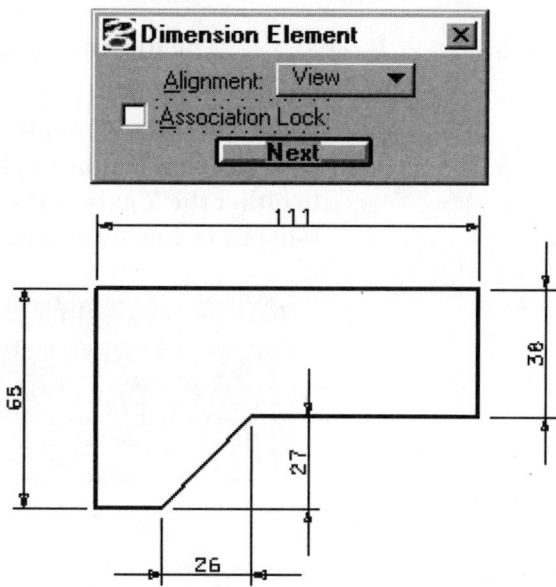

Fig. 11.10 Placing **View** alignment dimensions with the **Dimension Element** tool

The Dimension Radial tool

When this tool is selected, the **Dimension Radial** Element Selection box allows for several **Modes** as shown in Fig. 11.11. The five modes are shown in the dimensioning of a circle in Fig. 11.11. The method of placing the dimension consists of:

1. *Select* the tool **Dimension Radial**. In the Element Selection box, set the **Mode**.
2. *Left-click* on the circle to be dimensioned and *drag* the dimension to its required position under mouse control.

Arcs are dimensioned in a similar manner with this tool.

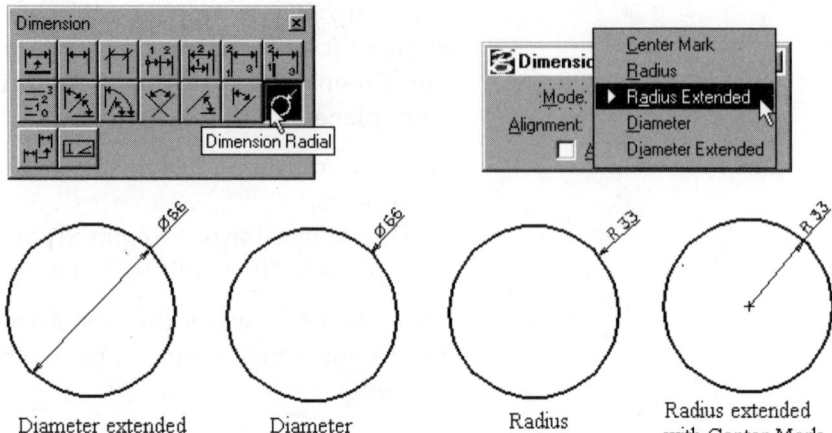

Fig. 11.11 Examples of using the **Dimension Radial** tool

The dimensioning of angles

Figure 11.12 shows three of the several methods of dimensioning angles. In these examples the actual angle is shown as dimensioned with the **Dimension Angle Between** tool and the angle a line makes to either the **X** axis or the **Y** axis with the appropriate dimensioning tools as indicated in Fig. 11.12.

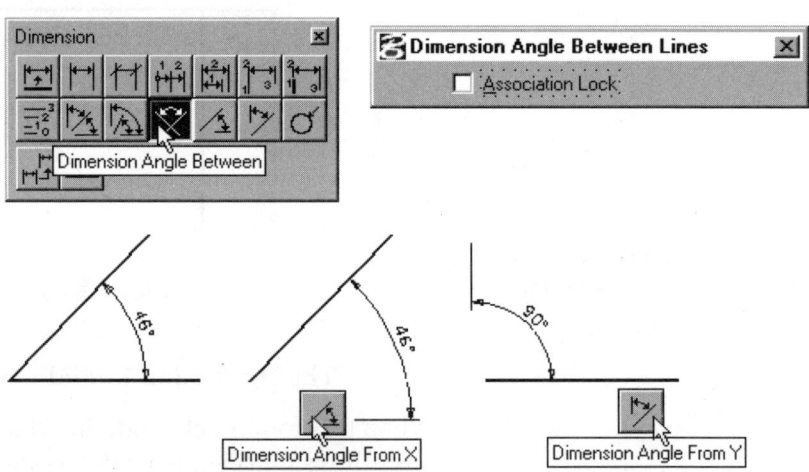

Fig. 11.12 Examples of methods of dimensioning angles

The Dimension Ordinates tool

Our final example from the many methods of adding dimensions to drawings shows the use of this tool (Fig. 9.13). Dimensions are taken from a datum both vertically and horizontally. When using the tool, care must be taken to follow the prompts as they appear in the Status Bar one after the other.

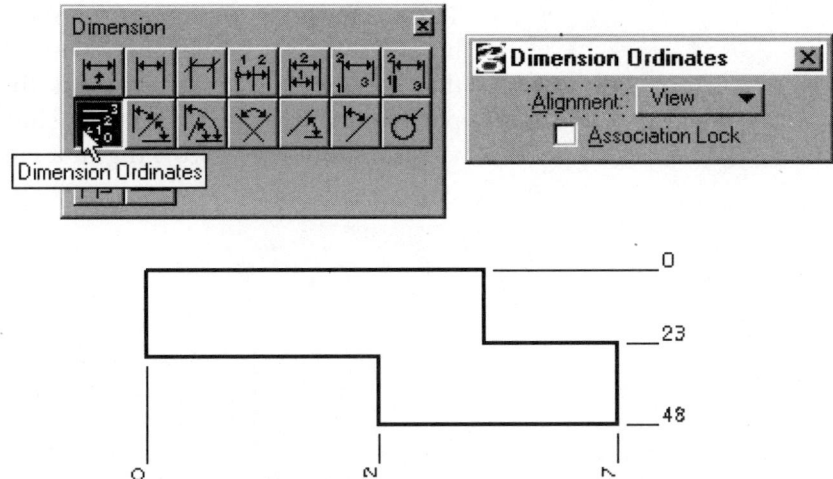

Fig. 11.13 An example of the use of the **Dimension Ordinates** tool

Dimension tolerances

To add tolerances to dimensions, recall the **Dimension Settings** dialogue box, and *left-click* on **Tolerance**. Figure 11.14 shows the tolerance settings for the dimensioned drawing in Fig. 11.15. Note the **Tolerance** settings in the dialogue box:

Type	Plus/Minus
Upper	tolerance 0.05
Lower	tolerance 0
Text Size	0.6 of **Text** height

Also note:

Tolerance Generation: set on (**X** in check box)
2 places of decimals in tolerance: thus **Units** must be amended to this.

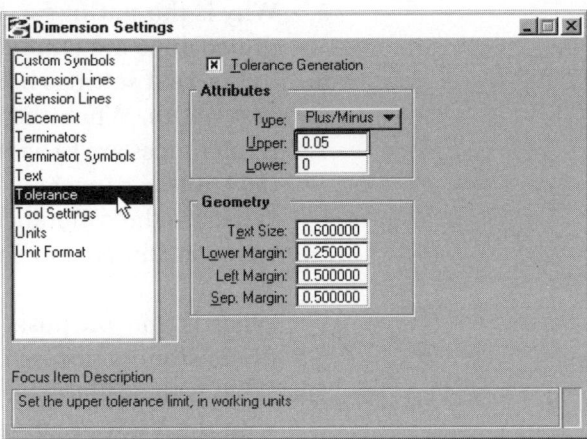

Fig. 11.14 Setting **Tolerance** settings in the **Dimension Settings** dialogue box

The example in Fig. 11.15 contains dimension figures of 6 mm height, which is higher than would normally be acceptable. This is due to wishing to ensure that the tolerances are clear in this particular illustration. A dimension text height of 4 mm is usually very suitable when working in a metric A3 size screen.

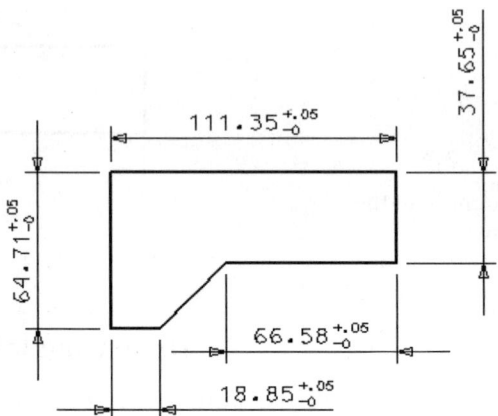

Fig. 11.15 An example of an outline in which dimensions include tolerances

Questions

1. Why are the **Terminators** in the examples given above set to a **Width** of only 0.5?
2. If you do not wish dimensions to be placed on a different level to that which holds outlines, how do you alter the settings to allow for this?
3. Look at settings for **Custom Symbols** in the **Dimension Settings** dialogue box. Why is it that we have ignored this setting in this book?
4. What is a **Terminator** with respect to the settings for dimensions?
5. Why is the setting for **Text Height** so important when settings for dimensions are entered?
6. In the **Text** settings box, a lock icon will be seen between **Height** and **Width**. What is its function?
7. If tolerances are to be included in a drawing, how does this affect the **Units** settings?
8. What are the differences between including angular dimensions between **Dimension Angle Between** and **Dimension Angle From X**?
9. What is the purpose of the **Mode** setting **Center Mark** when dimensioning circles or arcs?
10. What is the difference between adding a dimension to a drawing with the **View** alignment compared with the **True** alignment?

Exercises

Exercises set in previous chapters were assumed as being worked without adding dimensions. Recall some of the drawing answers and now add the dimensions.

1. Figure 11.16 is an unhatched sectional view through a small lathe faceplate. Construct the given view to the sizes given. Add hatching and fully dimension the view.

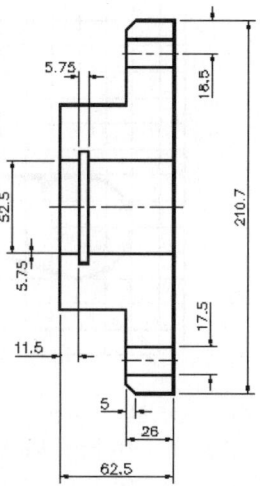

Fig. 11.16 Exercise 1

2. Figure 11.17 is a simple outline based on a grid of 10 mm squares. Counting the numbers of squares indicates the sizes of each part of the outline. Construct the outline twice. On the first outline add dimensions using the **Dimension Element** tool. On your second outline add dimensions taken from ordinates.

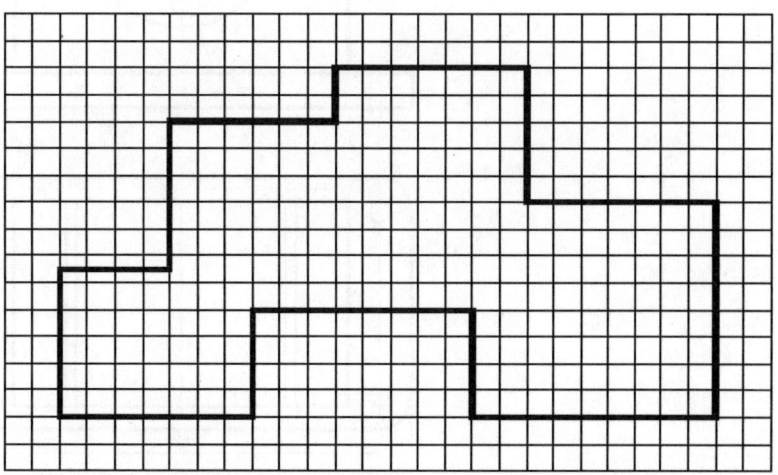

Fig. 11.17 Exercise 2

3. Construct the three outlines of Fig. 11.18 and fully dimension each one.

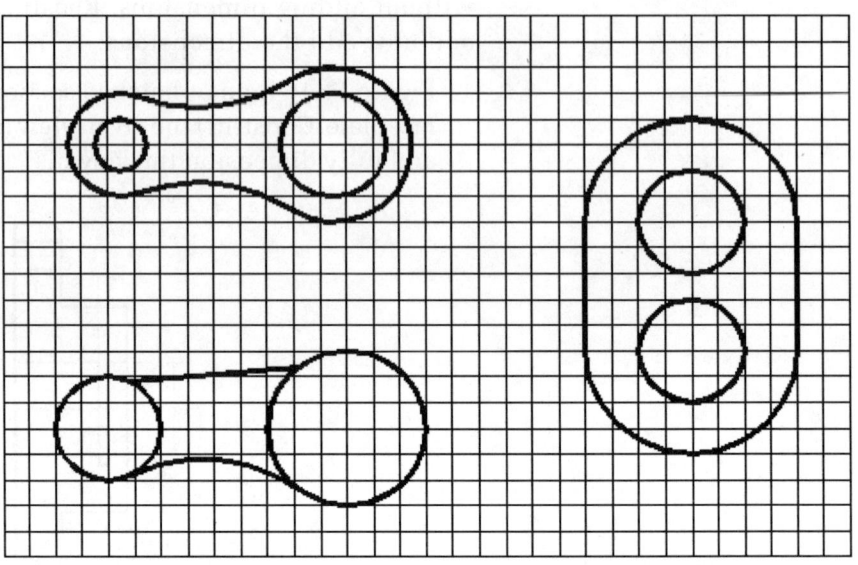

Fig. 11.18 Exercise 3

4. Construct the three-view first angle orthographic projection given in Fig. 11.19. Work in either first or third angle as wished. In place of the given dimensions, add dimensions with upper and lower tolerances of 0.05 mm.

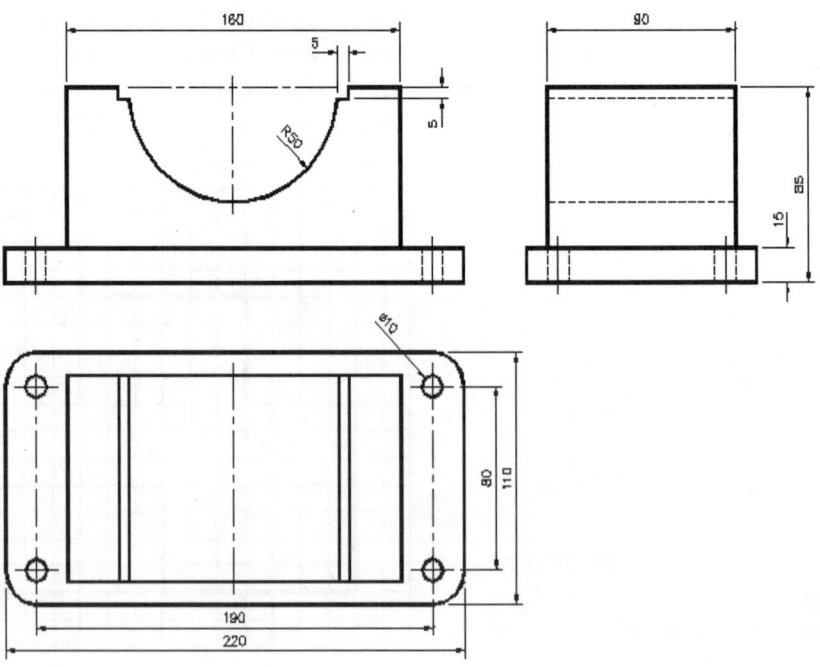

Fig. 11.19 Exercise 4

CHAPTER 12

The Pattern tools

Introduction

Some details about the use of tools in the **Pattern** tool palette were dealt with to a limited extent in Chapter 10. Further details are given in this chapter.

Figure 12.1 shows the flyout resulting from a *left-click* on the **Hatch Area** tool icon and Fig. 12.2 shows all the tool tips of the tools in the **Patterns** tool palette to which **Hatch Area** belongs.

Fig. 12.1 The flyout resulting for a *left-click* on the **Hatch Area** tool icon

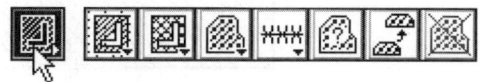

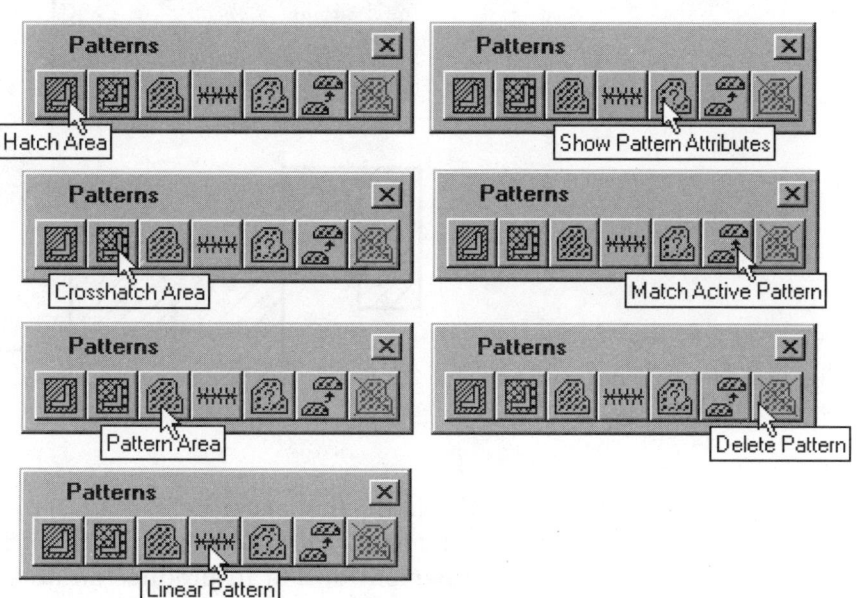

Fig. 12.2 The tool tips of the tool icons in the **Patterns** tool palette

The tools in the Patterns tool palette

The Hatch Area tool

The **Hatch Area** tool is for placing hatch lines within parts of a drawing at spacings and angles as determined by numbers *keyed-in* to the **Hatch Area** Element Selection box. A *left-click* on the tool icon and the Element Selection box appears. *Enter* relevant numbers in the **Spacing** and **Angle** boxes and set the **Method** by choosing an option from the pop-up list which appears with a *left-click* on the button to the right of the word **Method**. Two illustrations – Figs 12.3 and 12.4 – show the results of area hatching with the two options, **Element** and **Flood**.

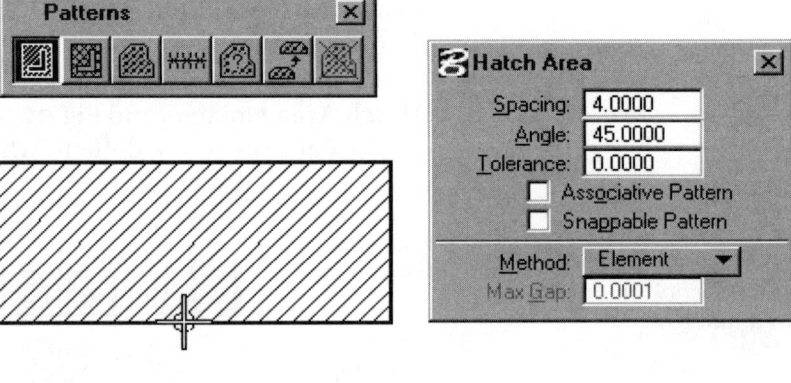

Fig. 12.3 Area hatching within an **Element**

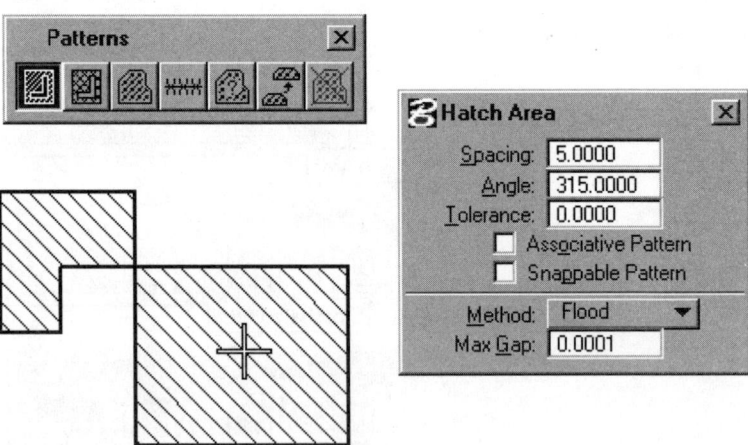

Fig. 12.4 Area hatching with the option **Flood**

In the first example (Fig. 12.3) the area being hatched must be an element. A graphic group will not function as an element for the **Element** option to produce an area which will be hatched, but a complex shape will. Just *left-click* somewhere on the element outline. The element outline ghosts. A second *left-click* and the area will be hatched. A third *left-click* confirms the hatching.

In the second example (Fig. 12.4) the area being flooded with hatch lines must be totally enclosed. The smallest gap within the outline will result in a statement in the error field – **No enclosing region found**. To flood the area with hatch lines *left-click* anywhere within the boundary. The boundary outline ghosts. A second *left-click* and the area is flooded with hatch lines.

There are other options within the **Hatch Area Method**. The method which will be used most frequently will probably be **Flood**. This is because so many sectional views which require the addition of hatch lines will be composed of areas surrounded with bounding elements. Other **Method**s have already been briefly described in Chapter 10.

Note

The **Weight** of hatch lines placed with the aid of the **Hatch Area** and the **Crosshatch Area** tools is dependent upon the setting of the line **Weight** from the **Element Attributes** dialogue box or from the pop-up list appearing with a *left-click* on the **Active Line Weight** button in the Status Bar. In the two examples given above, the line weight for the hatch lines was set at **0**, while the outlines of the areas being hatched were drawn with a line weight of **1**.

The Crosshatch Area tool

The same **Method** options are available when the **Crosshatch Area** tool is used. Figure 12.5 shows an example in which the area between two intersecting circles is flooded with cross hatching with lines at 5 units apart and at an angle of 0°. Hatch lines are of weight **0**.

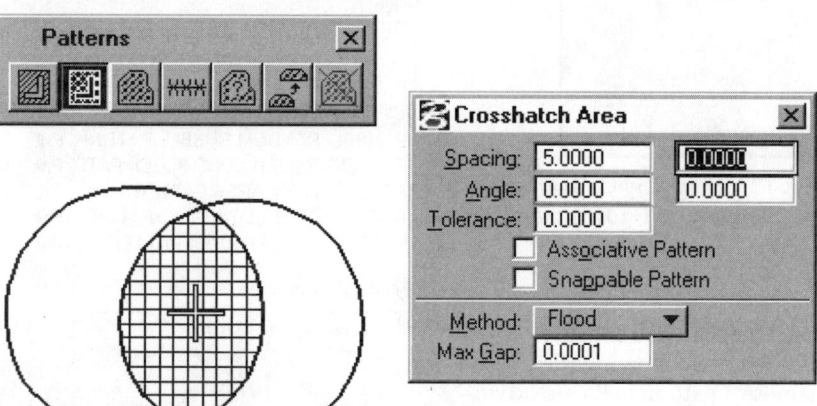

Fig. 12.5 An area **Flooded** with cross hatching

Figure 12.6 shows another example in which the one set of hatch lines are 5 units apart at an angle of 0°, while the second set of lines is 8 units apart at an angle of 45°. Note the settings made in the **Spacing** and **Angle** boxes of the **Crosshatch Area** Element Selection box for this example. Again, the hatch lines are of weight **0**.

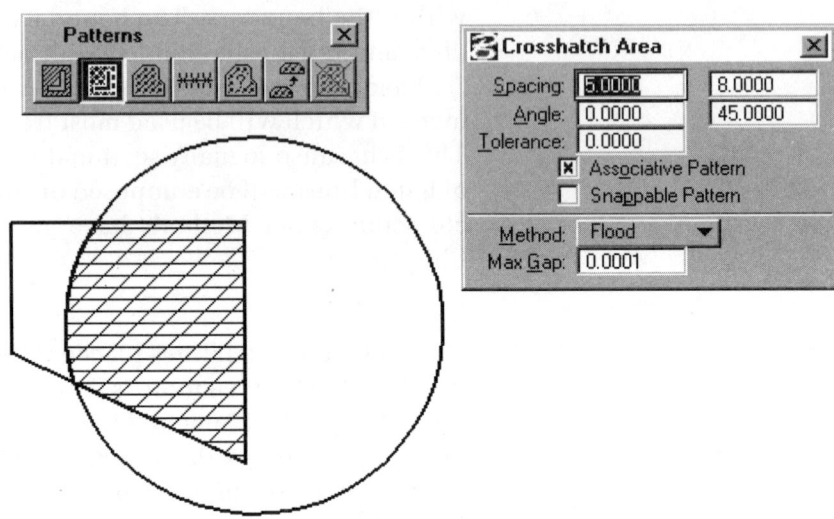

Fig. 12.6 Second example of **Crosshatch Area** hatching

The Pattern Area tool

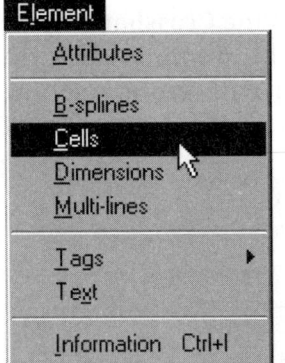

Fig. 12.7 Selecting **Cells** from the **Element** pull-down menu

Fig. 12.8 The **Cell Library** dialogue box showing the names of pattern cells already loaded

When an area is to be filled with a pattern, the name of the pattern must first be *entered* in the **Pattern Cell** box of the **Pattern Area**

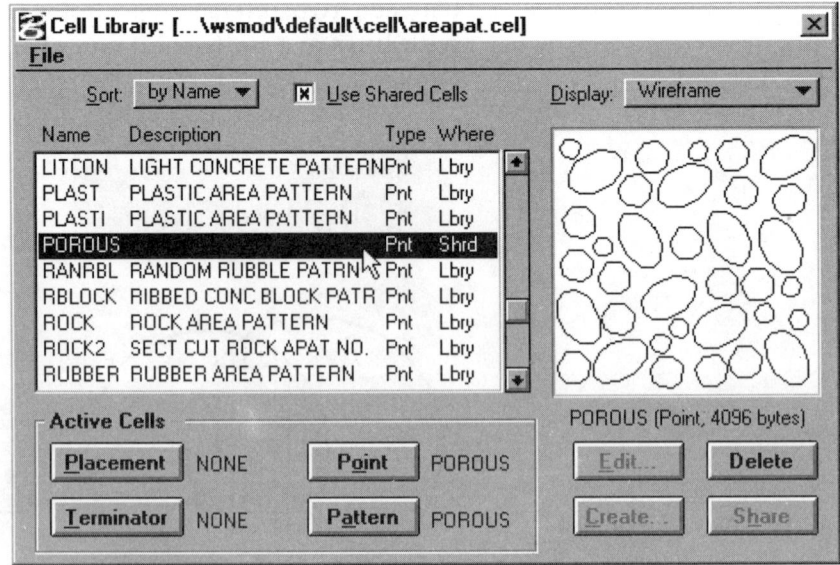

Element Selection box. To discover the name of a pattern cell, *left-click* on **Cells** in the **Element** pull-down menu (Fig. 12.7) and the **Cell Library** dialogue box showing the names of cells already loaded into the system will show on screen (Fig. 12.8). A *left-click* on any name in the list box brings its pattern into the window to the right of the list. This allows the operator to select the pattern required as well as its name.

An example of the use of the **Pattern Area** tool is given in Fig. 12.9, in which the name of the pattern cell **POROUS** has been *entered* in the **Pattern Cell** box of the **Pattern Area** Element Selection box and a **Scale** of **20** has also been *entered* against the **Scale** box. The area within the four lines of Fig. 12.9 has been **Flood** pattern hatched with the **POROUS** cell pattern.

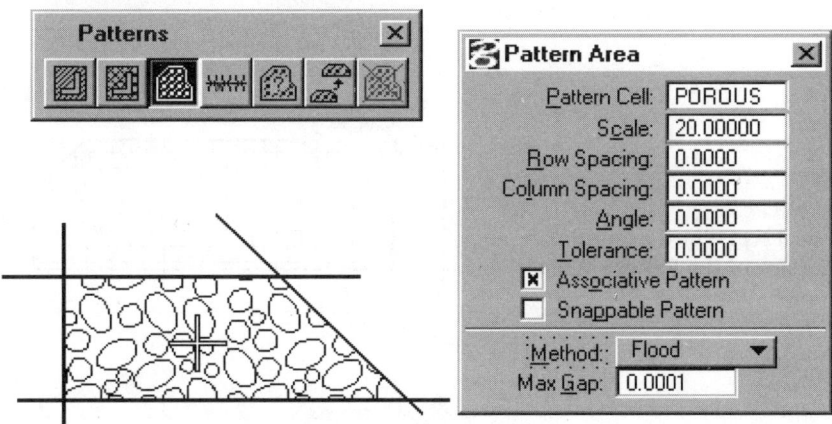

Fig. 12.9 First example of the use of the **Pattern Area** tool

A second example of the use of the tool **Pattern Area** is given in Fig. 12.10. In this example the **Method** selected from the pop-up list was **Difference**. Note that with this option the two elements in the drawing had to be selected to place the pattern in the required area between the two outlines. The pattern in this example, chosen from the **Cell Library** dialogue box, was **STARS**.

A third example of the use of this tool is given in Fig. 12.11, in which the chosen **Method** has been **Intersection**. Again, both elements in the drawing have been selected in order that the required area was hatched with the pattern. In this third example, this was the pattern cell **CMBOND**.

The Linear Pattern tool

Only a single example of the use of this tool is given – Fig. 12.12, in which an arc is patterned with the pattern cell **HBONE** with the

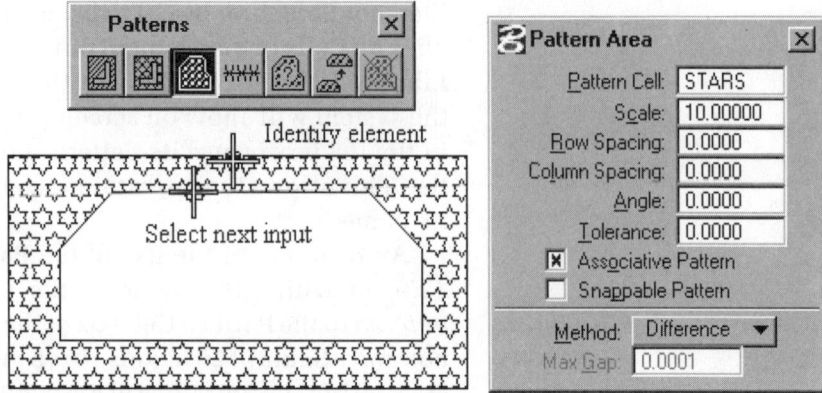

Fig. 12.10 Second example of the use of the **Pattern Area** tool

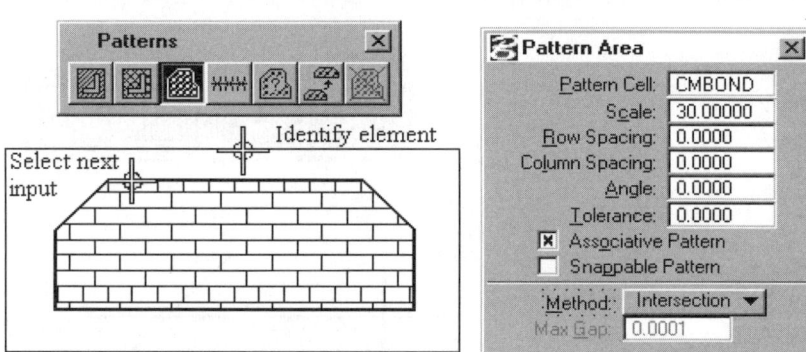

Fig. 12.11 Third example of the use of the **Pattern Area** tool

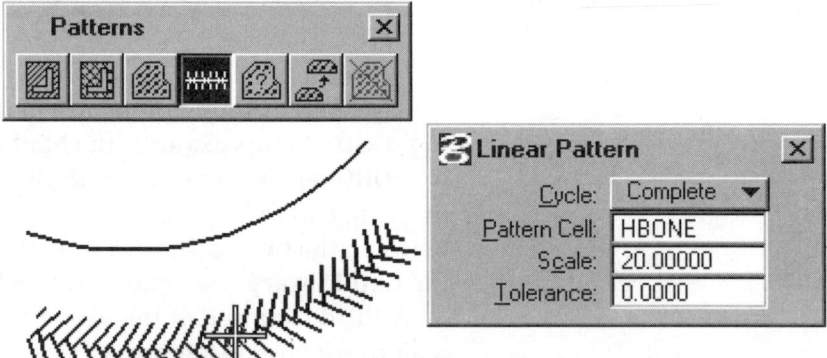

Fig. 12.12 An example of the use of the **Linear Pattern** tool

Complete method of **Cycle** chosen from the pop-up list which appears when the **Cycle** button is selected. When the **Cycle** has been selected and the name of the **Pattern Cell** has been *entered*, all that is required is a *left-click* on the element along which the **Linear Pattern** is to be placed.

Show Pattern Attributes tool

No examples are given, but when a pattern is selected, its name, scale and angle appear in the **Message** field of the **Command Window**.

The Match Active Pattern tool

If a pattern is placed within an area or on a line and the **Match Active Pattern** tool is selected, a *left-click* on the pattern will make that pattern active for the next area to be patterned. Thus a *left-click* on the **HBONE** pattern on the line (Fig. 12.12) will cause the **HBONE** pattern to appear in the **Pattern Area** Element Selection box when the **Pattern Area** tool is called.

The Delete Pattern tool

If one wishes to erase a pattern from a hatched area, select this tool and *left-click* on the pattern. The pattern will then all be deleted.

Cell Libraries

Pattern cells are held in cell libraries. There are a number of these in the files of MicroStation 95. To see the filenames, *left-click* on **Cell Selector** in the **Utilities** pull-down menu (Fig. 12.13). The **Cell Selector** dialogue box appears (Fig. 12.14). The required cell library can be called from the **Files** list box in the **Select Cell Library to Load** dialogue box which appears (Fig. 12.15).

Fig. 12.13 Selecting **Cell Selector** from the **Utilities** pull-down menu

Fig. 12.14 The **Cell Selector** dialogue box, with **Load Cell Library...** selected from its **File** menu

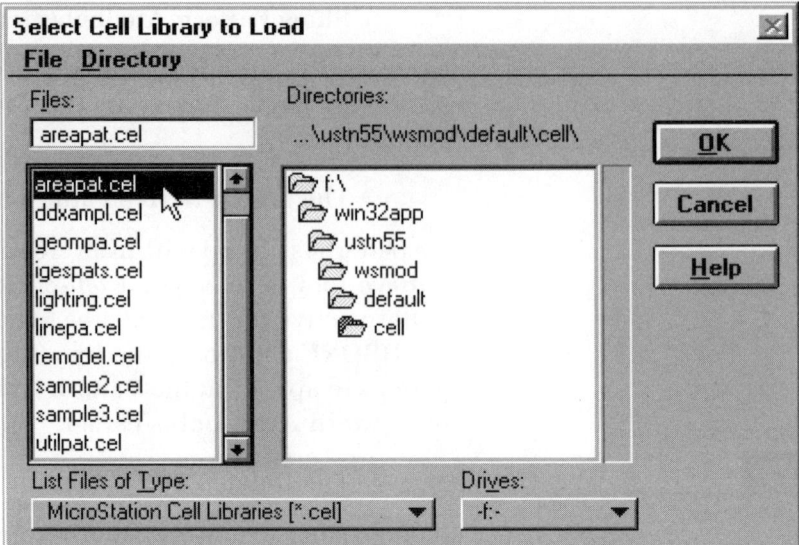

Fig. 12.15 The **Select Cell Library to Load** dialogue box

The Place Cell tool

From the **Cell Selector** dialogue box, a *left-click* on one of the patterns results in the **Place Cell** Element Selection box appearing. After *keying-in* a suitable **Scale** and possibly suitable **Angle** in the relevant places in the Element Selection box, the chosen cell pattern appears at the end of the cursor and can be dragged to any required position. Figure 12.16 shows two placements of the cell **DECD**, one of which has already been placed (*left-click*), the other about to be placed. This particular facility is of value when constructing circuits – electric, electronic, pneumatics, fluidic, etc.

A second example of using the **Place Cell** tool is given in Fig. 12.17. Note that the **Cell Selector** dialogue box has been made smaller by *dragging* its window corners to achieve a more suitable

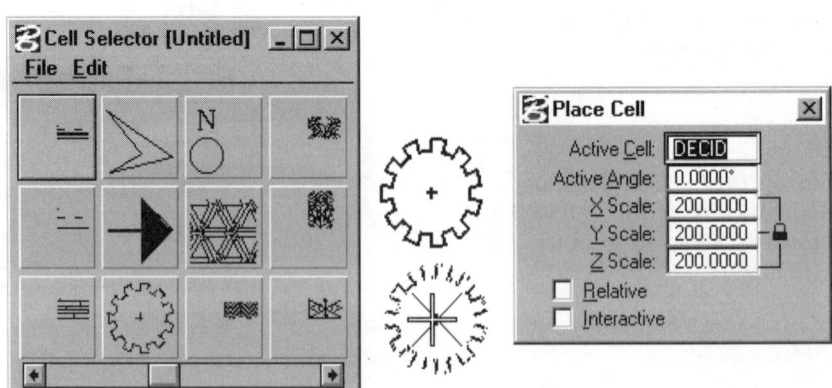

Fig. 12.16 Placing a cell with the aid of the **Place Cell** tool.

size for the work in hand. This example shows a plan of a set of easy chairs placed as cells around a circular table.

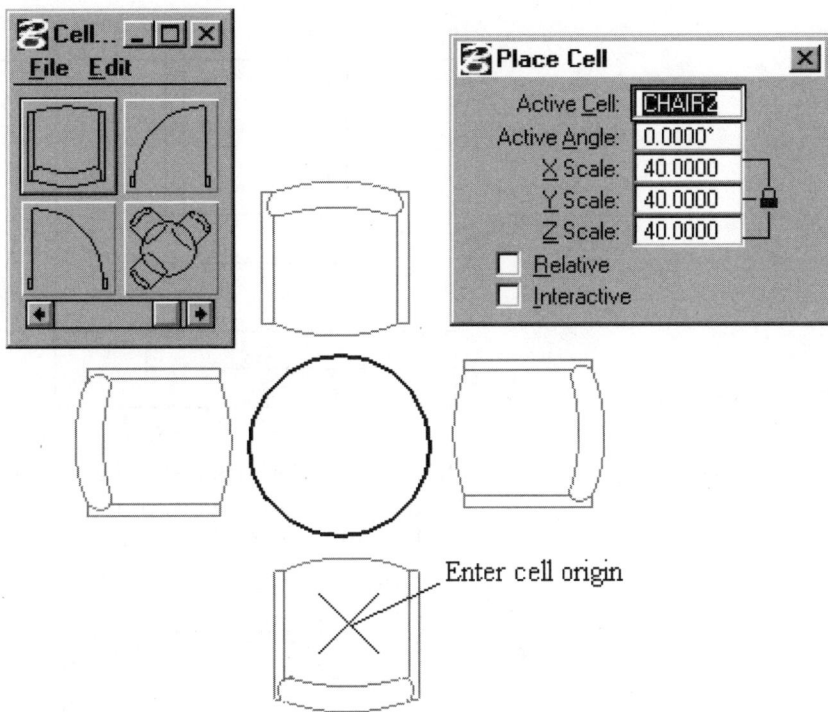

Fig. 12.17 A second example of the use of the **Place Cell** tool

Enter cell origin

Questions

1. Can the **Hatch Area** tool be used for placing a pattern within a drawing?
2. What are the differences between hatching with the **Hatch Area** tool and the **Crosshatch Area** tool?
3. What are the differences between **Flood** and **Element** which can be selected from **Method** in the **Hatch Area** Element Selection box?
4. How can hatch lines be drawn to a different **Line Weight** to the outlines within which the hatching is to be added?
5. How are patterns for use with the **Pattern Area** selected?
6. What is a cell?
7. Cells are held in libraries. How can a new cell library be selected.
8. What is the difference between placing a cell with the **Place Cell** tool and using a cell with the **Pattern Area** tool?

Exercises

1. The left-hand drawing of Fig. 12.18 shows a sectional view without its hatch lines. The right-hand drawing shows the sectional view

after hatching. Copy the view to the given dimensions and add the hatching.

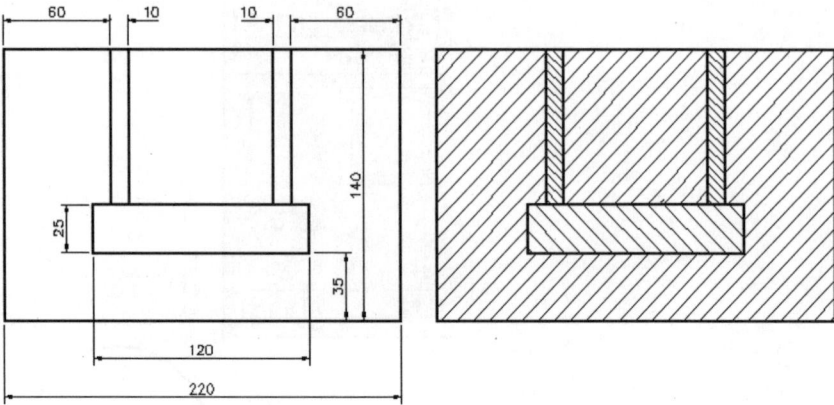

Fig. 12.18 Exercise 1

2. Figure 12.19 is a side view of a motor car. Either copy the given view to any suitable sizes, or construct a side view of another vehicle. Use any suitable cell pattern for the hatching of the side panels.

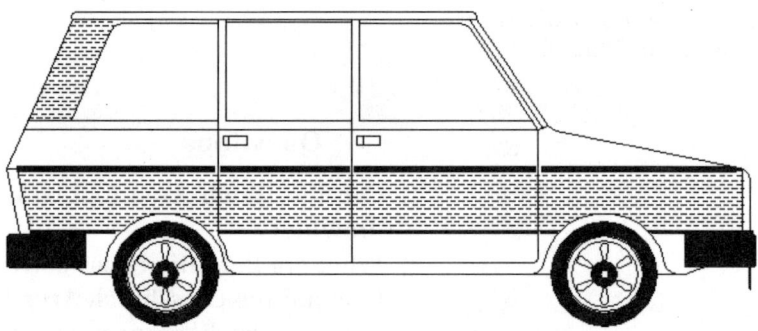

Fig. 12.19 Exercise 2

3. Figure 12.20 is a sectional view through a garden wall. Working to any suitable dimensions, construct the sectional view.
4. Figure 12.21 shows a sectional view through a double pulley assembly. Working to any suitable dimensions construct the given sectional view.
5. Construct the patterned outlines shown in Fig. 12.22 working to the given dimensions.
6. Construct the pattern shown in Fig. 12.23 to any suitable dimensions.
7. Figure 6.24 consists of two views of a bungalow. Construct the two views working to any suitable sizes.

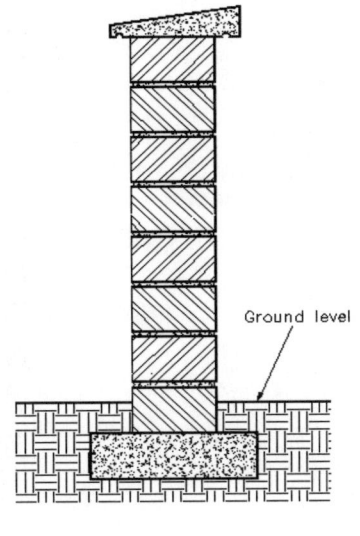

Ground level

Fig. 12.20 Exercise 3

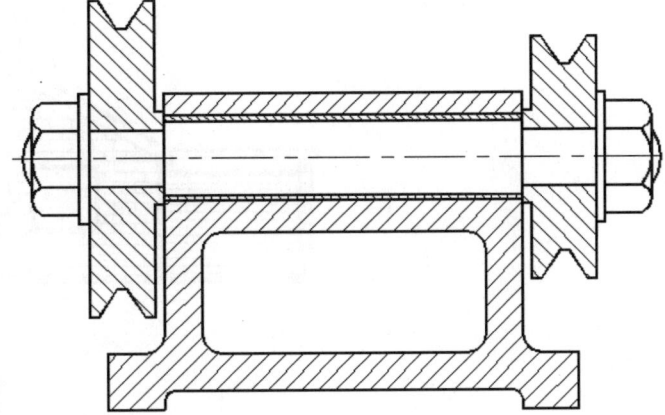

Fig. 12.21 Exercise 4

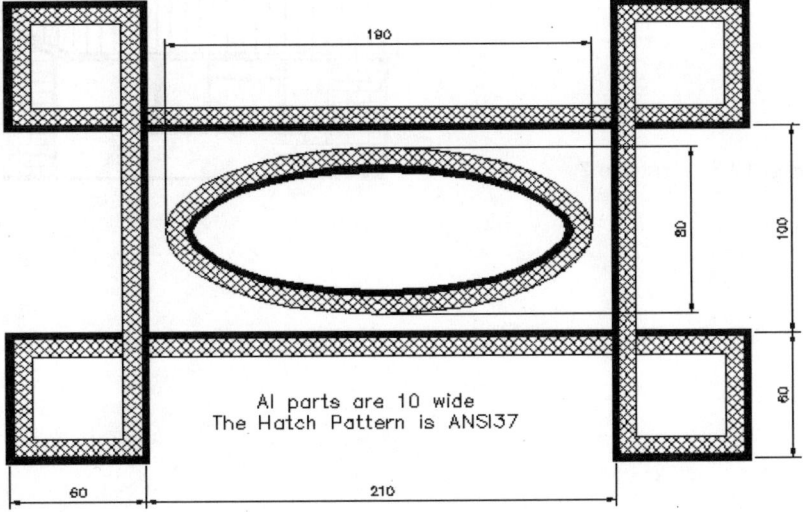

190

80

100

60

Al parts are 10 wide
The Hatch Pattern is ANSI37

60

210

Fig. 12.22 Exercise 5

Fig,. 12.23 Exercise 6

Fig. 12.24 Exercise 7

CHAPTER 13

Isometric drawing

Introduction

When constructing isometric drawings, it must be understood that they are not three-dimensional drawings, but only two-dimensional representations of 3D objects. MicroStation 95 has excellent tools for the construction of true 3D models. An introduction into the construction of 3D models is given in the following chapters.

Settings for isometric drawing

It is advisable to make the following settings when attempting the construction of isometric drawings.

Isometric tool box

Call the isometric tool box on screen – *left-click* on **Isometric** in the **Tools** pull-down menu (Fig. 13.1). The tool palette which appears only contains two tools: **Place Isometric Block** and **Place Isometric Circle**.

Isometric Grid

In the **Design File Settings** dialogue box, *left-click* on **Grid** and then set **Grid Config** to **Isometric** (Fig. 13.2). While in the **Design File Settings** box, the **Isometric Lock** can be set as indicated in Fig. 13.3. While the locking of the grid points is not essential, it may make a drawing easier to construct, so this setting is optional. In fact there are several ways of setting locks – from the **Settings/Locks** pull-down sub menu, from the **Design File Settings** box, or from the pop-up list appearing with a *left-click* on the lock icon in the Status Bar.

Isometric Full View cursor lines

Setting the **Full View** cursor and **Isometric** in the **Operation** box of **Design Settings,** causes the across screen cursor hairs to take up isometric positions on screen (Fig. 13.3).

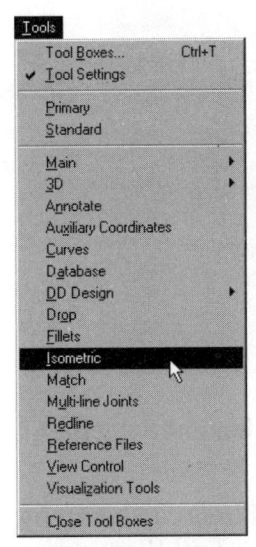

Fig. 13.1 Select **Isometric** from the **Tools** pull-down menu

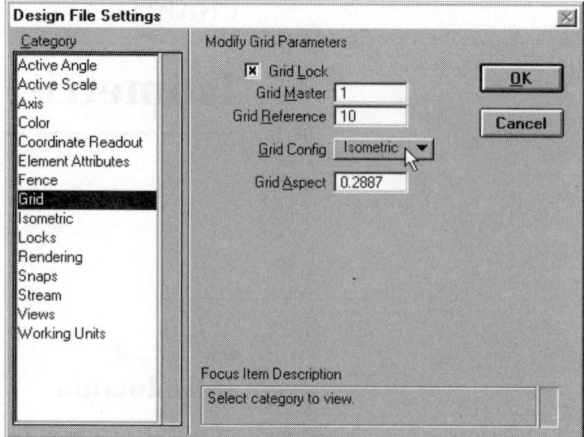

Fig. 13.2 Set **Grid Config** to **Isometric**

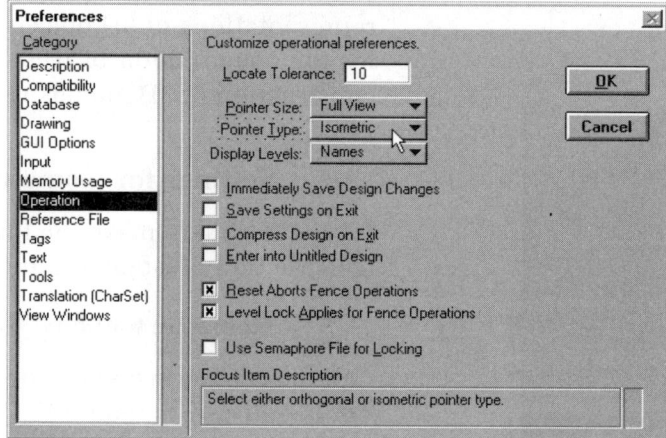

Fig. 13.3 Set Full View and **Isometric** in the **Operation** box of **Design File Settings**

The Place Isometric Block (or Circle) Element Selection box

In the Element Selection box of either tool, the **Plane** can be set for **Top**, **Right** or **Left** as shown in Fig. 13.4. When the **Full View** cursor lines are present on screen, they will be seen changing between the planes as each is selected from the **Plane** pop-up list. Figure 13.5 shows the effects of choosing different planes for three isometric circles.

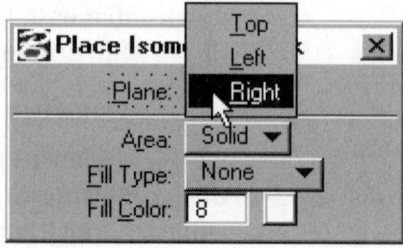

Fig. 13.4 The three **Planes** in the **Place Isometric** Element Selection boxes

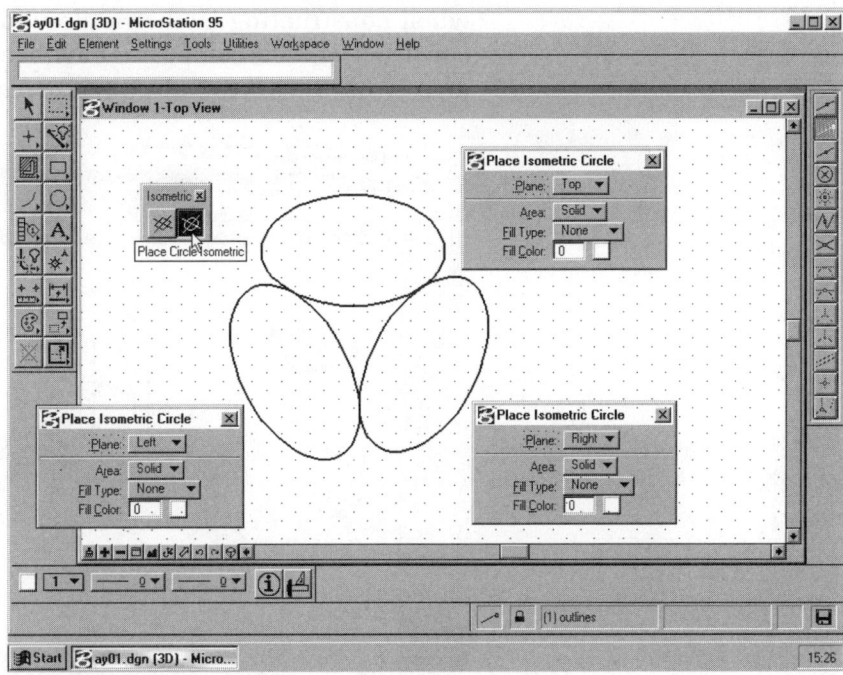

Fig. 13.5 Isometric ellipses on three different planes

Figure 13.6 shows the effects of the three planes using either of the two tools.

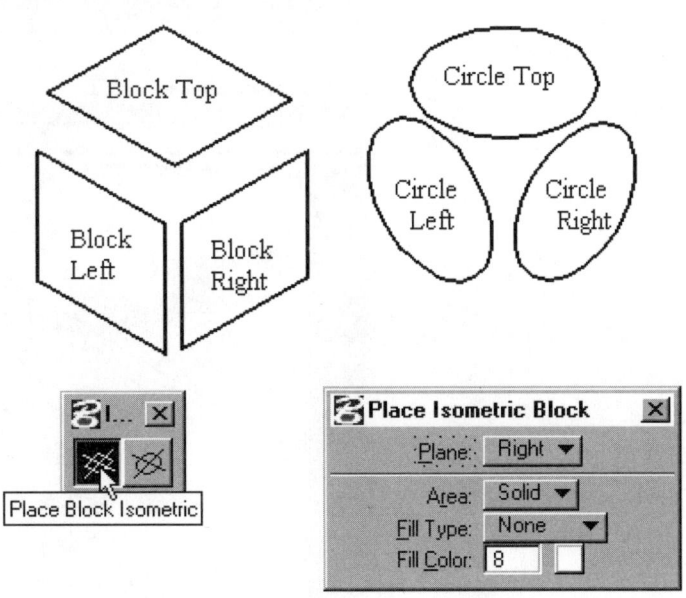

Fig. 13.6 The effects of the three isometric planes

AccuDraw

Although the AccuDraw compass has not been included in any of the illustrations shown in this chapter, AccuDraw works as effectively when constructing isometric drawings as with any other form of construction. The compasses have been left out from the illustrations merely for the sake of clarity of meaning in each illustration.

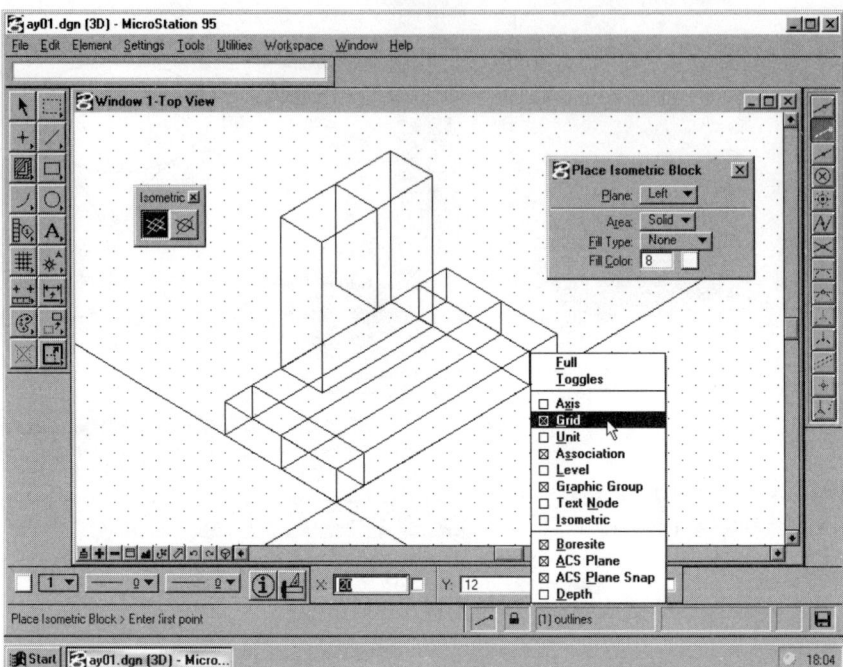

Fig. 13.7 The first stage in the construction of an isometric drawing

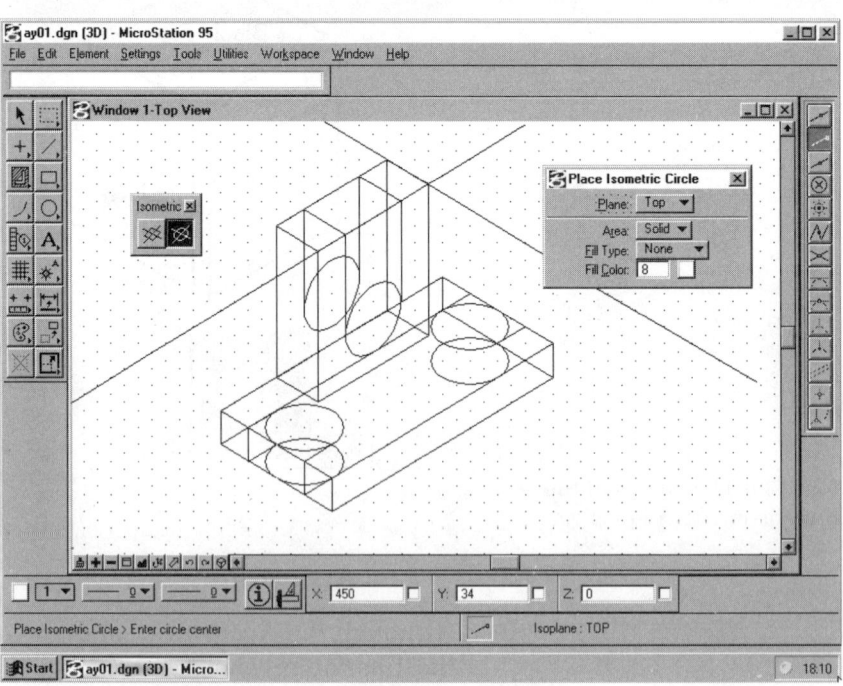

Fig. 13.8 The second stage in the construction of an isometric drawing

An example of a simple isometric drawing

Stage 1: Fig. 13.7

Set **Grid Lock** from the pop-up lock menu in the Status Bar if not already set. Set line weight to **0**.

With the **Isometric Block** tool in action and using AccuDraw, construct the outlines for the drawing as shown in Fig. 13.7. Some of the blocks have been included as constructions for the centres of the ellipses to be added during the second stage. *Left-click* the **Plane** options of **Top**, **Right** and **Left** when necessary as the blocks are placed on each of the planes. Although sizes have not been included in this drawing, use the AccuDraw to determine correct sizes for each block as it is placed in position.

Stage 2: Fig. 13.8

With the **Place Isometric Circle** tool add the ellipses as shown in Fig. 13.8. Use the construction blocks to aid the centring of the ellipses. When all the ellipses have been placed, erase the construction blocks. With the **Place Line** tool add tangential lines to the ellipse at the back and base of the drawing as shown. Use the grid locks to determine the centres and the tangential lines.

Stage 3: Fig. 13.9

Use the tools **Delete**, **Trim Element** and **Partial Delete** to delete, trim or partially delete to remove those parts of the construction not needed for the final drawing.

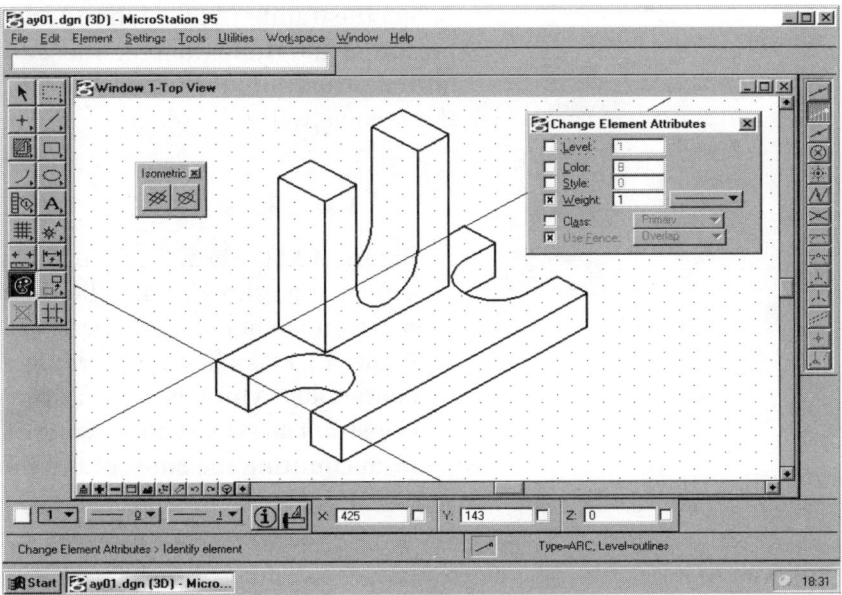

Fig. 13.9 The third stage in the construction of an isometric drawing.

Select the **Change Element Attributes** tool and in its Element Selection box set line weight to **1**. *Left-click* on each element in the drawing in turn to change its line weight to **1** as shown.

Note

Because MicroStation 95 contains such excellent 3D modelling tools, it is thought that the above explanation of how to construct an isometric drawing will suffice. However, a few exercises follow for the reader to practise this form of construction.

A note on function keys

The keyboard function keys – those marked with an **F**, usually from **F1** to **F12** along the top of the keyboard – can be configured to be used to cause certain effects. Some are already set as defaults. These are:

F1	Help
F3	backup
F5	choose element
F7	place fence
F9	update
F11	zoom in
F12	window area

I have added **F2** to call undo. If you wish to add, or alter the functions set for the keys, *left-click* on **Function keys...** in the **Function Keys** dialogue box, *left-click* on the button marked **F1**, which brings up a pop-up list showing all function key numbers. Select the number you wish to add (or change); *left-click* on the **Edit** button of the dialogue box and add the function for the key being edited. Finally *left-click* on the **OK** button of the dialogue box and the change will take place for the edited function key.

Exercises

1. Figure 13.10 shows an angle bracket. Working to the overall dimensions shown with the drawing and estimating other sizes, make an isometric drawing of the bracket.
2. Figure 13.11 is a first angle orthographic projection of an engineering component which has been drawn within a grid of sides 10 mm. Construct an isometric drawing of the component judging the sizes from counting the sides of the squares in the 10 mm grid.

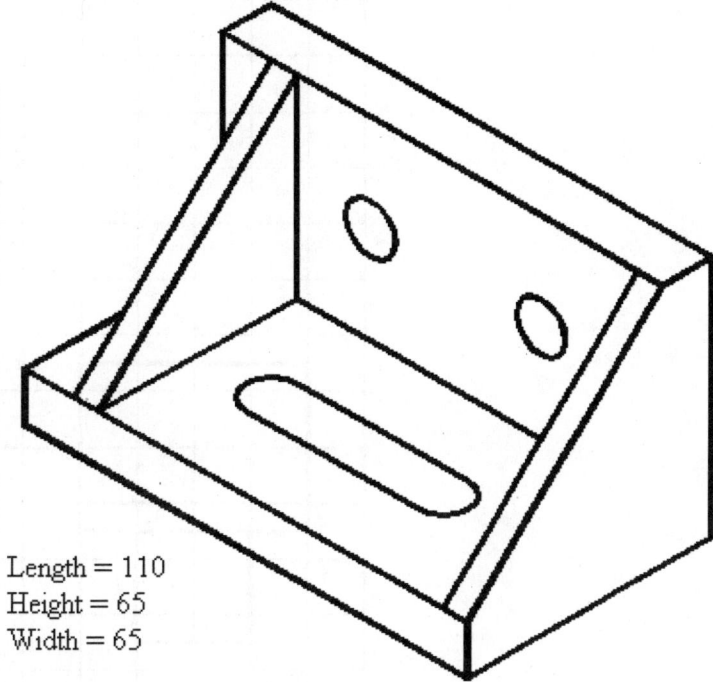

Length = 110
Height = 65
Width = 65

Fig. 13.10 Exercise 1

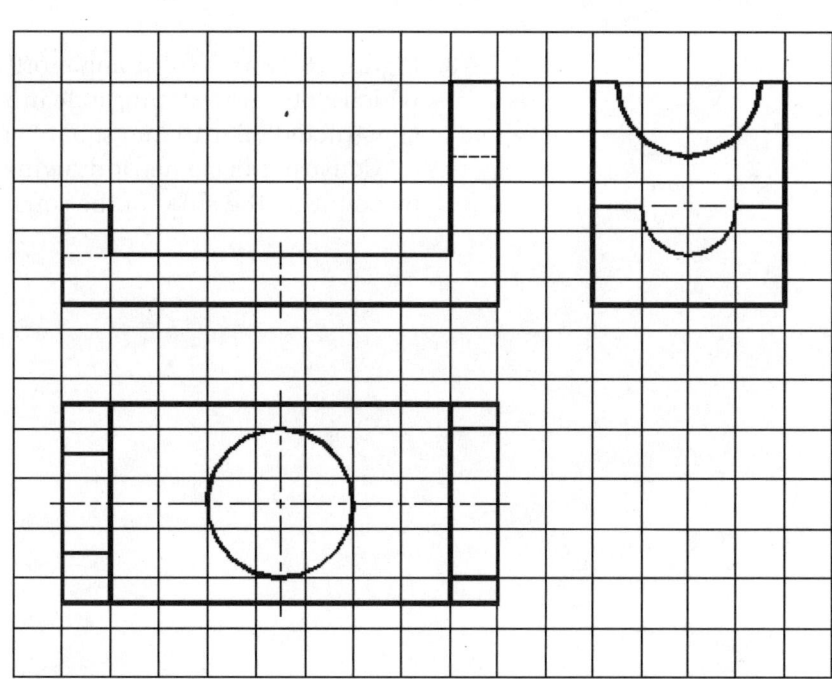

Fig. 13.11 Exercise 2

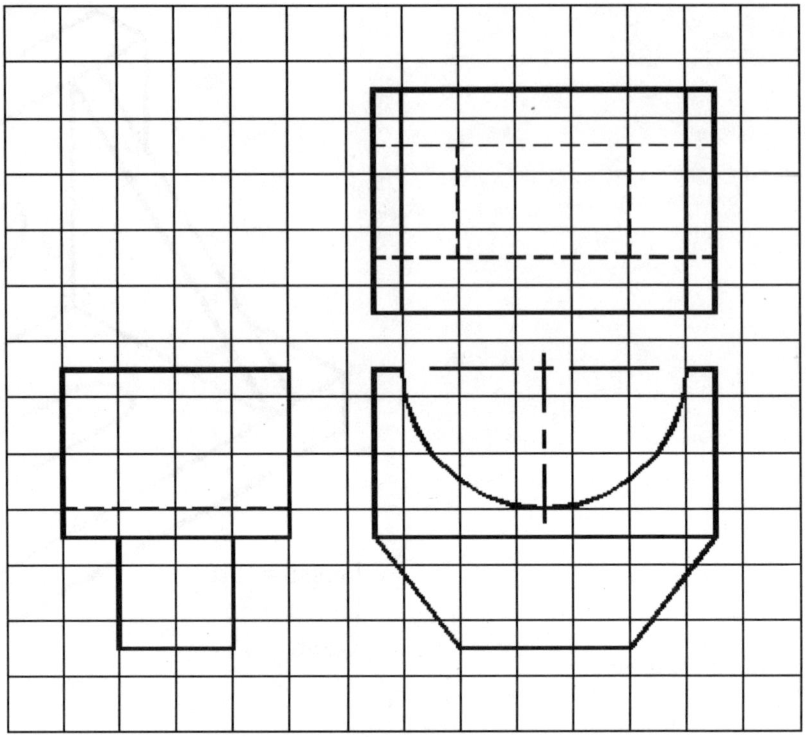

Fig. 13.12 Exercise 3

3. Figure 13.12 is a third angle orthographic projection of a guide which slots into a sloping hole in a machine. The drawing has been constructed on a 10 mm square grid.

Construct an isometric drawing of the guide judging dimensions by counting the sides of the square grid.

CHAPTER 14

3D modelling – a 3D design file

Introduction

In order to be able to start MicroStation 95 with a suitable design file for the construction of 3D models, it is suggested you set up a design file as described in the following pages. There are other methods of setting up a suitable design file for this purpose, but the following describes that in use in the following chapters.

Constructing the design file

On start-up MicroStation 95 opens with the **MicroStation Manager** dialogue box (Fig. 14.1). In the **Directories** list box, select the directory dgn\mechdrft. This brings up the design files in the **File** list box of the dgn\mechdrft directory. *Double-click* on the filename **a3form.dgn**. The dialogue box is then replaced with the screen of the design file of this name (Fig. 14.2). Add the following to this screen:

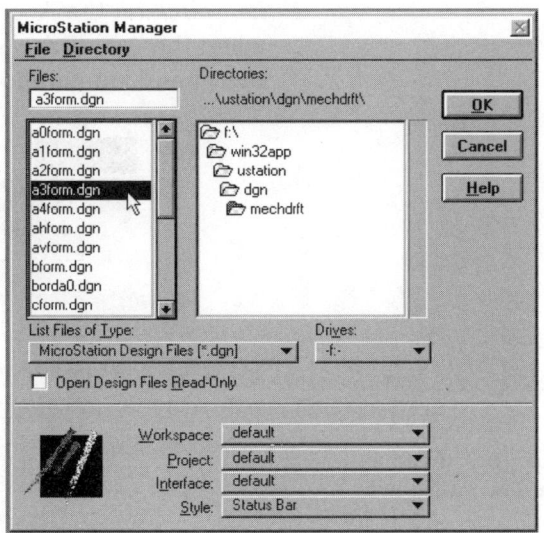

Fig. 14.1 The **MicroStation Manager** dialogue box

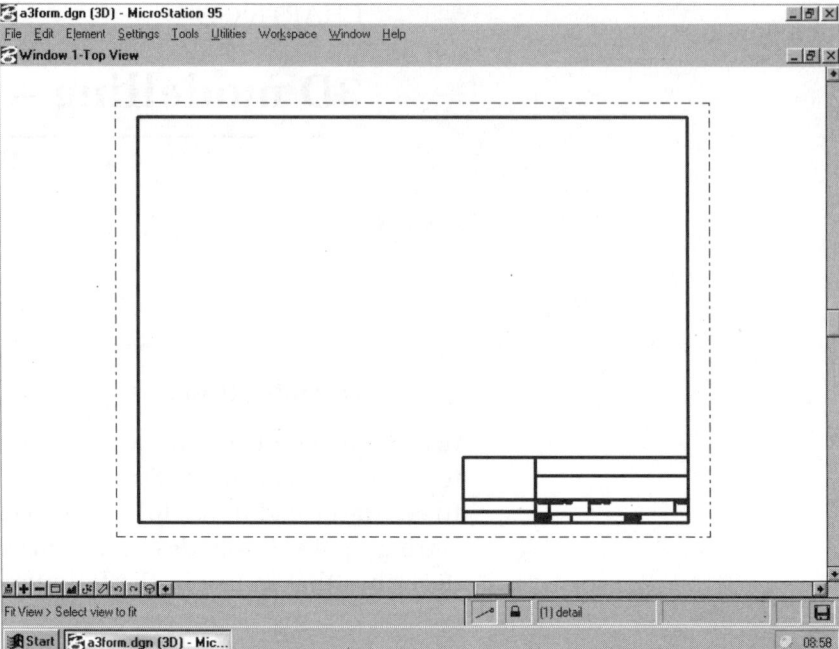

Fig. 14.2 The **a3form.dgn** screen as it first appears

1. From the **Tools** pull-down menu select the **Main** tool palette. When the tool palette appears on screen, *drag* it into the left-hand side of the screen.

2. From the **Tools** pull-down menu select the **3D Tools** tool palette. When the palette appears on screen, *drag* it into position just below the **Main** tool palette.

3. From the **Tools** pull-down menu select the **Primary** tool palette. When it appears, *drag* it into the left-hand side of the Status Bar.

4. *Left-click* on the **AccuDraw** icon in the **Primary** tool palette and when the **AccuDraw** coordinate window appears *drag* it into the right-hand side of the Status Bar.

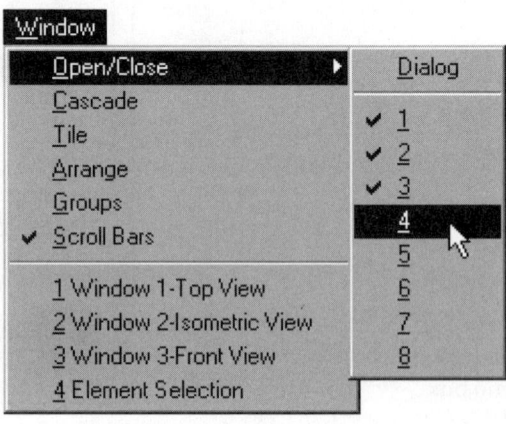

Fig. 14.3 Select **1**, **2**, **3** and **4** from the **Window** pull-down menu

5. From the **Utilities** pull-down menu select **Key-in**, and when the **Key-in** dialogue box appears reduce its window in size until only the **Key-in** window is showing. *Drag* the **Key-in** window into a position just below the menu bar.

6. With the **Delete** tool from the **Main** tool palette, delete the border lines and the title block from the screen.

7. From the **Window** pull-down menu select **Open/Close** and from the sub-menu **Dialog** select **1**, **2**, **3** and **4** in turn (Fig. 14.3).

8. *Left-click* on **Tile** in the **Window** pull-down menu. The screen now appears as shown in Fig. 14.4.

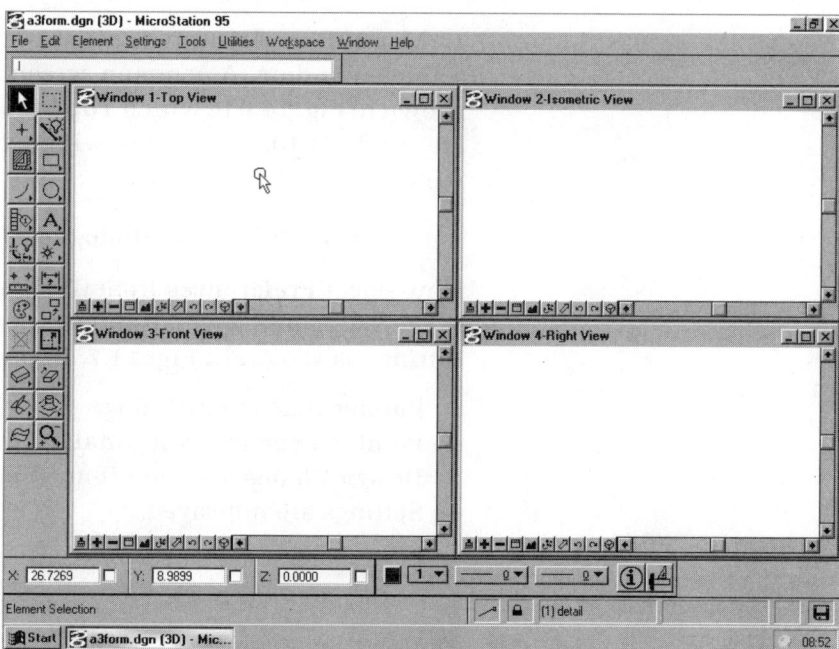

Fig. 14.4 The amended **a3form.dgn** screen

9. Save the file to a name such as **ay3d.dgn** in the directory dgn\default (Fig. 14.5). This is my initials followed by **3d**. The reader could use his/her own initials.

Number of windows in the 3D design file

It will be seen from Fig. 14.4 that, as a 3D model is being constructed, the four windows will show a **Top View** (Window 1), an **Isometric View** (Window 2), a **Front View** (Window 3) and a **Right View** (Window 4). It will also have been noticed that there are four further windows from which a choice could have been made from the **Window** pull-down menu – Windows **5** to **8**. The reader may care to experiment with these further windows, but for the time being we will be using all or some of the first four windows.

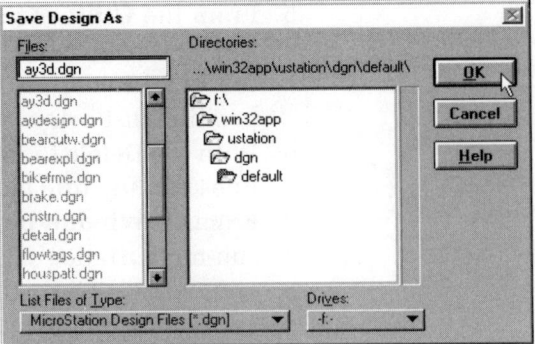

Fig. 14.5 Save the screen to a suitable filename

Many 3D models can be constructed in two windows, or even in a single window. A common screen in which to construct in 3D is shown in Fig. 14.6 in which **Top View** and **Isometric View** windows are used. At times a single window, perhaps the **Isometric View** window, may be preferred.

The Preferences dialogue box

Now select **Preferences** from the **Workspace** pull-down menu and in the dialogue box which appears, *left-click* on **Operation** and make settings as shown in Fig. 14.7. In particular note:

> **Pointer Size** is **Full View**
> **Pointer Type** is **Orthogonal**
> **Design Changes** are not immediately saved
> **Settings** are not saved

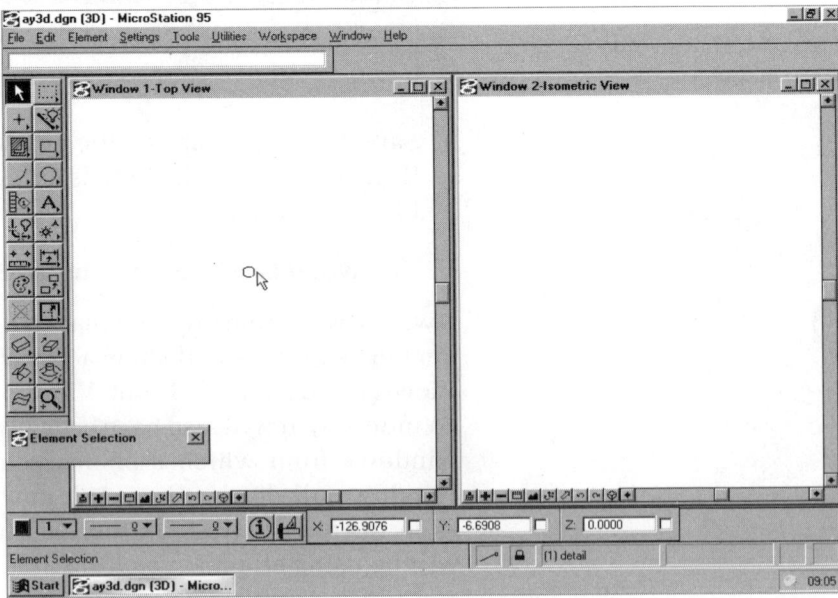

Fig. 14.6 A two-window 3D screen

It is up to the operator to decide these operation parameters. For the purpose of the designs in this book, the settings were those in Fig. 14.7.

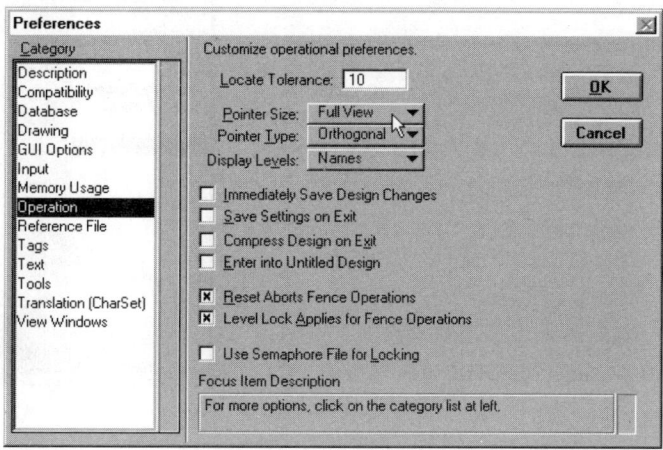

Fig. 14.7 Settings in the **Preferences** dialogue box

Left-click on **View Windows** in the dialogue box and set windows to show a white background (Fig. 14.8). Many operators will prefer working against a black background but for the purposes of illustrations in this book, features show up more clearly if drawn against a white background. Again, this setting is left to the preferences of the operator.

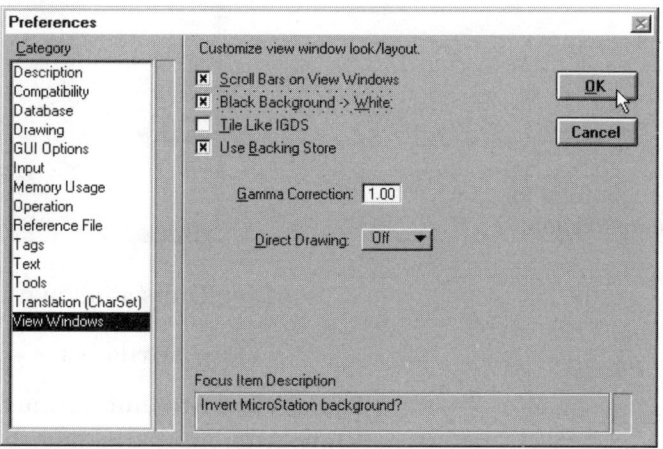

Fig. 14.8 Setting **View Windows** to show white

The Design File Settings dialogue box

From the **Settings** pull-down menu select **Design File**, and in the **Design File Settings** dialogue box which appears make the following settings:

1. **Grid** settings as shown in Fig. 14.9.

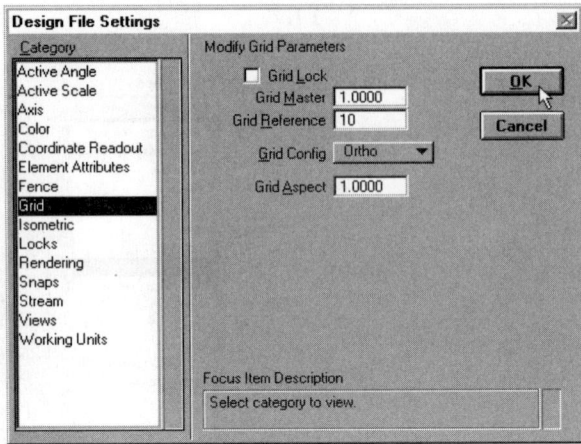

Fig. 14.9 Settings for **Grid**

2. **Coordinate Readout** as shown in Fig. 14.10.

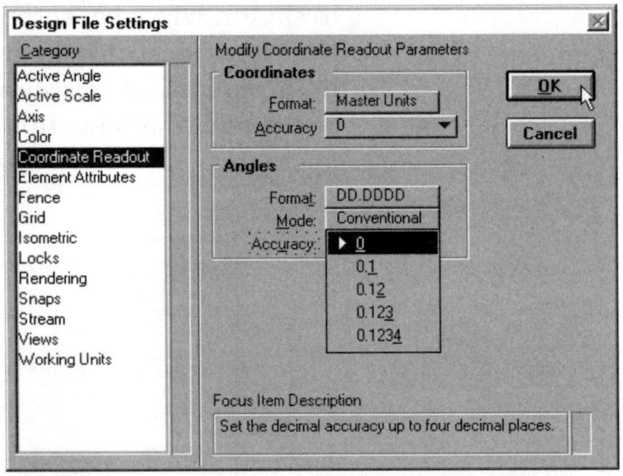

Fig. 14.10 Settings for
Coordinate Readout

3. **Working Units** as shown in Fig. 14.11.

View Attributes

Select **View Attributes** from the **Settings** pull-down menu and in the **View Attributes** dialogue box which appears set the check box against **ACS Triad** on (**X** in check box). Make sure the check box is on for each of the **View** windows. See Fig. 14.12. Figure 14.13 shows the triads on a simple 3D model in four windows. The triads appear with their apex at the coordinate position 0,0,0.

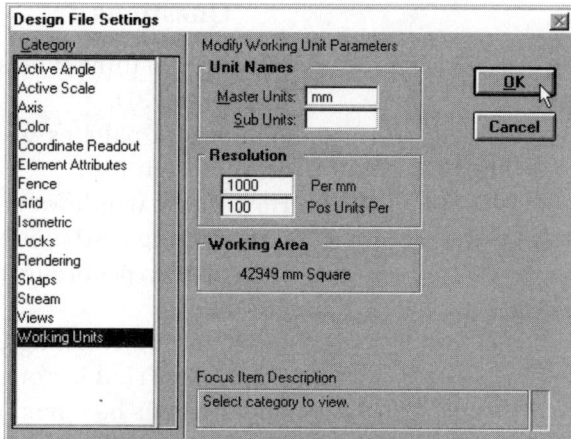

Fig. 14.11 Settings for **Working Units**

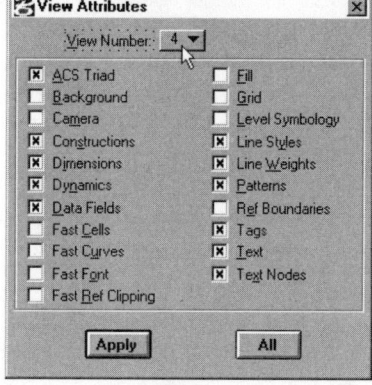

Fig. 14.12 Set check box against **ACS Triad** on for all four **View** windows

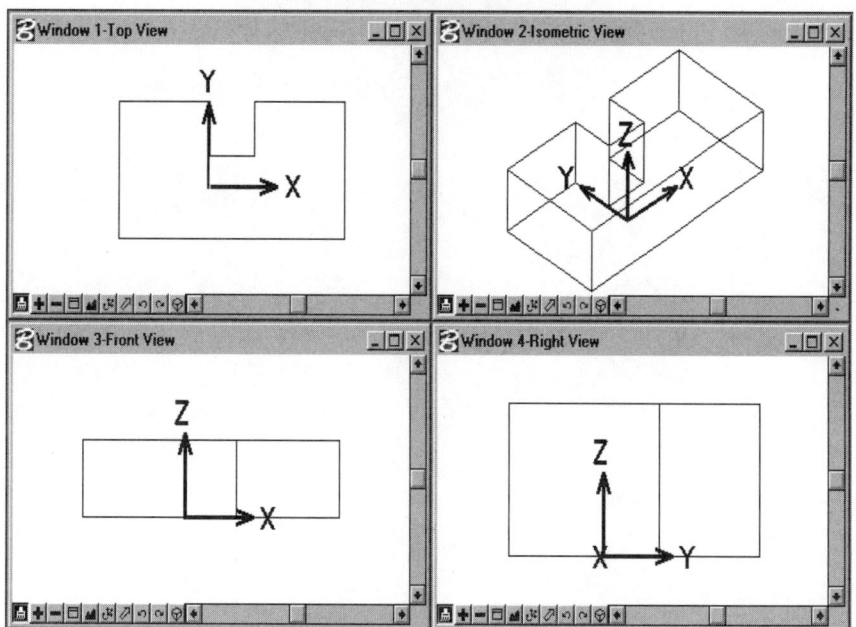

Fig. 14.13 The **ACS Triads** showing on a simple 3D model in four windows

Questions

1. Why do you think it necessary to set up your own design file when working in 3D?
2. Which tool palettes were added to the screen in making up the given design file?
3. How many windows do you think you will be working in when constructing a 3D model in MicroStation 95?
4. How many types of cursor are used in conjunction with MicroStation 95?
5. What are the **Working Units** setting for the suggested design file?
6. If an **ACS Triad** is not showing in one of the windows on screen, how can this be remedied?
7. How can you ensure that the **ACS Triads** are showing in a window?

CHAPTER 15

The Groups tool palette

Introduction

The tools of the **Groups** tool palette are important in the construction of 3D models because they allow the operator to group together elements prior to their being acted upon by the tools in the **3D Free-form Surfaces** palette. The tools in this 3D tool palette will be described at some length in Chapter 17. In this chapter **3D Free-form Surfaces** tools, as well as rendering tools, are used to illustrate some of the uses of the **Groups** tools. Several of the illustrations in this chapter show the tools in the **Groups** palette.

Tools in the Groups palette

The Create Complex Chain tool

This tool creates a chain element from a number of separate elements. Fig. 15.1 shows two semicircular arcs and three lines joined to form

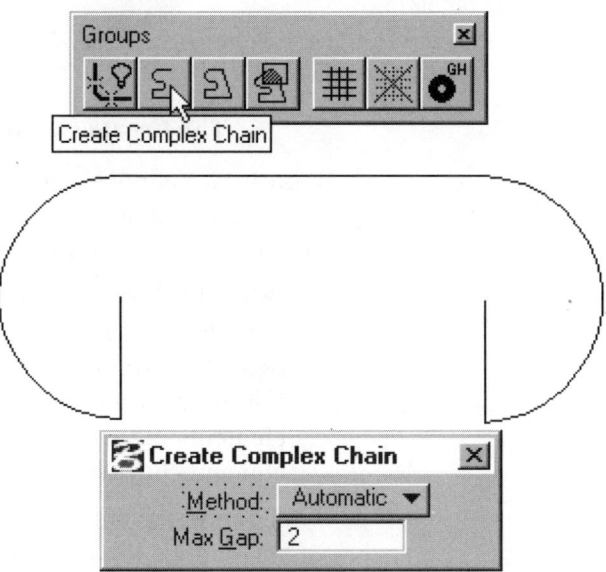

Fig. 15.1 The **Create Complex Chain** example

a complex chain under the action of the tool. The chain was constructed as follows:

1. With the aid of AccuDraw, draw the two semicircles and lines, using the **keypoint** snap to ensure they are joining at their ends.
2. *Left-click* on the **Create Complex Chain** tool icon. In the Element Selection box select **Automatic** from the **Method** pop-up list.
3. Following prompts in the Status Bar, *left-click* on each of the five elements in turn. They highlight as they are picked. When all the elements have been selected, *left-click* to complete the operation.

To show the value of this tool in connection with the construction of 3D models, the complex chain was acted upon by the **Construct Surface of Projection** tool from the **3D Free-form Surfaces** palette. The chain was formed into a 3D model. The model was then acted upon by the **Render Phong** tool from the **Utilities** pull-down menu. The resulting rendered model is shown in Fig. 15.2.

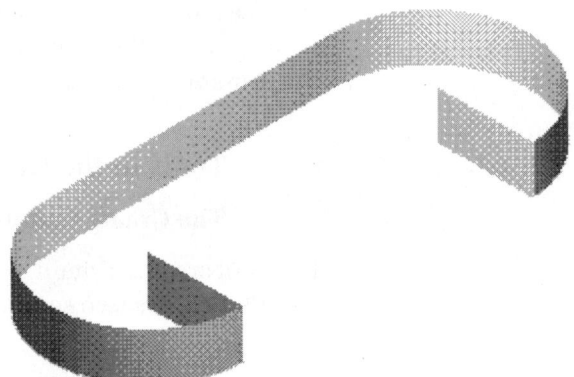

Fig. 15.2 The **Phong** rendering of the 3D model from Fig. 15.1

The Create Complex Shape tool

Figure 15.3 shows a group of elements forming a closed outline. They were acted upon by the **Create Complex Shape** tool to form a single element as follows:

1. Draw the eight elements forming the closed outline.
2. *Left-click* on the **Create Complex Shape** tool. In the Element Selection box select **Automatic** from the **Method** pop-up list.
3. Following prompts in the Status Bar, *left-click* on each of the eight elements in turn. They highlight as they are picked. When all the elements have been selected, *left-click* to complete the operation.

To show the value of this tool in connection with the construction of 3D models, the complex shape was acted upon by the **Construct**

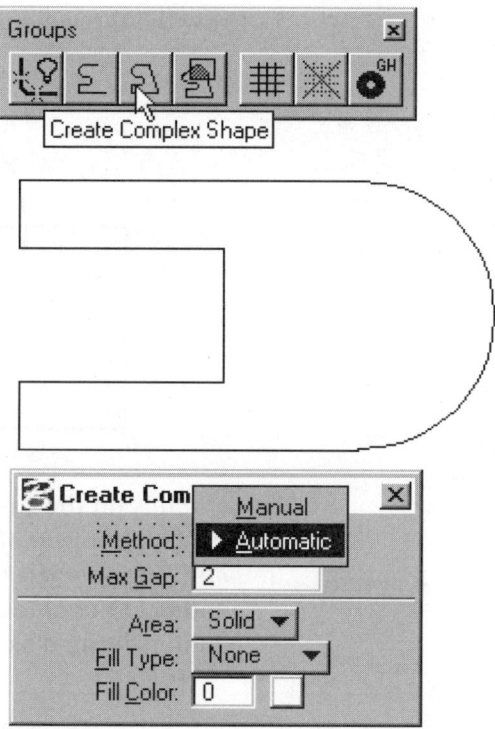

Fig. 15.3 The **Create Complex Shape** example

Surface of Projection tool from the **3D Free-form Surfaces** palette. The shape was formed into a 3D model. The model was then acted upon by the **Render Phong** tool from the **Utilities** pull-down menu. The resulting rendered model is shown in Fig. 15.4.

The Create Region tool

Figure 15.5 shows three elements – a block and two circles. To form the region shown in Fig. 15.6:

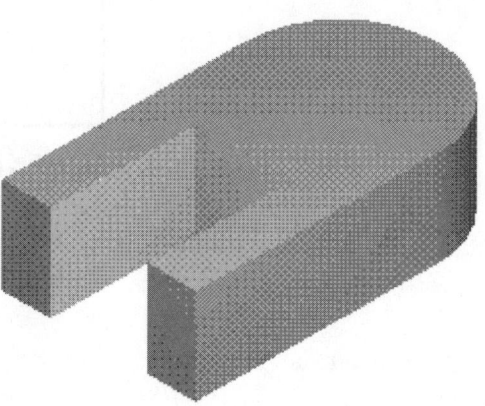

Fig. 15.4 The **Phong** rendering of the Complex Shape model

1. Draw the three elements – Fig. 15.5.

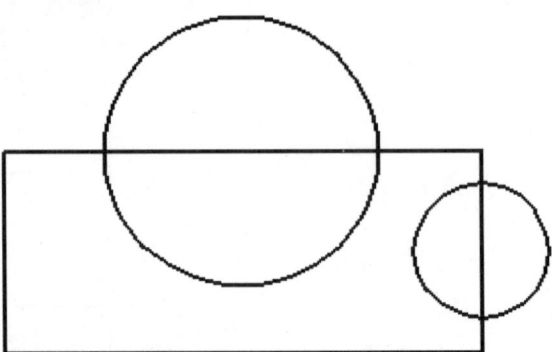

Fig. 15.5 The three elements
for the region

2. *Left-click* on the **Create Region** tool. In its Element Selection box select **Union** from the **Method** pop-up list.
3. *Left-click* on each element in the drawing in turn, followed by another *left-click* to confirm, followed by a *right-click*. The resulting region is formed as shown in Fig. 15.6.

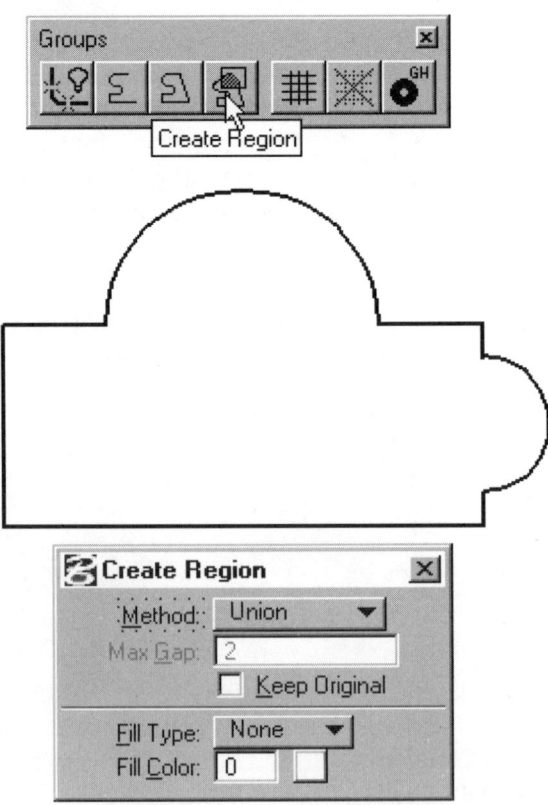

Fig. 15.6 The region formed by
the **Create Region** tool

Once again the resulting outline was acted upon by the **Construct Surface of Projection**, followed by rendering with **Phong** from the **Utilities** pull-down menu with the results as shown in Fig. 15.7.

Fig. 15.7 The **Phong** rendering of the region

The Group Hole tool

An outline created with the aid of the **Create Region** tool can have holes of any shape, which have been drawn within its outline, treated as holes in a **Surface of Projection** developed from the region. This is shown in Figs 15.8 and 15.9. The first illustration shows a circle drawn within the outline of the region, the second shows a **Phong** rendering of the region with its hole after being acted

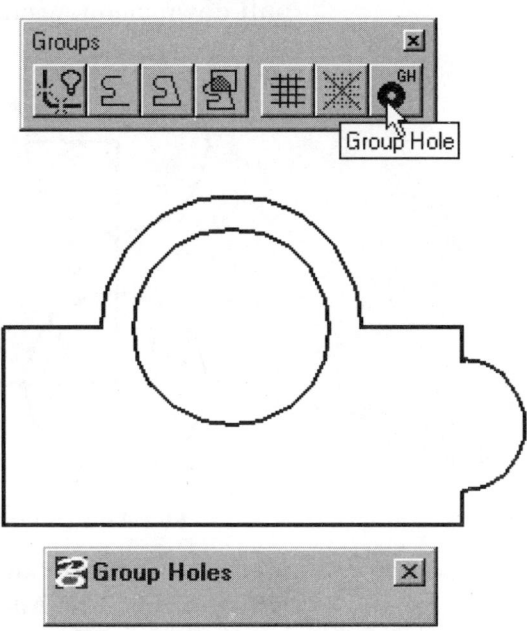

Fig. 15.8 Forming a **Group Hole** within a region

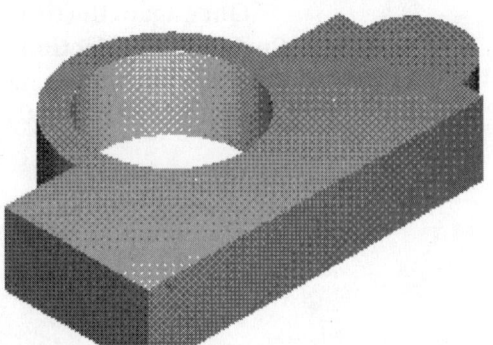

Fig. 15.9 A **Phong** rendering of the region with its group hole

upon by the **Construct Surface of Projection** tool. The process is carried out by first selecting the **Group Hole** tool, followed by a *left-click* on the region outline and another on the circle.

Another example of using the Group Region tool

Figure 15.10 shows four circles centred at the corners of a block. This drawing was acted upon by the **Group Region** tool, but this time with **Difference** selected from the **Method** pop-up list, as shown in Fig. 15.11. Another block was added inside the region already constructed and then the **Group Hole** tool was called to form the block into a hole within the region – Fig. 15.12. After being acted upon by the **Construct Surface of Projection**, the resulting 3D model was rendered with the **Phong Antialias** command from the **Utilities** pull-down menu, resulting in the illustration shown in Fig. 15.13.

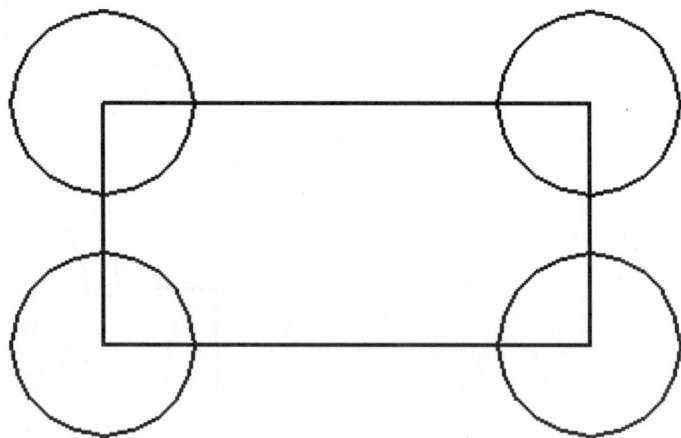

Fig. 15.10 Preliminary drawing showing the use of the **Create Region** tool

The Add to Graphic Group tool

Figure 15.14 shows an outline with its elements grouped together with the aid of the **Add to Graphic Group** tool. After selecting the

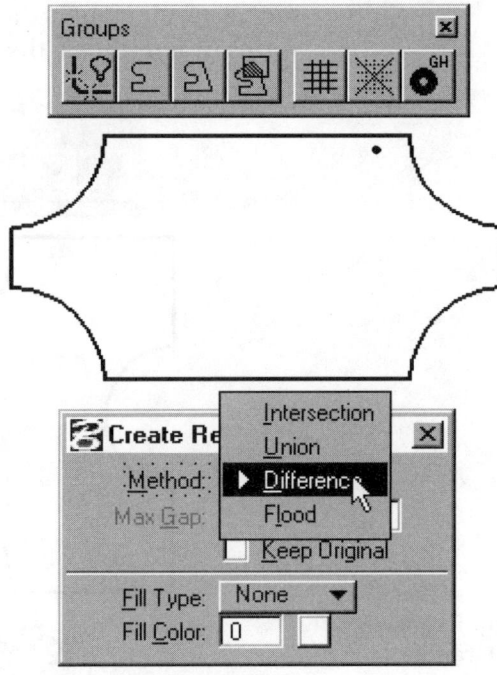

Fig. 15.11 Creating a **Region** with the method **Difference**

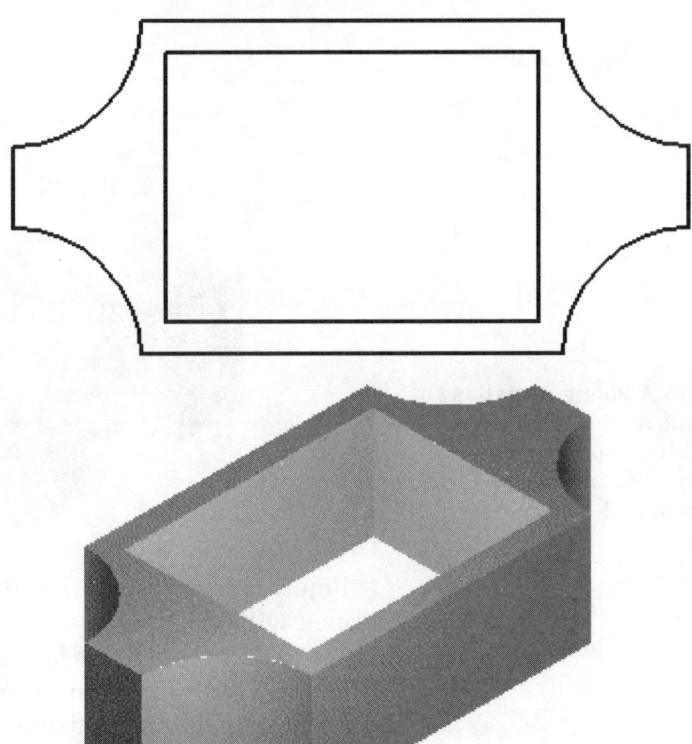

Fig. 15.12 An example of a hole formed in a region with the **Group Hole** tool

Fig. 15.13 A **Phong Antialias** rendering of the region with its hole after being acted upon with the **Construct Surface of Projection** tool

tool, each element is then selected with a *left-click.* At the end of the series of *left-clicks,* the group is formed.

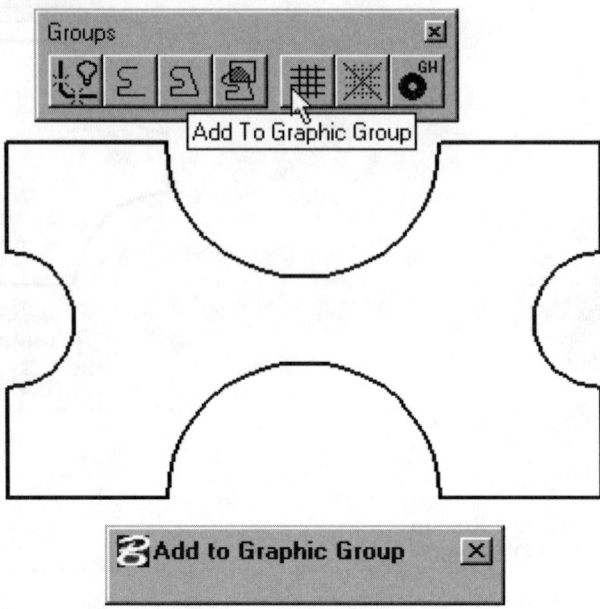

Fig. 15.14 A group formed with the **Add to Graphic Group** tool

Fig 15.15 A **Phong Antialias** rendering of Fig. 15.14 after being acted upon by the **Construct Surface of Projection** tool

Figure 15.15 shows the essential difference between a group formed with this tool and those resulting from the use of the other **Group** tools mentioned so far. When a **Construct Surface of Projection** 3D model is formed from the group, the resulting 3D model has no top or bottom. It is a solid, but a surface-only model, no matter what the setting is in the **Construct Surface of Projection** Element Selection box.

Other tools in the Groups palette

Two other tools in the palette are the **Drop Element** tool (Fig. 15.16) and the **Drop From Graphic Group** tool (Fig. 15.17). The actions of these two tools are shown in their names.

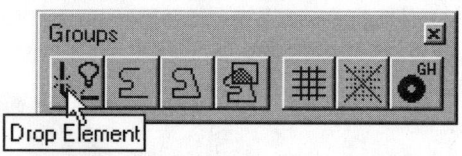

Fig. 15.16 The **Drop Element** tool

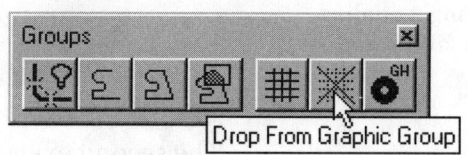

Fig. 15.17 The **Drop From Graphic Group** tool

When an element from a group is acted upon with the **Drop Element** tool active with a *left-click*, the chosen element is parted from the group. This may not be apparent at first, but can be proved if the selected element is acted upon with the tool **Move**, when it will be seen that the dropped element can be moved away from the group of which it was previously a part.

The **Drop From Graphic Group** tool has the same effect on elements from a group formed with the aid of the **Add to Graphic Group** tool, but not from other forms of group.

Further examples of the use of Groups tools

Two further examples of the use of these tools are given in Figs 15.18 to 15.20. Figure 15.18 shows a view of a clip. Its outline has been grouped with the **Create Region** tool and the circle of the hole has been acted upon with **Group Hole**.

The resulting outlines have then been acted upon with the **Construct Surface of Projection** tool and rendered with the **Phong**

Fig. 15.18 The **Create Region** and **Group Hole** outline of a clip

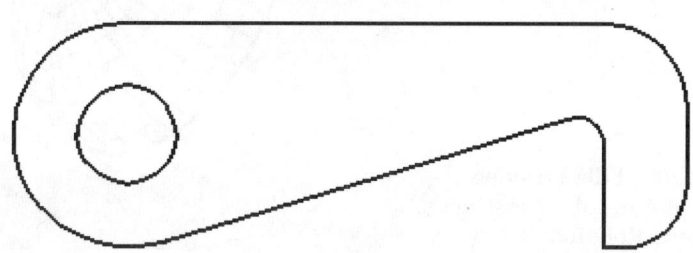

Antialias command from the **Utilities** pull-down menu, the results being shown in Fig. 15.19.

Fig. 15.19 A **Phong Antialias** rendering of the clip in Fig. 15.18

The second example shows an outline formed with the aid of the **Create Complex Chain** tool. The resulting chain was then acted upon by the **Construct Surface of Rotation** tool and rendered with the **Filled Hidden Line** command from the **Utilities** pull-down menu. See Fig. 15.20.

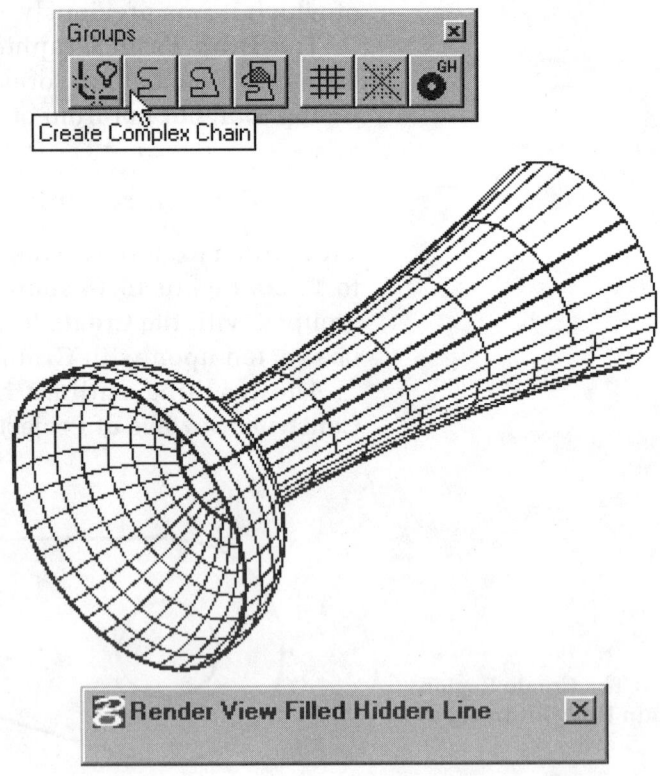

Fig. 15.20 A **Filled Hidden Line** rendering of a **Construct Surface of Rotation** model

Questions

1. What is the purpose of using the **Drop Element** tool?
2. What is the difference between the actions of the **Drop Element** tool and the **Drop From Graphic Group** tool?
3. Can the **Group Hole** tool be used in conjunction with the **Add to Graphic Shape** tool?
4. What is the difference between creating a **Surface of Projection** from an outline grouped with the aid of the **Add to Graphic Group** tool and one grouped with the **Create Region** tool?
5. Experiment with an open outline with both the **Create Complex Chain** tool and the **Create Complex Shape** tool. What happens?
6. When using the **Create Region** tool, there are a number of **Methods** which can be set from a pop-up list in the Element Selection box of the tool. Can you explain the action of each of these methods?
7. Some of the renderings shown in this chapter have been made with the **Phong** form of rendering. Try rendering a **Surface of Projection** with **Phong** and then with **Phong Antialias**. What differences can you see between the two renderings?
8. Now try rendering with the **Filled Hidden Line** type of rendering. What difference is there between this type of rendering and one of the **Phong** renderings?
9. Try the **Create Complex Shape** tool on an outline using the **Manual** method (selected from the tool's Element Selection box). What is the difference between using the **Automatic** and the **Manual** methods?
10. Why are the **Groups** tools so important in the construction of 3D models in MicroStation 95?

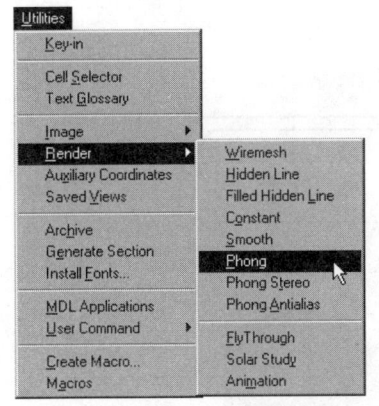

Fig. 15.21 Selecting rendering commands from the **Utilities** pull-down menu

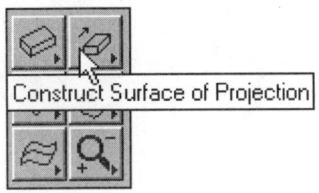

Fig. 15.22 The **Construct Surface of Projection** tool from the **3D Tools** palette

Exercises

After constructing each of the outlines and using the **Groups** tools to form them into groups, try using the rendering techniques from the **Utilities** pull-down menu, shown in Fig. 15.21.

Before rendering is possible, the grouped outline must first be acted upon by the **Construct Surface of Projection** tool from the **3D Tools** palette (Fig. 15.22). When the tool is selected its Element Selection box contains a pop-up list labelled **Type** (Fig. 15.23). It will be seen that the resulting surface of projection can either be solid (totally enclosed with a top and a bottom) or a surface (only surfaces without top or bottom). Note, however, that this **Type** will not function with some of the **Groups** tools.

Note also in the Element Selection box that the **Distance** box shows the height for the surface of projection. However this will not

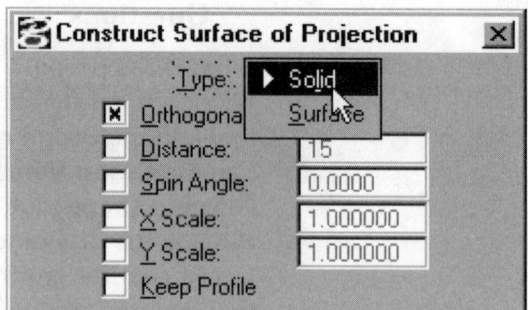

Fig. 15.23 The **Construct Surface of Projection** Element Selection box showing its **Type** pop-up list

be effective until the check box to the left of **Distance:** is checked (**X** in check box). Thus to set a height for your projection, *left-click* in the **Distance:** check box to set it on, followed by *entering* the required height in the **Distance** box.

1. Figure 15.24 shows the outline and a rendering of a window clip. Working to the given dimensions, construct the outline, produce a projection from your outline and then render with **Phong Antialias**.

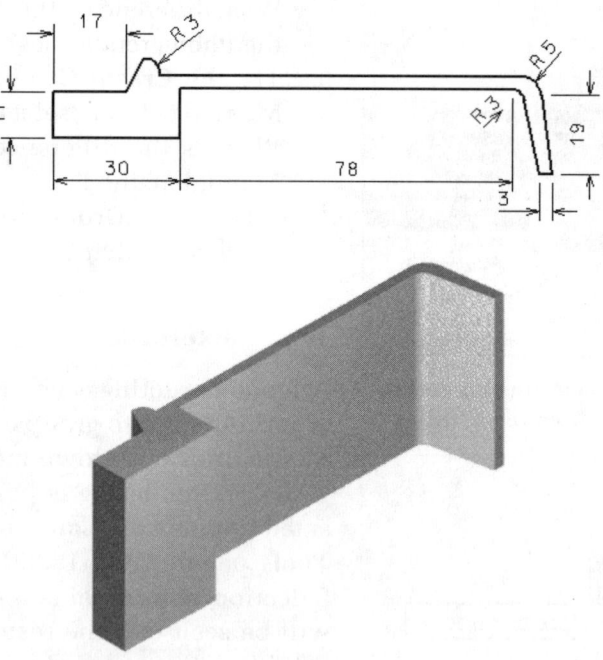

Fig. 15.24 Exercise 1

2. Figure 15.25 gives the outline and a rendering of a part for a pneumatic pump. Working to the dimensions given with the outline, construct the 3D model with a height of 25 mm. Then with **Phong Antialias**, render your model.

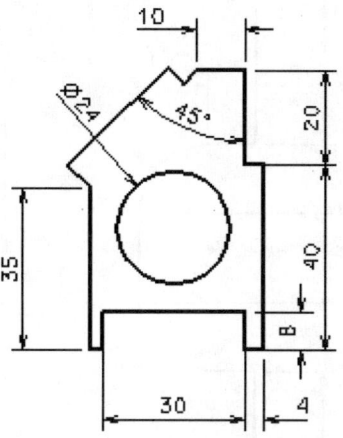

Fig. 15.25 Exercise 2

3. Figure 15.26 shows the outline and rendering of a pipe clip. Construct the given outline and group it with an appropriate **Groups** tool. Then form a projection of height 15 mm, which can be rendered with the aid of the **Phong Antialias** command.

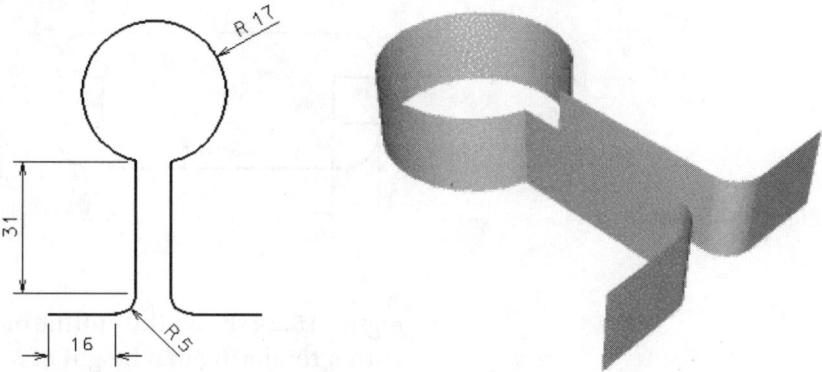

Fig. 15.26 Exercise 3

4. Figure 15.27 shows the outline of a clip, together with a **Filled Hidden Line** rendering of the projected clip. The height of the projection is 20 mm. Working to the given dimensions, construct the outline, group its elements and, after projecting the outline 20 mm high, render with the appropriate rendering command.

5. Figure 15.28 shows an outline for a mould tray, together with a rendering of the tray outline projected to a height of 8 mm. Construct the outline to the given sizes, project it 8 mm high and render with an appropriate rendering command.

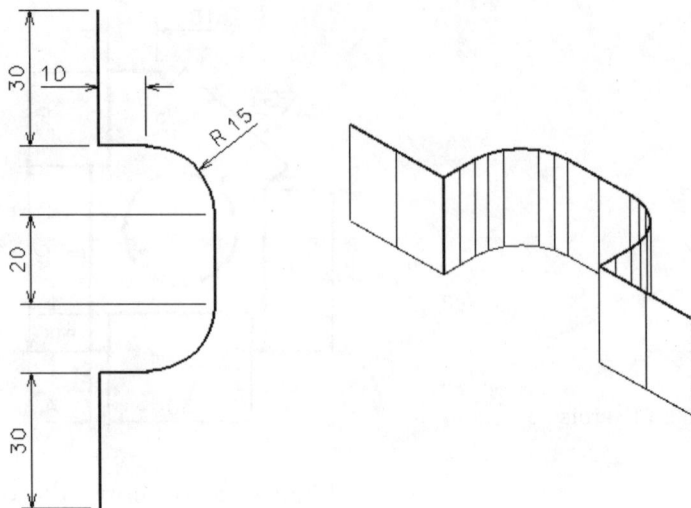

Fig. 15.27 Exercise 4

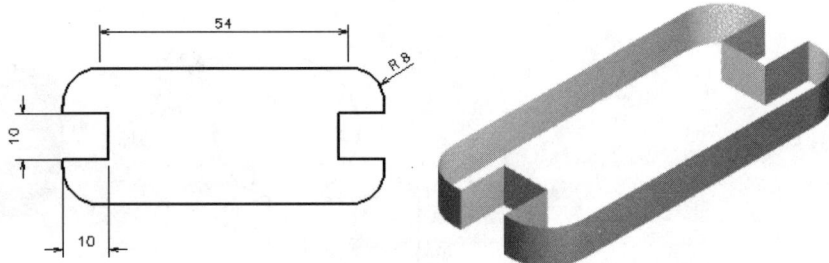

Fig. 15.28 Exercise 5

6. Figure 15.29 shows the outline of the handle for a tool box, together with a rendering of a height of 5 mm. Construct the outline to the given dimensions, group its elements, project it to a height of 5 mm and then render with an appropriate rendering command.

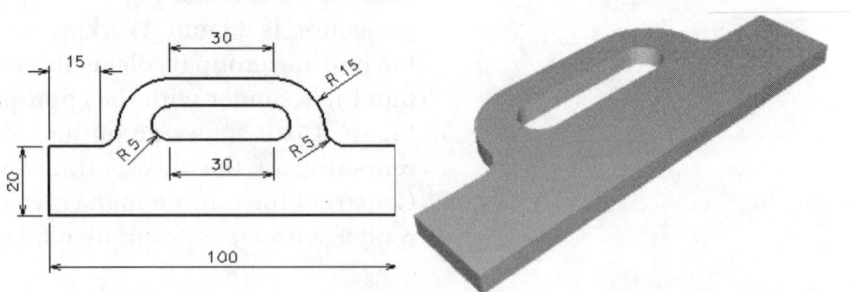

Fig. 15.29 Exercise 6

7. The drawing on the left of Fig. 15.30 shows a view of a clip for fitting to a pipe of 50 mm diameter. A 15 mm high rendering of the clip is given to the right of the drawing. Working to sizes based on the pipe diameter, construct the outline, group its elements and then render with **Phong Antialias**.

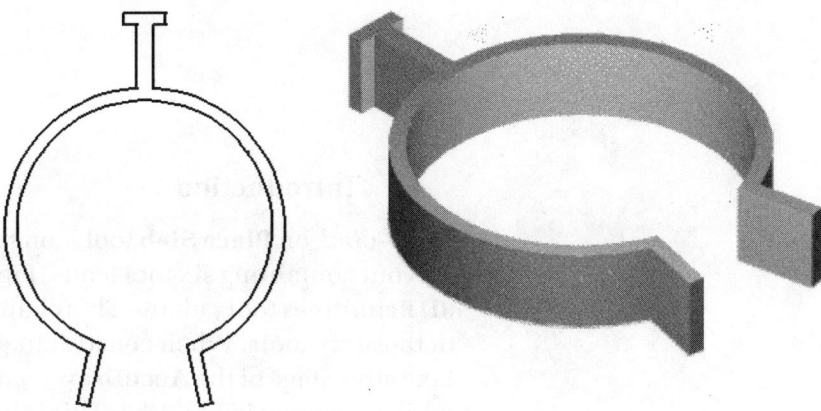

Fig. 15.30 Exercise 7

CHAPTER 16

3D Primitives

Introduction

A *left-click* on **Place Slab** tool icon in the **3D Tools** palette brings up a flyout containing six tool icons (Fig. 16.1) These are the tools in the **3D Primitives** tool palette. This chapter is concerned with the action of these six tools. When constructing any 3D model it is advisable to take advantage of the **AccuDraw** compasses, the **Rectangular** type of which is shown in Fig. 16.2. This is because accuracy of constructing to given sizes is much easier when AccuDraw is in operation. In Fig. 16.2 the AccuDraw coordinate window is shown on screen, but as indicated in Chapter 14, we will be working with the AccuDraw coordinate window in the Status Bar.

When working with the **3D Primitive** tools, the resulting 3D model can be in either a **Solid** or a **Surface** form. The differences between these two forms are shown in illustrations in this chapter.

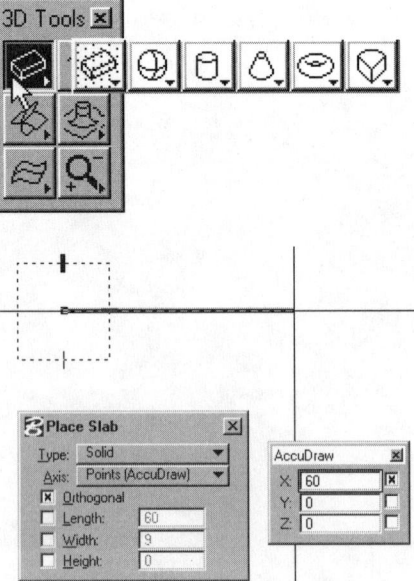

Fig. 16.1 The flyout resulting from a *left-click* on the **Place Slab** icon

Fig. 16.2 Use **AccuDraw** when constructing 3D models

The Place Slab tool

Figure **16.3** shows the **Place Slab** tool being selected from the **3D Primitives** tool palette, together with two slabs, one of which is in **Solid** form, the other in **Surface** form. The two slabs were constructed in a two-view window – **Top View** and **Isometric View**. In the **Isometric View** window the slabs have been rendered in **Phong Antialias**. To construct the two slabs.

First method

1. *Left-click* on the **Place Slab** tool icon. The tool's Element Selection box appears.
2. *Left-click* at a suitable point in the **Top View** window. The AccuDraw compass appears.
3. Move the cursors in the **X** direction of the AccuDraw compass. The prompt **Place Slab > Define length** appears in the Status Bar. A small vertical line blinking cursor appears in the **X** box of the AccuDraw window. *Enter* 40 and *left-click*.
4. Move the cursors in the **Y** direction (up or down). The Status Bar prompt changes to **Place Slab > Define width**. A small blinking line cursor appears in the **Y** box of the AccuDraw coordinate window. *Enter* 20 and *left-click*.
5. Move the cursors into the **Isometric View** window. The Status Bar will be showing **Place Slab >Define height**. *Enter* 15 and *left-click*.
6. *Right-click* and the AccuDraw compass disappears from the screen.

Second method

Instead of *entering* numbers in response to the blinking cursors appearing in the AccuDraw coordinate window, the sizes of the slab

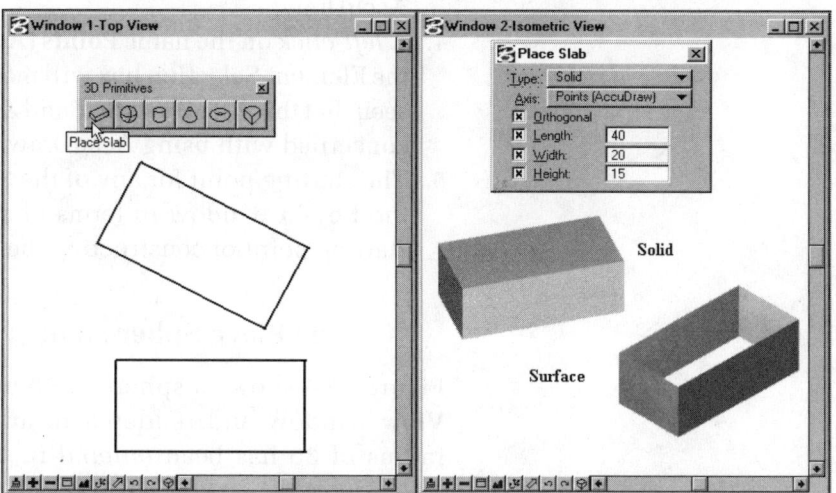

Fig. 16.3 Two examples of slabs – **Solid** and **Surface**

can be *entered* in the relevant boxes in the **Place Slab** Element Selection **Length**, **Width** and **Height** boxes. First, *left-click* in each of the check boxes against **Length**, **Width** and **Height**, followed by *entering* the required sizes in the boxes to the right of the words in the Element Selection box. Then:

1. In the **Top View** window, move the cursors in the **X** direction of the AccuDraw compass and *left-click.*
2. Move the cursors in the **Y** direction of the AccuDraw compass and *left-click.*
3. Move the cursors into the **Isometric View** window and move the cursors in the **Z** direction of the AccuDraw compass, followed by a *left-click.* Then *right-click* to complete the operation.

Notes

1. A **Surface** 3D model will be open at top and bottom, as illustrated by the lower slab in Fig. 16.3. A **Solid** 3D model will be totally enclosed as in the upper slab in Fig. 16.3. In order to construct a solid or surface model, set the **Type** in the pop-up list of the appropriate tool's Element Selection box. In Fig. 16.3, the **Type** is set for the upper slab to **Solid**. To set to **Surface** *left-click* on the word **Solid** and in the pop-up list which appears *left-click* on **Surface**.
2. When *entering* **Length**, **Width** and **Height** numbers in the AccuDraw coordinate window, there is no need to *click* in the boxes in the coordinate window. All that is required is to *enter* the required figures at the keyboard.
3. There is no need to *click* in the **X**, **Y** or **Z** boxes when working with AccuDraw, because when the AccuDraw compass is active, the directions in which the cursors are moved is 'recognised' by AccuDraw.
4. A *left-click* on the name **Points (AccuDraw)** in the **Axis** window of the Element Selection box will make a pop-up list appear. It will be seen that this list allows **X**, **Y** and **Z** axes to be used. Here we are only concerned with using AccuDraw.
5. The starting point for any of the **3D primitives** can be *keyed-in* in the **Key-in** window in terms of an X,Y,Z coordinate if the exact starting point of constructing the primitive is necessary.

The Place Sphere tool

Figure 16.4 shows a sphere of 30 mm radius constructed in a **Top View** window and rendered in an **Isometric View** window. The radius of 30 has been *entered* in the **Radius** box of the Element

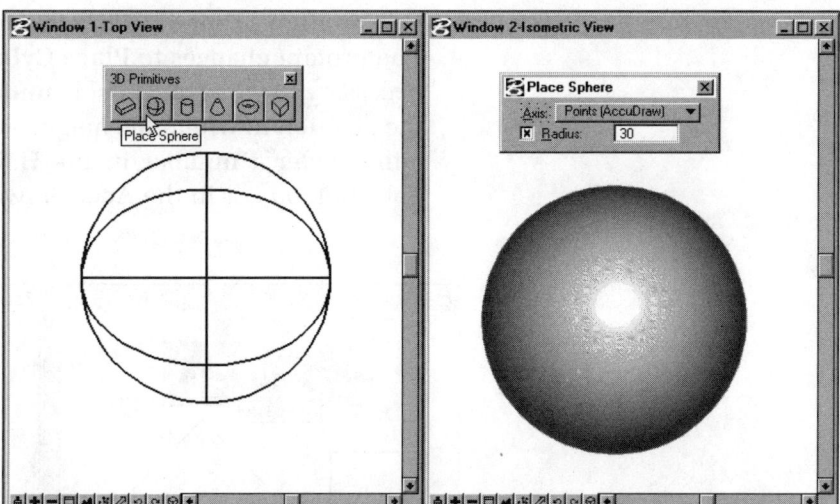

Fig. 16.4 An example of the use of the **Place Sphere** tool

Selection box, but it could equally as well have been *entered* in the AccuDraw coordinate window. To place a sphere:

1. *Left-click* on the **Place Sphere** tool icon in the **3D Primitives** palette. The prompt **Place Sphere > Enter center point** appears at the Status Bar. Either *left-click* at a suitable point or *key-in* X,Y,Z coordinates in the **Key-in** window.
2. Move the cursors in a suitable direction in the AccuDraw compass. The prompt **Place Sphere > Define axis and radius** appears. *Left-click* to set the already defined radius. *Right-click* to complete the operation.

The Place Cylinder tool

Fig. 16.5 shows three **Solid** cylinders of the same dimensions placed in various positions with the **Orthogonal** option set in the tool's Element Selection box in two windows of the screen. Figure 16.6 shows three **Surface** cylinders of the same dimensions, but with the **Orthogonal** option off. With the **Orthogonal** check box off, cylinders can be constructed on the skew, as will be seen in the given illustration.

To construct a cylinder:

1. *Left-click* on the **Place Cylinder** tool icon in the **3D Primitives** dialogue palette.
2. Either *left-click* at a suitable point in the window or, *key-in* coordinates.
3. The Status Bar prompt shows **Place Cylinder > Define radius**. Either *enter* a radius in the **Radius** box of the tool's Element

Selection box or *enter* a radius in the AccuDraw coordinate window.

4. The prompt changes to **Place Cylinder > Define height**. It will be necessary to move the cursors under mouse control in order to see the position in which the height axis of the cylinder will lie. Then either *enter* a number in the **Height** box of the tool's Element Selection box or in the AccuDraw coordinate window.

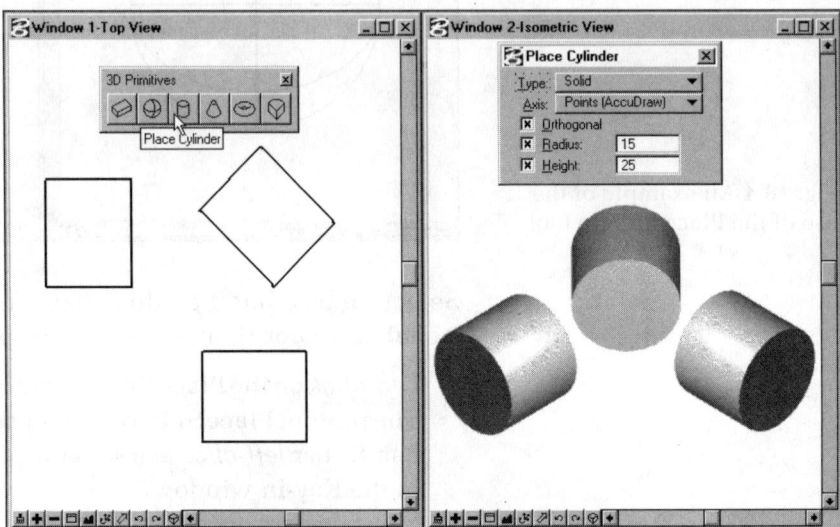

Fig. 16.5 Three **Solid Orthogonal** cylinders

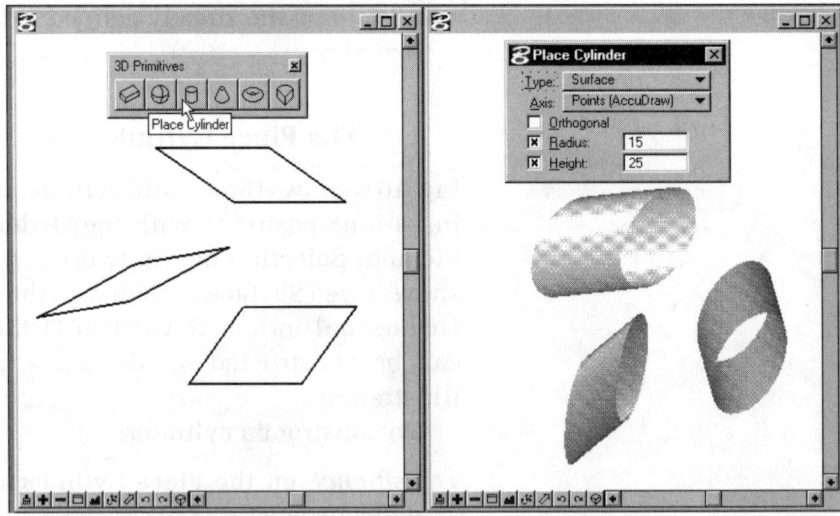

Fig. 16.6 Three **Surface** cylinders with **Orthogonal** set off

The Place Cone tool

Figure 16.7 shows two **Solid** cones and a **Surface** cone at a variety of angles in the **Top View** window, together with renderings of the cones in the **Isometric View** window. The sizes can again either be *entered* in the tool's Element Selection box or *entered* in the AccuDraw coordinate window. When the sizes have been predetermined by *entering* in the Element Selection box, the two prompts appearing in the Status bar when the tool is in action are:

Place Cone > Enter center point
Place Cone > Define axis

and when the centre point has been entered (*left-click* or *key-in* coordinates) the axis direction is determined by moving the top view of the cone which appears to a suitable direction.

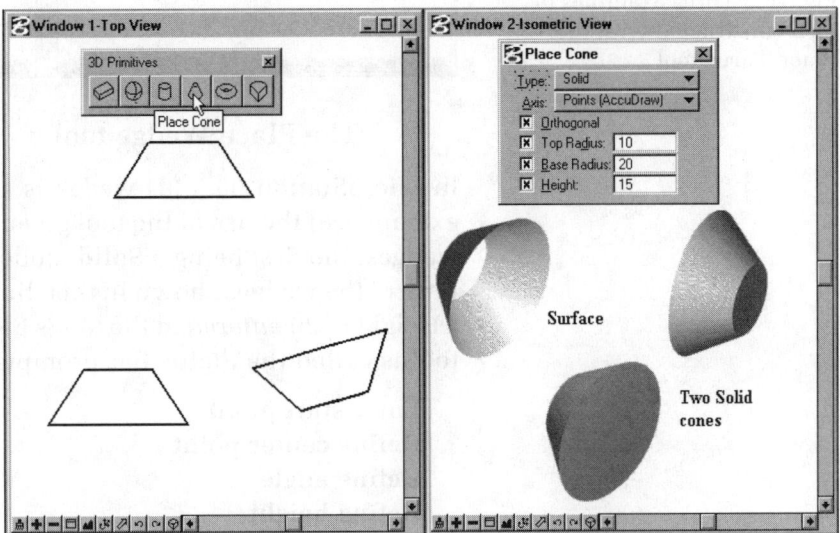

Fig. 16.7 Three examples of cones constructed with the **Place Cone** tool

The Place Torus tool

Figure 16.8 shows three torii – a **Surface** torus constructed with the **Angle** setting at 180° degrees, a **Solid** torus with the **Angle** setting at 270° and another with the setting at 360°. In each of these three examples the other settings in the tool's Element Selection box were as shown in Fig. 16.8. The Status Bar prompts associated with this tool are:

Place Torus > Enter start point
Define central point
Define axis of revolution

These prompts appear when the sizes of the **Primary Radius**, **Secondary Radius** and **Angle** have been predetermined by *entering* in the tool's Element Selection box.

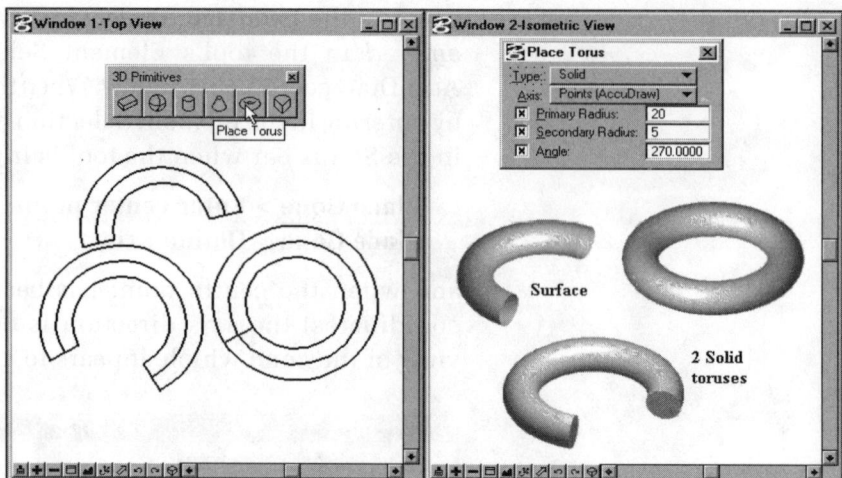

Fig. 16.8 Three examples of torii constructed with the **Place Torus** tool

The Place Wedge tool

In MicroStation 95 a 3D wedge is a sector of a cylinder. The two examples of the use of the tool given in Fig. 16.9 show 90° and 225° wedges, the first being a **Solid** model, the second a **Surface** model. Both of the wedges shown in this illustration had a **Radius** of 30 and a **Height** of 20 *entered* in the tool's Element Selection box. When the tool is called the Status Bar prompts show:

> **Enter start point**
> **Define center point**
> **Define angle**
> **Define height**

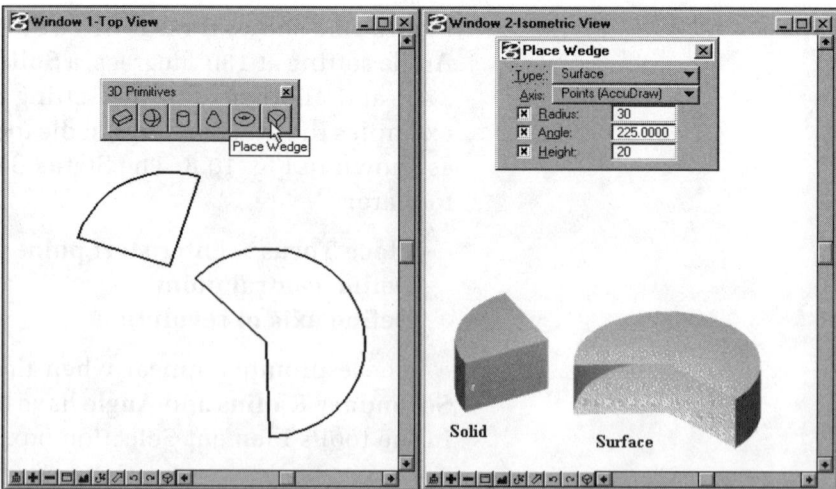

Fig. 16.9 Two examples of wedges constructed with the **Place Wedge** tool

If the sizes have previously been *keyed-in* to the Element Selection box, all that is required in response to each of the prompts is a *left-click*, with a movement in the direction of the **center point** after the second prompt. A *right-click* completes the operation.

Examples of 3D models

Example 1

Figure 16.10 shows a simple example of a 3D model constructed from four solid primitives – two cylinders, a torus and a slab. To construct the model draw its four parts in correct positions relative to each other in the **Top View** window. It will then be seen that, while the circular parts (the cylinders and the torus) are in line with each other in the **Front View** window, the slab requires to be moved to bring its centre in line with the other three component parts of the model. This can effectively be carried out with the aid of the **Move** tool from the **Manipulate** tool palette (Fig. 16.11).

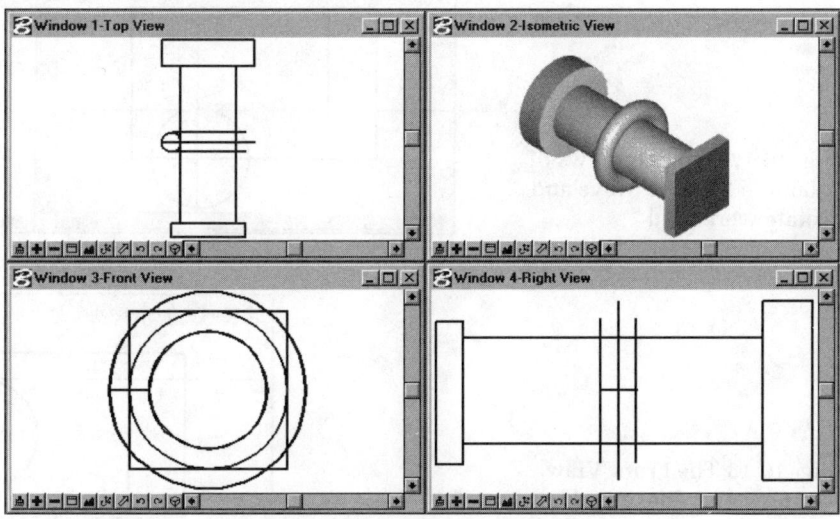

Fig. 16.10 Example 1

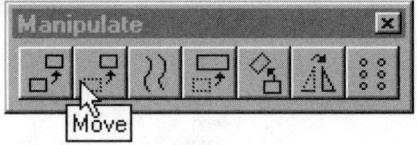

Fig. 16.11 The **Move** tool from the **Manipulate** palette

Note

The tools in the **Manipulate** palette – **Copy**, **Move**, **Move Parallel**, **Scale**, **Rotate**, **Mirror** and **Array** – can all be employed on 3D solids in any of the windows of MicroStation 95.

Example 2

Figure 16.12 shows a 3D model of a holder constructed in four windows. The four parts of the model – three slabs and a cylinder – were constructed in the **Top View** window. The cylinder was then moved in the **Front View** window to a central position within the two slabs of the model, giving the result shown in Fig. 16.13. Each part was then acted upon with the tool **Rotate** to rotate the whole model into a better viewing position. After rendering, the result is shown in Fig. 16.14.

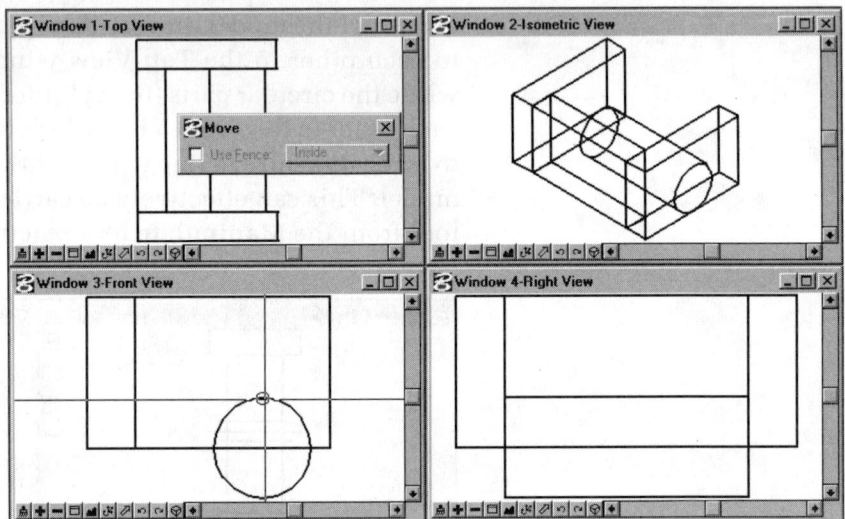

Fig. 16.12 The four views of Example 2 before **Move** and **Rotate** were used

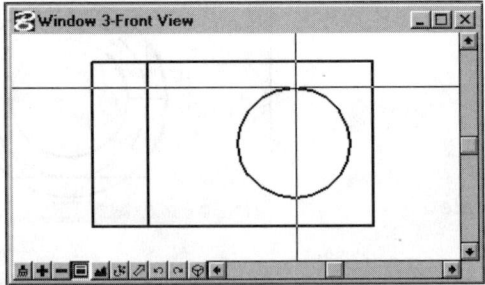

Fig. 16.13 The **Front View** window after **Move** had been used to place the cylinder in a central position

Example 3

Figure 16.15 shows the four parts of a 3D model placed at random in the **Top View** window. Figure 16.16 shows the same 3D model after all parts had been moved and then rotated. The moves and rotations took place in the windows most suited to the action taking place. Figure 16.16 includes a rendering of the completed model.

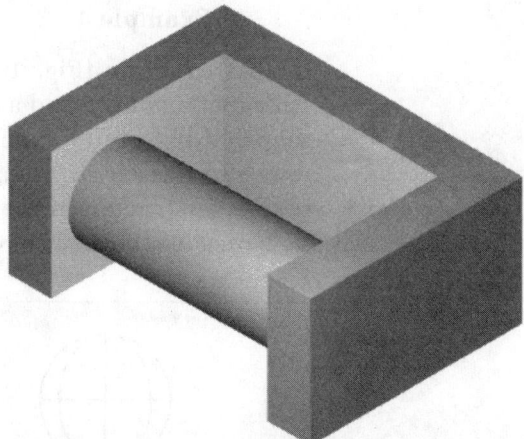

Fig. 16.14 A **Phong** rendering of Example 2 after all parts had been acted upon with **Rotate**

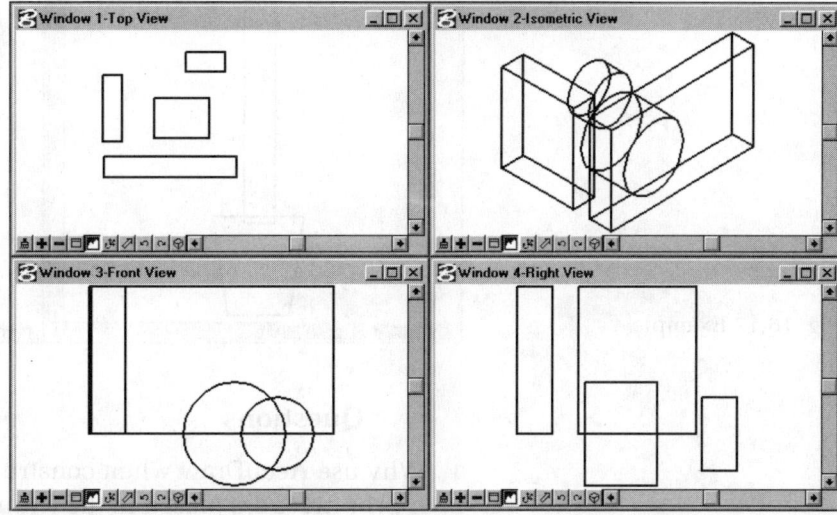

Fig. 16.15 The Example 2 before moving and rotating its parts

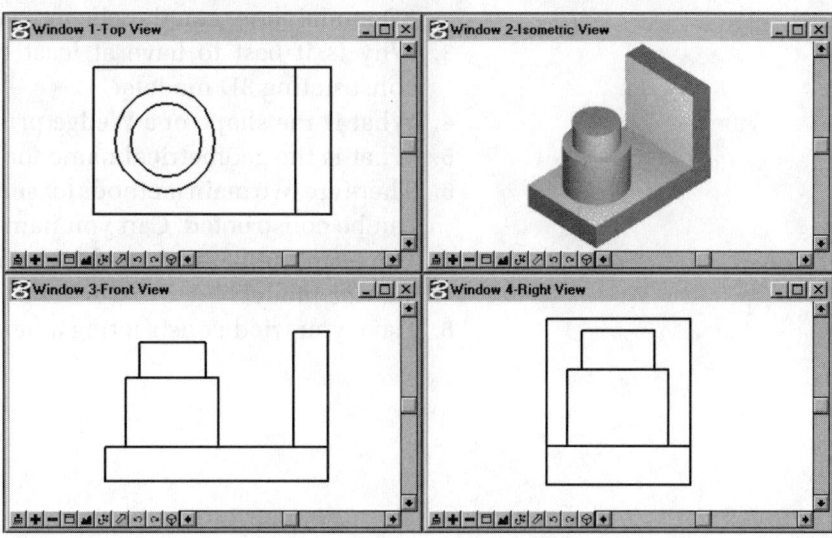

Fig. 16.16 The completed model after moving and rotating its parts

Example 4

In this example (Fig. 16.17), because each part was circular – a cylinder, a sphere and a cone – no action upon any of its parts was required before the completed model was rendered. All that was required was care in placing the three parts of the model as they were being constructed in the **Top View** window.

Note also that only two windows were necessary in this example.

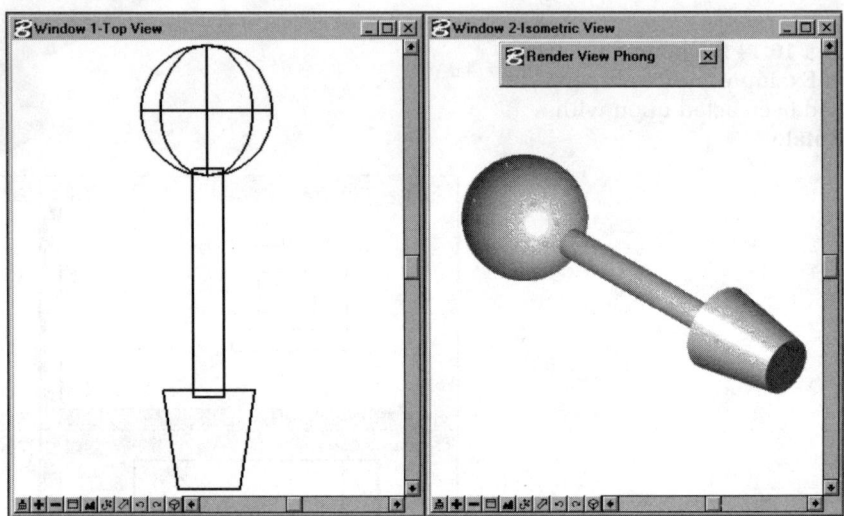

Fig. 16.17 Example 4

Questions

1. Why use AccuDraw when constructing 3D models?
2. If primitives are placed in the wrong position when constructing a 3D model, how can they be moved?
3. Why is it best to have at least two view windows open when constructing 3D models?
4. What is the shape of a **Wedge** primitive based upon?
5. What is the geometrical name for a slab?
6. There are two main methods for setting the sizes to which primitives can be constructed. Can you name them?
7. How can the parameters for a primitive be set so as to produce a surface model?
8. Have you tried constructing a hemisphere?

Exercises

1. Figure 16.18 is a dimensioned two-view orthographic projection of a bobbin. Working to the given dimensions, construct and render a 3D model of the bobbin.

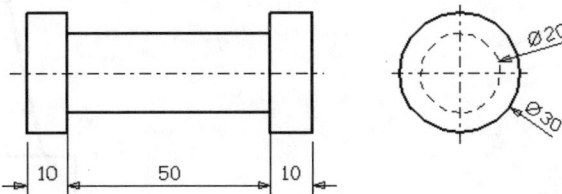

Fig. 16.18 Exercise 1

2. Figure 16.19 is a two-view orthographic projection of a turnkey with a square shank. Working to the dimensions given with the two views, construct and render a 3D model of the turnkey.

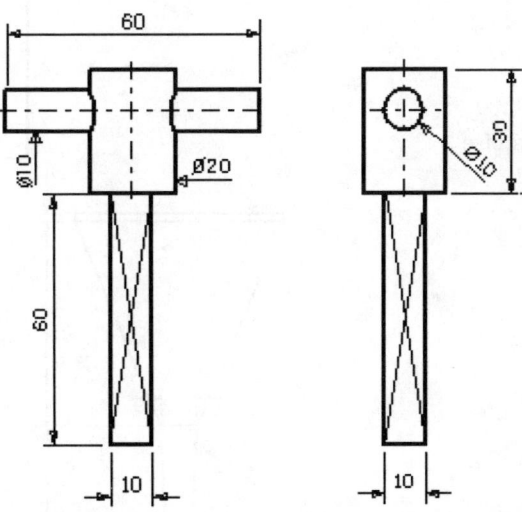

Fig. 16.19 Exercise 2

3. Figure 16.20 is a front view and plan of a stand made from a square base, a cone and a square prism. Working to the dimensions given with the two views, construct a 3D model of the stand.

4. Figure 16.21 is a front view of a funnel and Fig. 16.22 a rendering of the funnel. Working to the sizes in Fig. 16.21, construct and render a 3D model of the funnel.

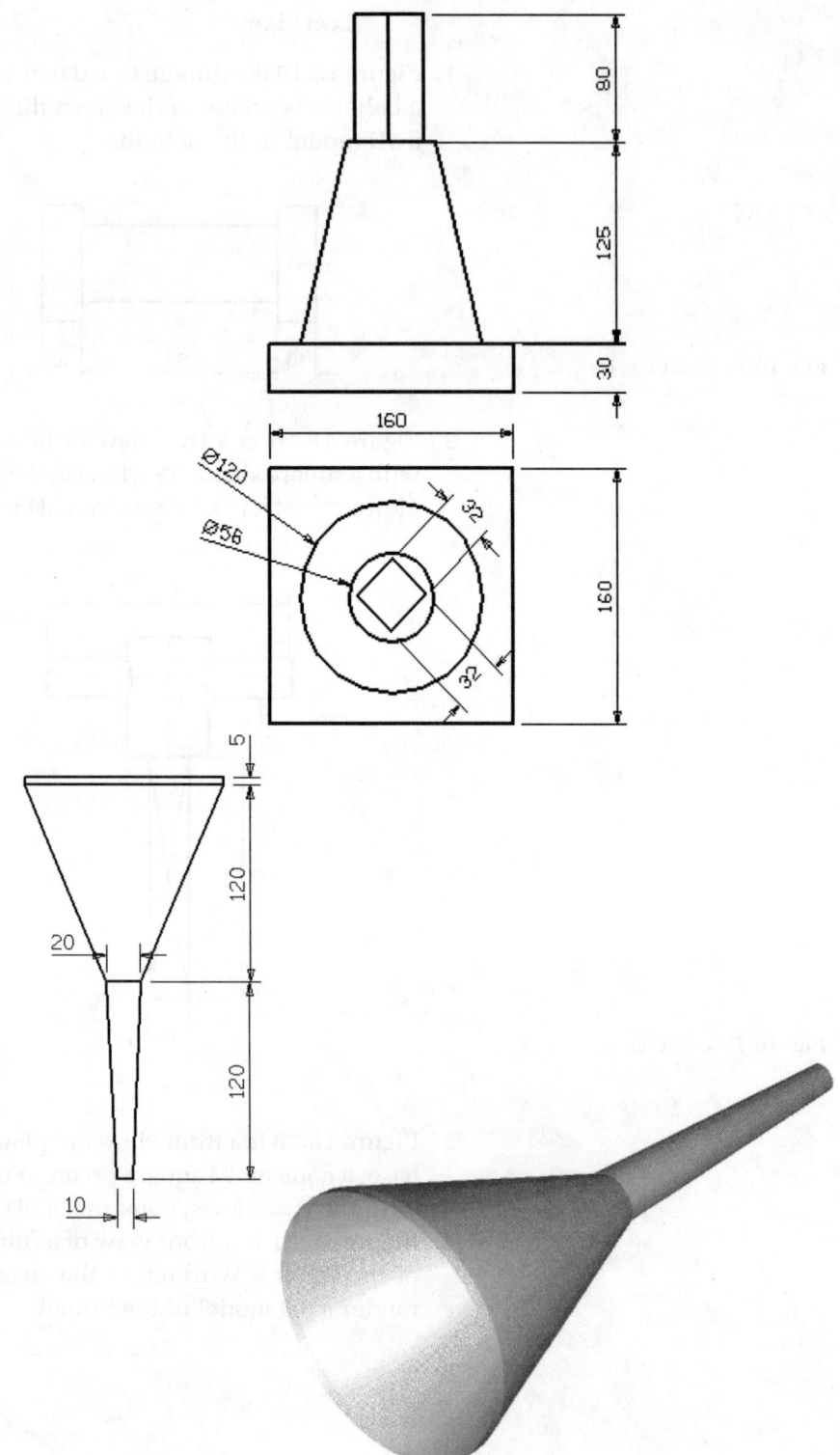

Fig. 16.20 Exercise 3

Fig. 16.21 Exercise 4

Fig. 16.22 A rendering of
Exercise 4

CHAPTER 17

3D Free-form Surfaces

Introduction

Left-click on the **Construct Surface of Projection** tool in the **3D Tools** palette and the **3D Free-form Surfaces** flyout appears (Fig. 17.1).

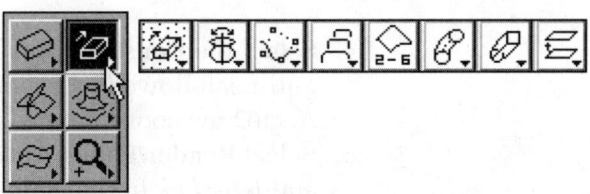

Fig. 17.1 The **3D Free-form Surfaces** flyout

We have already seen some of the results from using the **Construct Surface of Projection** tool from the **3D Free-form Surfaces** palette in a previous chapter (Chapter 15). Some further examples of the results of using this tool will be included in this chapter, together with examples of the use of the other tools in the palette.

The Construct Surface of Projection tool

Example 1

This is shown in Fig. 17.2. The procedure for constructing the 3D model for this example was:

1. In the **Top View** window, with AccuDraw active, construct the outline of the 3D model and add the rectangular and circular holes using the **Smart Line** and **Place Circle** tools.
2. Select the **Create Region** tool and *left-click* on the **Smart Line** outline.
3. Select the **Group Holes** tool and *left-click* on the outline, *right-click*, then *left-click* on each of the holes in turn.

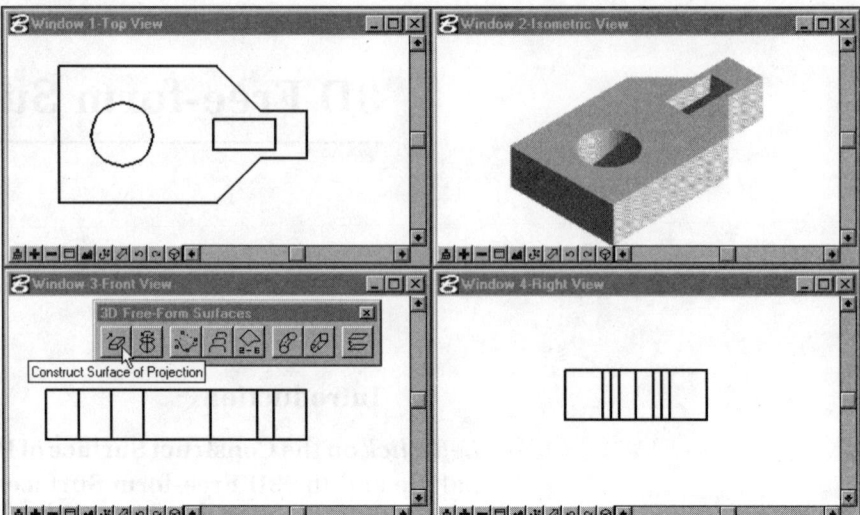

Fig. 17.2 Example 1. Using the **Construct Surface of Projection** tool

4. Select the **Construct Surface of Projection** tool, *left-click* on the outline, followed by *keying-in* the height figure in the Z box of the AccuDraw coordinate window.
5. Select **Render/Phong Antialias** from the **utilities** pull-down menu and *left-click* in the **Isometric** window to render the 3D model.

Example 2

This is shown in Fig. 17.3. To construct the 3D model:

1. In the **Top View** window and using the tools **Place Circle**, **Polar Array**, **Circular Fillet**, **Delete Part of Element** and **Trim Element** construct the outline.
2. *Left-click* on each element in the outline with the **Create Complex Shape** tool active.

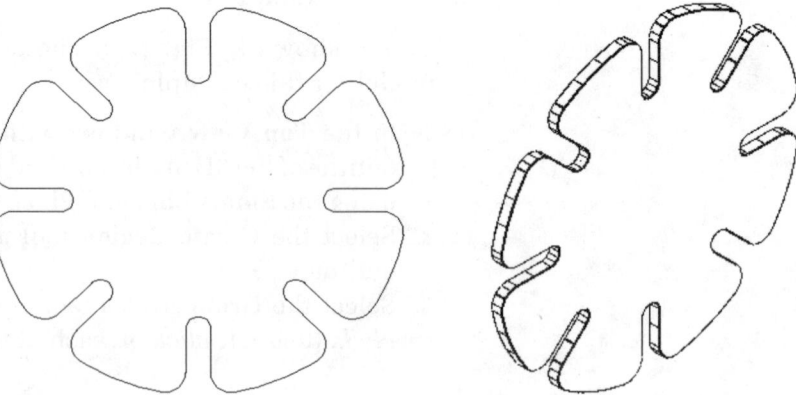

Fig. 17.3 Example 2. Using the **Construct Surface of Projection** tool

3. *Left-click* on the **Construct Surface of Projection** tool and *enter* an appropriate figure in the Z box of the AccuDraw coordinate window. *Left-click* on the grouped outline, followed by a second *left-click*. The 3D model appears in the **Isometric** window as shown in the right-hand drawing of Fig. 17.3.

Example 3

This is shown in Fig. 17.4. The procedure for constructing the 3D model was:

1. Construct the outline shown in the left-hand drawing of Fig. 17.4 in the **Top View** window – using the **Place Circle**, **Smart Line**, **Circular Fillet**, **Delete Part of Element** and **Trim Element** tools.
2. With the **Create Complex Shape** tool, form the outline into a complex shape.
3. With the **Construct Surface of Projection** tool, form a 3D model of height 120 mm from the complex shape.
4. With the **Place Block** tool, construct a second 3D model of sizes 140 mm by 80 mm by 10 mm for the base of the handle.
5. Use **Phong Antialias** to render the model.

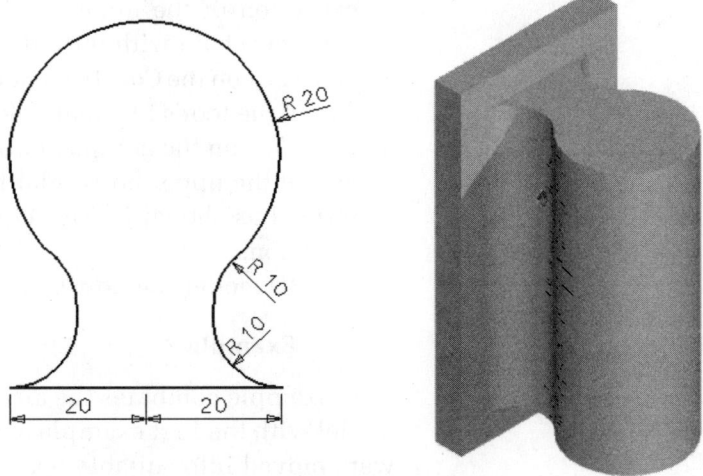

Fig. 17.4 Example 3. Using the **Construct Surface of Projection** tool

The Construct Surface of Revolution tool

Example 1

This is shown in Figs 17.5 and 17.6. Figure 17.5 shows the outline on which the surface of revolution was based and the screen in Fig. 17.6 shows the completed example in all four windows in which the example was constructed. The procedure for the construction was:

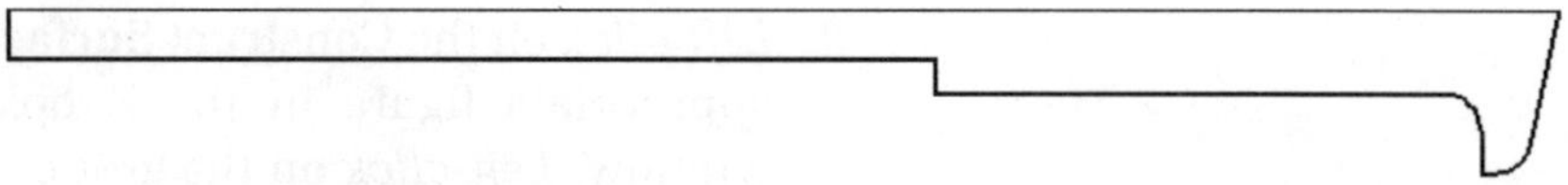

Fig. 17.5 Example 1. The outline from which the model was revolved

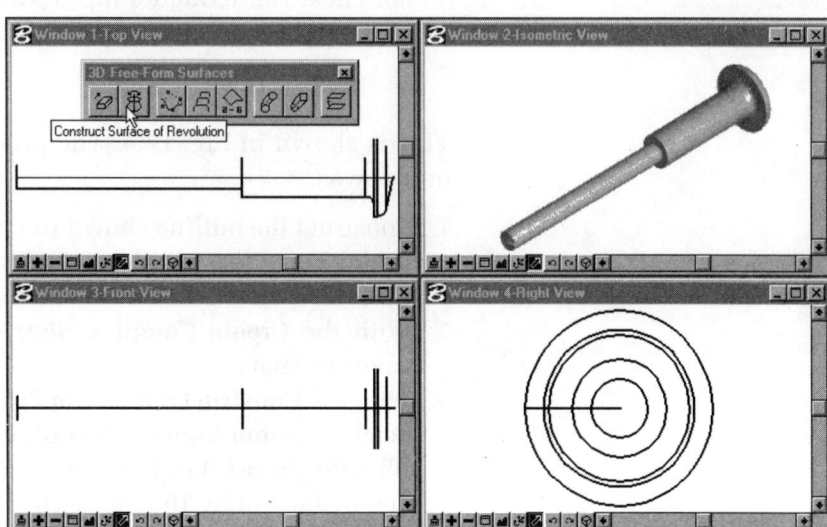

Fig. 17.6 Example 1. Using the **Construct Surface of Revolution** tool. The completed example

1. Using AccuDraw construct the outline Fig. 17.5, and with the exception of the upper horizontal line, turn the outline into a complex chain with the aid of the **Create Complex Chain** tool.
2. *Left-click* on the **Construct Surface of Revolution** tool. In the **Angle** box of the tool's Element Selection box *enter* 360.
3. *Left-click* on the grouped outline, followed by a *left-click* on each end of the upper horizontal line and the surface of revolution is formed as shown in Fig. 17.6. Use snaps to ensure accuracy of selection.
4. The 3D model can now be rendered in the **Isometric** window.

Example 2

This example combines the already described surface of projection model with the first example of a revolved 3D model. The two parts were moved into suitable positions relative to each other with the aid of the **Move Element** and **Revolve Element** tools in suitable windows of the screen before rendering. Figure 17.7 shows the four windows of the screen in which this example was developed and Fig. 17.8 the rendered model to a larger scale.

Example 3

Figure 17.9 shows the outline from which this example was formed. Figure 17.10 shows a **Filled Hidden Line** rendering of the completed

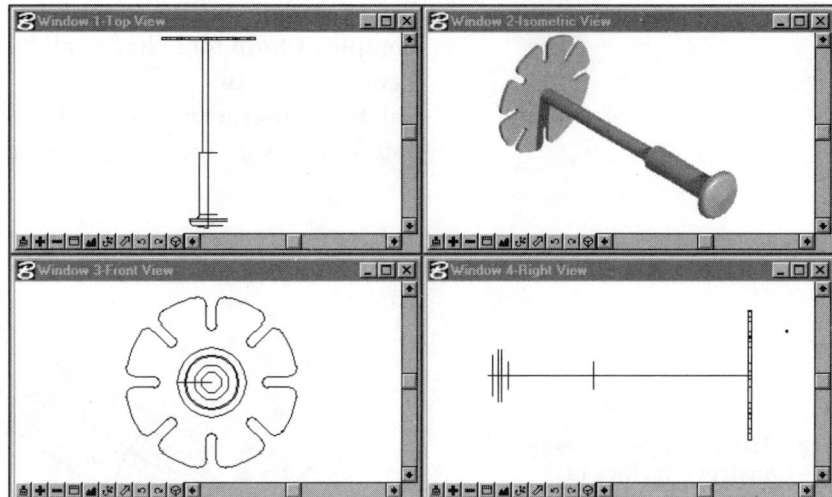

Fig. 17.7 Example 2. Using the **Construct Surface of Revolution**

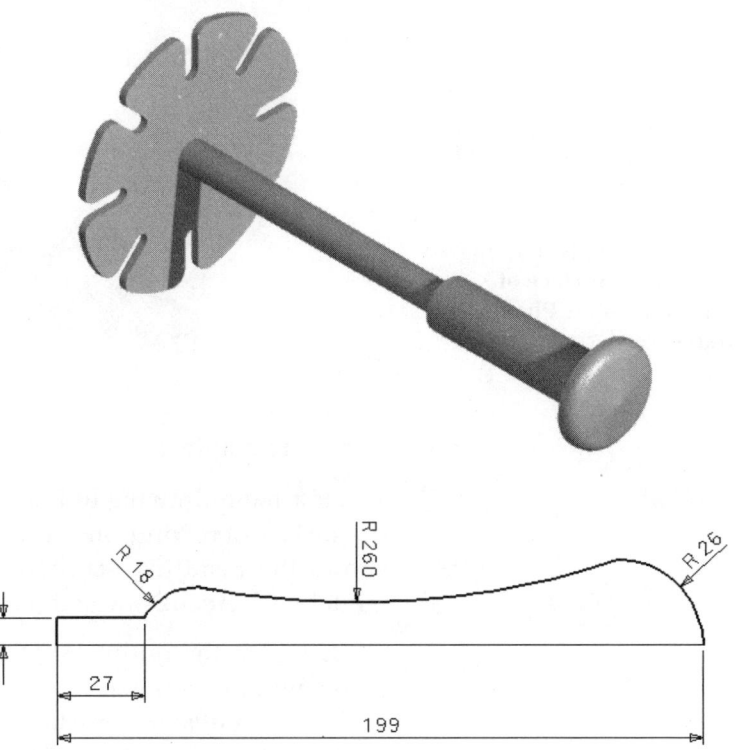

Fig. 17.8 Example 2. Using the **Construct Surface of Revolution** tool. A larger scale view of the rendering

Fig. 17.9 Example 3. Using the **Construct Surface of Revolution** tool. The complex chain outline

model after being acted upon by the **Construct Surface of Revolution** tool. Fig. 17.11 is a **Phong Antialias** rendering of the model. The procedure for constructing the example was:

1. Construct the outline shown in Fig. 17.9 and with the **Create Complex Chain** tool change all but the upper horizontal line into a complex chain.
2. Call the **Construct Surface of Revolution** tool. Set the **Angle** to 360 and *left-click* on the complex chain.

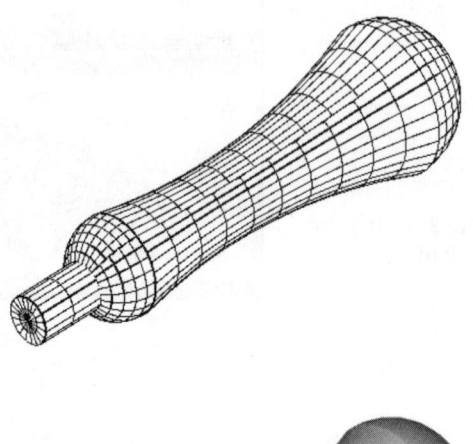

Fig. 17.10 Example 3. Using the **Construct Surface of Revolution** tool. A **Filled Hidden Line** rendering

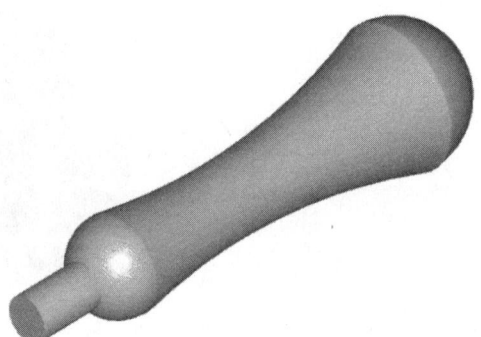

Fig. 17.11 Example 3. Using the **Construct Surface of Revolution** tool. A **Phong Antialias** rendering

Example 4

The left-hand drawing of Fig. 17.12 shows the outline from which the surface of revolution was formed and the right-hand illustration shows the resulting 3D model after rendering. To construct the model with AccuDraw active:

1. Construct the outline shown in Fig. 17.12 and add the axis of revolution as shown.
2. Call the **Construct Surface of Revolution** tool. *Enter* 360 in the **Angle** box of the tool's Element Selection box. *Left click* on the outline followed by *left-clicks* on each end of the axis of revolution line.
3. Render the model as thought fit. The right-hand illustration of Fig. 17.12 shows a **Phong Antialias** rendering.

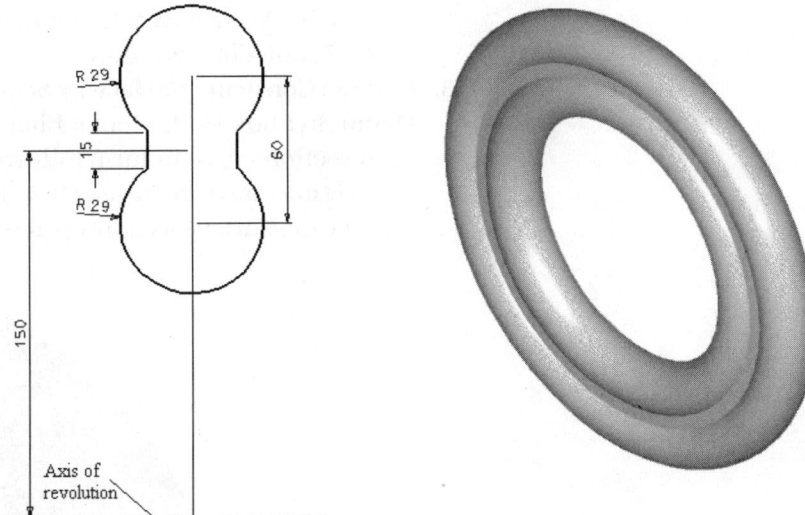

Fig. 17.12 Example 4. Using the **Construct Surface of Revolution** tool.

The Construct Surface by Section tool

Example 1

Figure 17.13 shows the four-window screen in which this example was constructed and Fig. 17.14 shows the resulting 3D model after rendering. To construct the model:

1. With AccuDraw active and with the **Vertex Type** set to **Rounded** in the tool's Element Selection box, and with a variety of radii *keyed-in* to the **Rounding Radius** box, draw five outlines as shown in the **Right View** window of Fig. 17.13.

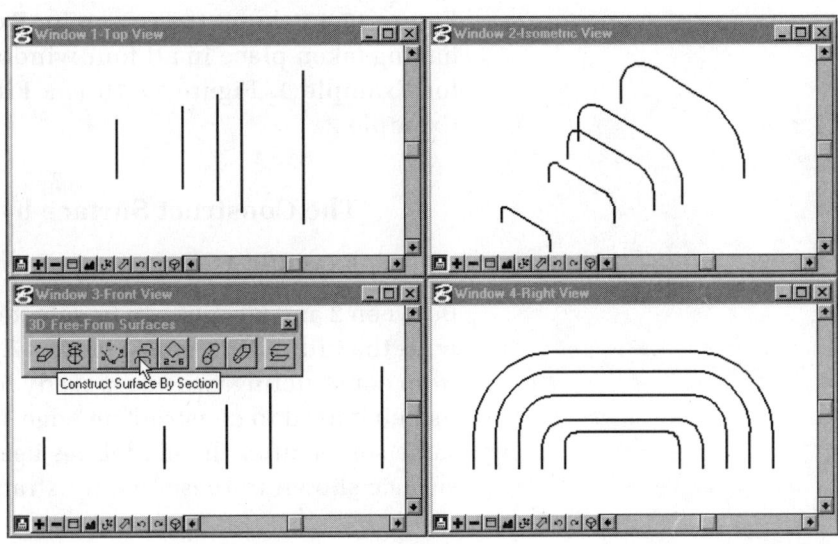

Fig. 17.13 Example 1. Using the **Construct Surface by Section** tool.

2. Again with AccuDraw active, move the outlines to suitable positions in the **Front View** window.
3. Call the **Construct Surface by Section** tool. Select **Section** from the **Define by:** box in the tool's Element Selection box. *Left-click* on each section curve in turn, followed by a second *left-click* after all the sections have been selected. The surface forms.
4. Render the surface as appropriate.

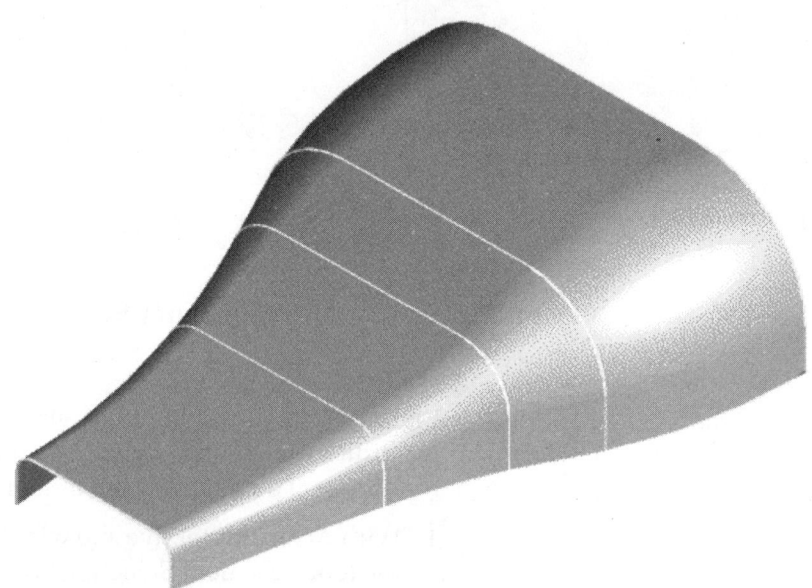

Fig. 17.14 Example 2. Using the **Construct Surface by Section** tool. A rendering

Example 2

Figure 17.15 shows the screen for Example 2 with the construction having taken place in all four windows in a similar manner to that for Example 1. Figure 17.16 is a **Filled Hidden Line** rendering of Example 2.

The Construct Surface by Edges tool

Example 1

Between 2 and 6 edges can be selected for the formation of a surface with the aid of this tool. Figure 17.17 shows the screen resulting from constructing two edges ready for selection by the tool prior to its being used to construct an edge surface. Figure 17.18 shows the same screen after the model has been completed. To construct the surface shown in these two illustrations:

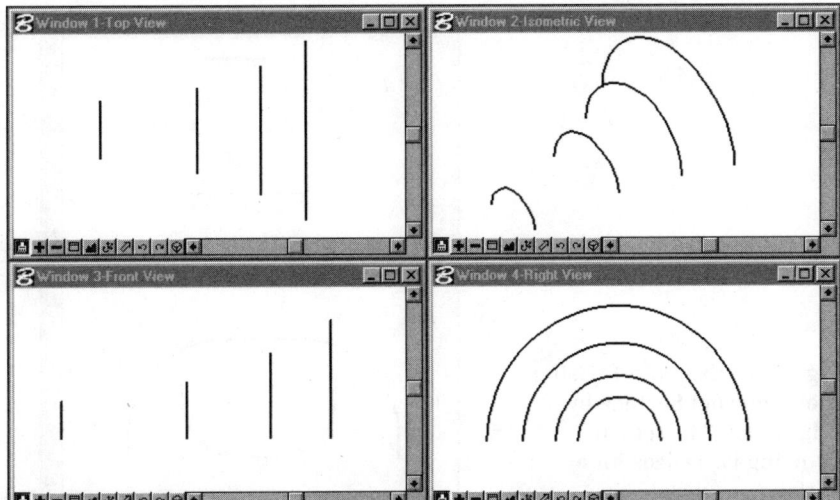

Fig. 17.15 Example 2. Using the **Construct Surface by Section** tool

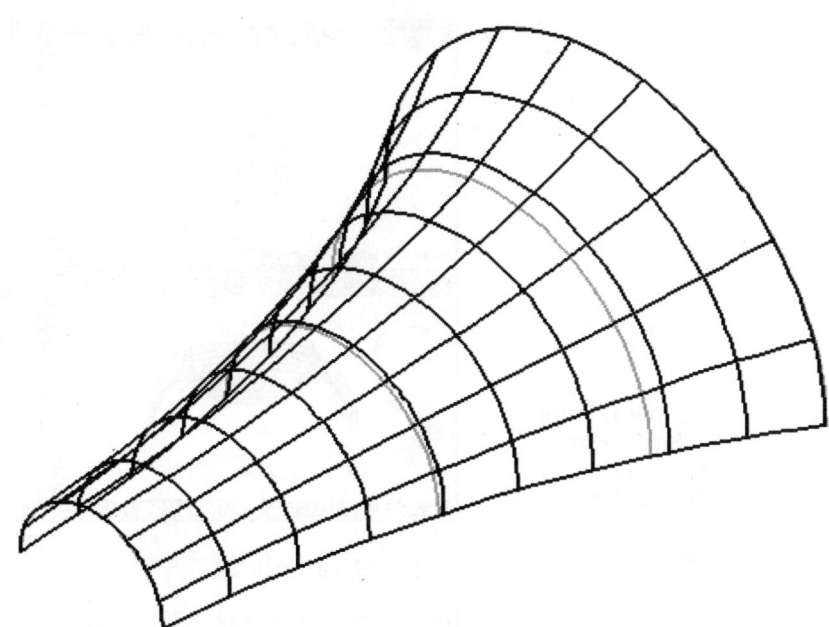

Fig. 17.16 Example 2. Using the **Construct Surface by Section** tool. A rendering

1. With AccuDraw in action and with **Vector Type** set to **Rounded** in the tool's Element Selection box, use **Smart Line** to draw the two edges shown in Fig. 17.17. With the **Move Element** tool move one of the smart lines to a new position.

2. Call the **Construct Surface by Edges** tool and select each edge one after the other with a *left-click* on each. The surface forms as shown in Fig. 17.18.

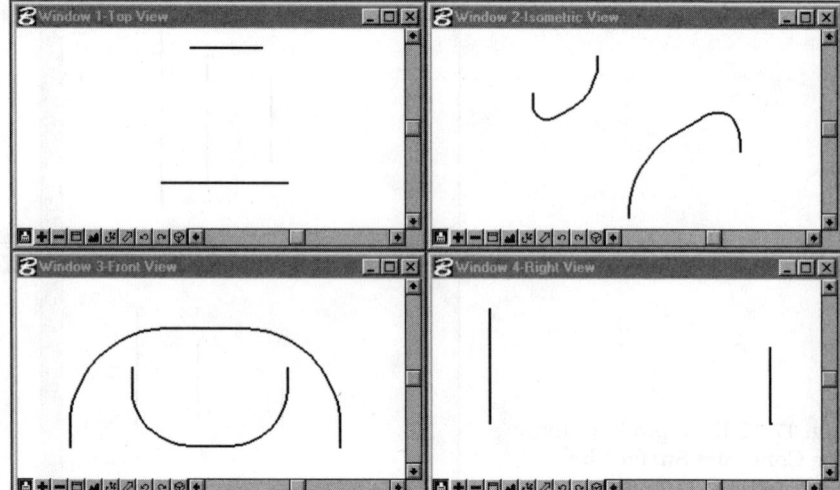

Fig. 17.17 Example 1. Using the **Construct Surface by Edges** tool. The screen showing two edges for a surface

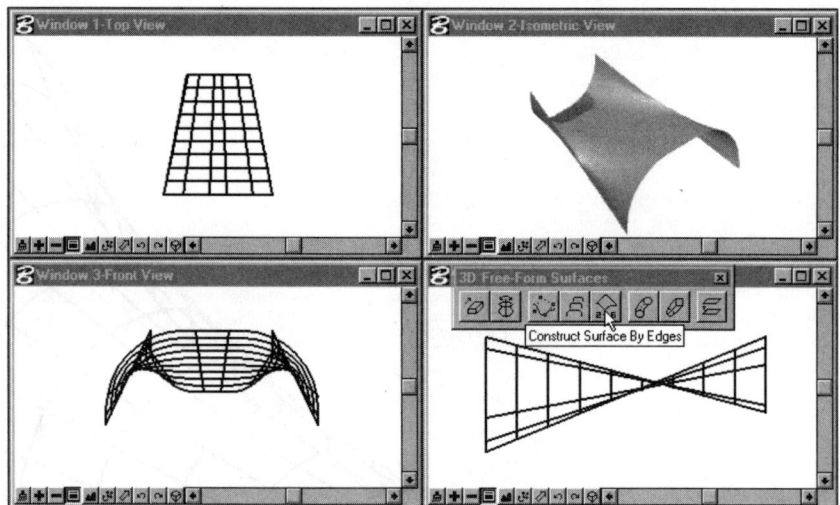

Fig. 17.18 Example 1. Using the **Construct Surface by Edges** tool. The screen after the action of the tool

Example 2

In this example (Fig. 17.19) the surface was formed from four edges. It must be noted that when using more than two edges to form a surface, the ends of each of the edges must be touching and in contact with the end of their adjacent edges. Failure to ensure this will result in the message **Unable to perform operation** appearing in the Status Bar. To make sure that the ends of edges for a surface do touch, use an appropriate **Snap** and work in the most suitable window when constructing the edges.

Apart from this proviso – that ends of edges must be touching – the construction of surfaces by more than two edges is carried out by selecting appropriate edges in turn, one after the other.

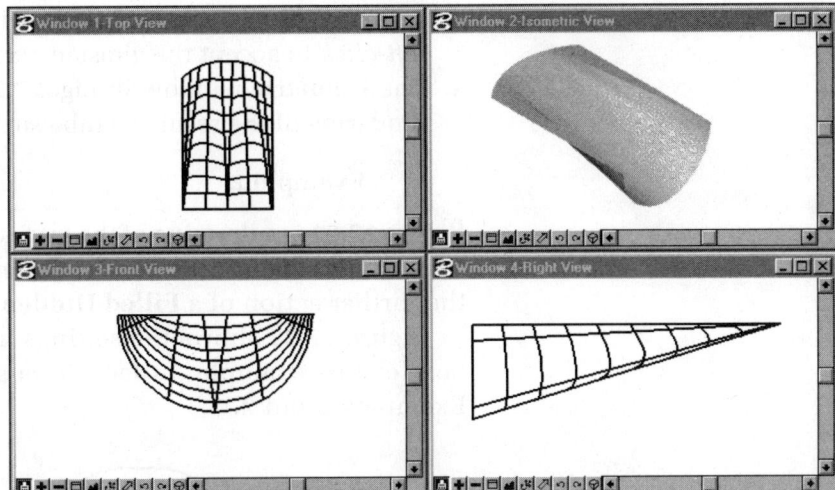

Fig. 17.19 Example 2. Using the **Construct Surface by Edges** tool

The Construct Tubular Surface tool

Example 1

The settings in the tool's Element Selection box for this example (Fig. 17.20) were – **Type** Solid; **Define by:** Circular; **Inside Radius** 10; **Outside Radius** 12. The construction of this example followed the procedure:

1. Draw the trace curve for the tube surface. This is shown in the lower drawing in the **Top View** window of Fig. 17.20. **Smart Line** was used.
2. Make the necessary settings in the tool's Element Selection box.

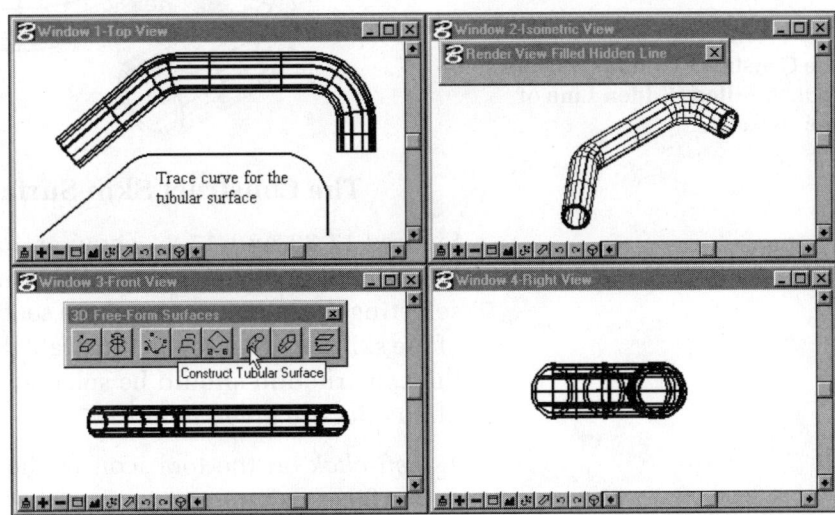

Fig. 17.20 Example 1. Using the **Construct Tubular Surface** tool

3. *Left-click* on the trace curve already drawn, followed by a second *left-click* to accept the ghosted surface which appears.

4. The **Isometric** window in Fig. 17.20 shows a **Filled Hidden Line** rendering of the resulting tube surface.

Example 2

Figure 17.21 is a drawing of the trace curve for this example and Fig. 17.22 shows the resulting surface after the action of the tool and after the further action of a **Filled Hidden Line** rendering.

Figure 17.22 shows the settings in the tool's Element Selection box for this example. In fact these settings are the same for both Examples 1 and 2.

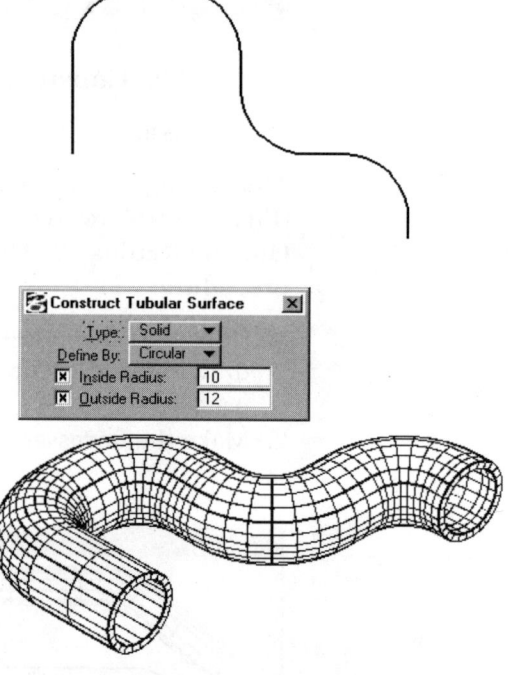

Fig. 17.21 Example 2. Using the **Construct Tubular Surface** tool. The trace curve for the example

Fig. 17.22 Example 2. Using the **Construct Tubular Surface** tool. A **Filled Hidden Line** of the surface

The Construct Skin Surface tool

Figures 17.23 and 17.24 show an example of the use of the tool. When employing the tool to form a surface some care is needed when selecting the trace curve and the section curves making up the parts of the skin. In order to demonstrate the order in which these parts of the construction should be selected, the prompts appearing in the Status Bar are given below:

1. *Left-click* on the tool icon in the flyout or in the **3D Free-form Surfaces** palette.

2. The following prompts appear in the Status bar:

> **Construct Skin Surface > Identify trace curve:** *left-click* on the curve (Fig. 17.23).
> **Construct Skin Surface > Identify first section line:** *left-click* on one of the lines (Fig. 17.23).
> **Construct Skin Surface > Identify second section line:** *left-click* on the second of the lines (Fig. 17.23).
> **Construct Skin Surface > Accept/Reject:** *left-click* (to accept). The surface appears in ghosted form.
> **Construct Skin Surface > Accept/Reject:** *left-click* (to accept). The surface appears in full colour.

3. The surface can be rendered as thought fit. Figure 17.24 is a **Phong Antialias** rendering of the surface.

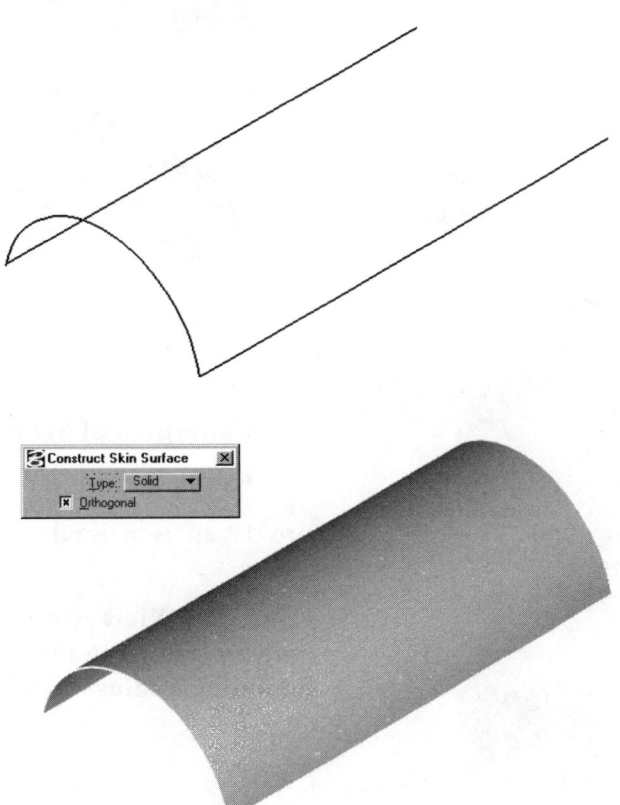

Fig. 17.23 An example of using the **Construct Skin Surface** tool. The trace curve and section lines

Fig. 17.24 An example of using the **Construct Skin Surface** tool. A rendering of the surface

The Construct Offset Surface tool

Figure 17.25 shows an example of the use of this tool. The offset can be inside or outside the original from which the offset is being made. As the surface to be offset is selected, arrows appear indicating the direction in which the offset is to be made. If on the wrong side, move the mouse until the directional arrows appear on the required side. When using the tool only two prompts appear in the Status Bar:

Construct Offset Surface > Identify Surface: *left-click* on the surface and *drag* until arrows appear on required side.

Construct Offset Surface > Accept/Reject: *left-click* (to Accept).

Settings must be made in the tool's Element Selection box as indicated in Fig. 17.25. If the **Tolerance** setting is made, check on the result before accepting the **Accept/Reject** prompt. Some experimentation is advisable before setting a **Tolerance**.

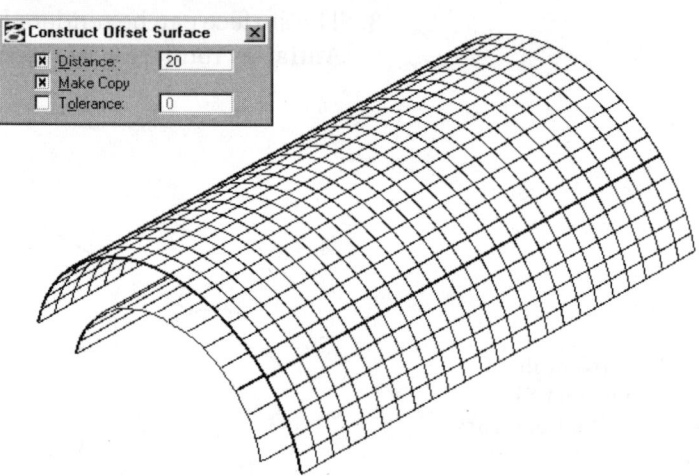

Fig. 17.25 An example of using the **Construct Offset Surface** tool

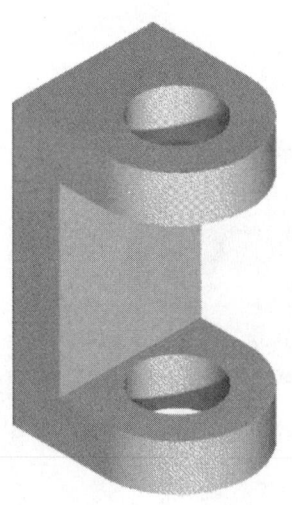

Fig. 17.26 Example 1. A rendering

Fig. 17.27 Example 1. The drawing for the top and bottom

Examples of 3D models from several surfaces

Example 1

Figure 17.26 is a rendering of this example. To construct this example:

1. In the **Top View** window, with AccuDraw active construct the drawing shown in Fig. 17.27 with the aid of **Smart Line**. Use a **Rounding Radius** of 15 for the outer curve.

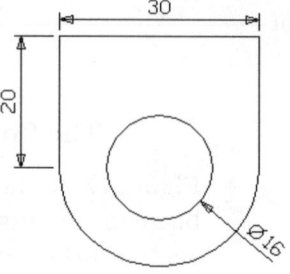

2. With **Create Region** and **Group Hole** change the drawing to a **Group**.

3. Call **Construct Surface of Projection** and create a projection of a height of 10 of **Type** with **Solid** showing (Fig. 17.28).

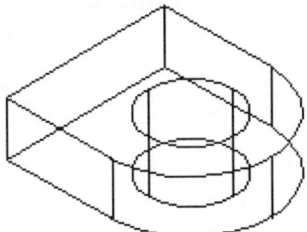

Fig. 17.28 Example 1. The surface of the top as it appears in the **Isometric** window

4. In the **Front View** window **Copy** the surface 50 mm below the existing surface (Fig. 17.29)

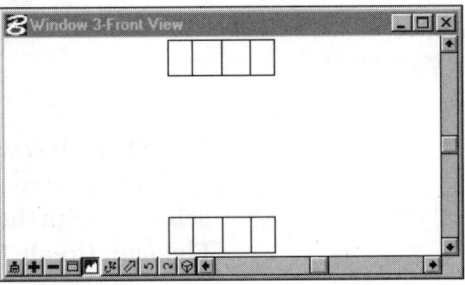

Fig. 17.29 Example 1. **Copy** top to bottom in the **Front View** window

5. Construct a surface of projection from a block 50 mm by 30 mm and 10 mm high in the **Front View** window. **Move** this surface as required in any of the windows in order to place the surface in its correct position as shown in Fig. 17.30.

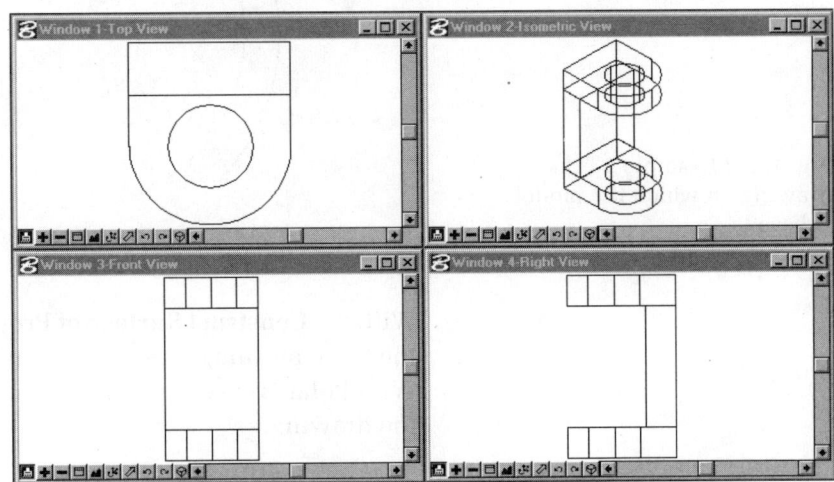

Fig. 17.30 Example 1. Constructing the back of the model

6. Render as necessary.

Example 2

Figure 17.31 is a rendering of this example. The procedures were as follows:

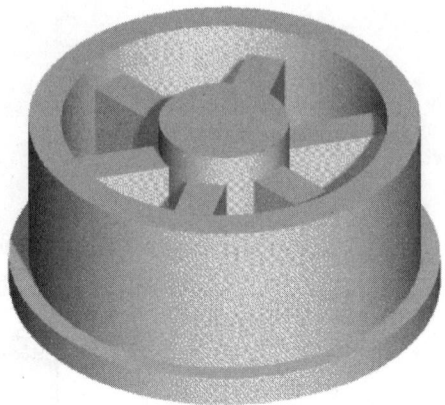

Fig. 17.31 Example 2. A rendering of the example

1. In the **Top View** window construct the drawing as in Fig. 17.32. The 'arm' of the view must be constructed as a group. This can be best achieved with the aid of tools such as **Trim Element**, **Delete Part of Element**, **Create Complex Shape**.

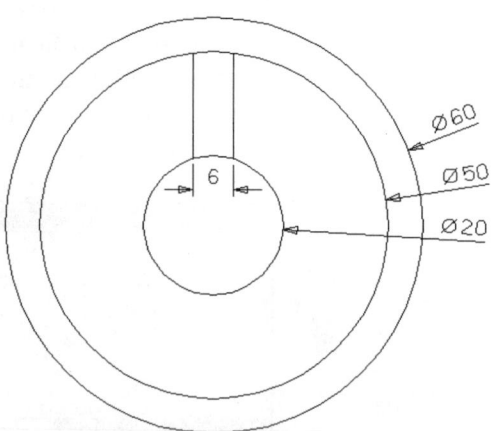

Fig. 17.32 Example 2. The drawing on which the model is based

2. With the **Construct Surface of Projection**, construct a surface from the 'arm' outline of height 50 mm.
3. With **Polar Array**, array the surface six times around the centre of the drawing.

4. Construct surfaces of projection 60 mm high from the two circles of diameters 20 and 50.
5. Construct a surface of projection –10 mm high from the circle of diameter 60.
6. The resulting windows now appear as in Fig. 17.33.
7. Rendering can now take place as required.

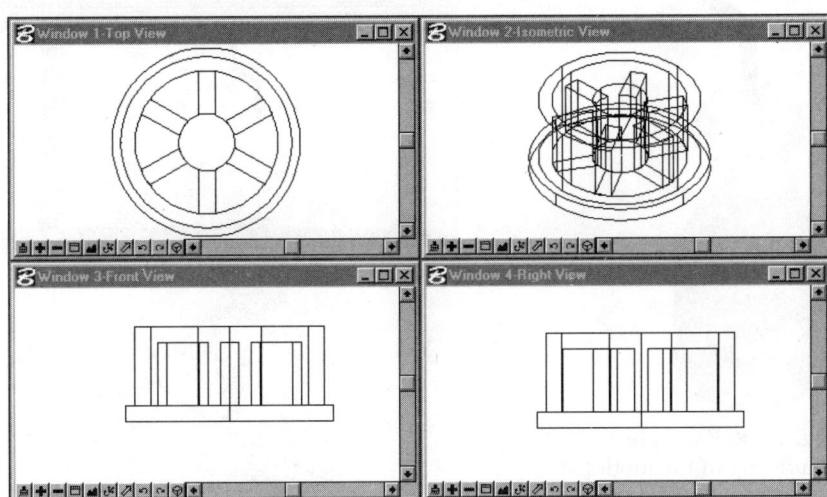

Fig. 17.33 Example 2. All the surfaces of projection

Example 3

Three illustrations – Figs 17.34 to 17.36 – show the basics for the construction of this model. The model was constructed with the aid of the **Construct Surface of Revolution** and **Construct Tubular Surface** tools. The outline on which the surface of revolution was based is shown in Fig. 17.33, the four windows showing the results of including a 'cork' and a tube are shown in Fig. 17.34 and a rendering of the completed model in Fig. 17.35. The reader may wish to attempt constructing this model from the information given in the drawings.

Fig. 17.34 Example 3. Dimensions for the surface of revolution

Example 4

Three illustrations – Figs 17. 37 to 17.39 – show the basic construction for this example. It is suggested the reader attempts the construction of the model from the information given in these three illustrations. The height of the main web is 10 mm, of the thinner web 5 mm and of the cylinder 30 mm.

It will be seen in Fig. 17.39 that it may pay to work in windows that have been altered in size by *dragging* existing windows to a different shape with the aid of the mouse and the windows movement cursors.

Fig. 17.35 Example 3. The completed model in four windows

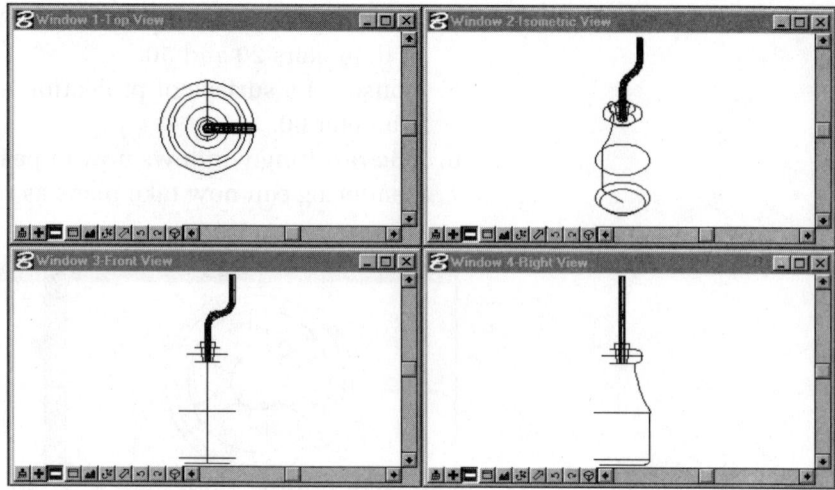

Fig. 17.36 Example 3. A rendering of the model

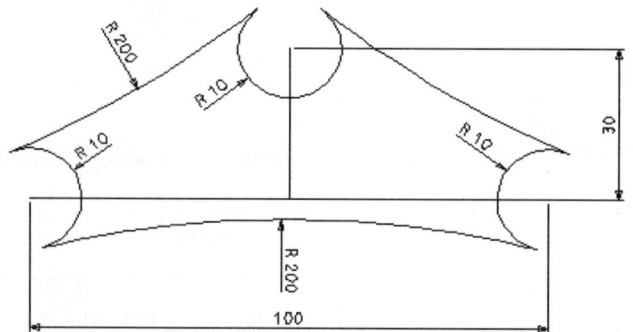

Fig. 17.37 Example 4. Dimensions for the main web

Fig. 17.38 Example 4. The surfaces of projection for the cylinders and main web

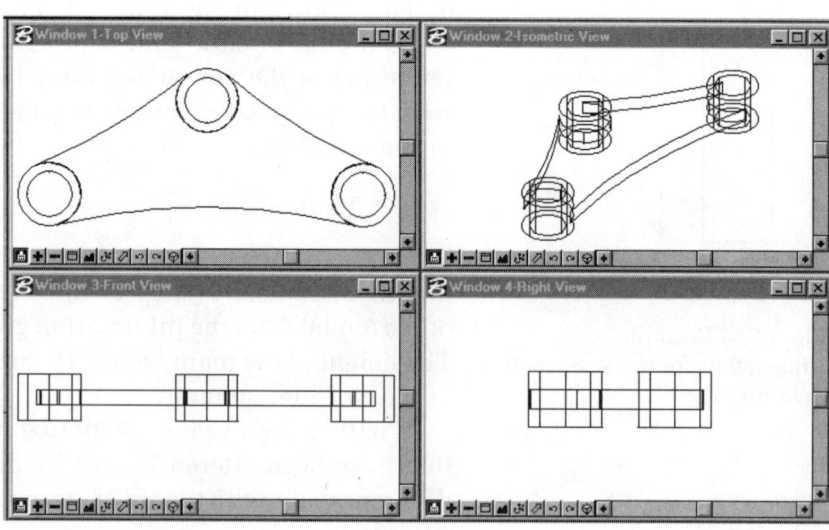

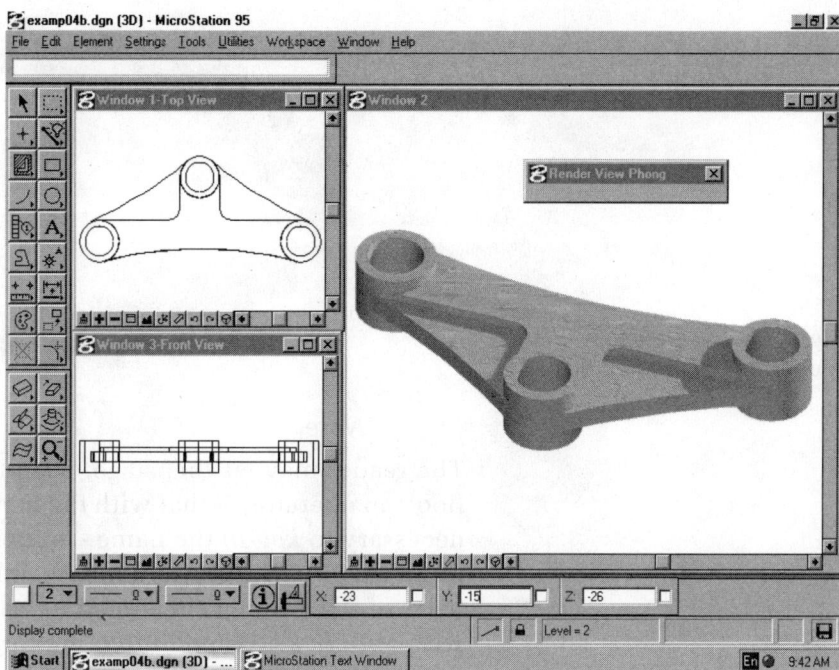

Fig. 17.39 Example 4. The
resulting model in three
windows

Example 5

A final example is given in Figs 17.40 and 17.41. The gear was
constructed from a complex shape formed into a region with a group
hole (Fig. 17.39). The complex shape involved the use of a number
of 2D tools such as **Place Circle, Circular Fillet, Trim Element, Polar
Array.** When the drawing had been completed a surface of projection
was formed from the region and then rendered (Fig. 17.41).

Fig. 17.40 Example 5. The
region from which the surface
of projection was formed

Fig. 17.41 Example 5. A
rendering of the example

Note

The reader may, at this stage, wish to experiment with one of the
Boolean operators – that with the name **boolean surface union**. It is
necessary to *key-in* the name – either in full or as the abbreviation
bo su un into the **Key-in** window, followed by *Return*. Then select
pairs of the parts of the model to be formed into one by the union
with *left-clicks*. When unions are formed in this manner the model
will act as a single unit.

Notes on renderings in this chapter

1. Some of the renderings in colour are included in plates in the
    colour section (between pages 114 and 115).
2. All the renderings were taken from screens in which settings in the
    Global Lighting dialogue box were as shown in Fig. 17.42. This
    dialogue box is called to screen by a *left-click* on **Rendering** in the
    Settings pull-down menu, followed by another *left-click* on the
    Global Lighting sub-menu which then appears.

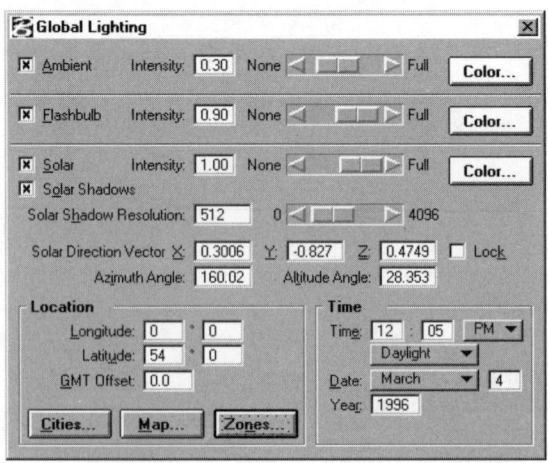

Fig. 17.42 The **Global Lighting**
dialogue box

Questions

1. Why is it important to have AccuDraw in operation when constructing 3D models?
2. It is better to use **Smart Line** when constructing the outlines from which 3D surfaces are formed. Why is this?
3. The **Group** palette of tools is very important in connection with the constructing of surfaces using the **3D Free-form Surfaces** tools. Why is this?
4. From which menu are the render tools called?
5. Can you state the difference between **Smooth** rendering and a **Phong** rendering?
6. How many edges can a surface be constructed from when using the **Construct Surface by Edges** tool?
7. Have you tried constructing a tubular surface with the **Section** selected from the **Define by:** box? If so what differences are there between such surfaces and those drawn with **Circular** chosen from this box?
8. What problems might arise if wrong selections are made from elements on screen when using the **Construct Skin Surface** tool?
9. Can an offset surface be added inside an existing surface?
10. What are the uses of the **boolean surface union** command?

Exercises

If you have not already done so, it is suggested you attempt all the examples given throughout the chapter.

APPENDIX

Printing or plotting

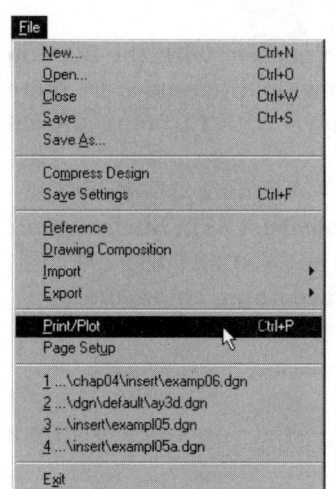

Fig. A1 Selecting **Print/Plot** from the **File** pull-down menu

Introduction

Printing can be carried out very easily if the default Windows 95 printer is used for the purpose. Other drivers – printers or plotters – can be loaded for use if required. This appendix will describe the printing of a drawing constructed in MicroStation 95 to the default Windows 95 printer driver.

Procedure

1. *Left-click* on **Print/Plot** in the **File** pull-down menu (Fig. A1).
2. The **Plot** dialogue box appears over the drawing to be plotted (Fig. A2).
3. Make sure the printer is switched on and that there is paper in its tray.
4. *Left-click* on the **Plot** icon in the **Plot** dialogue box.

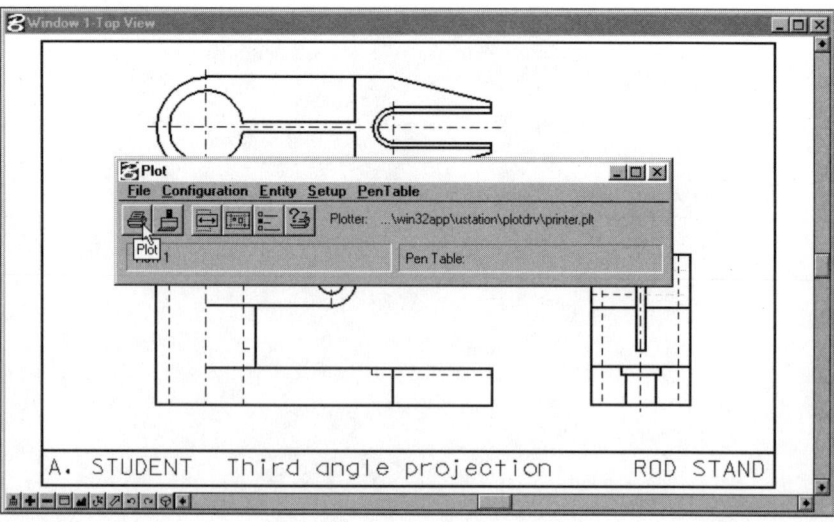

Fig. A2 The **Plot** dialogue box

Other tools in the Plot dialogue box

Figure A3 shows tools from the **Plot** dialogue box palette. These have the following functions:

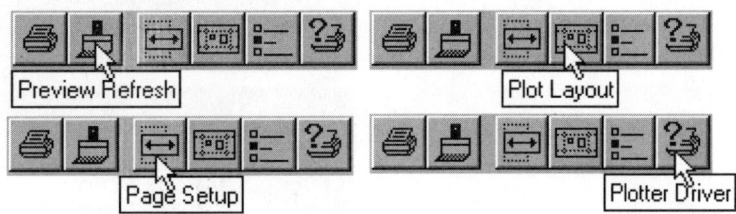

Fig. A3 Tool icons in the **Plot** dialogue box

1. **Preview Refresh**: *Left-click* in the icon and the **Plot Preview** box appears (Fig. A4) showing the position of the drawing as it will be printed on the drawing sheet in the printer tray.

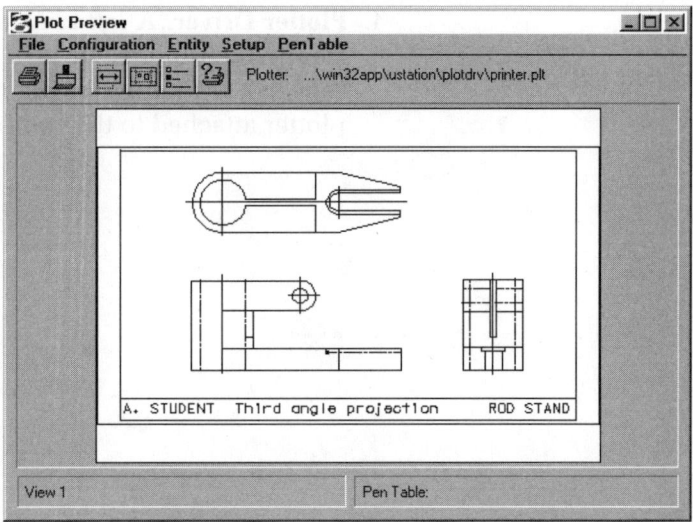

Fig. A4 The **Plot Preview** box

2. **Page Setup**: *Left-click* on the icon and the **Print Setup** box appears showing details of the printer, paper size and whether the drawing is to be printed in landscape or portrait orientation. In the example given (Fig. A5) the Windows 95 default printer is a laser printer – HP LaseJet IIIP, printing to A4 size sheets. The printing is to be in the landscape orientation.
3. **Plot Layout**: If a plotter is being used instead of a printer, a *left-click* on this icon brings up the **Plot Layout** dialogue box, to show how the plot will appear on the drawing sheet in the plotter.

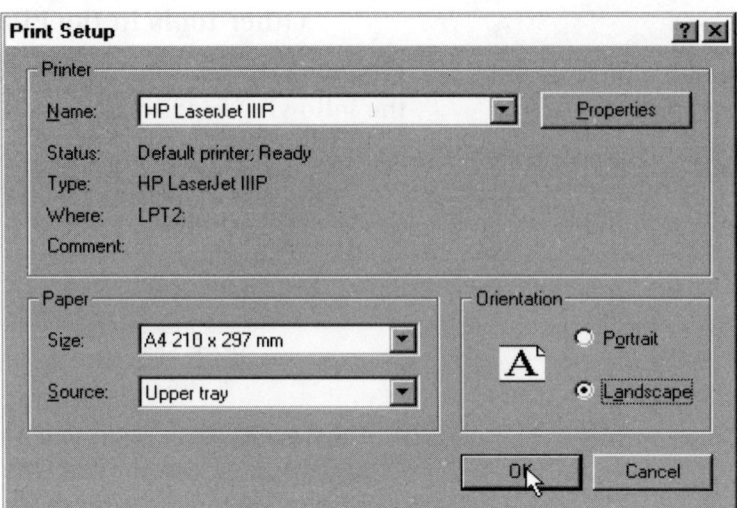

Fig. A5 The **Printer Setup** box

4. **Plotter Driver**: A *left-click* on this icon brings up a dialogue box from which plotter drivers loaded with MicroStation 95 can be selected. If plotting, select the name of the plotter driver for the plotter attached to the computer being used.

Product information

For more information on the MicroStation family of products and services please contact your nearest Bentley dealer or your nearest Bentley office.

WWW: http://www.bentley.com/
Compuserve: GO MSTATION
e-mail: family@bentley.com

UK

Bentley Systems (UK) Ltd
l'Avenir
Opladen Way
Bracknell
Berkshire RG12 0PF
UNITED KINGDOM
Tel: 01344 412233
Fax: 01344 412386

For further details of the academic edition of MicroStation 95, contact:

3DI Systems
Mill House
Main Street
Hillsborough
Co. Down
NORTHERN IRELAND
Tel: 01846 689217
WWW: http://www.3di.co.uk

Europe

Bentley Systems Czech Republic
Brehova 1
110 00 Praha 1
CZECH REPUBLIC
Tel: (+42) 2 231 6591
Fax: (+42) 2 232 8444

Bentley Systems Finland Oy
Innopoli, Tekniikantie 12
02150 Espoo
FINLAND
Tel: (+358) 04354 3604
Fax: (+358) 04354 3605

Bentley Systems Scandinavia AS
Lyngbyvej 24
DK-2100 Copenhagen
DENMARK
Tel: (+45) 392 71001
Fax: (+45) 392 71041

Bentley Systems France SaRL
CNIT, 2 Place de la Defense
92800 Puteaux
FRANCE
Tel: (+33) 1 46924092
Fax: (+33) 1 46924093

Bentley Systems Germany GmbH
Carl-Zeiss-Ring 3
85737 Ismaning
GERMANY
Tel: (+49) 899 624320
Fax: (+49) 899 6243220

Regerstrasse 5 (for Eastern Europe)
73479 Ellwagen
GERMANY
Tel: (+49) 7965 90050
Fax: (+49) 7965 900520

Bentley Systems Italia Srl
Strada 1, Palazzo WTC
Milanofiori
20090 Assago, Milano
ITALY
Tel: (+39) 257 500254
Fax: (+39) 257 500270

Bentley Systems Europe BV
Polarisavenue 33
2132 JH Hoofddorp
THE NETHERLANDS
Tel: (+31) 23 5685588
Fax: (+31) 23 5685595

Bentley Systems Iberica SA
C/Ochandiano 8
Centro Empresarial el Plantio
28023 Madrid
SPAIN
Tel: (+34) 1 372 8494
Fax: (+34) 1 307 6285

USA

Bentley Systems, Inc.
690 Pennsylvania Drive
Exton PA 19341
USA
Tel: (+1) 610 458 5000
Fax: (+1) 610 458 1060

Asia-Pacific

Bentley Systems Pty Ltd
Suite 8, 51 City Road
South Melbourne VIC 3205
AUSTRALIA
Tel: (+61) 3 9699 8699
Fax: (+61) 3 9699 8677

Far East

Bentley Systems South East Asia
Lot 5.01 5th Floor
Wisma HLA Jalan Raja Chulan
Kuala Lumpur 50200
MALAYSIA
Tel: (+60) 3 242 6233
Fax: (+60) 3 242 7233

Mid-World

Bentley Systems Mid-World Ltd
28 Kennedy Avenue
Suite 401
1087 Nicosia
CYPRUS
Tel: (+357) 2 459936
Fax: (+357) 2 365765

Middle East

Bentley Dubai
PO Box 28149
Dubai
UAE
Tel: (+971) 4 312666
Fax: (+971) 4 312802

Bentley Bahrain
PO Box 10001
Office 32 (Floor 3)
Building 20 Al Khalifa Avenue
305 Manama
BAHRAIN
Tel: (+973) 212 595
Fax: (+973) 214 882

Africa

Bentley South Africa
22 Athlone Road
Parkview 2193
Johannesburg
SOUTH AFRICA
Tel/Fax: (+27) 11 486 0687

Index